# Mobile and Sensor-Based Technologies in Higher Education

Oytun Sözüdoğru
*University of City Island, Cyprus*

Bülent Akkaya
*Manisa Celal Bayar University, Turkey*

A volume in the Advances in Educational Technologies and Instructional Design (AETID) Book Series

Published in the United States of America by
IGI Global
Information Science Reference (an imprint of IGI Global)
701 E. Chocolate Avenue
Hershey PA, USA 17033
Tel: 717-533-8845
Fax: 717-533-8661
E-mail: cust@igi-global.com
Web site: http://www.igi-global.com



Library of Congress Cataloging-in-Publication Data

Names: Sozudogru, Oytun, 1985- editor. | Akkaya, Bulent, 1980- editor.
Title: Mobile and sensor-based technologies in higher education / Oytun Sozudogru and Bulent Akkaya, Editors.
Description: Hershey, PA : Information Science Reference (an imprint of IGI Global), [2023] | Includes bibliographical references and index. | Summary: "This book explores the current state of practice of how mobile and sensor-based technologies are helping higher education, providing a roadmap for harnessing the artificial intelligence, online learning, distance learning and other modern technologies to aid dealing with the education aspects"-- Provided by publisher.
Identifiers: LCCN 2022024513 (print) | LCCN 2022024514 (ebook) | ISBN 9781668454008 (hardcover) | ISBN 9781668454046 (paperback) | ISBN 9781668454015 (ebook)
Subjects: LCSH: Mobile communication systems in education. | Detectors. | Education, Higher--Effect of technological innovations on. | Educational technology.
Classification: LCC LB1044.84 .M582 2023 (print) | LCC LB1044.84 (ebook) | DDC 371.33/4--dc23/eng/20220622
LC record available at https://lccn.loc.gov/2022024513
LC ebook record available at https://lccn.loc.gov/2022024514

This book is published in the IGI Global book series Advances in Educational Technologies and Instructional Design (AETID) (ISSN: 2326-8905; eISSN: 2326-8913)

British Cataloguing in Publication Data
A Cataloguing in Publication record for this book is available from the British Library.



For electronic access to this publication, please contact: eresources@igi-global.com.

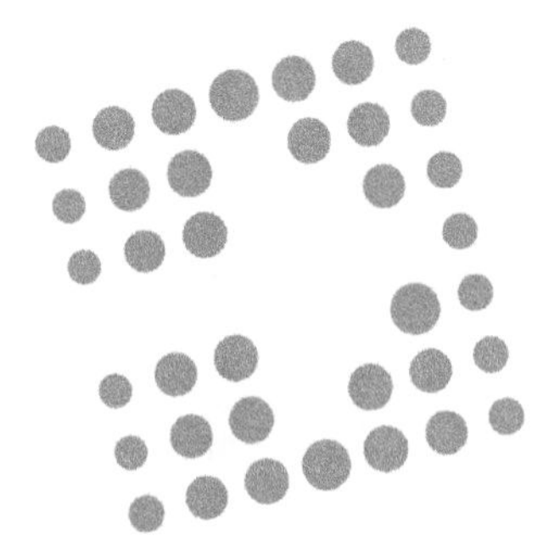

# Advances in Educational Technologies and Instructional Design (AETID) Book Series

ISSN:2326-8905
EISSN:2326-8913

Editor-in-Chief: Lawrence A. Tomei Robert Morris University, USA

## MISSION

Education has undergone, and continues to undergo, immense changes in the way it is enacted and distributed to both child and adult learners. In modern education, the traditional classroom learning experience has evolved to include technological resources and to provide online classroom opportunities to students of all ages regardless of their geographical locations. From distance education, Massive-Open-Online-Courses (MOOCs), and electronic tablets in the classroom, technology is now an integral part of learning and is also affecting the way educators communicate information to students.

The **Advances in Educational Technologies & Instructional Design (AETID) Book Series** explores new research and theories for facilitating learning and improving educational performance utilizing technological processes and resources. The series examines technologies that can be integrated into K-12 classrooms to improve skills and learning abilities in all subjects including STEM education and language learning. Additionally, it studies the emergence of fully online classrooms for young and adult learners alike, and the communication and accountability challenges that can arise. Trending topics that are covered include adaptive learning, game-based learning, virtual school environments, and social media effects. School administrators, educators, academicians, researchers, and students will find this series to be an excellent resource for the effective design and implementation of learning technologies in their classes.

## COVERAGE

- Curriculum Development
- Adaptive Learning
- Collaboration Tools
- Web 2.0 and Education
- Virtual School Environments
- E-Learning
- Hybrid Learning
- Bring-Your-Own-Device
- K-12 Educational Technologies
- Digital Divide in Education

IGI Global is currently accepting manuscripts for publication within this series. To submit a proposal for a volume in this series, please contact our Acquisition Editors at Acquisitions@igi-global.com or visit: http://www.igi-global.com/publish/.

The Advances in Educational Technologies and Instructional Design (AETID) Book Series (ISSN 2326-8905) is published by IGI Global, 701 E. Chocolate Avenue, Hershey, PA 17033-1240, USA, www.igi-global.com. This series is composed of titles available for purchase individually; each title is edited to be contextually exclusive from any other title within the series. For pricing and ordering information please visit http://www.igi-global.com/book-series/advances-educational-technologies-instructional-design/73678. Postmaster: Send all address changes to above address. 

## Titles in this Series

*For a list of additional titles in this series, please visit:*
*www.igi-global.com/book-series/advances-educational-technologies-instructional-design/73678*

***Handbook of Research on Advancing Teaching and Teacher Education in the Context of a Virtual Age***
Aaron Samuel Zimmerman (Texas Tech University, USA)
Information Science Reference • © 2023 • 405pp • H/C (ISBN: 9781668484074) • US $270.00

***Technology Integration and Transformation in STEM Classrooms***
Christie Martin (University of South Carolina – Columbia, USA) Drew Polly (University of North Carolina – Charlotte, USA) and Bridget T. Miller (University of South Carolina, USA)
Information Science Reference • © 2023 • 335pp • H/C (ISBN: 9781668459201) • US $215.00

***Advancing STEM Education and Innovation in a Time of Distance Learning***
Roberto Alonso González-Lezcano (Universidad CEU San Pablo, Spain)
Information Science Reference • © 2023 • 359pp • H/C (ISBN: 9781668450536) • US $205.00

***Promoting Next-Generation Learning Environments Through CGScholar***
Matthew Montebello (University of Malta, Malta)
Information Science Reference • © 2023 • 310pp • H/C (ISBN: 9781668451243) • US $215.00

***Implementing Rapid E-Learning Through Interactive Materials Development***
Mohammad Issack Santally (University of Mauritius, Mauritius) Yousra Rajabalee (Mauritius Institute of Education, Mauritius) and Ravi Rajputh (University of Mauritius, Mauritius)
Information Science Reference • © 2023 • 300pp • H/C (ISBN: 9781668449400) • US $215.00

***Computer-Assisted Learning for Engaging Varying Aptitudes From Theory to Practice***
R. Dhaya (King Khalid University, Saudi Arabia) and R. Kanthavel (King Khalid University, Saudi Arabia)
Information Science Reference • © 2023 • 229pp • H/C (ISBN: 9781668450581) • US $195.00

701 East Chocolate Avenue, Hershey, PA 17033, USA
Tel: 717-533-8845 x100 • Fax: 717-533-8661
E-Mail: cust@igi-global.com • www.igi-global.com

This book is dedicated to our brilliant and beautiful daughters, Adel Sözüdoğru and Şule Akkaya.

# Table of Contents

# Detailed Table of Contents

preferred all over the world. As it was used lacking sufficient skills, knowledge, and enough training for many teachers, some drawbacks and challenges were faced. This chapter focuses on different assessment approaches and practices (with examples) that can be used to overcome the difficulties encountered in digital learning.



Learning in today's world is equipped with novel ways and techniques to make learners attracted towards learning. Mobile-assisted language learning (MALL) has been considered as a primary tool for enhancing the performance of learners. However, this phenomenon is missing in developing nations. This chapter, therefore, will attempt to investigate the efficacy of MALL on Pakistani English language learners. Data were collected from the population of 120 learners belonging to private institutes in Lahore, Punjab, Pakistan. Firstly, a pre-test was performed, and two groups were formed, which were equally divided into 60 learners (experimental and controlled). After that, a post-test was conducted, and performance of conventional group and MALL learners was compared. It was found that the experimental group showed significant variations in their performance as compared to conventional learners. Therefore, from the results, it can be concluded that MALL can be integrated and effectively utilized in a local context.



Assessment techniques are essential for utilization in both digital and online classrooms. The online evaluation must be viewed to evaluate a student's academic performance. Educational institutions are being held to a greater standard of accountability, and learning about online assessment is critical. Perhaps the information presented here can assist teachers in selecting assessment approaches that are appropriate for the pedagogy of online courses. Technology, delivery, pedagogy, learning styles, and learning outcomes must all be balanced in online assessment efficiently and comprehensively assess student learning, while meeting the problems of accountability, reform, and students' learning requirements, a diverse set of online components, methods, assessment criteria, and tools are required. Educators should continue to investigate various types of digital tools and methods for evaluating students in higher education in order to develop novel, efficient, and effective evaluation procedures that will hold institutions accountable for student outcomes in the online environment.



This chapter reviews research studies conducted on emergency remote teaching in foreign language education in higher education and presents the results of the qualitative study which evaluates the effectiveness of emergency remote teaching in English as a foreign language instruction. The data were elicited from 15 undergraduate students studying at the English language teaching departments in North Cyprus. The textual data gathered through self-reports revealed that a great majority of the participants were in favor of hybrid instruction after the pandemic. The rationale behind this result was found to be the fact that both in-person and online education had their own merits and demerits in their own way and that hybrid education had a potential to exploit the merits while avoiding the demerits. It was an unexpected result to find that the participants were in favor of the digitalization of language education.



One of the most important problems of our age is the lack of effective and efficient use of human resources. In this context, it is important to establish the human resources profile of the education sector, which has the highest human resources in the public sector, and to investigate whether this resource is used efficiently and effectively. In terms of the quality of education, it is important to evaluate the correct employment, motivation studies, and performance of school employees. However, in the evaluation of the performance of teachers and school staff, who will be involved, according to which criteria and how to evaluate, and the way of using the results of the evaluation are among the answers required. The aim of this research is to meet the expectations and needs of the education system by suggesting the importance, functioning, and applications of human resources in educational practices and by proposing a human resources employment strategy model.

This chapter provides a variety of different perspectives regarding inclusive education practice in higher education settings. It provides an introduction into learning in the field of higher education. Then, the background information about the field of inclusive education practice follows. Furthermore, it emphasizes the needs that should be met and suggests some ways for inclusion practice to better provide students with different approaches and methods. The chapter also provides a wide explanation in terms of building an appropriate curriculum in higher education for both students with and without disabilities. Finally, it points out the necessary acts to be taken and provides implications in terms of e-learning and inclusion for those to succeed in the field. The chapter will provide insight for educators in the field of inclusive education.



The COVID-19 pandemic has forced the higher education sector to move from traditional in-person teaching and learning to hybrid pedagogical practices. Presently, almost all higher education institutions have commenced transiting from the physical classroom space to the online teaching and learning space. Hence, the impact of the fourth industrial revolution (4IR) has started manifesting in higher education, as evident in the modus operandi adopted recently by the service providers. In other words, as the world advances, higher education institutions are incorporating Industry 4.0 (I4.0) technologies. This transition is part of the evolution of higher education for the 21st century, referred to as Education 4.0 (EDUC4). Hence, this chapter presents a discus on promoting EDUC4 for effective post-pandemic higher education, considering the essential role of I4.0 technologies and meaningful hybrid e-training.

Digital transformation has forced higher education institutions to adapt new models of education and learning. In pandemic times, higher education institutions have started to practice online learning experiences. In this respect, the time comes to consider the active learning in higher education by the merits of online learning environments. Experiences of graduate school students were examined on the use of six hats and station methods in online course activities. These experiences and thoughts were gathered through story-based reflections through reflection task. It is revealed that active learning in higher education models is possible by integrating different learning activities in the online context. Learners developed research and project management skills through personalized learning and collaborative learning. They gained the ability to look at topics from different angles and ability to accept criticism.



As part of the curriculum at the Department of Tourism, Brawijaya University, Malang City, Indonesia, the authors are conducting a virtual tourism course to understand the interrelation of virtual reality (VR) and augmented reality (AR) in the tourism and hospitality fields. Moreover, this course also included practicums to create and use varied, immersive systems such as Web-VR, 3D VR, Multiplayer 3D VR, Marker-Based AR, and Marker-Less AR content in the context of tourism business etiquette and procedures as a virtual tour guide. In continuation, under the coordination of the tourism laboratory, they initiated a virtual living lab together with students and stakeholders that focus on strengthening Malang's City identity as a heritage city by using AR/VR technologies. Therefore, this chapter aims to define and recognise basic insights of the concept, types, and characteristics of remote practicum methods. Specifically, this review also describes with examples required equipment and best practice software and explains the advantages and limitations that may occur.

This chapter discusses the challenges for the higher education sector during the coronavirus pandemic. It examines the advantages of information and communication technology (ICT) tools in advancing higher education and students' changing communication practices during the recent pandemic. The chapter identifies research gaps, highlighting the consequential effect on lesser-developed countries, the psychological effect on the student community, and the vital role of management in handling distributed software development practice. It also presents that the main objective should be to develop more resilient higher education teaching and learning provisions that are responsive and adaptive to future crises. For example, an undergraduate software development case study describes a group of computer science students' views on digital communication channel utilization behaviour during the coronavirus pandemic. Finally, a multiple-choice questions and answers method provides the students' views regarding the relevant research issues and a view of university students' communication channel utilization patterns.



In this chapter an endeavour has been established to capture the pre-COVID-19 and COVID-19-related educational transformation and adaptability of the teaching-learning community to embrace the exigency-based changes along with the exploration of the community of inquiry model (CoI) with its three basic elements: social presence, cognitive presence, and teaching presence. The chapter also delves into the learners' and teachers' reactions and adaptability towards the change to acquire it as a permanent solution to the traditional teaching procedure. There would be a discourse on the use of ICT (information and communications technology) to address the issues of coping mechanism with the virtual platform, making it a seamless process. In this chapter, the target audience gets a fair cognitive familiarity with the present state and future prediction of the COVID-19-driven pandemic and ramification of it in the future for academic discourse and referencing.

# Preface

This book will bring together the current work of well-established and well-known researchers in the field of the role of distance education in shaping the nature of education. At all educational levels, innovation is progressively becoming an intrinsic aspect of learning. As online education continues to grow, we need curriculum and training that prepares teachers for online course design and delivery. One major challenge accompanying the growth in online education is that many teacher educators find themselves under pressure and underprepared to teach online courses. Digital media has transformed and continues to change teaching and learning. The proliferation of mobile devices and sensor-based technologies increased the possibilities for learning and pushed it into institutions. To sum up, in this book we intend to explore the current state of practice of how mobile and sensor-based technologies are helping higher education, roadmap for harnessing the artificial intelligence, online learning, distance learning and other modern technologies to aid dealing with the education aspects.

## ORGANIZATION OF THE BOOK

This book is including 12 chapters. It begins with a chapter of "Artificial Intelligence in Higher Education" by Tanaya Krishna Jupalli, Mulka Sai Tharun Reddy, Hari Kishan Kondaveeti. It covers, AI was not playing a pivotal role in technology. But now, artificial intelligence is a key part of the revolution of technology. AI has become a powerful tool in recent years, enabling machines to think and act like humans. AI helps in developing a better approach to teaching students i.e. adaptive learning where a computer algorithm identifies the rate of learning of a student and adapts itself so that the student learns efficiently. The aim of implementing AI in education is not to replace tutors, but to assist them in understanding the potential and limitations of each student individually. This chapter will cover the introduction, existing applications, and new applications of Artificial Intelligence in Higher Education. The prime focus of the chapter will be on the approaches to different product developments and their implementation using artificial intelligence in the educational sector. It provides a brief idea of how the existing applications solve the problems in Higher Education and new approaches to make Higher education more efficient.

Second chapter of the book, "Practical Suggestions for the Digital Assessment Challenges," by Ramadan Eyyam, Ipek Menevis, Nazan Dogruer. It discusses of after the pandemic traditional instruction was forced to evolve and become digitalized. Consequently, the assessment changed shape and digital assessment was preferred all over the world. As it was used lacking sufficient skills, knowledge and enough training by many teachers, some drawbacks and challenges were faced besides its benefits. This chapter focuses on different assessment approaches and practices (with examples) that can be used to overcome the difficulties encountered in digital learning.

The third chapter, "Mobile-Assisted Language Learning: A Boon or a Bane for Pakistani ESL Learners?" by Dr. Muhammad Mooneeb Ali, covers the learning in Today's world is equipped with novel ways and techniques to make learners attracted towards learning. Mobile Assisted Language learning (MALL) has been considered as a primary tool for enhancing the performance of learners since long. However, this phenomenon is missing in developing nations. This chapter, therefore, will attempt to investigate the efficacy of MALL on Pakistani English language learners. Data were collected from the population of 120 learners belonging to private institutes in Lahore, Punjab Pakistan. Firstly, a pre-test was performed and two groups were formed which were equally divided into sixty learners (experimental and controlled). After that, a post-test was conducted and performance of conventional group and MALL learners was compared. It was found out that experimental group showed significant variations in their performance as compared to conventional learners. Therefore, from the results it can be concluded that MALL can be integrated and effectively utilized in local context

The fourth chapter of the book is "Methods of Evaluation and Assessment in Digital Learning" by Hameed Khan, Kamal Kumar Kushwah, Kanchan Khare, Sujeet Mahobia, Jitendra Thakur. It stated the assessment techniques are essential for utilization in both digital and online classrooms. The online evaluation must be viewed to evaluate a student's academic performance. Educational institutions are being held to a greater standard of accountability, learning about online assessment is critical. Perhaps the information presented here can assist teachers in selecting assessment approaches that are appropriate for the pedagogy of online courses. Technology, delivery, pedagogy, learning styles, and learning outcomes must all be balanced in online assessment efficiently and comprehensively assess student learning while meeting the problems of accountability, reform, and students' learning requirements, a diverse set of online components, methods, assessment criteria, and tools are required. Educators should continue to investigate various types of digital tools and methods for evaluating students in higher education in order to develop novel, efficient, and effective evaluation procedures that will hold institutions accountable for student outcomes in the online environment.

Chapter 5, "Emergency Remote Teaching in Language Education: Opportunities and Challenges," by Nurdan Atamturk, reviews research studies conducted on emergency remote teaching in foreign language education in higher education and presents the results of the qualitative study which evaluates the effectiveness of emergency remote teaching in English as a foreign language instruction. The data were elicited from fifteen undergraduate students studying at the English language teaching departments in north Cyprus. The textual data gathered through self-reports revealed that a great majority of the participants were in favor of hybrid instruction after the pandemic. The rationale behind this result was found to be the fact that both in-person and online education had their own merits and demerits in their own way and that hybrid education had a potential to exploit the merits while avoiding the demerits. It was an unexpected result to find that the participants were in favor of the digitalization of language education.

The sixth chapter of the book is "Evaluation of the Impact of Technology and Human Resources on Quality in Higher Education" by Meryem Baştaş. It covers the one of the most important problems of our age is the lack of effective and efficient use of human resources. In this context, it is important to establish the human resources profile of the education sector which has the highest human resources in the public sector, and to investigate whether this resource is used efficiently and effectively. In terms of the quality of education, it is important to evaluate the correct employment, motivation studies and performance of school employees. However, in the evaluation of the performance of teachers and school staff, who will be involved, according to which criteria and how to evaluate, and the way of using the results of the evaluation are among the answers required. The aim of this research is to meet the expectations and needs of the education system by suggesting the importance, functioning and applications of human resources in educational practices and by proposing a human resources employment strategy model.

Chapter 7 is "Inclusive Education Practice" by Halil Ercan and Razge Zorba. This chapter provides a variety of different perspectives regarding inclusive education practice in higher education settings. It provides an introduction into learning in the field of higher education. Then, it is followed with the background information about the field of inclusive education practice. Furthermore, it emphasizes the needs that should be met and suggests some ways for inclusion practice to better provide students with different approaches and methods. The chapter also provides a wide explanation in terms of building an appropriate curriculum in higher education for both students with and without disabilities. Finally, it points out the necessary tackles to be taken and provides implications in terms of e-learning and inclusion for those to succeed in the field. Once and for all, it is considered that the chapter will provide an insight for educators in the field of inclusive education.

Chapter 8 of the book is "Education 4.0 for Effective Post-Pandemic Higher Education: The Capacity of Industry 4.0 Technologies and Meaningful Hybrid E-Training" by John Aderibigbe. It discusses the COVID-19 pandemic has forced the higher education sector to move from traditional in-person teaching and learning to hybrid pedagogical practices. Presently, almost all higher education institutions have commenced transiting from the physical classroom space to the online teaching and learning space. Hence, the impact of the Fourth Industrial Revolution (4IR) has started manifesting in higher education, as evident in the modus operandi adopted recently by the service providers. In other words, as the world advances, higher education institutions are incorporating industry 4.0 (I4.0) technologies. This transition is part of the evolution of higher education for the 21st century, referred to as education 4.0 (EDUC4). Hence, this chapter presents a discus on promoting EDUC4 for effective post-pandemic higher education, considering the essential role of I4.0 technologies and meaningful hybrid e-training.

Chapter 9, "Merits of Six Hat Metaphors and Station Techniques for Project Management Skills in Online Courses: Learner Engagement to Online Courses," by Fahriye Altinay, Zehra Altinay, Gokmen Daglı, Mehmet Altinay, Mutlu Soykurt, discusses digital transformation has forced higher education institutions to adapt new models of education and learning. In pandemic times, higher education institutions have started to practice online learning experiences. In this respect, the time comes to consider the active learning in higher education by the merits of online learning environments. Experiences of graduate school students were examined on the use of six hats and station methods in online course activities. These experiences and thoughts were gathered through story-based reflections through reflection task. It is revealed that active learning in higher education models are possible by integrating different learning activities in online context. Learners developed research and project management skills through personalized learning and collaborative learning. They gained ability to look at topics in different angles and ability to accept criticism.

Chapter 10 is "Actual Practicum Course vs. Virtual Living Lab in Tourism Education: Alike and Unlike at Once" by Aniesa Bafadhal, Muhammad Hendrawan. As part of our curriculum at the Department of Tourism, Brawijaya University, Malang City, Indonesia, we are conducting a Virtual Tourism course to understand the interrelation of Virtual Reality (VR) and Augmented Reality (AR) in the tourism and hospitality fields. Moreover, this course also included practicums to create and use varied, immersive systems such as Web-VR, 3D VR, Multiplayer 3D VR, Marker-based AR and Marker-less AR content in the context of tourism business etiquette and procedures as a virtual tour guide. In continuation, under the coordination of the Tourism Laboratory, we initiated a Virtual Living Lab together with students and stakeholders that focus on strengthening Malang's City identity as a Heritage City by using AR/VR technologies. Therefore, this paper aims to define and recognise basic insights of the concept, types and characteristics of remote practicum methods. Specifically, this review also describes with examples, required equipment, best practice software, along with explaining the advantages and limitations that may occur.

Chapter 11 is "Coronavirus's Impact on Digital Technology Use in a University Student Software Engineering Project Management" by Kamalendu Pal. This chapter discusses the challenges for the higher education sector during the coronavirus pandemic. It examines the advantages of information and communication technology (ICT) tools in advancing higher education and students' changing communication practices during the recent pandemic. The chapter identifies research gaps, highlighting the consequential effect on lesser-developed countries, the psychological effect on the student community, and the vital role of management in handling distributed software development practice. It also presents that the main objective should be to develop more resilient higher education teaching and learning provisions that are responsive and adaptive to future crises. For example, an undergraduate software development case study describes a group of computer science students' views on digital communication channel utilization behaviour during the coronavirus pandemic. Finally, a multiple-choice questions and answers method provides the students' views regarding the relevant research issues.

Chapter 12 is "COVID-19 Reactions, Responses, and Ramifications for the Future of Education" by Oindrila Chakraborty. Through this chapter an endeavour has been established to capture the pre-Covid and Covid related educational transformation and adaptability of the teaching -learning community to embrace the exigency-based changes along with the exploration of the Community of Inquiry Model (CoI) with its three basic elements- Social Presence, Cognitive Presence and Teaching Presence. The chapter should also delve into the learners' and Teachers' reaction and adaptability towards the change to acquire it as a permanent solution to the traditional teaching procedure. There would be a discourse on the use of ICT (Information and Communications Technology) to address the issues of coping mechanism with the virtual platform, making it a seamless process. Through this chapter the target audience would get a fair cognitive familiarity with the present state and future prediction of the Covid driven pandemic and ramification of it, in the future times for academic discourse and referencing purpose.

We think each of the 12 chapters in this book contributes interesting and significant viewpoints to the body of knowledge already available on the subject of Mobile and Sensor-Based Technologies in Higher Education. The fact that each contributor made an effort to go beyond simple declarations of technological prowess and discuss how mobile and sensor technology has affected higher education in distinctive and significant ways greatly impressed and pleased us as editors. The key accomplishment of the book, in our opinion, is its focus on the more subtle and intricate facets of technology. Mobile and Sensor-Based Technologies in Higher Education explores how mobile and sensor-based technologies are shaping higher education and creating a roadmap for harnessing artificial intelligence, online learning, distance learning, and other modern technologies to aid education. Covering key topics such as assessment, inclusive education, and social distancing, this reference work is ideal for policymakers, researchers, scholars, academicians, practitioners, instructors, and students.

*Oytun Sozudogru*
*University of City Island, Cyprus*

*Bulent Akkaya*
*Manisa Celal Bayar University, Turkey*

# Acknowledgment

Dr. Oytun Sözüdoğru and Dr. Bülent Akkaya, the editors of *Mobile and Sensor-Based Technologies in Higher Education*, would like to express their heartfelt appreciation to everyone who contributed their time, energy, and experience to compiling this significant collection of research and practice. The chapter contributors, peer reviewers, and the IGI Global staff assigned to this project are among those persons. This book would not have been possible without the collaborative work, dedication, and support of each of these groups.

First and initially, the editors would like to thank each chapter contributor for their knowledge as well as their persistence during the editing process This book is built on your belief in the project and your important input. Thank you for sharing your skills in a way that adds to the increasing knowledge base for anyone interested in learning more about assisting learners born into technology environment.

Second, the editors like to express their appreciation to the reviewers. Your involvement added another layer of quality feedback. This assistance aided in the development of *Mobile and Sensor-Based Technologies in Higher Education*, which will benefit instructors as a quality resource.

Last, the editors would wish to express their gratitude to their families. Thank you for understanding and supporting us. For the editors, family has been at the center and the heart of this project.

*Oytun Sözüdoğru*
*University of City Island, Cyprus*

*Bulent Akkaya*
*Manisa Celal Bayar University, Turkey*

# Chapter 1
# Artificial Intelligence in Higher Education

**Tanaya Krishna Jupalli**
https://orcid.org/0000-0002-4409-7540
*VIT-AP University, India*

**Mulka Sai Tharun Reddy**
https://orcid.org/0000-0002-6369-1625
*VIT-AP University, India*

**Hari Kishan Kondaveeti**
https://orcid.org/0000-0002-3379-720X
*VIT-AP University, India*

## ABSTRACT

*In the past decades, AI was not playing a pivotal role in technology. But now, artificial intelligence is a key part of the revolution of technology. AI has become a powerful tool in recent years, enabling machines to think and act like humans. AI helps in developing a better approach to teaching students (i.e., adaptive learning where a computer algorithm identifies the rate of learning of a student and adapts itself so that the student learns efficiently). The aim of implementing AI in education is not to replace tutors, but to assist them in understanding the potential and limitations of each student individually. This chapter will cover the introduction, existing applications, and new applications of artificial intelligence in higher education. The prime focus of the chapter will be on the approaches to different product developments and their implementation using artificial intelligence in the education sector. It provides a brief idea of how the existing applications solve the problems in higher education and new approaches to make higher education more efficient.*

DOI: 10.4018/978-1-6684-5400-8.ch001

## INTRODUCTION

Technology has been evolving tremendously over the decades. It is now an inevitable entity in our everyday life. One such technology which has boomed in recent years is Artificial Intelligence(AI). In the year 2016, Klaus Schwab, the author of the book "World Economic Forum" (Schwab, 2017). *The fourth industrial revolution.* Portfolio Penguin.) stated that AI is a part of The Fourth Industrial Revolution (4IR). AI has evolved into a powerful tool, empowering robots and computers to think and act like humans over the years. AI has grown into a powerful appliance in current years, permitting robots to suppose and act like humans. Almost Every market adopted AI into its products and services. Numerous problems have been solved and automated rigorously with AI. Every opportunity is associated with a challenge and AI has become capable of solving them. Many organizations and enterprises are solving day-to-day tasks with the help of AI. Products and services are integrated with AI to make them reliable and efficient for the consumer. Education is a field where AI is being adapted. This helps in developing a better approach to teach students i.e. adaptive learning where a computer algorithm identifies the rate of learning of a student and adapts itself so that the student learns efficiently. The aim of implementing AI in education is not to replace tutors, but to assist them in understanding the potential and limitations of each student individually.

Before the COVID-19 pandemic, students used to have physical classes. Universities and schools use a number of Machine Learning (Subset of AI) algorithms for tracking the performance of students in academics, interactions with the university website feed, emails, usage of resources in the university and ensure in giving optimum facilities. Another application is to balance the course load of a student based on his majors and previous similar student's data profiles on how they performed for a particular course. This pandemic had a huge toll on almost every field and the educational system is one of them. This impact forced the education system to switch from physical to online. All the universities and schools started to use virtual platforms for teaching and delivering practical experience using various tools. A number of features are integrated into e-learning platforms that provide videos, course suggestions based on interests, and also a chatbot to assist students. If we look into the future, there is going to be massive growth in the use of AI in the educational field.

Currently, the accuracy of the new notions of deep learning algorithms are turning out to be very high. Inferences for the future are being done by deep learning algorithms, which are accomplished by analyzing image data from phenomena of interest. Deep learning goes into a thorough analysis of such cases, examining their traits deep into their genetic makeup. As a whole, it is precise to say that AI is empowering education in an immeasurable manner. There are various applications of

AI in education, such as profiling and prediction, admission predictions and course scheduling, dropout and retention, Natural Language Processing (NLP) applications in education, Adaptive learning, and exam proctoring using gaze tracking. In this chapter, we are going to discuss such applications and analyze which techniques work the best.

## BACKGROUND

### Artificial intelligence

An Intelligent entity capable of solving tasks and thinking and acting rationally and humanly without training explicitly. Artificial Intelligence (AI) is applied to almost all fields like healthcare, navigation, lifestyle, etc. AI is divided into six sub parts as shown in Figure 1.

### Machine Learning (ML)

Machine Learning (ML) coined by Arthur Samuel (Roberto Iriondo & Pratik Shukla, 2022), is a subset of AI that helps a computer to acquire data automatically and learn from the experiences or instances it has encountered. ML helps us in completing a task or work without any extensive programming.

ML accentuates the development of algorithms that can analyze data and generate predictions. There is significant use of MLin the Health Care Industry.

### Types of Machine Learning

Like any method, there are multiple approaches to training ML algorithms.

It is categorized into three types, they are

1. Supervised Learning
2. Unsupervised Learning
3. Reinforcement Learning

### Deep learning

Deep learning is a subset of ML and the word deep refers to the total count of layers the data is sent and transformed through. It is a type of ML method where output is a prediction for a given input and it uses multiple layers to pull out high-level features from the provided data. An algorithm based on deep learning allows computer

*Figure 1. Subsets of AI*

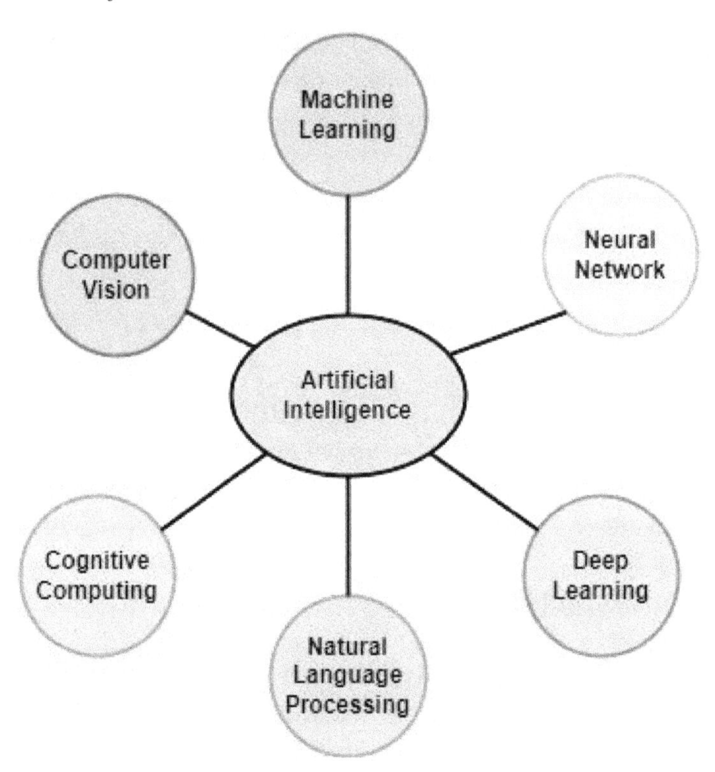


systems to enhance their performance with experience and data. The algorithms in deep learning resemble the functioning of the human brain. The structure of the algorithm based on which it is built is called artificial neural network (ANN). These algorithms learn how human performs a task by trying to mimic the human brain. Ultimately, the algorithm understands and gains some intelligence (similar to human intelligence), known as AI. The world's first functioning deep learning algorithm was proposed in the year 1967 (Ivakhnenko et al., 1967). After that, multiple methods and deep learning architectures have been and are being developed. They made human life easy by providing solutions for various problems which could not be solved or computed by humans.

## Neural Networks

Neural Networks also referred to as Artificial Neural Networks(ANNs) are a part of ML and are the crux of Deep Learning algorithms. As the name suggests, it's motivated by the structure and functioning of the human brain. The ANNs mimic the biological neurons of humans which send signals from one neuron to another.

ANNs consist of a node or neuron layers. The first layer of the node layers is an input layer. The layer at the end which is the final layer is known as the output layer. The layers present in the midst of the input and output layers are termed hidden layers which can be one or more. Nodes are connected to one another and have associated weight and the threshold value for each connection. If the value of the threshold is less than the output of that particular node, then the node is activated and transfers the data to the next layers of the neural network. But if the output value of a node doesn't, exceed its threshold value, then that neuron is not activated and no data is sent to the next layers.

## Natural Language Processing (NLP)

Natural Language Processing (NLP) is a subset of AI whose ability is to make the computer understand natural language i.e the human language that is written and spoken. NLP makes computers comprehend natural language that humans can. Be it written or spoken, NLP uses MLto take the input, train and process it, and make the computer understand. Humans have ears to listen, eyes to see, and brains to process information. Similarly, computers have a program to take input and process it. During this process, the input is converted into a code that the computer understands.

NLP is separated into two phases scilicet Data Preprocessing and Algorithm Development.

In data preprocessing phase, cleaning is done on text data for the computer to study it. Preprocessing converts the raw data into a workable form through various techniques such as tokenization, stemming, stopword removal, parts of speech tagging, etc. Algorithms use this preprocessed data and process it so the computer can understand this data.

Out of multiple NLP algorithms, the two main and most commonly used types are

### Rule-based systems

In this system, the linguistic rules are predefined. Based on the grammar, the text is processed. This method was considered early on in NLP and is also applied in the current day.

### Machine Learning-Based System

This system uses MLalgorithms that are derived from statistical methods. These MLalgorithms are fed with the training data, they process the data and understand it.

## Existing Applications of AI

AI is stretched into different Areas, and with its applications, different problems are solved every day. There are various applications in different sectors.

### Health sector

AI transformed the entire health sector. From developing New medicines to Robotic surgeries. We know that Covid-19 affected the entire world very badly, to get unaffected vaccination is the only weapon to defeat it, Generally to discover a vaccine or a drug takes 10-12 years of time, but the pandemic accelerated the rapid discovery of vaccines. World wide Pharmaceutical companies used AI to discover the vaccine, especially MLalgorithms to find the right base component to build immunity against the virus. Cancer detection at early stages is made possible by analyzing general screenings and blood samples. The advantage of robotic surgeries is they don't get fatigued no matter what activity they're doing. Notes are the most important entity for doctors, they help in diagnostic and patient health tracking purposes. NLP helps in transforming unstructured data into structured data very accurately, error-free and information is transferred very fastly. (Comito & Pizzuti, 2022; Huang et al., 2022)

### Automobile sector

AI made a huge impact on the Automotive sector in recent years from vehicle maintenance recommendations to self-driving cars.

- Drivers' Behaviour Analytics is aiding a lot of people which assists in finding the issues with driving by analyzing the driver and road conditions.
- Analyzing road conditions gives assistance to drivers by determining the best path for the journey based on potholes, humps, and road closures.
- Self-driving car is one of the greatest inventions that the automobile industry has ever witnessed. They are capable of driving the car without any assistance from a person. These vehicles use image recognition frameworks. Neural networks will distinguish the patterns in the input data and based on the patterns they teach themselves how to detect traffic signals, trees, animals etc. All this magic happens in a matter of milliseconds, that's how the system is built. Tesla has succeeded in developing the best possible autonomous cars and more is to be done. (Izci & Ekinci, 2022; Manimuthu et al., 2022)

### Economics and finance

Investing in stocks and cryptocurrencies increased in recent years. There is a huge rise in investments and mining of cryptocurrency, although China banned mining in view of environmental issues. AI Algorithms are used to observe the changes in the market, ups and downs much earlier using different Recurrent and Neural networks. Banking Services analyze the user's behaviour and provide the best possible personalized suggestions. (Gigante & Zago, 2022; Rodrigues et al., 2022)

Recently, a study was done by the authors (Dampitakse et al., 2021) on the adoption of AI in the Association of Southeast Asia Nations (ASEAN) countries. The study mainly focused on the following areas, namely Economic Growth (EG), Financial Development(FD), Financial Performance(FP), and Capital Growth(CG). The study outcome states that there is a positive influence on the adoption of AI. These organizations have strong EG, FD, and FP. Combining the innovation with AI adoption made their EG, FD, and FP much stronger. While increasing the danger of disruption by automation, AI has decreased repetitive tasks in many sectors, including manufacturing, healthcare, transportation, IT, retail packaging, financial services, and shipping. For instance, according to a recent study by Capgemini, AI in retail may save $340 billion in costs.

Another study was on the Economic impact of AI by (Haseeb et al., 2019). The study mainly focuses on the capability of AI in business operations. The findings of this study make it clear that AI has the potential to be the primary engine of economic growth in the Asia-Pacific region. The gross domestic product (GDP) of the major Asia-Pacific nations and the net and gross effects of AI on labor markets show that by the year 2030, AI may result in a 16-percent growth in the output, indicating an estimated sum of $13 trillion.

### Defense and military

AI Algorithms are used in Surveillance systems by using computer vision and Neural networks to analyze the footage to detect hostile activity. The airforce is using the F-35's Autonomic Logistic Systems to get notified about maintenance and replacing the damaged parts. This system extracts the data from all the sensors installed in the aircraft and passes them to a Prediction model which is trained with large data. (Robinson et al., 2021; Kiakalayeh, M. 2022)

## Machine Learning Applications in Education

There are a wide range of applications of ML in the field of education. Here are a few out of many applications.

The authors *(Sharma & Harkishan, 2022)* segregated the applications of AI in education into three categories

1. Personal instructors,
2. Intelligent support for collaborative learning
3. Intelligent virtual reality.

Intelligent tutoring systems (ITS) are used in one-to-one personalized teaching. The aim is to provide personal instructions and feedback to the users i.e students in our scenario. These are designed to help students master difficult areas of study and skills by using powerful algorithms that adapt to the learner based on their learning rate. These systems have a wide range of potential to track a student, analyze and respond to them with appropriate level of resources, so that they are able to master the concepts.

ITS also includes a feature to look at the clues to solve the problem. If the learner is willing to know the solution, the solution is instantly made available and a new question is given to the learner in order to test their knowledge. Along with this, the learner has access to the history of their activities. The system takes the help of this history and determines the capability of the student and gives questions accordingly.

Interaction and collaboration with different minds are the core entities in the learning process. AI can be integrated into online collaborative learning, adaptive groups are formed based on learner models. Based on the discussion data tutors can guide the students towards their aim.

Similarly, virtual reality has become famous and its usage is becoming prominent. Intelligent Virtual Reality (IVR) is used to help students to learn using environments that contain content made with games.

## Profiling and prediction

According to authors *(Papanicolau-Sengos & Aldape, 2022)*, Profiling, is a technique used to analyze and get a better understanding of the raw data. This can determine what insights can be interpreted when this data is used in ML algorithms. This is the important step in preparing the data for a predictive model. This technique is used to record the patterns and classify the patterns of a student's performance to build profiles. These profiles are used to predict the probability of a student dropping out of a course or a student getting admitted to a programme. Many studies by researchers have applied different MLalgorithms to detect patterns and classify them and build each student model to make predictions like the probability of students dropping out etc.

## Admission Decisions and Course Scheduling

Academic performance plays a vital role in admission decisions. Few studies tried to predict whether a student will get an admit to a university or not using MLalgorithms. (Acikkar & Akay, 2009) selected a few candidates based on GPA, National selection for a school of Physical education and sports in turkey, they predicted admission decisions and classified students using the SVM (Support Vector Machine) algorithm with an accuracy of 97.17% and 90.5%.

When it comes to course scheduling, MLalgorithms and Artificial Neural Networks are used to predict the student course selection behaviour to assist new students in course planning. Several factors are considered while selecting a course such as faculty, examination time, slot, workload etc. (Kardan et al., 2013) developed a model to predict the course selection with ANN in two master programs. These admission decisions are predicted at a higher accuracy level, this decreases the workload on administrative staff and relieves them to spend time on other work.

## Drop-out and retention

Dropouts are dangerous and affect the student badly, if the dropouts can be predicted at an earlier stage then students can make appropriate decisions on how to proceed with a particular course. ML and deep learning algorithms can be used to predict dropouts and some researchers have already done this in this field. Dataset is the most important for an algorithm to work, it should not contain outliers and also features are more important, what kind of features is also a key part of dataset selection. For this Dropout Scenario Features such as financial support, personal info, past and current academic info. (Delen, 2011) applied ANN to predict the student's dropout based on the above-mentioned features and he came to know that students' past and present academic achievements influenced a lot in prediction.

They have applied algorithms like ANN (Artificial Neural Networks), SVM (Support Vector Machine), NB (Naive Bayes), etc and compared their final prediction accuracy against the LR (Logistic Regression), it came to be known that these methods outperformed LR discussed below.

(Acikkar & Akay, 2009) used SVM (Support Vector Machines) algorithm to predict the Admission decisions and they achieved results with 93.8%. (Delen, 2011) applied different algorithms namely ANN (Artificial Neural Networks), SVM (Support Vector Machines), LR (Linear Regression) and (RF) Random Forest for predicting the likelihood of an undergraduate student dropping out from university, and his predictions were pretty good with 86.5%, 87.2%, 86.1%, 87.2% respectively. (Bahadır, 2016) applied both ANN (Artificial Neural Networks) and LR (Linear

Regression) to predict the student's academic performance, he achieved the results with good accuracy of 93.0% and 90.8% respectively.

## NLP In Education

In the present times, NLP is being hailed as one of the most ingenious and surprising ways to improve learning in day-to-day lives and in the future as well. In the past few years, it was already proven that NLP is successful in the field of education. This technology, which is being used to improve students' reading and writing abilities, is already in use and has shown a lot of great outcomes.

The benefits of NLP are truly starting to show, whether it's parsing and summarising arguments inside writing, motivating essay revisions, or increasing general writer's prose, but one basic question remains on the minds of many developers, service managers and organizations.

### Using NLP for Writing

NLP is presently being utilized in schools and colleges to assist pupils to improve their reading and writing skills. Here are some typical applications for writing and reading. Consider a scenario where a six-paragraph essay is submitted by a student, language learning technology based on NLP can provide practical guidance to help the student in improving and writing a better version. This favour refers to the grammar, general writing mechanics and prose. NLP is widely used in education and Grammarly is a good instance of this. It's a software that makes writing precise and errorless.

Nevertheless, a suitable practice for NLP and education to unite is for instructors to utilize NLP to monitor what is ensuing with the pupils and their distinctive skills, rather than merely helping pupils to submit better quality work to their instructors.

The use of NLP will be crucial for both students and teachers as technology advances. It helps them to assist and define the mental process of a student's writing, which tends in giving advice on how to enhance on a basic level, be it writing mechanics or the format of the task. (Lin & Yuxin, 2022)

### Using NLP and Education for Improved Reading

There are NLP tools or applications to assist students if they are having a problem reading. NLP algorithms can catch weaknesses in the pupil's reading abilities instantly and provide automated feedback on areas of improvement. It is obvious that it is impossible for an instructor to go around all pupils and provide feedback that the NLP tools are able to give. NLP tools are coming into the limelight for this sole reason.

NLP in education can also suggest reading content to students based on what suits them, considering how challenging and productive it will be. It is difficult for the teachers to figure out and suggest reading content that suits each student by themselves. This is the reason NLP tools are appreciated. NLP techniques have shown that the increase in grade of student reading scores is more significant than the traditional methods like the Flesch-Kincaid Grade Level exam. (Lee & Lee, 2022)

### Using NLP for Motivating Behavior

The most difficult task for a teacher is motivating the students to build up the interest in them. A student needs to get distracted for a small duration of time before he/she entirely loses track of the rest of the class. This is why teachers struggle a lot to get students motivated and interested. NLP technologies are widely used in education.

NLP technologies are used to determine the languages used by students and professors in a classroom environment and also their state of mind during class time. This information helps a lot for teachers to analyze how the students are reacting to specific concepts and what can be done to make the class interesting.

NLP technology has the ability to analyze the language used by both teachers and students in a class to define their states of mind during learning times. Using this analysis, teachers can see, in real-time, how students are reacting to the teaching methods and what can be done to be more engaging. These technologies are used to track, record and analyze students' behaviour and attention while learning. Naturally, stealth testing may be necessary for the most accurate findings, but NLP examples for education will need to be built up and evaluated to determine how successful this may be. NLP experts are probably definitely working on the case. If adopted, there may be rules that need to be investigated before commercializing these services.

Natural language software and solutions are growing prospects in all of these sectors, and once the benefits have been established (which is progressively happening and being worked on all the time), this will undoubtedly be an industry and line of technology that thrives. (Feldhus et al., 2022)

## Adaptive Learning in Education

***Definition:*** Adaptive learning is the process of providing a custom learning experience to each student individually as each of them has their own lapses that require special care to mitigate through regular feedback, pathways, and resources (instead of delivering a one-size-fits-all learning experience). (Smart Sparrow, n.d.)

Consider a scenario where a teacher is tutoring a student. The teacher is using the best of their abilities to make the student understand the concept, but the student is unable to fully grasp it. Let's see how Adaptive Learning makes a difference and is effective in such a scenario. The teacher observes the verbal and non-verbal cues from the learner and makes the hints and advice according to the learner based on the analysis of cues to make the learner understand better. This helps the student in understanding the concept in an effective way. As the teacher is adapting to the learner's responses, this is called Adaptive Learning.

For a small number of groups, Teachers can manage to understand each learner's response cues and adapt to them accordingly to tutor individually, but for larger groups, it's very hard and teaching efficiency will be degraded and will not meet the standards.

To make this possible Adaptive learning Technology is built into a model, basically a web-based platform and also made available on multiple platforms. These applications review learners' behaviours and experiences based on the specific factors called "Adaptivity factors". These factors can be past experiences of students in a particular situation, content knowledge, or misconceptions. These factors are analyzed and will be used to create courseware for each individual. These systems are capable of developing a unique learning experience for each student based on factors and classifying their responses to the lessons and performance reviews are provided to the instructors. Instructors use these reviews, they can manage the way an individual learns.

Some famous applications are built on Adaptive Learning Technology.

1. Knewton's Alta - Alta is a courseware i.e educational materials, and courses provider. Knewton is the best Adaptive Learning Technology, this technology is integrated with the Alta to provide the best-personalized experience to the learner. If a student is struggling to solve an assignment on Alta, newtons technology dynamically diagnoses the students' weak points, and strengths by interacting and providing the respective content to fill the gaps. (knewton.com)
2. Smart Sparrow - Recent Pandemic forced every educational institute to move from physical teaching to online teaching. Most of the students like online learning due to the flexibility and accessibility although, students and teachers get uneasy with online learning at some point of time. To solve this problem smart sparrow made a unique Adaptive learning technology that replicates in-person experience while teaching to make the learning as hands-on as possible (Smart Sparrow, n.d.)

## Analysis of Student Performance

In the present day, educational institutions are more concerned about their prestige and quality of education in society. For an educational institution, students are the core stakeholders, the management gives students' academic progress with utmost priority and takes required measures. Taking care of each and every student is impossible for a single teacher in a class, to solve this, various applications are built using ML algorithms. These applications will monitor each student's progress and inform the teacher if there is a chance for a student in acquiring a bad result in a particular course. Prediction of results of a course at an early stage helps students to rework for getting good results.

(Khan et al., 2021) applied a set of ML algorithms namely KNN, artificial neural networks, naive bayes and decision tree. These models are trained using a dataset with 151 instances with features like CGPA, attendance, marks for each course, grades, etc. Out of all the algorithms, Decision tree performed well with 86% accuracy. This model can be applied after the first set of exams to predict who is struggling and how many students are on the border to fail. According to the predictions, suitable measures can be taken like additional classes, modifying the content delivery, etc.

## Evaluating Student's Interest and Interaction in the Classroom

The effectiveness of listening to the concepts and interacting with the teachers governs the entire learning process. When it comes to offline education students and teachers learn and teach physically with face-to-face interaction, Teachers cannot observe each and every student in the classroom whether they understood the concepts. Asking questions to evaluate their grasp of the concept may not give the true outcomes, students try to restrict themselves by not saying true feedback about their understanding. Each student is different. Some students may not be interested in the lecture and other students may be interested but may not listen to the lecture due to a lack of motivation and circumstances. This cluster of emotions puts the teacher into a confused state about whether the students are understanding or not which leads to an inefficient lecture. To tackle this situation, Adaptive learning is needed to be incorporated into day-to-day learning. Adaptive learning makes learning personalized for every student individually can help them. The fundamental principle of adaptive learning environment is that learning will be effective when presented in the context of learners.

There a numerous ways of building an adaptive learning environment. Here is one such method to tackle the above scenario. The motive of this method is to have a better understanding of students' interests and interactions in the classroom and the end goal is to achieve personalized learning.

*Figure 2. Standard set of emotions*
*Source: (Angelica Perez, 2018)*

Interest in the learners can be acquired through carefully-designed learning environments that enable students to concentrate on the subject they are learning (Renninger & Hidi, 2011). Some of the researchers (Ainley et al., 2002; Flowerday et al., 2004) showed that presenting content in the context of learners' interests is effective, impacting persistence, concentration, and engagement. Figure 2 depicts the standard emotions.

From the Computer's perspective, the image will look like a matrix of pixel values. In order to classify an image as an emotion, the computer needs to discover the patterns in the matrix, different patterns are generated for the same emotion too. The process is rigorous and hard because with a few minute changes in the pattern emotions can vary. There are various image classification problems like numbers identification etc, but the Facial Emotion Recognition (FER) is difficult compared to the other image classification problems.

Deep Learning is suitable for the above scenario. The reason to choose deep learning is, that when logistic regression is applied on the non-linear data, then the MLalgorithm learns the linear decision boundary, it cannot create a non-linear boundary for the classification problem. Every ML algorithm is not capable of learning all the functions that can solve a problem. There are two types of Neural Networks that can be used: Convolutional Neural Networks (CNN) and Recurrent Neural Networks (RNN).

## Artificial Neural Networks (ANN)

ANN is capable of learning any nonlinear function, unlike ML algorithms. These Networks can learn the weights that map any inputs to outputs. The reason behind why ANNs can learn any nonlinear function is because of Activation functions, they add the nonlinear properties to the network. This makes it possible to learn any complex relationship between input and output.

The most important step before feeding the input to the neural network in image classification problems is to convert a 2-Dimensional image into a 1-Dimensional vector, but the issue is the number of training parameters at each hidden layer will be increased, which results in an increase in computation power. To solve this problem CNN can be used.

## Convolutional Neural Networks (CNN)

The CNNs are being used a lot in deep learning projects, especially in image and video processing-based projects. The whole CNN is entirely governed by the kernels, which are used to extract the relevant features from the input. The kernel is in the form of a matrix which contains random values which are multiplied with the input to extract the relevant features. After applying the kernels, activation matrices are formed and passed into the next layer in the network. In this way, CNN processes the more granular elements within the image, making them better to distinguish between two similar classifications. Here, it refers to the emotions. The main advantage of CNN is they capture spatial features which refer to the arrangement of pixels and relations between them, this helps a lot in classifying an image.

To get more accurate results considering the previous image frame makes a lot of difference in classification and we can get more information from this approach. Let's say a person is smiling, if we consider the previous frame the model will capture the lips expression from neutral to smiling expression. Overall we are trying to capture the transitions in the expressions.

Considering the previous intervals data can be done using the Long Short-Term Memory (LSTM) and extracting data from the images can be done using CNN. Combining both produces a perfect algorithm (ConvLSTM) for image classification. But the performance is completely dependent on the input data, training parameters, emotions-set and the system requirements.

Many Researchers worldwide took this area as a challenge, worked a lot and contributed to the research community.

## Facial Emotional Recognition (FER)

FER model was developed by (Yang et al., 2018). They used the Japanese Female Facial Expression (JAFFE) database consisting only of Japanese women's faces. Six emotions considered are as follows

- Sadness
- Happiness
- Surprise
- Fear
- Anger
- Disgust

For Extracting the Facial Features, it completely depends on the type of classification method and environment that is being used. Filtering and edge detection are considered for feature extraction.

### Filtering

Filtering helps in removing noise in the image, To get optimistic characteristic values of an image filtering should be applied accordingly.

### Edge detection

Edges define the boundaries for an object. To detect objects in an image edge detection is a very important step in the pre-processing stage. There are many edge detection kernels available out there.

Initially, the image is analyzed and observed for whether any face is present or not. This is done using the Haar Cascades method. This method uses edge detection techniques. The Haar Algorithm computes the sum of all the image pixels lying in the darker area of the haar feature and the sum of all the image pixels lying in the lighter area of the haar feature., and then find out their differences. Now if the image has an edge separating dark pixels on the right and light pixels on the left, then the haar value will be closer to 1. That means we say that there is an edge detected if the haar value is closer to 1. (Girija Shankar Behera, 2020)

If the face is detected, then eye and mouth locations are located and then cropped, and these characteristic values are obtained and trained the model. The model used

*Figure 3. Proposed Framework*

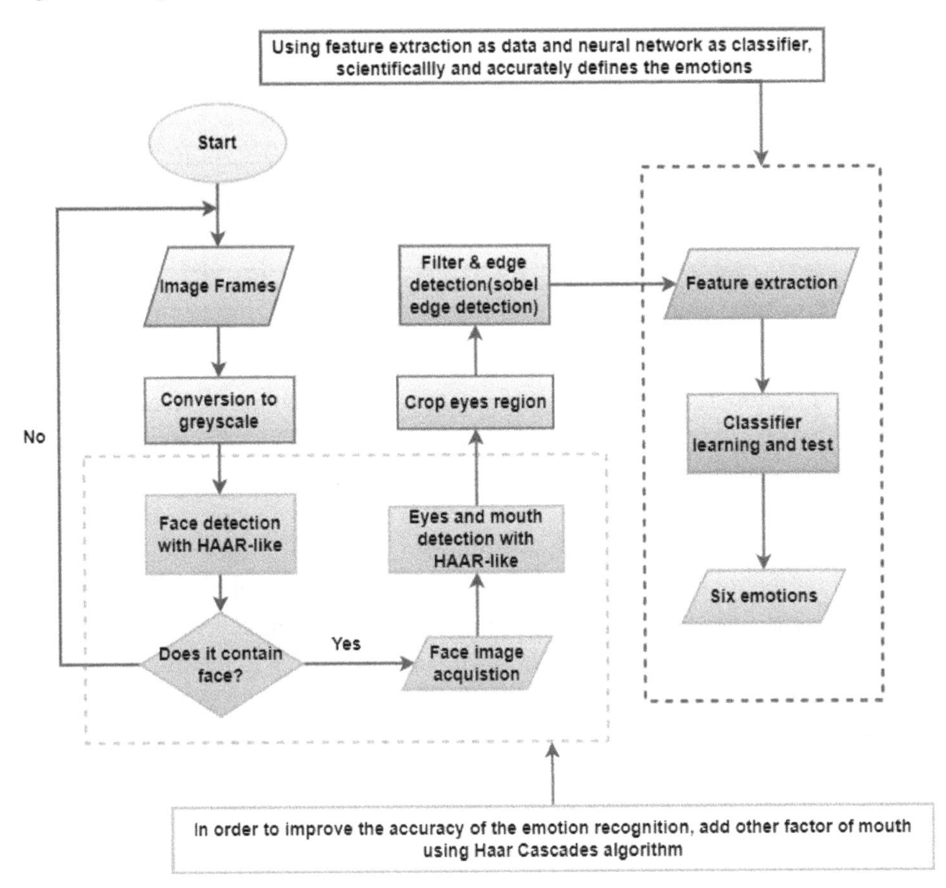


is Neural Networks with a 1 input neuron structure model, the 1 hidden layer has 20 neurons and 7 output neurons. Also, back propagation technique is used to reduce the errors weights in the hidden layers are updated.

This approach is not efficient for the student's emotion recognition as the approach didn't consider the different poses of the image. Poses of the face in the images will influence a lot of facial emotion recognition.

CNN usage increased a lot by researchers in this image classification and emotion recognition research area. It is observed that among the many advanced ML techniques, CNN is proved to be much more optimal in terms of lesser input, great accuracy and automated feature extraction.

In the approach proposed by (Dachapally, 2017), two emotion detection methods have been compared named Autoencoder and CNN. Out of those two CNN performed very well compared to Autoencoder in emotion recognition and also in (Ng et al., 2015) CNN predicted the emotion with better accuracy even on a small dataset

*Table 1. Learner's states of mind*

| State of mind of learner | Progress in learning | Assortment of emotions |
|---|---|---|
| Confused | Student has lack of clarity for understanding a concept | Surprised + Anticipation |
| Satisfied | Successfully understood the concepts | ———— |
| Dissatisfied | Difficulty in understanding the topic and not satisfied with the progress | Surprise + Sadness |
| Frustrated | Repeated unsatisfactory performance in a course | ———— |

(EMotiW). CNN is capable of detecting important features in a face, this can be achieved by tuning the parameters in Network.

(Mukhopadhyay et al., 2020) developed an approach that can be included in the Learning Systems. This approach is different from what we have seen in previous approaches in regards to identifying emotions.

Human emotions change according to various events that occur internally as well as externally. We experience and project basic emotions every day, In the same way, learners' emotions in the classroom change according to learning actions he/she encounters. They are hard to identify because they change continually before one could identify them.

During the process of learning different emotions will be developed which reflect different states of mind in the learner. State of mind can be referred to as overall experience, feedback of a learner whereas the emotions developed during this learning are just dots in a connected network which represent the state of mind. Rather than capturing these frequent changes in emotions which anyways doesn't conclude the actual feeling of the learner, capturing the long-lasting state of mind is a more optimistic way than temporary emotions.

Different states of mind are mentioned in the below table.

To find the emotions composition for the rest of the states of mind, an experiment was conducted on 150 students at the undergraduate level by providing them with learning materials composed of reading and puzzles. This material was chosen in a way that evokes all kinds of states of mind. Facial emotions were captured while learning the process and noted by an expert. Later, feedback was taken from the students about their emotional states and matched against the recorded ones. Out of 150 candidates, only 115 were found to have similar feedback.

These recorded videos were analyzed using standard emotion detection API (Windows Azure) by providing the image frames of each student for finding the basic emotions. These emotion patterns were used to define the combination of emotions for each state of mind and the combinations are as follows.

*Figure 4. Combination of emotions mapped to States of mind*

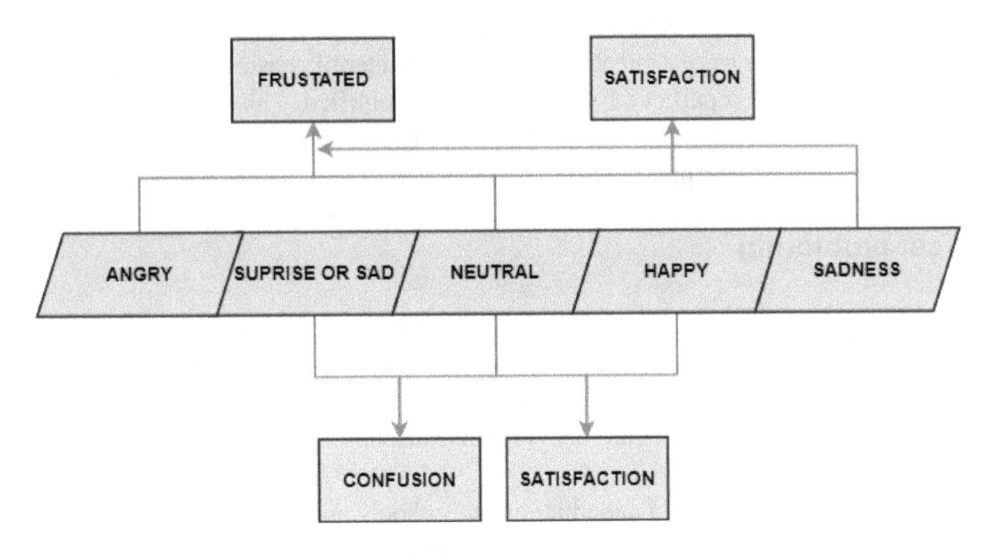


Now the main part comes here identifying emotions in an image, CNN is a supervised deep-learning algorithm that is generally used for image classification. Here they too used CNN for identifying the emotion in an image.

The Neural network is developed as follows:

- Five Convolutional layers with ReLu Activation Function f(x)=max(0,x), this Activation function is responsible for preventing the exponential growth in the computation required to operate the neural network.
- Three pooling layers, these layers help in reducing the dimension without losing the essential features and patterns in the data.
- Two fully connected layers and one output layer (7 nodes, each node refers to an emotion).

After the emotion identification, the state of mind needs to be interpreted using the set of emotions. As a reason, the state of mind cannot be identified using a single image because the learner exhibits multiple emotions in a short span of time, so a timeframe of 6 seconds needs to be considered. A face image can portray numerous shades of emotion, a score is predicted for each emotion of a particular image. To normalize this a threshold is set to 10%.

Predicted emotions of each image are taken and calculated the mean of each emotion of all images and a set is created i.e $M_{E=}$ {$M_A$, $M_d$, $M_f$, $M_h$, $M_n$, $M_s$, $M_r$, Now three emotions are considered out of these means i.e $E_1 = max(M_E)$ $E_2 = max(M_E$-

$E_1$) $E_3 = \max(M_E - E_2)$ such that $E_1 > E_2 > E_3$. Based on these prominent emotions are chosen and the state of mind is identified.

This approach is a good one. Instead of trying to identify basic emotions, a mixed emotion leading to a particular state of mind is identified. This helps a teacher to know his/her gaps in teaching, and at what point students are struggling to understand. Everything can be interpreted.

## Test proctoring

According to the author (Tyler Stike, 2021), the term proctoring is nothing but invigilating examinees attending an examination. A proctor is someone with honesty and ethics whose work is to make certain that the examinee or examinees he/she is proctoring during the test is/are obeying the rules and is/are not undertaking any kind of malpractice.

Due to the COVID-19 pandemic, all the schools and colleges were shut and everything was shifted to online mode. Teachers began to give lectures on Zoom meetings and Microsoft teams. This has solved a part of the issue of teaching online but the main problem was evaluating the students in online mode. Back then when classes were in offline mode, the evaluation was done by conducting written examinations. Based on the tests the teachers came to know the performance of a student in that particular course. But conducting written exams from home was next to impossible as it is very difficult for the teachers to monitor each and every student sitting at home and there is a high chance of malpractice. This was when online proctoring tools came into the picture. Many schools and colleges used proctoring softwares to conduct tests in online mode. During the pandemic, this transpired to become the new normal for conducting examinations.

## Online Proctoring using Gaze Tracking

Eyes are the opening to the spirit, but on the other hand, they're the doorway to knowledge about how individuals retrieve information and what affects their actions and decisions. The idea of contemplating where we look has been around since the 18th century, and in the present-day eye-tracking technology permits us to gather an unparalleled measure of knowledge into the human brain.

Gaze tracking is nothing but the process of measuring eye activity i.e the method of measuring either the point of gaze (where one is looking) or the motion of an eye relative to the head.

Eye gaze technology has taken truly a jump lately, moving away from the more generic eye trackers, which actually required physical contact with the person it's being used on, to an eye-tracking technology where no physical contact is necessary and everything is computerized and is based on digital video examination of eye movement.

Gaze tracking is applied in multiple fields and education is one of them. Here are a few applications built or methods proposed based on gaze tracking.

1. Real-time Attention Span Tracking

This method proposed by (RK et al., 2021) makes use of five attributes to compute the attention-span level of the learner listening to the digital lecture. Firstly attendance of the student is validated using facial recognition. The following parameters are considered.

- eye gaze
- background noise
- facial expression,
- body posture
- blink rate

Using the above 5 parameters, the attention span score is computed and is constantly updated every 5 seconds. The values of the parameters are calculated simultaneously rather than through sequential execution as soon as the lecture begins. Computing all parameters parallelly is attained by applying multithreading for all the methods. This plays a vital role in lowering the time complexity of algorithms also including the whole system. For every 5 seconds of duration, the model will show the attention span score and live feedback is provided to the students by plotting all the parameters on live graphs and also including the attention span score.

Here is the architecture for the above system.

**2. An Intelligent System For Online Exam Monitoring** *Source:* (Prathish et al., 2016)

As many courses are provided digitally on various educational platforms, there are a number of proctoring softwares built. Here is a table showing the existing online proctoring tools.

A system is proposed in which the actions like face movements of the candidate are monitored using a webcam. Also, the system usage and audio usage are monitored. To detect the occurrences of malicious activities that can occur, a rule-based inference system is designed and all the extracted features are fed into the system. Hence based on the students' actions, the system makes a decision.

*A. System usage analysis*

Window or tab switch in the computer that the examinee is writing the exam in is detected with the help of the primary module i.e system usage capture. The process capture detects if the examinee is taking the help of any other software or searching for answers by opening the browser. The result of active window capture

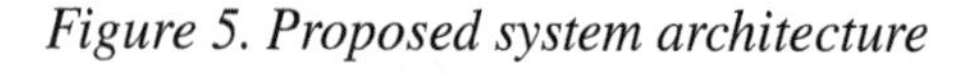
*Figure 5. Proposed system architecture*

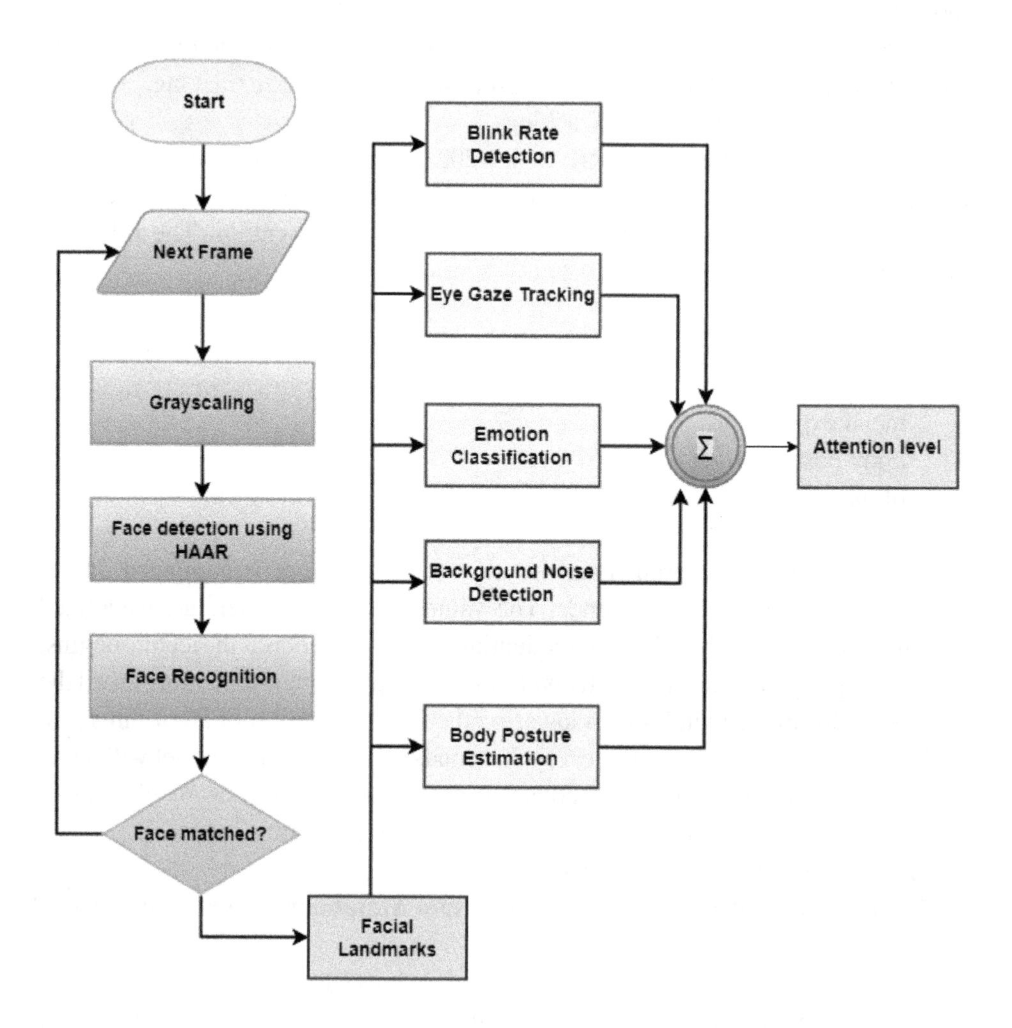


while the exam is going on with the beginning and ending time of the processes, is a log with the active processes. The process capture detects if a student tries to connect any gadgets to the system via Universal Serial Bus(USB).

*B. Video analysis*

Video input processing is the next module. To implement this, a webcam is adequate as it's enough to capture the student's facial expressions and movements during the exam. The input is nothing but the video captured and later analyzed. During the analysis of the video, it is broken or split into frames with a certain fixed frame rate. With the help of these frames, the head pose estimation and feature point extraction are accomplished.

*Figure 6. Each module's flowchart*

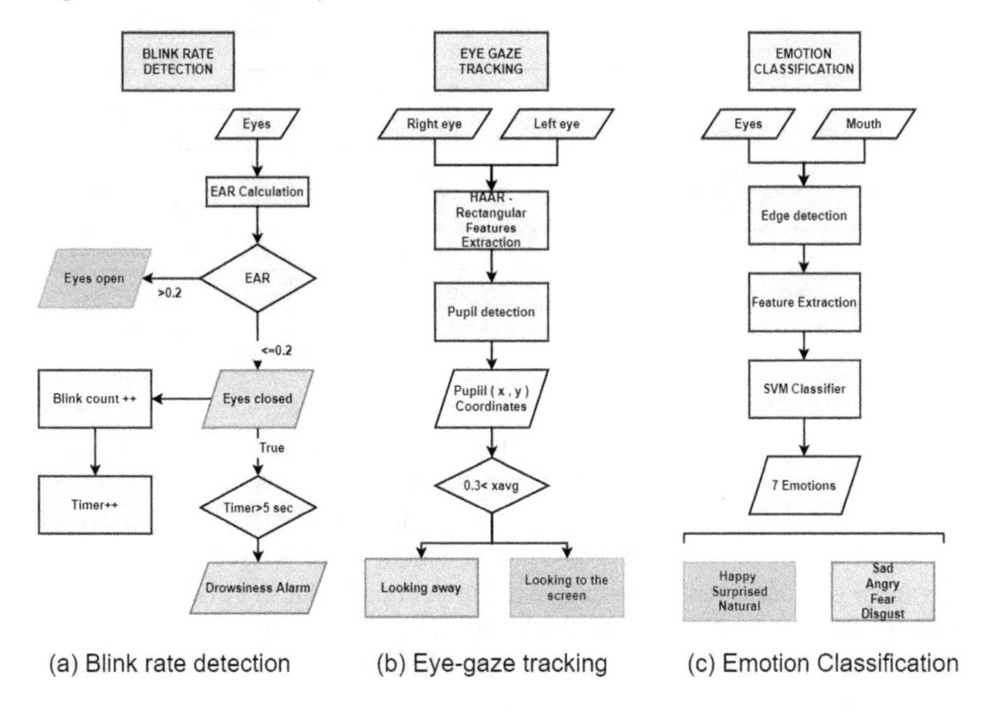


(a) Blink rate detection (b) Eye-gaze tracking (c) Emotion Classification

*Figure 7. Each module's flowchart*

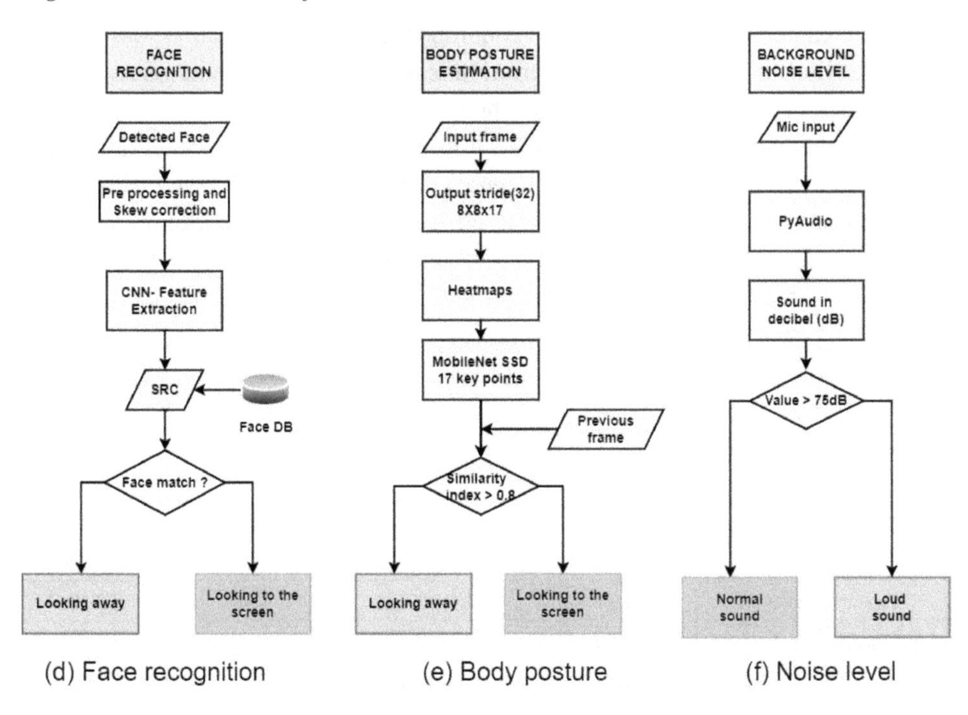


(d) Face recognition (e) Body posture (f) Noise level

*Table 2. The accuracy table for the above-proposed system*

| *Module* | *Inference time* | *Accuracy* |
|---|---|---|
| Facial Landmarks | 0.033 ms | 89.67% |
| Blink rate detection | 0.026 ms | 91.02% |
| Eye gaze tracking | 0.032 ms | 75.33% |
| Emotion classification | 0.057 ms | 82.55% |
| Facial recognition | 0.052 ms | 90.11% |
| Body posture | 0.048 ms | 79.06% |
| **Overall System** | **0.258 ms** | **84.6233%** |

Landmark localization and Face detection has been done together with the help of the methods proposed by (Xiangxin Zhu & Ramanan, 2012). A harmonious model is proposed for landmark localization and facial detection. The model considers each and every landmark of the face. The model is built based on tree structure. Each mixture is part of the model. 13 unique mixtures are introduced by the model. They are unique due to their viewpoint. Having the input which is an image, it is feasible for us to calculate the summation of the score for appearance evidence for placing a template. Along with this, the score for the spatial arrangement of parts is also computed. The best appropriate mixture for the given input is delivered as output.

*C. Audio analysis*

Audio capture is the third module. A number of malpractices can be done by the examinee during the exam. Audio variation is useful in some scenarios to identify malpractice. Possible scenarios are when the examinee tries to initiate verbal communication with the person next to him or calls them when the examinee is sitting alone in the room, or a person comes near to the examinee and tries telling him/her the answers. Definitely, there is some background noise when the exam is conducted but the malpractice can be detected as there will be a deviation in the

*Table 3. Comparison of different features in existing proctoring tools*

| **Features** | **Kryterion** | **Software Secure** | **Proposed System** | **ProctorU** |
|---|---|---|---|---|
| Physical Proctor for monitoring | YES | YES | NO | YES |
| Voice recognition | NO | NO | YES | NO |
| Usage of webcam | YES | YES | YES | YES |
| Continuous internet | YES | NO | YES | YES |
| Automatic active window capture | NO | NO | YES | NO |

*Figure 8. Multi-Model Online Proctoring System Architecture*

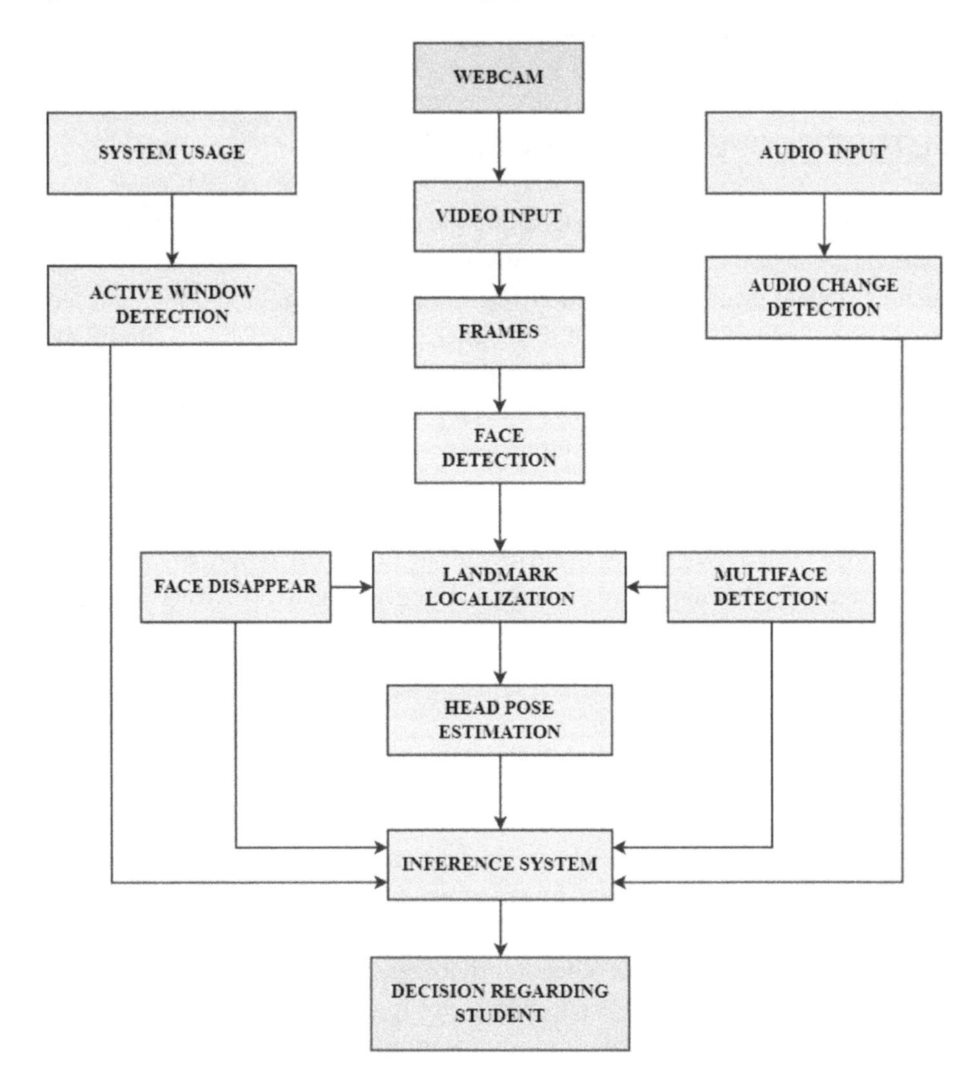


audio (exceeding the threshold value). The audio level at each time is measured i.e the output of audio capture (Raj et al., 2015). The respective frames having the audio level exceeding the threshold value are indicated as threats.

*D. Inference system*

After each method is applied and processed outputs are obtained, they are fed as input for the rule-based inference system. The system then classifies the outputs and detects the possibilities for malpractice that can occur. An output log is produced which consists of all frames with timestamps and audio variation exceeding the threshold and the frames with the yaw angle. Based on the output log, the model finally gives the sign of occurrence of malpractice with the respective time frame.

## FUTURE SCOPE FOR RESEARCH

In education, there are several use cases for the applications of AI. Above discussed techniques can be used to unravel multiple issues that are encountered in education, such as student evaluation, attention span detection, exam proctoring, and facial emotion recognition. The student data collected such as facial data can be more school or college-specific i.e data is collected within the school or college. This helps in giving better results from the AI applications and more over the data can be stored in a database and used for future AI-powered applications. These AI-based algorithms can be blended into mobile and computer applications to increase their reach and make them more available to schools and colleges. Especially, there is a lot of scope for improvement in exam proctoring platforms as they are increasingly being used. Deep learning architectures can be developed to do a better job at facial detection.

## CONCLUSION

AI applications are reviewed in this chapter. AI consists of ML, deep learning, and neural networks, here we showed how AI can be integrated into specific scenarios to solve problems. Some of the scenarios are course scheduling, dropouts and retention, adaptive learning to help students and decrease the workload on teachers, gaze tracking, etc. It has been observed that technology has transformed more or less in every sector compared to the last decade, education sector is also transforming at a faster pace, specifically, we have seen applications related to neural networks and ML algorithms. From students' perspective, they feel shy and fear in the classroom to ask doubts. This affects the student which results in poor results. In this scenario, we discussed about detecting students' emotions using FER and their states of mind like whether they are confused, satisfied, etc. For online examinations to help with proctoring gaze tracking was implemented using Deep learning, and computer vision. Day by day Proctoring tools are becoming more and more intelligent and effective (Nigam et al., 2021). There's much out there to learn and develop new innovative solutions to the problems in the Educational industry. There is no doubt deep learning algorithms will be blended with education and the results will get better.

## REFERENCES

Acikkar, M., & Akay, M. F. (2009). Support vector machines for predicting the admission decision of a candidate to the School of Physical Education and Sports at Cukurova University. *Expert Systems with Applications*, *36*(3), 7228–7233. doi:10.1016/j.eswa.2008.09.007

Ainley, M., Hidi, S., & Berndorff, D. (2002). Interest, learning, and the psychological processes that mediate their relationship. *Journal of Educational Psychology*, *94*(3), 545–561. doi:10.1037/0022-0663.94.3.545

Bahadır, E. (2016). Using Neural Network and Logistic Regression Analysis to Predict Prospective Mathematics Teachers' Academic Success upon Entering Graduate Education. *Educational Sciences: Theory and Practice*. Advance online publication. doi:10.12738/estp.2016.3.0214

Comito, C., & Pizzuti, C. (2022). Artificial intelligence for forecasting and diagnosing COVID-19 pandemic: A focused review. *Artificial Intelligence in Medicine*, *128*, 102286. doi:10.1016/j.artmed.2022.102286 PMID:35534142

Dachapally, P. R. (2017). *Facial Emotion Detection Using Convolutional Neural Networks and Representational Autoencoder Units*. Academic Press.

Dampitakse, K., Kungvantip, V., Jermsittiparsert, K., & Chienwattanasook, K. (2021). The Impact of Economic Growth, Financial Development, Financial Performance and Capital Growth on the Adoption of Artificial Intelligence in the ASEAN Countries. *Journal of Management Information and Decision Sciences*, *24*(4), 1–14.

Delen, D. (2011). Predicting Student Attrition with Data Mining Methods. *Journal of College Student Retention*, *13*(1), 17–35. doi:10.2190/CS.13.1.b

Feldhus, N., Ravichandran, A. M., & Möller, S. (2022). *Mediators: Conversational Agents Explaining NLP Model Behavior*. Academic Press.

Flowerday, T., Schraw, G., & Stevens, J. (2004). The Role of Choice and Interest in Reader Engagement. *Journal of Experimental Education*, *72*(2), 93–114. doi:10.3200/JEXE.72.2.93-114

Gigante, G., & Zago, A. (2022). *DARQ technologies in the financial sector: artificial intelligence applications in personalized banking*. Qualitative Research in Financial Markets. doi:10.1108/QRFM-02-2021-0025

Girija Shankar Behera. (2020, December 24). *Face Detection with Haar Cascade*. Towardsdatascience.

Haseeb, M., Sasmoko, Mihardjo, L. W. W., Gill, A. R., & Jermsittiparsert, K. (2019). Economic Impact of Artificial Intelligence: New Look for the Macroeconomic Assessment in Asia-Pacific Region. *International Journal of Computational Intelligence Systems, 12*(2), 1295. doi:10.2991/ijcis.d.191025.001

Huang, J., Shlobin, N. A., Lam, S. K., & DeCuypere, M. (2022). Artificial Intelligence Applications in Pediatric Brain Tumor Imaging: A Systematic Review. *World Neurosurgery, 157*, 99–105. doi:10.1016/j.wneu.2021.10.068 PMID:34648981

Iriondo, R., & Shukla, P. (2022, May 6). *What is Machine Learning (ML)?* Towards AI. https://towardsai.net/p/machine-learning/what-is-machine-learning-ml-b58162f97ec7

Izci, D., & Ekinci, S. (2022). *A Novel Hybrid ASO-NM Algorithm and Its Application to Automobile Cruise Control System*. doi:10.1007/978-981-16-6332-1_29

Kardan, A. A., Sadeghi, H., Ghidary, S. S., & Sani, M. R. F. (2013). Prediction of student course selection in online higher education institutes using neural network. *Computers & Education, 65*, 1–11. doi:10.1016/j.compedu.2013.01.015

Khan, I., Ahmad, A. R., Jabeur, N., & Mahdi, M. N. (2021). An AI approach to monitor student performance and devise preventive measures. *Smart Learning Environments, 8*(1), 17. doi:10.118640561-021-00161-y

Kiakalayeh, M. (2022). 'Military Use of Artificial Intelligence under International Humanitarian Law: Insights from Canada'. World Academy of Science, Engineering and Technology, Open Science Index 184. *International Journal of Law and Political Sciences, 16*(4), 213–217.

Lee, B. W., & Lee, J. H. (2022). *Auto-Select Reading Passages in English Assessment Tests?* Academic Press.

Lin & Yuxin. (2022). *Rhetoric, Writing, and Anexact Architecture: The Experiment of Natural Language Processing (NLP) and Computer Vision (CV) in Architectural Design*. Academic Press.

Manimuthu, A., Venkatesh, V. G., Shi, Y., Sreedharan, V. R., & Koh, S. C. L. (2022). Design and development of automobile assembly model using federated artificial intelligence with smart contract. *International Journal of Production Research, 60*(1), 111–135. doi:10.1080/00207543.2021.1988750

Market Trends. (2021, May 27). *Use cases of AI in diverse sectors*. Analytics Insight.

Mukhopadhyay, M., Pal, S., Nayyar, A., Pramanik, P. K. D., Dasgupta, N., & Choudhury, P. (2020). Facial Emotion Detection to Assess Learner's State of Mind in an Online Learning System. *Proceedings of the 2020 5th International Conference on Intelligent Information Technology*, 107–115. 10.1145/3385209.3385231

Ng, H.-W., Nguyen, V. D., Vonikakis, V., & Winkler, S. (2015). Deep Learning for Emotion Recognition on Small Datasets using Transfer Learning. *Proceedings of the 2015 ACM on International Conference on Multimodal Interaction*, 443–449. 10.1145/2818346.2830593

Nigam, A., Pasricha, R., Singh, T., & Churi, P. (2021). A Systematic Review on AI-based Proctoring Systems: Past, Present and Future. *Education and Information Technologies, 26*(5), 6421–6445. doi:10.100710639-021-10597-x PMID:34177348

Papanicolau-Sengos, A., & Aldape, K. (2022). DNA Methylation Profiling: An Emerging Paradigm for Cancer Diagnosis. *Annual Review of Pathology: Mechanisms of Disease, 17*(1), 295–321. doi:10.1146/annurev-pathol-042220-022304 PMID:34736341

Perez. (2018, August 30). *Recognizing human facial expressions with machine learning*. Thoughtworks.

Prathish, S., S., A. N., & Bijlani, K. (2016). An intelligent system for online exam monitoring. *2016 International Conference on Information Science (ICIS)*, 138–143. 10.1109/INFOSCI.2016.7845315

Raj, R. S. V., Narayanan, S. A., & Bijlani, K. (2015). Heuristic-Based Automatic Online Proctoring System. *2015 IEEE 15th International Conference on Advanced Learning Technologies*, 458–459. 10.1109/ICALT.2015.127

Renninger, K. A., & Hidi, S. (2011). Revisiting the Conceptualization, Measurement, and Generation of Interest. *Educational Psychologist, 46*(3), 168–184. doi:10.1080/00461520.2011.587723

RK. (2021). Real-time Attention Span Tracking in Online Education. Academic Press.

Robinson, N., Hardy, A., & Ertan, A. (2021). Estonia: A Curious and Cautious Approach to Artificial Intelligence and National Security. SSRN *Electronic Journal*. doi:10.2139/ssrn.4105328

Rodrigues, A. R. D., Ferreira, F. A. F., Teixeira, F. J. C. S. N., & Zopounidis, C. (2022). Artificial intelligence, digital transformation and cybersecurity in the banking sector: A multi-stakeholder cognition-driven framework. *Research in International Business and Finance, 60*, 101616. doi:10.1016/j.ribaf.2022.101616

Sharma, P., & Harkishan, M. (2022). Designing an intelligent tutoring system for computer programing in the Pacific. *Education and Information Technologies*, *27*(5), 6197–6209. Advance online publication. doi:10.100710639-021-10882-9 PMID:35002465

Sparrow, S. (n.d.). *Let's Talk About Adaptive Learning*. Smart Sparrow.

Stike, T. (2021, June 3). *What is Proctored Testing?* HonorLock. https://honorlock.com/blog/what-is-proctored-testing/

Yang, D., Alsadoon, A., Prasad, P. W. C., Singh, A. K., & Elchouemi, A. (2018). An Emotion Recognition Model Based on Facial Recognition in Virtual Learning Environment. *Procedia Computer Science*, *125*, 2–10. doi:10.1016/j.procs.2017.12.003

Zhu, X., & Ramanan, D. (2012). Face detection, pose estimation, and landmark localization in the wild. *2012 IEEE Conference on Computer Vision and Pattern Recognition*, 2879–2886. 10.1109/CVPR.2012.6248014

# Chapter 2
# Practical Suggestions for the Digital Assessment Challenges

**Ramadan Eyyam**
https://orcid.org/0000-0003-0265-1459
*Eastern Mediterranean University, Turkey*

**Ipek Menevis**
*Eastern Mediterranean University, Turkey*

**Nazan Dogruer**
*Eastern Mediterranean University, Turkey*

## ABSTRACT

*Especially after the pandemic, traditional instruction was forced to evolve and become digitalized. Consequently, the assessment changed shape, and digital assessment was preferred all over the world. As it was used lacking sufficient skills, knowledge, and enough training for many teachers, some drawbacks and challenges were faced. This chapter focuses on different assessment approaches and practices (with examples) that can be used to overcome the difficulties encountered in digital learning.*

## INTRODUCTION

Today, it is clearly understood that learning has been digitalized to keep up with the current age. Current students are now learning with digital methods rather than learning information from teachers in traditional classrooms. Just like the change in learning, the evaluation of students' performances has kept up with the times; it has had to adapt and evolve. Even though the digitalization of the teaching, learning, and assessment processes has been preferred by innovative educators for several decades,

DOI: 10.4018/978-1-6684-5400-8.ch002

especially after the pandemic that began in March 2020, all educators were forced to recognize the importance of digitalization and focus more on digital learning and assessment in education. Thus, they used technology while lacking sufficient skills, knowledge, and training. Consequently, the rapid transformation was not a success for many. Instead, they had to learn by doing and develop the necessary skills while using the technology for education and assessment. Based on the experiences during that period and the shared knowledge gathered, this chapter aims to shed light on the importance of assessment in both face-to-face instruction and the digital world. Therefore, it aims to provide examples of the different assessment approaches and practices that can be used to overcome the difficulties encountered in digital learning.

## ASSESSMENT AND DIGITAL ASSESSMENT

As we entered the era of online learning, the recent Covid-19 pandemic period and its lockdowns secured the longevity of online learning. Digital assessment became the topic to discuss in the education world. One of the most important parts of online learning is digital assessment and the "how" of it, but before all that, digital assessment and assessment need to be defined. For more than half a century, the concept of assessment has been defined by many scholars in various ways. In its simple form, assessment refers to a student's performance; it allows teachers to determine whether students are learning and where they need to improve (Australian Catholic University, 2014).

As a broader definition, assessment means "[making] judgements about students' work, inferring from this what they have the capacity to do in the assessed domain, and thus what they know, value, or are capable of doing" (Joughin, 2009, p.16). In other words, during or at the end of learning processes, it is vital to test learners' abilities and knowledge and make a judgment about them to guide them better and help them maximize their learning. The importance of appropriate assessment in course planning cannot be overstated. Assessment is so crucial to defining the course experience that some teacher/learner designers put it first on their design priority list. Some critical questions are important and need to be answered:

- What is the role of assessment in learning?
- What is the purpose of assessing?
- How can we tell if we are doing a good job?
- Does the assessment support our learning objectives? -Perhaps most important to be considered is the value of constructive alignment and ensuring that assessment is designed to support our learning objectives (or intended learning outcomes).

The assessment decisions made are very critical. In a practical sense, the learning experience is defined by how learners are expected to perform in order to demonstrate understanding of the course content. Students receive a strong message about the course from the assessment, and they figure out what the course expects from them and decide how much work they are willing to put in to meet those expectations. While good students are those who are eager to learn, their drive is not always based on a genuine interest in the subject. On the other hand, for some students, assessment is a hindrance rather than a valuable learning opportunity. As a result, it is difficult to create assessment tasks that appeal to a wide range of learners and are relevant to them.

The main point is that modifying evaluation can significantly impact a student's development, both positively and negatively. Because the major goal of assessment is to evaluate learning outcomes for specific topics, analyzing what is looked for in the results can help teachers clarify what skills and knowledge to ask students to display. It can also guide the selection of the type of assessment to employ. Other academic skills, such as communication, digital and information literacy, ethics, and reflective practice, can also be included. These competencies are frequently incorporated into topic learning outcomes and can also be used towards other graduate learning outcomes since subject learning outcomes include:

- knowledge of a content area
- a context or professional environment or practice in which the student can apply the skills and knowledge
- a student action or skill (usually identified through a verb such as describe, analyze, evaluate, design, or create, which indicates the development of skill) which can be a cognitive skill or one used in professional practice

Digital assessment has become more popular as a slightly different form of assessment, especially after the Covid-19 pandemic started and lockdowns interrupted regular teaching and learning processes and assessment practices. Digital assessment had already begun to spread all over the world when technology was integrated into the field of education, but the Covid-19 pandemic was the milestone for that since the Covid-19 pandemic accelerated its use. As a comprehensive definition, digital assessments are the tests administered online to evaluate, measure, and archive students' academic readiness, progress, skill acquisition, and educational needs (EasyLMS, 2022). Digital assessment, in the context of digital learning platforms, provides a fast, reliable, and easy way to evaluate learning with the help of technology on computers, tablets, or mobile phones. Digital assessment has made it possible to reach archived evaluation results easily and quickly, and to shorten the evaluation process for teachers and students.

## TYPES OF DIGITAL ASSESSMENT

Traditional assessment types can also be implemented in digital learning. Students can learn in a variety of ways, including face-to-face, distance (asynchronous or synchronous), and blended learning. In the past, assessments were usually given in paper printouts and had to be handed out and evaluated manually. Nowadays, all types of assessments can be created online. However, digital assessment is not just a matter of digitalizing educational information but also a set of educational methodologies (IPAG Business School, 2021).

Digital assessment should be carefully planned and implemented into the teaching and learning process to provide information about learning. It also must be arranged according to the learning outcomes and student needs. Although these evaluations, which are created using digital technologies, may seem different, the objectives of the evaluations and the expected standard should still be the same. In other words, this is not about the type of evaluation but how it is done effectively. In addition, there are many different formats for digital assessments, such as open book exams, online tests, virtual presentations, and essays (Trinity College Dublin, 2022). However, these various assessment types can be classified into three main categories that are systematically implemented and provide an overall view of students' individual achievement. These are named "assessment for learning," "assessment as learning," and "assessment of learning."

A. ***Assessment for learning***: This type of assessment aims to gather evidence to assess what students know and what they can do. It also tries to determine where students should go as a next step and how best to get them there. It is a formative and teacher-centered type of assessment. In addition, it is usually done before and during instruction, and it is frequently done while students are still learning and practicing skills. The information gathered is used to differentiate and personalize instruction and assessment, engage with students to develop appropriate learning objectives, monitor students' progress, provide feedback, scaffold next steps, and differentiate instruction in response to student needs.

B. ***Assessment as learning***: In this type of assessment, which is another type of formative assessment, the student takes an active role under the supervision of the teacher. In other words, it is student-centered with the guidance and help of the teacher. Here, the student reflects specifically on their own learning and monitors their own progress. It takes place throughout the learning process and gives students the task of critically analyzing themselves according to their learning outcomes.

C. ***Assessment of learning:*** Assessment of learning, also known as summative assessment, involves evaluating a student's learning against a predetermined learning outcome. The time for this type of assessment is determined during teaching and it takes place at the end of the learning process, so a final grade is given to the student. These grades are often used to evaluate and differentiate students' levels of achievement based on learning outcomes. It is also used to summarize the learning done during the period, to judge the quality of student learning based on established criteria, to assign a value to represent that quality, to see evidence of success in learning outcomes, and to share achievement information with students, parents, and others (NSW Government, 2021).

## KEY QUALITIES OF DIGITAL ASSESSMENT

Due to the pandemic, educators found themselves in the online teaching and learning process so suddenly that most of them were only able to focus on bringing education to the digital environment. Digital assessment was the last thing on their minds at the time due to the fact that they could not pay the necessary attention to it because they either lacked time or resources. As it was mentioned by Race, Brown, and Smith (2005), "Nothing we do to, or for our students is more important than our assessment of their work and the feedback we give them on it. The results of our assessment influence students for the rest of their lives." In other words, assessment locates where students' learning is and whether it is a success or a shortage. It also helps the syllabus designers evaluate their learning outcomes, so it leads to a curriculum review too. Assessment has recently been reconsidered and accepted as a tool that shapes learning rather than as a life-threatening incident. In 2005, Morgan and Reilly mentioned 10 key qualities that need to be considered for a good practice of digital assessment:

1. ***A clear rationale and consistent pedagogical approach***: Starting from the very first step, teachers should be very clear about what is aimed to be assessed, including approaches to be followed, as well as the understandings and skills to be gained. Any assessment should also be consistent with the learning outcomes and the curriculum to avoid complicated messages to students. If a syllabus aims at critical thinking, but the assessment supports memorization, students get confused, and the assessment is trivialized.
2. ***Explicit values, aims, criteria, and standards***: Students should be familiar with what is expected from them, and this can be achieved with clear descriptions of aims and requirements. Teachers need to be able to justify why certain standards are included in the assessment criteria so that students can feel more secure and confident in their performances. For instance, in digital assessment, some technical knowledge and/or abilities are needed besides the students' subject

knowledge, and the explanation of why such performances are needed is vital for students to fulfill their responsibilities.

3. ***Relevant authentic and holistic tasks***: The students in traditional classrooms are usually homogenous compared to those in online classes. The students attending online lessons might have different interests, contexts, and experiences. Thus, more authentic and relevant assessment tasks should be selected while designing on both classroom and assessment tasks and/or materials. In addition, online students benefit more when their backgrounds, life experiences, social interactions, personal and academic interests, and motivations are taken into account in this process.
4. ***Awareness of students' learning contexts and perceptions***: While organizing online exams, consider students' contexts beyond the subject at hand, such as competing assessment commitments in parallel disciplines and prior learning experiences and knowledge that they bring to the learning encounter. Students that are overburdened with assessments are not sufficiently stimulated by a range of assessment activities.

Furthermore, Ramsden (1997) reminds us that students' judgments of assessment tasks may differ significantly from our own, prompting not-in-depth approaches to learning despite our best efforts. Students can be forced to cut corners if they believe there is inadequate time, if they have received insufficient assistance or involvement, if they have previously been rewarded for reproducing strategies, or if their prior knowledge is insufficient. Evaluation weightings should be distributed among a variety of modalities to guarantee that students experiencing online techniques for the first time are not at a disadvantage.

5. ***Sufficient and timely formative feedback***: Formative assessment differs from summative assessment as it aims to improve students' understanding, motivate them, and inform them about their own progress. In digital learning, formative and summative assessments are applied together as a form of continuous assessment to ensure students' understanding and to provide them with adequate and timely feedback. As a result, students can develop their skills and understanding by receiving continuous and timely feedback, thus maximizing the practice of formative assessment. In addition, instead of summative assessment, which is the "last event" that follows learning, motivating and insightful assessments are made that are divided into manageable parts. Thanks to the feedback given to small groups during both extracurricular and online office hours (Rowe, 2003), the teacher takes on a task that facilitates learning rather than merely examining the success of the students.

6. ***A facilitative degree of structure***: Gibbs (1995) coined this concept to characterize the fluid balance we seek in online assessment between structured activities and learner autonomy. Self-direction may not be a natural trait in students, especially given the many years of teacher-centered experiences that have tended to socialize students in the other direction. Rather, it is viewed as a quality that can be nurtured in learners by a gradual shift from teacher to learner control over the course during a program of study, as students gain competency in information retrieval, goal planning, critical thinking, self-management, and self-evaluation (Brockett & Hiemstra, 1990; Candy, 1991). Thus, in online evaluation, a "facilitative" degree of structure is one that intentionally develops these abilities with the stated objective of self-direction and finds a balance between structure and self-direction at any given time that is most beneficial (Gibbs, 1995). In online contexts, finding a balance between structure and self-direction is critical. In terms of learning paths and assessment outcomes, students' early encounters may be extremely regimented. Learning paths and assessments become more customizable and self-directed as learners develop, which is the reason why pre-made, restrictive course materials with a focus on content transmission will operate against a learner-centered experience. Understanding how to make the most of the inherent flexibility offered by online learning and assessment is a difficult task. The subject of assessment flexibility necessitates determining to what extent we can sustain an assessment system that accommodates the diverse needs of students, staff, professors, and any applicable accrediting organizations.
7. ***Appropriate volume of assessment***: How much evaluation is required? You may be tempted to raise your assessment load if you believe assessments are a major driver of learning. Consider the consequences of overassessment before adopting such dramatic measures and raising your own workload. Anxiety and a superficial or survival attitude to learning result from too much examination of a subject (Ramsden, 1997). Although some assume that comprehensive assessment adds rigor to a subject, it may have the opposite effect on students. It could also be affecting students' abilities to meet assessment standards in other areas. To begin, an instructor should have a good understanding of how much time students will spend on each of the many activities, such as reading, interacting online, researching, and studying for exams; this information should be conveyed to students as a benchmark. Naturally, pupils will differ in terms of ability, prior learning, conflicting obligations, and so on, but a rough estimate is a useful guide for instructors and students (Chambers, 1992, 1994). Although there are often established norms within an institution or faculty, there is no universal formula for determining the proper volume of assessment. Teachers must determine what needs to be formally assessed to

obtain a balanced sampling of the subject while avoiding putting pupils on a treadmill.

8. ***Valid and reliable***: The terms "validity" and "reliability" are frequently used in educational measurement. Validity refers to whether assignments portray the most accurate image of the specific knowledge and abilities being evaluated by the assessment task. When it comes to reliability, it is important to consider whether assessment items can be marked consistently and objectively, especially if other instructors are evaluating the assessment. For high validity, assessments should sample students' performance on each target, employ an appropriate mix of assessment methods, and pick assessment methods based on delivering the most accurate image possible. The way assessments measure the target objective must be consistent and precise for reliability to be high. It is frequently stated that the online environment has enabled the evaluation of new skills and capabilities such as web-based research, design, and development, as well as text-based conversation and collaboration between distant and different pupils (McLoughlin & Luca, 2000). In general, validity is likely to be high if your online evaluations are real and holistic, with a high level of application to learners' actual experiences. Authentic assessments, on the other hand, have dependability issues due to higher levels of learner autonomy and a range of ways in which learners might demonstrate their learning. Even when content and evaluation are relatively stable and constrained, there is frequently a surprising amount of disagreement across markers about the relative quality of student work (Newstead & Dennis, 1994). Because authentic assessment involves complicated activities with several variables, judgments of student accomplishment are more likely to be subjective when compared to smaller, discrete tasks.
9. ***Certifiable as student's own work***: While it has always been important to confirm that the enrolled student is the one who has completed the prescribed assessment tasks or attended the exam and is thus the one who deserves to be graded, the adoption of electronic forms of assignment completion and submission has clearly increased the importance of certifying the student's identity. In this setting, where technology has exacerbated the problem, it is tempting to look for technological answers, according to Carroll and Appleton (2001). However, since intricate and potentially expensive technological solutions, many educators concur with the authors and recommend using both pedagogical and policy methods to reduce plagiarism and cheating in online assessment assignments. In some circumstances, students are simply unaware that they have broken the plagiarism guidelines. Some students have been observed to assume that duplicating the work of other authors is an appropriate representation of their understanding of the field's literature (Lok Lee & Vitartas,

2001). In this instance, it is critical to devote some time to teaching students about academic integrity and the institution's intellectual property and copyright policies. When teaching students about the proper approach to collaborative writing and attribution, it is best to do so within the disciplinary domain, with worked examples and the optimistic assumption that students are primarily enrolled with us to learn, and that they are willing to accept responsibility for exercising self-direction and progressing toward the goals to which they have committed. The key is to create mutually beneficial and desired processes that encourage commitment to learning and assessment goals. If an instance of plagiarism or cheating is discovered, however, it is critical to deal with it responsibly and transparently. Determining an acceptable course of action may be a case-by-case process at first, with referral to an examination board only if early actions are insufficient. Carroll has a comprehensive discussion and list of recommendations (2002).

10. ***Subject to continuous improvement via evaluation and quality enhancement***: A student's main focus is always on summative assessment processes, which are limited in their implications for institutional change in teaching and learning (American Higher Education Association, n.d.). In digital assessments, it is of great importance to evaluate the entire curriculum and not separate these assessments from the quality improvement process. As an institution, tools need to be developed to receive student and teacher feedback. It is also helpful to compare approaches to digital learning with other institutions teaching the same subjects. Comparisons can be made about teaching, learning, and assessment strategies from sources that can also be obtained on the internet. In addition, it is important for the institution to provide guidelines for designing, developing, and implementing evaluation strategies. Finally, it is beneficial to collect feedback, implement improvements, and share teacher insights on assessment practice.

## BENEFITS & OPPORTUNITIES OF DIGITAL ASSESSMENT

The introduction of all kinds of interactive technologies has opened up new possibilities for more engaging instruction and new modes of assessment. Technology has led to the ability to create new types of assessment or new ways to link assessment and learning more closely (Çelik & Aytin, 2014). Undoubtedly, technology has opened new horizons in everyone's life, but it has played an inevitable role in the lives of educators and students. For language teachers, being interactive is very important, and technology plays an integral part by providing students the opportunity to interact.

Some of the major benefits of technology integration in language classrooms include effective time management, an easy and detailed evaluation process, interesting and interactive presentation techniques, support for students' individual development and assessment, home-learning opportunities, and the use of various materials that address multiple intelligences (Çelik & Aytin, 2014). Some of the benefits of technology being integrated into assessments include:

- ***Effective time management***: One of the most significant advantages of employing assessment software over human performance evaluation is the cost and time savings. Previously, scoring and grading tests required a lot of manual effort; however, software may drastically reduce or completely remove manual effort, and results can be instantaneous (Hricko & Howell, 2006). In other words, it is possible to see the responses and outcomes of the test takers, and students can receive immediate feedback on the selected topic. With traditional paper-based assessments, more time is spent on grading the papers manually, and this process is burdensome for teachers. Reducing or taking away this burden from teachers allows them to spend more time dealing with students' problems or preparing new materials for them.
- ***Access from everywhere***: Organizing exams for large groups is always a logistical problem for educational institutions. Difficulties such as finding enough classrooms and assigning enough invigilators may need to be tackled. In addition, the number of papers used in printed exams is too high to be estimated. On the other hand, when digital assessment is taken into consideration, numerous candidates can take online tests at the same time, and they do not need to be in the same location. Therefore, with the help of software and the internet, assessments can be offered wherever and whenever they are needed. Since digital technologies also offer the possibility of less time-sensitive and location-specific examinations, individual needs and preferences can be accommodated by varying the location, timing, and length of examinations. Where, when, and how often work is assessed can all be organized to meet the needs of certain groups of students. Also, various mobile devices that test takers have can be used to conduct assessments in several places and during a variety of timeframes (Timmis et al., 2016). When different components of assessment are taken into consideration, digital assessment is also very useful for the students, as it enables students in remote areas to learn and take assessments in their own environments. It may also be completed at any time, giving students greater freedom in scheduling their tests (Alruwais et al., 2018).
- ***Easy and detailed evaluation process and effective feedback***: With the help of automated tests, the scores can be obtained more quickly and easily

(Jurāne-Brēmane, 2021). This is an advantage for both students and teachers because they can easily see the progress and problematic areas through immediate feedback. Also, digital assessment assists teachers in improving the quality of feedback provided to students. Since the tests are evaluated with ease, teachers can save their energy to provide effective and efficient feedback. With the help of these results, teachers track students' performance and analyze data from multiple assessments. The direct feedback from digital assessment allows the teacher to identify and correct any misconceptions that the students may have before the final exam. With all this information, it can be claimed that using digital assessment can relieve teachers of the burden of assessing a large number of students (Alruwais et al., 2018).

- ***Support students' individual development and assessment***: While both traditional and digital representations have advantages, more dynamic media has been demonstrated to be more effective at activating students' prior knowledge, allowing for the assessment of more complicated abilities (Perry, Meissel, and Hill, 2022). Activating students' prior knowledge and using different modes during the assessment can increase the efficiency of the tests and tools used in the digital assessment world. Teachers and test designers can use different graphic representations while preparing tests, and these graphic representations can provide contextual information that can help students who don't have enough prior knowledge to complete a question through an inquiry process. Different functions, such as drag-and-drop, can be used during test design, leading to increased interaction, engagement, and advanced problem-solving skills (Perry, Meissel, and Hill, 2022). Additionally, in today's world, collaboration and learning from peers are important for effective learning. Co-evaluation and peer-to-peer assessment are two collaborative learning and assessment approaches that can be supported by digital technology, such as mobile devices and tablets. Peer-to-peer data sharing, collaborative knowledge production, and peer review are all possible with networking and Web 2.0 technologies. By utilizing digital tools that facilitate social engagement and collaborative knowledge creation across contexts, assessment can become less individual and more closely tied to real-world problem solving (Alruwais et al., 2018). One of the foremost goals of education is to prepare students for real life, where they apply different strategies to solve the problems they will encounter, as well as to cooperate with the people around them while solving these problems. Digital assessment provides opportunities for students to practice this problem solving and collaboration.
- ***Individualized learning support***: Educators always want to encourage lifelong learning and are eager to have autonomous learners. That is why one of the main advantages of digital technologies is that students can learn anywhere

and anytime they want. This differs from the traditional model, where the teacher is the central figure in the classroom and instruction is limited to the school day. The teacher is no longer at the heart of the learning process when mobile devices are used, and instructional time can easily exceed the school day (Dias, 2017). Text, image, video, audio, data visualizations, and haptics (touching) are among the many types of media and modalities made available by digital technologies. These technologies allow new kinds of representation and the use of many modalities to convey achievement. They enable students to track their successes and development in various methods and over different timeframes and build exams in multiple formats (Timmis et al., 2016). Using visuals enhances the learning and motivation of students. When they have the opportunity to visualize the given information or are exposed to different media, they can understand the content better.

There are opportunities to extend decision-making in assessment through the social affordances of digital technologies such as social media, blogs, wikis, e-portfolios, and electronic voting for assessment. This can be done by sharing assessment challenges or problems across a larger group, providing mechanisms for aggregating collective, crowd-sourced grades, and allowing learners to choose which artifacts they present for assessment to which audiences (Timmis et al., 2016). In traditional assessment, the methods are standard, but for digital assessment, various alternatives may be suitable for students with different learning styles; therefore, their chances of success may be increased. Traditional testing methods may not appeal to all students, and this would put them in a disadvantageous position compared to other students in the exams. But in digital assessment, the students' varying personalities, learning styles, and needs are catered to more comprehensively. With the help of technology, tailored assessment is possible, and the students with learning abilities have the chance to showcase their abilities more. The integration of multimedia in digital assessment makes it more relevant because it allows the assessment to be tailored to individual candidates (Perry, Meissel, and Hill, 2022).

- ***Tracking students' progress and performance easily***: With the help of the data taken from digital assessment, individual or group responses to longitudinal research can be tracked using data warehouses (Hricko & Howell, 2006). To put it differently, with the help of the data collected, researchers, recruiters, instructors, or trainers gain a better understanding of their users, and they can adjust their curriculum and/or syllabus to meet their needs, capabilities, and weaknesses easily. It is one of the foremost goals of education to follow the progress of students, to understand the problems experienced as soon as possible, and to produce solutions. Since digital assessment provides immediate data, it becomes very useful for educators to track the progress and performance of students and deal with the necessary amendments.

- ***User friendly***: In today's world, the younger generation is digitally native. In other words, they have grown up in the electronic age and are more familiar and at ease with everyday technology than the previous generations. That is why students of today's world like digital assessment. It gives them more control, has user-friendly interfaces, and allows them to take tests in the form of games and simulations that mimic their learning environment and recreational activities (Alruwais et al., 2018).

## CHALLENGES OF DIGITAL ASSESSMENT

Technology has been a part of the field of education for a long time, and it is one of the greatest aids to both educators and learners. Its use has been further endorsed by the Covid-19 pandemic and lockdowns all over the world. Almost all educators have been forced to transition to digital instruction, which naturally led to digital assessment and evaluation. Although it has various benefits, it comes with a number of challenges too. Naturally, studies were conducted, and research papers were written on such challenges, and certain difficulties were mentioned in a number of writings. This section discusses the main challenges related to digital assessment:

1. It is a fact that where formative assessment is concerned, the implementation of digital assessment makes teachers' lives easier, as many things can be assessed by comprehensible assessment tools via computers and the internet. However, it is difficult to assess long answers or open-ended questions through digital assessments when it comes to summative assessment and when multiple choice questions are not an option. Assessing such types of questions requires experience, a well-structured answer key, and clear grading criteria. It also brings up the issue of subjectivity.
2. The traditional assessment system needs to be adapted to the new digital instruction. Therefore, a transition from the traditional assessment method to a digital one requires an investment in online teaching and assessment software. It is also important to handle the resistance of some staff and students. Digital teaching and assessment require some training on the teachers' part before they arrange any training for the students. People are programmed to resist change, especially when initially it seems it is increasing their workload. Institutions should ensure a smooth change from traditional to digital instruction and assessment. They should emphasize its advantages to help overcome its challenges and difficulties.

3. Poor technical infrastructure is one of the major challenges and may be the most vital one, as some locations do not have stable electricity and internet connections (Alruwais et al., 2018). A poor internet connection may also cause problems with taking an assessment, and it might even require the teacher to make a new version (an equivalent of the same test) since the student may have seen the previous version before they lost the internet connection.
4. Finances or the socio-economic status of some countries, institutions, and individuals (Kiernan, 2020; Jurane-Bremane, 2021) is another challenge that needs attention, as the cost of some necessary technological equipment can be quite high. Even if the institutions do their best to provide learners with digital instruction and assessment opportunities, the learners are required to have a smartphone, a tablet, or a computer with access to the internet to be able to become a part of these learning processes. Therefore, the implementation of digital assessment is costly (Osuji, 2021; Appiah & Van Tonder, 2018) for educators and institutions. Another drawback, which can be considered a serious challenge for teachers, is how rapidly the technological devices change. The developments in technology require all people to possess a device in good condition, but the definition of "good condition" changes almost monthly or with each upgrade.
5. The traditional summative assessment was administered under the invigilation of teachers, so students were not able to have various resources available during the tests. However, the digital assessment evolved assessment into an open-resource testing. In other words, when students started taking digital assessments, they were often allowed to use resources, and this led to testing security problems. Students prefer being assessed digitally, as it has become more fun and resembles a learning environment rather than a testing environment. Also, they might be sitting next to classmates or getting help from anyone at the time of the assessment since they are able to access it anywhere (Brink & Lautenbach, 2011). Similarly, resources such as books or other websites related to the assessment topic can be open in front of them, so it affects test security negatively (Wall, 2000). Another concern is whether the test takers are themselves, meaning the students may ask someone else to take the test instead. Therefore, cheating or concerns about the test taker's identity become important challenges when considering digital assessment. Unless high-security programs or installments (proctoring programs or browser lockdown systems) are used, the identity of the test taker cannot be guaranteed (Wall, 2000).
6. One of the biggest challenges of digital assessment is the unfamiliarity of both teachers and students with the technological tools and programs used for digital assessment (Alruwais et al., 2018; Jurane-Bremane, 2021). Insufficient knowledge of technology or computer illiteracy (Alruwais et al., 2018) might be

a reason for poor assessment performance even if the subject is understood well. In addition, technological assistance during assessments is often unavailable, and this is another challenge since such assistance can be provided during the usual/traditional instruction. So the available assistance for the supervision of technology to both students and teachers on site (Shim & Lee, 2020) is another challenge since such assistance can be provided during the usual/traditional instruction. However, in digital assessment, both the subject knowledge and digital knowledge are necessary for success. Many teachers and students are not proficient with technology, resulting in failure or low achievement rates. Therefore, technological and administrative assistance for both students and teachers is vital in this regard.

7. Teachers need to plan everything down to the tiniest detail and be extremely well prepared. This includes creating e-assessment tasks and working on the details in the task settings. For digital assessment it can be really tiring and time-consuming as it usually require significant time and energy for digital assessments (Mishra et al., 2020; Jurane-Bremane, 2021). Just preparing the digital assessment is not enough for teachers, as they need to secure the test and ensure its functionality, too (Dias, 2017). Therefore, time and workload constraints can be considered a big challenge for teachers and test designers.
8. Privacy/confidentiality (Wall, 2000) should also be mentioned within the list of challenges since the internet is not very secure. Either the tests, the test results, or both can be accessed, and the private information of people can be used or shared against those people's wishes or consents, so confidential information can be publicized. Such an action might also humiliate the test takers and cause psychological damage or other damages, depending on the severity of the situation.
9. The use of digital assessment might cause inequality or unfairness (Clairana & Wallace, 2002) to students or a certain group of students, such as students with learning or intellectual disabilities, speech/language disabilities, and hearing or visual impairments. Students from poor regions of the world or students from families with lower socio-economic status may also be at a disadvantage. It may not be one of the most obvious challenges of digital assessment, but even the gender, color, or ethnic backgrounds of some students (Wall, 2000) might cause disadvantages in their learning or assessment. If a certain group of students is more advantageous than other students in terms of having access to the internet or technological devices, this difference can create a big gap between the learners and/or test takers and result in inequality and unfairness.

## DIGITAL ASSESSMENT TOOLS FOR EFFECTIVE EVALUATION

Well-designed assessment procedures provide useful information regarding student learning, such as what students learned, how well they learned it, and where they struggled. Assessment becomes a lens through which teachers can better comprehend student learning, find hidden obstacles, and enhance their teaching methods. In this section, some very popular and well-known digital assessment methods for online learning are discussed under two sub-headings: assessment for learning and assessment of learning.

### (1) Examples for Assessment for Learning

Teachers want to scaffold what their students have already known about the given topic, or they want to see how much they get from the given lesson. There are different applications and teaching-learning tools that can be used to assess students' background knowledge about the topic and find out how much of the lesson is understood by students. The following online tools have similar purposes. In general, they are used to get feedback and help teachers see the progress of their students in specific areas. In some ways, these online tools are more effective than paper-based ones since they can be evaluated immediately and give teachers information.

(a) ***Kahoot!***: It is a cloud-based quiz tool designed specifically for students and teachers. It allows teachers to develop new quizzes from scratch, and teachers can be more creative and provide students with more personalized learning possibilities. More information can be reached at https://www.techlearning.com/how-to/what-is-kahoot-and-how-does-it-work-for-teachers. Like in face-to-face education, a tool like Kahoot! helps teachers to assess students' progress throughout the lesson by providing them with an online, synchronous quiz. With the help of this tool, both teachers and students can see the problematic areas and personalize the learning experiences of the students. It also helps teachers to deal with these areas more easily and prepare a remedial lesson to address them.

(b) ***Padlet***: It is an internet bulletin board. It allows teachers to create their own platforms and include a variety of media resources such as films, photographs, helpful links, school newsletters, amusing classroom updates, lesson materials, and answers to queries. Students can use it as a classroom bulletin board to reference a lesson topic, look back at daily lessons, keep up with school activities, or utilize it as a class document center. It is a one-stop sharing platform for students and teachers with collaborative creation, high security and privacy, and a variety of sharing options. More information can be reached at https://www.teachingexpertise.com/technology/what-is-padlet-and-how-does-it-work-for-teachers-and-students/. Padlet is a tool that helps teachers to evaluate their students' progress as it promotes the active participation of students to answer the given questions. It can be used as a reflection tool and helps teachers discover topics that need more explanation.

(c) ***AnswerGarden***: It is a web-based tool that may be used to collect text-based feedback (up to 40 characters) from students in a matter of seconds. When teachers ask students to respond to a subject or topic by posting it on the board, a word cloud is created upon numerous students entering their responses to the same cloud. It can be used for collecting short responses to a question or topic, checking homework, or mind mapping. It can also be used as a discussion starter or a brainstorming or reflection activity. More information can be reached at https://www.montevallo.edu/wp-content/uploads/2018/08/answer_garden__help_sheet.pdf . This tool is good for teachers when they check homework so that they can see all the students' answers at once. When it is used for the brainstorming stage of a lesson, it helps teachers find out what they know about the topic and provides teachers with ideas for developing the lesson around the knowledge of the students. If it is used as a reflection activity, it helps teachers get a clear picture of how much their students get from the topic.

(d) ***Wikis***: This is described as "websites created collaboratively which allows its users to add, modify, or delete its content via a web browser." More information can be reached at https://www.igi-global.com/dictionary/cybercells-integration-actual-virtual-groups/32586. While students are creating their own works collaboratively, teachers have the chance to observe the students' involvement.

(e) ***Socrative***: This is a digital platform designed for teachers and students to facilitate online learning interactions. It concentrates on quiz-style questions and answers to keep things simple. It gives teachers immediate feedback from live student responses, whether it is a multiple choice quiz or a question-and-answer poll. It has a wide range of evaluation applications, from in-class to remote learning. More information can be reached at https://www.techlearning.com/how-to/what-is-socrative-and-how-does-it-work-best-tips-and-tricks

(f) ***Mentimeter***: This is a digital presentation tool that may be used in real time. It is designed to be used in the classroom as well as for online learning. Unlike PowerPoint or Slides, this application allows educators to communicate with students in real time, take polls, present quizzes, and more. More information can be reached at https://www.techlearning.com/how-to/what-is-mentimeter-and-how-can-it-be-used-for-teaching-tips-and-tricks

(2) **Examples for Assessment of Learning**

At the end of a term, teachers need to know how much their students have learned, and they want to evaluate their knowledge. In face-to-face education, different types of exams are used for evaluating students. As online education needs to be evaluated similarly, a variety of assessment tools are needed to evaluate students. As students are not in the same room with teachers, some different strategies and tools are used. The online platforms offer teachers some opportunities to assess students' performances. For language learning, knowing the rules are not enough, and assessing students' performance on different skills becomes important. The online platforms used for synchronous teaching offer some tools which can be used for assessing different aspects of students' performance.

(a) ***Google Forms***: This is a simple and quick method to use the form-based system to create quizzes and speed up and simplify grading. Because everything is stored in the cloud, sharing forms is as simple as sending a link. It enables teachers to work with other teachers and exchange quizzes so that they can be edited to fit the needs of the subject or the learning outcomes. More information can be reached at https://www.techlearning.com/how-to/what-is-google-forms-and-how-can-it-be-used-by-teachers. Google Forms can be used to create multiple-choice tests, and it allows teachers to share these tests easily with students. It also allows teachers to see the grades or results instantly, which saves time and increases efficiency.

(b) ***Microsoft Teams Forms***: This is used for creating surveys, quizzes, and polls, as well as sharing quizzes with students via any web browser, including mobile devices. It can also be used to create formative assessments using branching, evaluate students' quiz results using built-in analytics, create assessments as a team by sharing a quiz draft with other educators, and export data (such as quiz results) to Excel for further analysis or grading. More information can be reached at https://support.microsoft.com/en-us/topic/microsoft-forms-for-education-8580c114-fae7-4f3c-9c18-9db984f3d547.

(c) ***A Learning Management System (LMS)***: This is a computer program or web-based technology that is used to design, implement, and evaluate the learning process. A learning management system often allows an instructor to generate and deliver curriculum, track student involvement, and evaluate student performance. Students may be able to use interactive features like threaded conversations, video conferencing, and discussion forums using a learning management system. More information can be reached at https://www.techtarget.com/searchcio/definition/learning-management-system. Within the learning management system, it is possible to prepare tests with different purposes. It can be used to prepare tests with higher face validity. It gives opportunities for creating different tasks. Also, an LMS gives the opportunity to limit students' time and movement, also enhancing the security of the exams. Shuffling the questions or the answer choices are options given to the test designer, and it provides the option to have a variety of exams.

(i) ***Multiple-choice items***: In LMS, it is very easy to prepare multiple-choice questions, and there are different ways of doing it. It can be prepared in advance and transferred into the LMS. When the "shuffle" option is selected, each student sees the questions in a different order. Moreover, there is an option to shuffle the answers, so the correct answer appears in different places for different students.

(ii) ***True–false questions***: This is a good option, especially when the aim of the test is to find out the general knowledge the students have or when the teachers want to see how much the students know about a specific topic. It is easy to prepare since transferring the sentences into the system is very easy.

(iii) ***Short answers***: Sometimes, the aim of a test is to match short answers to the given questions. If all the choices are loaded in as answers, it reduces teacher working time, and the results can be received instantaneously. For the test designer and teacher, it is important to remember that students should be familiar with this type of task.

(iv) ***Essays***: Within a given space, students are required to write their essays, and the length of the essay can be identified by the test designer. The evaluation is done by the teacher after submission.

(v) ***Drag and drop into text***: This is a good option for questions about vocabulary. Students can see all the options, and by dragging and dropping, they can select the answers they think are correct.

(vi) ***Select missing words/sentences/phrases***: It can be used for matching headings or for creating a "cloze test." Cloze tests are commonly used by language teachers, and learning management systems are one of the most effective tools for creating them.

(d) ***Written Assignments***: This is important to evaluate a student's performance. Both Microsoft Teams and LMS give a chance to collect students' written responses, and as a checking mechanism against plagiarism, *Turn-it-in* can be embedded into these assignments. This allows the grader/teacher to have the chance to check plagiarism in advance and grade their students' written assignments accordingly.

(e) ***Recorded Speaking Activities***: To find out a student's level of competence in speaking, one of the options is to give them assignments to prepare their own speeches and record them. Both Microsoft Teams and LMS provide the option for students to upload their own recordings.

(f) ***Online oral presentations***: This can be done with a program that has meeting options. One of these programs is Microsoft Teams. Students can share their own work and talk about it, and at the end of presentations, both teachers and peers have a chance to ask questions.

(g) ***Online speaking exams***: Speaking is an important skill to be tested, as some of the programs have the chance to meet students via video chat. During these chats, more than one examiner can be online and listen to the examinee to grade the performance with the given criteria.

## CONCLUSION

In conclusion, this chapter aims to discuss the practices used to suggest alternative solutions to the challenges faced in digital assessment through considering what assessment and digital assessment are, the different types of digital assessment, the key qualities of digital assessment, and the benefits and challenges of digital assessment. The chapter then provides information about various types of digital assessment tools; the tools are effective for student evaluation and are preferred by a huge number of scholars, educators, and teachers. Assessments have rapidly changed and become digitalized, especially after the Covid-19 virus affected the world. The education system completely changed and evolved as learners could not go to schools, and there was a need for more online education.

As in face-to-face education, the evaluation of what is taught in the course also has an important place in the digital environment. Educators need to make sure the subjects covered during a course are actually learned by the students. Teachers must be able to give detailed feedback to their learners, and this is a matter of evaluation and assessment. Although digital assessment and evaluation show similarities with face-to-face education, the fact that it is done in an online atmosphere remotely and the students and teachers are not in the same environment creates the biggest difference and may cause some difficulties.

Regarding the key qualities of digital assessment, the first point discussed in this chapter was the importance of assessment for learning. Assessment is one of the key elements of the learning process. Since active participation of students is important at every stage of learning, it is important to be a part of the assessment conducted during the learning process. That is why it is important for students to use the assessment processes for their learning. First, the criteria used for different types of digital assessment should be clear and should be applied equally to everyone. Knowing that these criteria will not change and having a clear understanding of the criteria will enable students to prepare for assessments properly. Also, in the world of education, a commonly accepted and respected truth is that learning is individual, and personal factors affect students' learning process and their progress. Therefore, with the help of digital assessment, personalized progress can be achieved by taking students' individual characteristics into account.

Most digital assessment tools provide instant feedback for students, and with the help of such feedback, students can easily observe their own improvement and see their weaknesses so that they can focus on them. These assessment tools are the ones which give the opportunity to see the improvement of each student and it focuses on the students' development. For learning, contribution and participation are vital, and digital assessments provide the opportunity for students to participate actively. Students need to talk and write; they need to communicate with their peers and with their teachers. They need to use the given input effectively in order to accomplish the given tasks. In general, students can get immediate feedback, and digital checking procedures also help speed up this process, so students get feedback and their results more quickly. This is not only a benefit for students but also for teachers since it minimizes the load of teachers.

Assessment in digital learning can vary based on the teacher's preferences and students' needs. The main methods of assessment used in digital learning are rubrics, portfolios, student-teacher conferences, online quizzes, drag-and-drop activities, online presentations, peer and self-assessment, forum posts, audio and video assessment, and one-on-one conferences. Most of these assessment methods can also be implemented in classrooms, even though some emerged to fulfill a need in digital learning. Stannard and Basiel (2013) emphasized that teachers can gain more experience with technology today through new technological tools. They also listed a number of Web 2.0 tools mentioned above to provide evidence of learning.

The assessments that functioned well in a face-to-face classroom may need to be changed or even replaced to be effective in an online environment because typical evaluation implementations may be challenging in the digital teaching and learning environment. One of the biggest challenges in digital assessment is security issues, as the real performance of students may not be reflected in the assessment. Therefore, studies were conducted on this problem, and they suggested some alternatives. For example, Foster and Layman (2013) compared the features of eight secure online assessment systems. Arnò et al. (2021), on the other hand, have examined the features of 29 online assessment systems and compared automatic and live proctoring online assessment systems. Recently conducted research by Topuz et al. (2022) revealed that the question types mentioned in this chapter are the most effective question types in digital assessment.

The digital assessment tools mentioned in this chapter and used in online practices show that students participate more in the learning process, and the stages of assessment become part of their learning. With the given advantages and qualities of digital assessment, it seems that digital assessment tools will be used in parallel with face-to-face education since it enhances learning and participation. This chapter explains how these tools are beneficial and effective for learning.

Overall, with the pandemic-endorsed online learning trends, although there are some points to consider in digital assessment and evaluation, the undeniable necessity of it means that it is here to stay. Digital assessment also offers numerous benefits, such as being in tune with the everyday requirements of our modern lives and allowing learners to continue their learning from anywhere at any time. This proves that digital assessment and evaluation will continue to be a part of our lives in the foreseeable future, too. Digital assessment tools will continue to be examined, and what we learn will continue to move education and assessment forward. The effect of any such tools on success or students' learning can be investigated. Also, a possible further consideration can be a study which examines whether there is a difference between traditional assessment and digital assessment or how accurate digital assessment tools are in measuring students' learning.

## REFERENCES

Alruwais, N., Wills, G., & Wald, M. (2018). Advantages and challenges of using e-assessment. *International Journal of Information and Education Technology (IJIET)*, *8*(1), 34–37. doi:10.18178/ijiet.2018.8.1.1008

American Association of Higher Education. (n.d.). *Assessment forum: 9 principles of good practice for assessing student learning*. Retrieved from https://www.aahe.org/assessment/principl.htm

Appiah, M., & Van Tonder, F. (2018). E-Assessment in Higher Education: A Review. *International Journal of Business Management and Economic Research*, *9*(6).

Arnò, S., Galassi, A., Tommasi, M., Saggino, A., & Vittorini, P. (2021). State-of-the-art of commercial proctoring systems and their use in academic online exams. *International Journal of Distance Education Technologies*, *19*(2), 41–60. doi:10.4018/IJDET.20210401.oa3

Australian Catholic University. (2014). *Assessment and evaluation approaches and methods for the online environment*. Retrieved from https://leocontent.acu.edu.au/file/22207b30-7a02-4e71-8948-7ed523bef6fd/3/html/ddv_3_60.html

Brink, R., & Lautenbach, G. (2011). Electronic assessment in higher education. *Educational Studies*, *37*(5), 503–512. doi:10.1080/03055698.2010.539733

Brockett, R. G., & Hiemstra, R. (1991). *Self-direction in adult learning: Perspectives of theory, research and practice*. Routledge.

Candy, P. (1991). *Self-direction for lifelong learning*. Jossey-Bass.

Carroll, J. (2002). *A handbook for deterring plagiarism in higher education*. Oxford Centre for Staff and Learning Development.

Carroll, J., & Appleton, J. (2001). *Plagiarism: A good practice guide*. Oxford Brookes University Press.

Çelik, S., & Aytin, K. (2014). Teachers' Views on Digital Educational Tools in English Language Learning: Benefits and Challenges in the Turkish Context. *Tesl-Ej*, *18*(2), n2.

Chambers, E. A. (1992). Workload and the quality of student learning. *Studies in Higher Education*, *17*(2), 141–152. doi:10.1080/03075079212331382627

Chambers, E. A. (1994). Assessing learners' workload. In F. Lockwood (Ed.), *Materials production in open and distance learning*. Chapman.

Clariana, R., & Wallace, P. (2002). Paper–based versus computer–based assessment: Key factors associated with the test mode effect. *British Journal of Educational Technology*, *33*(5), 593–602.

Dias, L., & Victor, A. (2017). Teaching and learning with mobile devices in the 21st century digital world: Benefits and challenges. *European Journal of Multidisciplinary Studies*, *2*(5), 339–344. doi:10.26417/ejms.v5i1.p339-344

EasyLMS. (2022). *Advantages and disadvantages of online assessments*. Retrieved from https://www.onlineassessmenttool.com/knowledge-center/online-assessment-center/advantages-and-disadvantages-of-online-assessments/item12518

Foster, D., & Layman, H. (2013). *Online proctoring systems compared*. Retrieved from https://caveon.com/wp-content/uploads/2013/03/Online-Proctoring-Systems-Compared-Mar-13-2013.pdf

Gibbs, G. (1995). *Assessing student-centred courses*. Oxford Centre for Staff Development, Oxford Brooks University.

Hricko, M., & Howell, S. L. (2006). *Online assessment and measurement*. IGI Global. doi:10.4018/978-1-59140-720-1

IPAG Business School. (2021). *What is digital learning?* Retrieved from https://www.ipag.edu/en/blog/definition-digital-learning

Joughin, G. (2009). Assessment, learning and judgement in higher education: a critical review. In G. Joughin (Ed.), *Assessment, learning and judgement in higher education* (pp. 13–27). Springer Netherlands. doi:10.1007/978-1-4020-8905-3_2

Jurāne-Brēmane, A. (2021). The digital transformation of assessment: Challenges and opportunities. *Human, Technologies and Quality of Education*, 352.

Kiernan, J. E. (2020). Pedagogical commentary: Teaching through a pandemic. *Social Sciences & Humanities Open*, *2*(1), 1–5. doi:10.1016/j.ssaho.2020.100071

Lok Lee, Y., & Vitartas, P. (2001, November 15). *Teaching and learning in Asia.* Unpublished Seminar hosted by Teaching and Learning Centre, Southern Cross University.

McLoughlin, C., & Luca, J. (2000). Assessment methodologies in transition: Changing practices in Web-based learning. *ASET-HERDSA*, *5*, 16–526.

Mishra, L., Gupta, T., & Shree, A. (2020). Online teaching-learning in higher education during lockdown period of COVID-19 pandemic. *International Journal of Educational Research Open*, 1–24, doi:10.1016/j.ijedro.2020.100012

Morgan, C., & O'Reilly, M. (2005). Ten key qualities of assessment online. In *Online assessment and measurement: Foundations and challenges* (pp. 86–101). IGI Global. doi:10.4018/978-1-59140-720-1.ch004

Newstead, S. E., & Dennis, I. (1994). The reliability of exam marking in psychology: Examiners examined. *The Psychologist*, 216–219.

NSW Government. (2021). *Approaches to assessment.* Retrieved from https://education.nsw.gov.au/teaching-and-learning/professional-learning/teacher-quality-and-accreditation/strong-start-great-teachers/refining-practice/aspects-of-assessment/approaches-to-assessment

Osuji, U. S. (2012). The use of e-assessments in the Nigerian higher education system. *Turkish Online Journal of Distance Education, 13*(4), 140–152.

Perry, K., Meissel, K., & Hill, M. F. (2022). Rebooting assessment. Exploring the challenges and benefits of shifting from pen-and-paper to computer in summative assessment. *Educational Research Review*, *36*, 100451. doi:10.1016/j.edurev.2022.100451

Race, P., Brown, S., & Smith, B. (2005). *500 tips on assessment.* RoutledgeFalmer.

Ramsden, P. (1997). The context of learning in academic departments. In *The experience of learning* (2nd ed.). Scottish Academic Press.

Rowe, S. (2003). *A virtual classroom: What you CAN do to enrich the learning experience.* Paper presented at the NAWeb, New Brunswick, Canada.

Shim, T. E., & Lee, S. Y. (2020). College students' experience of emergency remote teaching due to COVID-19. *Children and Youth Services Review*, *119*, 1–7. doi:10.1016/j.childyouth.2020.105578 PMID:33071405

Stannard, R., & Basiel, A. (2013). A practice-based exploration of technology enhanced assessment for English language teaching. In G. Motteram (Ed.), *Innovations in Learning Technologies for English Language Teaching* (pp. 145–174). British Council.

Timmis, S., Broadfoot, P., Sutherland, R., & Oldfield, A. (2016). Rethinking assessment in a digital age: Opportunities, challenges and risks. *British Educational Research Journal*, *42*(3), 454–476. doi:10.1002/berj.3215

Topuz, A. C., Saka, E., Fatsa, Ö. F., & Kurşun, E. (2022). Emerging trends of online assessment systems in the emergency remote teaching period. *Smart Learning Environments*, *9*(1), 1–21. doi:10.118640561-022-00199-6

Trinity College Dublin. (2022). *Advantages and disadvantages of online assessments.* Retrieved from https://www.tcd.ie/academicpractice/Gateway_to_Assessment/staff/digital_assessment_types

Wall, J. E. (2000). *Technology-delivered assessment: Diamonds or rocks?* ERIC Clearinghouse on Counseling and Student Services.

# Chapter 3
# Mobile-Assisted Language Learning:
## A Boon or a Bane for Pakistani ESL Learners?

**Muhammad Mooneeb Ali**
*Punjab Higher Education Commission, Pakistan*

## ABSTRACT

*Learning in today's world is equipped with novel ways and techniques to make learners attracted towards learning. Mobile-assisted language learning (MALL) has been considered as a primary tool for enhancing the performance of learners. However, this phenomenon is missing in developing nations. This chapter, therefore, will attempt to investigate the efficacy of MALL on Pakistani English language learners. Data were collected from the population of 120 learners belonging to private institutes in Lahore, Punjab, Pakistan. Firstly, a pre-test was performed, and two groups were formed, which were equally divided into 60 learners (experimental and controlled). After that, a post-test was conducted, and performance of conventional group and MALL learners was compared. It was found that the experimental group showed significant variations in their performance as compared to conventional learners. Therefore, from the results, it can be concluded that MALL can be integrated and effectively utilized in a local context.*

## INTRODUCTION

English is regarded as a second language in Pakistan and it is quite impactful on

DOI: 10.4018/978-1-6684-5400-8.ch003

the larger population of the people. It is an official language and the language of the law, administration, commerce, mass media, and higher education in Pakistan. Tariq et al., (2013) stated that in Pakistan, the status of English rose higher even after independence from the British. Here English executes different purposes i.e., for attaining jobs, for media reporting, in the offices and in the local and foreign policy matters as well. Actually, English here became "vernacularized" and "natisized" because of social, political, mobility, and economic reason and most of the people here exploit English for the said reasons (Schneider, 2020).

All these aspects direct that without English it can be hard to have a high status in the local vicinity.

## BACKGROUND

English in Pakistan enjoys popularity and high status. It is a language of communication in almost all disciplines and areas (Ali et al., 2021). The western classrooms, are learner-centered and teacher is a mentor. Whereas, in eastern classrooms, the conventional strategies and teacher centered classrooms are practiced. The customary strategy generally centers upon repetition which is opposed to the development of information and ideas. Ali, Malik and Rehman (2016) expressed that the classes in Pakistan is dominated by teachers with conventional techniques for teaching English. The students work individually and there is no utilization of innovation for ESL learning and educating. Hardly any latest tool is utilized. Whereas the use of white or Blackboards are typically used in colleges, yet projectors are used in universities, but the utilization of innovative devices are primarily missing in schools, colleges and universities.

With the changing demands of learning contexts and communication for learning, the world has shifted from orthodox methods to newer ones involving communication, technology, interaction, collaboration and independence in learning (Renau, 2018). So, English learning and teaching is no longer related to the structure only but it is now the development of new concepts while adapting different contexts and learning styles to make new realities of teaching and learning. As the demand for learning is constantly changing, there is a strong need to change the approach and methods for teaching and learning with time as well (Attar & Chopra, 2010).

In South Asia, specifically in Pakistan the conventional mode of teaching and learning is a common practice. Particularly, in ESL learning situations, the learners are usually dependent upon teachers who are the central figure inside the classroom. Grammar Translation Method and Direct Method are the most common methods used for teaching English. There is no concept whatsoever to discuss, teach and learn outside the classroom. In Pakistan where English is the most important language of the country, the desire to learn English is quite strong in people, yet the customary methods of learning and teaching English have become least effective without meeting the objectives of the learners. The teachers are accustomed to customary ways which resultantly are affecting the learners' efficiency regarding ESL learning. For teaching formal syllabus there is a dire need to introduce the latest methods dipped with technology and innovation so that the learner may be attracted towards studies. Induction of modern tools is common practice in the world and adaptation of this modern method may increase learners' productivity. The inclusion of technological tools like mobile phones can make learners independent, agile and active participators in different language learning activities. It will also enhance collaboration among them and will improve their communication level with the teacher so that maximum learning outcomes can be achieved.

Many investigations have been done on MALL focusing upon its various aspects. Precisely some studies focused upon finding the impact of MALL on English language writing but there is a scarcity of doing an investigation on the impact of MALL in connection with local context amongst English as a Second Language learners.

## MAIN FOCUS OF THE CHAPTER

This chapter is actually a baseline to view the efficacy of MALL in Pakistani context. This chapter will be pivotal as it opens up new avenues for learning connected with technology and MALL. Thus, it attempts to initiate transformation in the educational ambiance and classrooms in Pakistan. This chapter will have its implication for the policymakers in Pakistan as this will be one of the initial investigations using MALL in the formal language learning process. This study will be supportive for the institutional heads to utilize MALL and its benefits according to their own objective and aims of courses, syllabus and learning situations. This chapter will also be significant to create a trend by influencing orthodox methods and creating a new arena and space of modern techniques for learning. The idea of learning and mentoring beyond time and place will totally change the concept of learning in Pakistan. This study will also be a benchmark to provide an opportunity to develop a way forward for autonomous and student-centered learning contexts.

### Research Questions

1) Does MALL influence the performance of ESL learners in Pakistan?
2) Is there any significant difference in the performance of controlled and experimental group learners?

## REVIEW OF LITERATURE

### English as Second Language

Presently the horizon of communication and interaction in English language has become widened in a technology-driven society where most communication is now internet-based. Now more than 80% of communication and medium of language is English which occurs through the internet and other modes of communication (Balla, 2018). It clearly suggests that for attaining social awareness and knowledge of the various cultures, contexts, aspects, trends in education and people, ESL learning is extremely important. It also mirrors that with the upcoming challenges in global academia where there is strong competition among learners, the value of ESL has increased to present the individual as well as societal perspective (Reddy et al., 2016).

ESL learning has different dimensions in ESL countries. Sometimes ESL learning is performed by infusing certificate level, special language learning courses, ESP, TEFL, TESL and other academic purposes in different learning centers to equip learners with the latest ESL methods. The aim is to provide awareness to learners regarding the latest English language propensities. On the other hand, sometimes English is learnt for other competitive examinations to seek lucrative positions and to uplift social status. This notion is also supported by Cogo (2012) who was of the view that English is learnt for uplifting the social class and status. Furthermore, it is also taught as a compulsory subject in the curriculum from the initial level to the highest level of learning (Peng, 2019). So, in Pakistani ESL learning ambiance, English is a compulsion in curriculum and is being taught at different levels up till graduation. After the graduation it is an optional subject.

### Mobile Assisted Language Learning (MALL)

Initially the major breakthrough of technology came from the integration of computers in classrooms precisely in English language learning situations. This method was termed as computerized assisted language learning (CALL). Gradually the advancement of technology gave a way to the advancement in the tools of learning also. The inclusion of Mobile phones in society and later into English language learning brought a new phenomenon called as Mobile assisted language learning (MALL). The ubiquity, easy access and portability are the pivotal elements which can structure a perfect learning condition. Ali et al., (2021) stated that MALL is new way of learning English through various suitable gadgets like hand-held devices and palmtops. So, learning with all these gadgets are called MALL. This resourceful technology' bent has given provided an opportunity to the Academia where they can use variety of devices. Paris et al., (2021) compared CALL with

MALL and illustrated that MALL devices can increase the chance of learning due to their structure, size, and variety of softwares offered. The devices like mobile phones have music players, recorders, camera and play store for downloading and using different apps for making anywhere and anytime learning concept practicable. Therefore, MALL can be utilized either online, face to face or as blended learning (Shortt et al., 2021). There is no compulsion for the learners to sit in the class all the time. So, it provides practical solutions for English learning contexts. The major elements of MALL are ubiquity, ambient and pervasiveness. Ubiquity relates to the presence of MALL devices all around. Ambient is the feature related to the structure (weight and size). Pingping et al., (2021) stated that social interaction, sensitivity of the context, connectivity, and collaboration are also considered as major aspects of MALL. Further, cheaper cost and easy user interface are also taken as one of the major features (Hou & Arya Doust, 2021) pointed out some important characteristics related to mobiles used for language learning purposes.

## Advantages of Applying MALL

The advancement of MALL has provided numerous opportunities for learning the language. Some scholars (Puangrimaggalatung et al., 2022; Puebla et al., 2022; Puebla & Garcia, 2022; Wardak, 2020) proved the efficiency of MALL particularly in ESL contexts. MALL can be utilized in various language learning environments and the learners can be engaged simultaneously in different activities that can be formal and informal in nature (Morgana & Kukulska-Hulme, 2021). MALL is rather an acquiring appreciation because it offers so many features to its users for language learning purposes. Kukulska-Hulme et al., (2021) also indicated two important advantages of MALL which are connectivity and portability. Connectivity permits the user to be connected with peers, teachers, related communities and other social media for relevant information and learning. It also promotes ubiquitous learning like email, SMS and WhatsApp chatting. Moreover, the advantage of portability helps the learners to use mobile devices without place restriction and they can utilize material from anywhere. Xiaolong & Qian (2022) stated that MALL expedites learning outside the ambiance of classrooms as it provides real-life experiments. Another advantage of MALL is that it offers motivation and autonomy to the learners (Li et al., 2022). Çakmak (2022) asserted that MALL motivates learners with autonomy, ownership, communication and interaction and a fun learning ambiance. MALL also features the facility of downloading and accessing various relevant materials. García Botero et al., (2022) stated that despite technical issues the downloadable facility and the various kinds of material available on the internet, even the access and downloading of various videos help the learners to increase their learning efficiency. Furthermore, the sharing of knowledge and information through various applications like Bluetooth, Wi-Fi is also an added advantage of MALL (Dağdeler, 2020). Additionally, some other features like Google play, Google drive and social media also contribute to the sharing of academic resources and information. Audio files, voice messages and every type of text file can be shared among teachers and learners. Lei et al., (2021) also shared some benefits of MALL stating that the physical aspects of MALL tools like weight, size, in as well as output features and screen size uplifts the learning significantly. Viberg et al., (2020) also added some merits of MALL tools such as flexibility, low cost, small size and user-friendliness. also stated that collaborative learning is an attributive feature and benefit of MALL which has impacted learning ambiance.

## MALL in Pakistan

Being a multilingual state, there are various languages that exist in Pakistan. However, the status of English is always a discussion point amongst masses. It can be said that elite status is assigned to English by society though the major language is Urdu. The issue to first and second language has created a lot of problems with local learners. Resultantly no training and formal teaching is there as far as English and Urdu languages are concerned. Particularly in English which has been an area of trouble since independence. Though in formal learning situations English is taught as a compulsory subject yet the ways and techniques to teach English are quite poor. Using drill method and Grammar Translation Method the local learners are taught. These methods have affected the learners' performance negatively (Ali et al., 2021).

Keeping in view, there were some explorations that were conducted on computerized assisted language learning in the past decade i.e., a study carried out by Nadeem, Mohsin and Hussain (2012) using CALL for the improvement of pronunciation of teachers. Likewise, Irshad and Ghani (2015) conducted research for exploring the efficacy of CALL. Moreover, Bhatti (2013) performed research for the improvement of reading of 12th grade learners in Karachi using CALL. All these researches concluded that CALL is a fruitful method of learning.

MALL integration in Pakistan is getting noticed because of the popularity of Mobile phones. Moreover, the portability, affordability and ubiquity has also made mobile phones the most preferred tool for MALL researches. The major utilization of Mobile phone amongst Pakistani community is for social interactions. Yet to exploit it for English language learning is a perfect idea. Only few researches like Rashid, S. (2018) was conducted on the impact of training in MALL which successfully explored that MALL is an effective tool for training in ESL context. Moreover, Khan and Tufail (2020) studied the efficacy of MALL in COVID 19 situations. They concluded that MALL is the most important tool in ESL situations during COVID 19. Ali et al., (2020) and Ali, Gulzar and Anwar investigated the worth of

MALL in connection with grammar. They explored that MALL is an influential tool in English language learning.

## THEORETICAL FRAMEWORK

### Constructivist Learning Theory

Constructivism as an educational theory holds that teachers should first consider their students' knowledge and allow them to put that knowledge into practice (Mvududu & Thiel-Burgess, 2012). In addition to that, the environment is also focused and critical because the particular interaction between environment and learner is actually the reason of creating knowledge. So, in this learning situation the pivotal point for learning is that it must occur in a real context and the tasks of learning should be pertinent to the learners (Ertmer & Newby, 1993). Knowledge is constructed individually but mediated socially (Felix, 2005). So, the learning environments in constructrivism should aim at providing rich opportunities that motivate the learners for learning. The theories of Piaget and Vygotsky can specifically be viewed as a baseline for constructivist theories of learning. Both in particular, can be seen in the background of constructivist learning theories. Both Piaget and Vygotsky viewed actions as an initial point for further advancement. However, their understanding about actions was different. Piaget viewed action as a natural aspect of event which is occurring in a natural ambiance whereas Vygotsky stated that action is a meaningful and rich humanly act which is constructed by society and history (Tryphon & Vonèche, 1996).

The theory presented by Piaget is known as the theory of genetic epistemology which focuses upon the individual aspect of learning, on the other hand, the cultural-historic theory presented by Vygotsky focused upon the social aspect in learning. Thus, constructivist learning theories can be segregated into two important categories i.e., social and cognitive constructivist approach. Vygotsky perceived social constructivist theory and originated it. Vygotsky (1962) emphasized that it is not possible to segregate learning from its social aspect and context and he further stated that the real way to develop thinking comes from the social side to the individual not from the individual to the social side.

From the perspective of language learning the application of constructivism according to Ziglari and Birjandi (2012) is that learners exchange cooperative and collaborative meaning between them. This learning paradigm is a trend that is appreciated to be used in the language learning process. The basic principle of this theory states that individuals construct and interpret their knowledge and understanding actively by communicating with their earlier knowledge and the present information (Sweller, 2003). Likewise, Candy (1991) pointed out that during the language learning process in constructivism the role of the teacher has changed as he/she is not solely authoritative and in this learning paradigm the learners have the leading role. Knowledge is constructed by the students rather than being taught to them. MALL also shows as a subset of constructivist classroom by the inclusion of different online possible connection that can help along with face-to-face interactions and sessions. Sturm, Kennel, McBridem and Kelly (2009) emphasized that social constructivism is an appropriate theory for online as well as distance learning process. The constructivist scholar explored that technology is supportive for the realization of constructive process of learning (Bonk & King, 2012). The recent literature related to m-learning in connection with constructivism explains that constructivism may refer to the general theory of constructivism or social side i.e., social constructivism; it means constructivism and social constructivism both are similar (Friesen, 2008). Constructivism offers a concrete baseline for altering the method of delivery of knowledge as well as the construction of learning ingredients along with the role of the participants. So, it is relevant to m-learning.

## Past Researches on the Impact of MALL

Looking at the researches from around the globe it can be said that MALL has been an effective tool for teachers, students and educationists in various genres of education. The successful employment of MALL with positive results has been presented by various researches in different language skills like writing (Gharehblagh, & Nasri, 2020), listening (Salih, 2019, 2010), reading (Li, 2022), grammar (Parsa & Fatehi Rad, 2021), pronunciation and speaking (Darmawati, 2018; Saran et al., 2009) and vocabulary (Zhang & Perez-Paredes, 2021; Abbasi & Hashemi, 2013;; Başoğlu & Akdemir,2010; Song & Fox, 2008). Kiernan and Aizawa (2004) performed research that can be taken as one of the initial studies on MALL. The researchers combined MALL and task-based method of learning and pointed out a number of advantages of mobile phones for the purpose of learning languages. Thornton and Houser (2005) studied the impact of mobile phones on the vocabulary and found out that the learners who studied from the same repertoire of vocabulary have learnt more as compared to the other ones who learnt in the class through the conventional method. An identical study was conducted by Lu (2008) in which he found out that the use of mobile phones for learning language i.e., vocabulary is more impactful than the usual paper and pen-based learning method. Hayati, Jalilifar and Mashhadi (2013) focused upon using SMS and utilized it in the delivery of idioms lesson to the students on their mobile phones in an Iranian college and resultantly they were more enthusiastic in learning idioms and outperformed those who learnt through classroom traditional methods. The feature of SMS was applied in the delivery of assessment of learners on their mobile phones in a Malaysian context as well that enhanced the access and flexibility to education (Ziden & Rahman, 2013). In Jordan, the exchange of emails through mobile phones was done by the learners who were learning English as a foreign language. It was explored that their exposure was increased towards foreign language use through interactive and collaborative learning opportunities. It also increased the communication amongst the learners which helps to improve the writing and acquisition of vocabulary of language (Alzu'bi & Sabha, 2013). Thus, it explains the efficacy of MALL in EFL contexts. Whereas in recent time the world has been convinced to utilize MALL in English language learning situations. Lei et al., (2022) conducted a study on EFL learners to explore the role of MALL in vocabulary learning. By employing quantitative research design data were collected. It was found out that MALL improves the vocabulary learning of the learners and it also provides a positive impact on learning attitudes of the EFL learners. Likewise, Li, performed a study to explore reading comprehension of lESL learners it was validated through the results that MALL applications are significantly helpful to achieve desired results in reading comprehension s compared to conventional ways. It was also explored that MALL engages the readers in a way that they become energetic and active. Ghorbani, and Ebadi, (2020) explored the feedback of teachers regarding the grammatical development on EFL learner. Data were analyzed through qualitative method where the themes were extracted to find the results. It was found out that MALL applications are useful in improving the grammatical knowledge of learners.

Gharehblagh and Nasri (2020) investigated the effectiveness of MALL in contrast with paper pencil instructional methods. The data were collected from the EFL learners studying at elementary level. They explored that experimental group learners were vividly better in performance in comparison with controlled group thus this research ascertained that MALL is an important tool in ESL and EFL setting to achieve desired results. Ali et al., (2020) in local context examined the utility of MALL in COVID-19 situations. Through an online survey data were collected from university learners and instructors. It was concluded that MALL was found to be effective and impactful tool in English language learning situations

## MATERIALS AND METHODS

### Research design

The design of any research can be positivist and interpretivist or can be a mixture of both for taking the objective and subjective viewpoint of the particular subject under observation. Both are equally important as they efficiently entertain different research designs (Corbetta, 2003; Marcon & Gopal, 2005; Kroeze, 2012).

The main objective of this research work is to investigate the impact of MALL on ESL learners' performance in the Pakistani context, particularly in Lahore. The first important element was to connect relevant research design to my study. Therefore, for finding the impact of MALL on ESL learners' performance, positivist (quantitative) research paradigm is used for the collection of data and analysis. Creswell and Poth (2017) stated that the quantitative design of research elaborates a specific aspect by numeric data collection that can be analyzed by using some statistical methods.

## Population and Sampling of the Study

The population for data collection comes from Lahore, precisely all the private sector colleges of Lahore. These learners were studying English as their compulsory subject in BS English semester 2. Out of all BS English learners, 120 students were chosen as a sample for this study. Each group consisted of 60 learners. From each college 20 learners were part of the study (10 each in the controlled and experimental group). Both of these groups in each college were assigned a teacher. Therefore, the cumulative number of teachers assigned to both experimental group learners and controlled groups was 12(6 in each group).

## Instrument used for Data Collection

The instrument for used data collection was

- Pre-test
- Post-test

The pre-test is important as it is a tool utilized for assessment for determining already existing subject knowledge of the learners (Berry, 2008). Usually, they are conducted at the initial stage of any course (Angelo & Cross, 2012). Similarly, on 120 learners of this study, a pre-test was conducted which comprised of 10 short questions according to the syllabus of BS English compulsory subject. Firstly, the content validity of the data was established and these questions were chosen randomly from the whole syllabus. This pretest was conducted for the purpose of randomization and to distribute learners according to their test scores thus making sure that both groups (controlled and experimental) had mixed ability learners. This Pre-test was of 50 minutes. The pattern of the short questions was already known by the learners as it was part of their final paper pattern. This will also eliminate any variable effect on learners. Strict monitoring was done during the test to avoid copying.

On the basis of their pre-test scores, the learners' groups were made. The normal class group was not carried out rather a special class was made according to the learners' performance in the pre-test. It was made sure that each group (control and experimental) had (60 each) mixed ability students. This was done to create homogeneity amongst the groups. It was made sure that no group should only have either high or low-performance learners to avoid bias in experimentation.

### Treatment

After the experimentation process of learning the controlled group was taught conventionally and the experimental group learnt through MALL by the facilitation of their teachers. Furthermore, after the conclusion of the teaching and learning sessions of both groups which lasted for a month, a post-test was conducted identically to the pattern of the pre-test. The reason for conducting a post-test was to explore the impact of learning through MALL. The time, test pattern and all other arrangement all were identical to pre-test for the participants of both groups.

## RESULTS AND DISCUSSION

The results reflect the answers of two major research questions of the study i.e., investigating the impact of MALL on ESL learners' performance in Pakistan and finding the significant difference in the performance of the conventional (controlled) group and experimental (MALL) group. This hints at exploring that how MALL can uplift the learners' performance better than the conventional method of learning. To address this question a quantitative analysis will be done by applying two different tests (independent sample t-test and paired sample t-test) using SPSS 23.

### Experimentation Process to Explore the Impact of MALL

Here two groups of learners are equally divided into 60 students each. One group named as controlled group is taught conventionally whereas the other group learnt through MALL. The results of the pre and post-test have been presented initially through an independent sample T-test and later on by comparing both of them through paired sample T-test.

### Pretest Results of Independent Sample T-test (Controlled and Experimental Group)

The assumption of homogeneity of variance was found to be assumed as $F = .494$ $p > .05$ which indicated that the variance of pre-test was found to be invariant across both groups i.e., experimental and control. The above table-2 revealed that

*Table 1. Independent Samples t-test Comparing Pre-test Assessment across Experimental and Control Groups (N=120)*

| Variable | Experimental Group (n = 60) | | Control Group (n = 60) | | *t (118)* | *P* | *95% CI* | | *Cohen's d* |
|---|---|---|---|---|---|---|---|---|---|
| | *M* | SD | *M* | *SD* | | | *LL* | *UL* | |
| Pre-Test | 9.85 | 1.29 | 9.18 | 1.28 | -2.84 | .007 | -1.13 | -0.20 | 0.52 |

*Note.* CI = Confidence Interval, *LL*= Lower Limit, *UL* = Upper Limit.

there were significant differences of pre-test was found in experimental and control groups (t = -2.84, p<.01). This showed that the mean score of experimental group on pre-test (M = 9.85, SD = 1.29) was higher than the mean score on control group (M = 9.18, SD = 1.28).

## Post-Test Results of Independent Sample Test (controlled and experimental group)

The assumption of homogeneity of variance was found to be assumed as F = .051 p > .05 which indicated that the variance of pre-test was found to be invariant across both groups i.e., experimental and control. The above table-3 revealed that there was significant difference of pre-test was found in experimental and control groups (t = -26.88, p<.001). This showed that that the mean score of experimental group on pre-test (M = 16.83, SD = 0.98) was higher than the mean score on of control group (M = 11.82, SD = 1.10).

## Pretest and Post-test Result of Paired Sample T-test (Controlled Group Results)

The above table-4 revealed that there were significant differences found in pre-test and post-test assessment of the control group (t = -25.43, p<.001). This show that

*Table 2. Independent Samples t-test Comparing Post-test Assessment across Experimental and Control Groups (N=120)*

| Variable | Experimental Group (n = 60) | | Control Group (n = 60) | | *t (118)* | *P* | *95% CI* | | *Cohen's d* |
|---|---|---|---|---|---|---|---|---|---|
| | *M* | SD | *M* | *SD* | | | *LL* | *UL* | |
| Post-Test | 16.83 | 0.98 | 11.82 | 1.10 | -26.88 | .000 | -5.38 | -4.65 | 4.94 |

*Note.* CI = Confidence Interval, *LL*= Lower Limit, *UL* = Upper Limit.

*Table 3. Paired Samples t-test Comparing Pre and Post Test of Control Group (N=60)*

| Variable | Pre-test | | Post-test | | *t (149)* | *P* | *95% CI* | | *Cohen's d* |
|---|---|---|---|---|---|---|---|---|---|
| | *M* | SD | *M* | *SD* | | | *LL* | *UL* | |
| Control Group | 9.18 | 1.28 | 11.82 | 1.07 | -25.43 | .000 | -2.84 | -2.3 | 4.34 |

*Note.* CI = Confidence Interval, *LL*= Lower Limit, *UL* = Upper Limit

the mean score of post-test assessment (M = 11.82, SD = 1.07) was higher than the mean score on of pre-test assessment (M = 9.18, SD = 1.28) of the control group.

## Pretest and Post-test Result of Paired Sample T-test (Experimental Group Result

The above table revealed that there were significant differences found in the pre-test and post-test assessment of the experimental group (t = -60.62, p<.001). This showed that that the mean score of post-test assessment (M = 9.85, SD = 1.29) was higher than the mean score on of pre-test assessment (M = 9.85, SD = 1.29) of the experimental group

Furthermore, effect size (magnitude of the differences) for the experimental group across pre-test and post-test assessments was 6.39. The Cohen's d value showed that the size of effect falls under the range of large magnitude of differences (Cohen, 1988).

## Findings

The results investigate the impact of MALL on learners' performance in the Pakistani ESL context. The findings of this experimental process on both the controlled and experimental groups reveal some important facts.

Initially, normal distribution was examined with skewness and kurtosis and it can be seen from the results that the data is normally distributed. Moreover, the

*Table 4. Paired Samples t-test Comparing Pre and Post Test of Experimental Group (N=60)*

| Variable | Pre-test | | Post-test | | *t (149)* | *P* | *95% CI* | | *Cohen's d* |
|---|---|---|---|---|---|---|---|---|---|
| | *M* | SD | *M* | *SD* | | | *LL* | *UL* | |
| Experimental Group | 9.85 | 1.29 | 16.83 | 0.98 | -60.62 | .000 | -7.21 | -6.75 | 6.39 |

*Note.* CI = Confidence Interval, *LL*= Lower Limit, *UL* = Upper Limit

evidence of skewness and kurtosis of the distribution showed that the values fall under the acceptable ranges of normal distribution. Similarly, the Shapiro Wilk test was found to be non-significant, which also validated that the distributions of pre and post-test assessments across control and experimental groups were normality distributed. Moreover, the values of the effect size for both the tests also come under the range of acceptance (see tables above).

Further, there are two tests applied on the collected data. Independent sample t-test and paired sample t-test. Both Independent sample and paired sample tests are applied on pre-test and post-test scenarios. The independent sample t-test actually compares two means of two different groups. It also validates that both of the samples are collected independently. The objective of applying both the test is to investigate the impact of MALL by finding out the significant difference (if any) in the performance of both the controlled and experimental group in pre and post-test results. It can be seen in above tables that the experimental group performed slightly better than the controlled group. The statistic value presented in the tables above clearly validates that both sample groups belong to different population. Viewing the values in pre-test above it can be seen that both experimental and controlled groups performed almost equally. The difference of mean between both the groups in their pre is not significantly great.

## Discussion

The results of this study reflect that there is a vivid difference in the performance of the students of experimental group as compared to controlled group students. Though, the performance both groups is higher in the post test results yet the performance of the experimental group is significantly better than controlled one. This validates the fact the MALL does create a positive impact on learners. The outcomes of the study are similar to the investigation conducted by Ghorbani and Ebadi (2020) who was of the view that mobile phones develop a constructive relationship with the learning of language. The utility of MALL is because of its structure, softwares, and various qualities that engages the reader positively. Particularly in the case of this research where the Pakistani learners were prone to learn through old method. They found MALL an attractive and innovative learning method. This view is also explained in some past researches by (Baleghzadeh and Oladrostam, 2010; Sole and Neijmann, 2010; Thornton and Houser, 2005). The results collected from this study also explained that MALL which is already popular in western classrooms is equally liked and appreciated by the Pakistani learners and teachers. The clear difference in the performance of the experimental group as compared to the controlled one is a proof that MALL does impact learners and their performance.

One of the major reasons that can be extracted from the better performance of the students in the experimental group is that MALL provides variety in the learning methods. Shortt et al., (2021) claimed that the orthodox ways of presenting course contents are usually monotonous and thus affects the interests of the learners. Usually, MALL methods are trendy, exciting and modern. These learning methods sometimes breakout the conventional mode of learning and attract the learners. It also supports the learners to improve their concentration level. All these methods actually increase the interest and keep them energetic in the learning process (Pingping et al., (2021). The experimental group learners performed better as the latest ways support the learners to understand concepts in an easier way. MALL activities are structured and designed to provide ease regarding comprehension of any concept and syllabus content and create learning in the formal and informal environments (Hou & Aryadoust, 2021). The outcomes of this study are identical to the aspect that MALL is appreciative amongst learners because it offers so many learning paths to its users for language learning purposes (Puebla et al., 2022).

Another important reason that can be extracted from the significant performance of experimental group learners in this research is that MALL has a pivotal feature of mobility, portability and ubiquity. This viewpoint is similar to the statement of Morgana and Kukulska-Hulme (2021) who pointed out features like lower cost, flexibility and user-friendliness are the benchmarks of MALL. It can be said after viewing the results of this experimental study that in elevating the performance of ESL learners in Pakistan, mobility and portability significantly supported the learners. The aspects of MALL which provided benefit to Pakistani ESL learners are also supported by Kukulska-Hulme et al., (2021) who were of the view that mobility and flexibility promote learning by providing luxury in learning methods and these are hallmarks of MALL. This is identical with the argument presented by Xiaolong & Qian (2022) who indicated that the chief advantages of MALL to learners are the aspects of mobility and portability.

Then the feature of ubiquity is also an important fundamental element of MALL. This anytime-anywhere learning facility helps them to learn willfully with their convenience and hence it enhances their performance. Pakistani learners also benefitted from this facility and ubiquity supported them to learn outside the classroom. This transformed their concept of learning as in Pakistan the learning (in conventional settings) is environment bound i.e., occurs within the classrooms. This feature also helped them to be more efficient learners (Çakmak, 2022). This viewpoint is also supported by Li et al., (2022) who stated that ubiquity truly helps the learner to have learning outside the classroom anytime which motivates them. It also provides them with the sense of responsibility and self-paced learning process. It also makes them autonomous in their learning.

Another important aspect that contributed to the better performance of the experimental group learners was the facility of social interaction and collaborative learning. The results reflect that collaborative learning impacts learning positively. The benefits achieved from this feature also connects with the study by García Botero et al., (2022) who stated that collaboration in learning increase mutual interaction and eliminate any conceptual difficulty of the learners. The exchange of information promoting social interactions supported Pakistani ESL learners to learn in a new way which not only made them interested but also helped to improve their knowledge by exchanging various ideas on similar areas of syllabus or content. It has also promoted beyond time and place learning opportunities and aided them to evaluate each other. This feature connects to the argument given by Dağdeler (2020) who were of the view that collaborative learning also helps in evaluating one another to achieve learning goals. This feature of collaborative learning actually overhauled the learning atmosphere and concept in this research. Viberg et al., (2020) also stated that collaborative learning is an attributive feature and benefit of MALL which has impacted learning ambiance. It also allows them to construct their own meanings regarding different learning concepts

Apart from these findings the overall outcomes of this experiment reveal that students appreciated learning through MALL. MALL though is a new concept yet all the learners took interest and participated in the activities.

The outcomes revealed in this investigation are identical to the studies conducted by various other researchers like Khan & Tufail (2020) who claimed that MALL is an impactful method to improve the learning of the students. also stated that MALL creates a positive impact on the learners and makes them interested and focused upon learning which consequently makes them motivated and affects their performance. Ali et al., (2022) also pointed out that mobile phones as MALL tools help to develop and construct the knowledge of the students. Though, there are some opposing researches regarding MALL yet they were at the start of this century i.e., Viberg (2020) stated that learning and especially language learning is a complex process that needs concentration and focus and MALL tools are least important and valuable for learning as it can distract the learners' attention. Gradually with the technological development, there are several kinds of research that claimed and proved the importance of MALL and mobile phones for language learning and teaching purposes. The results of this particular study richly present that MALL significantly improves the academic performance of the learners and this viewpoint is supported by number of researchers who claimed that as MALL offers variety and innovation in different language learning genres so it influences the learners and urges them to perform better. These genres are writing (Gharehblagh, & Nasri, 2020), listening (Salih, 2019), reading (Li, 2022), grammar (Parsa & Fatehi Rad, 2021), pronunciation and speaking (Darmawati, 2018; Saran et al., 2009) and vocabulary (Zhang & Perez-Paredes, 2021; Abbasi & Hashemi, 2013;; Başoğlu & Akdemir,2010; Song & Fox, 2008).

In connection with the constructivist theory these results aptly illustrates the aspects of constructivism. Constructivist approach states that learning is active while the context is important and collaborative learning and activities are used to elevate learning. Moreover, the relations between a student and instructor are perfect whereas the role of the teacher is to facilitate learning procedure while making learner autonomous. This research has followed all the aspects of constructivist theory and it can be seen from the results that all the learners in MALL group actively participated in the learning process. Moreover, the learning way and context was also changes. Now the learning was not in-class only, rather it was ubiquitous so learners enjoyed this facility. Further, all the learners were connected with each other through social groups when they are outside classrooms. This developed a sense of collaboration between them which ultimately improved their learning performance. The teacher worked as their helped and focus was on the learners' autonomy rather than teacher control. So, viewing all this it can be said that this research perfectly directs the features of constructivism. The results of this study in connection with constructivism are connected with the study by Fernando and Marikar (2017) who stated that constructivism is an active path of learning and learning is deeply rooted and embedded in the social interactions and collaboration. Wang (2014) also claimed that using MALL based constructivist activities elevates the learners" performance by aiding the process of learning and uplifting the confidence and motivation of learners through collaboration and interaction. Moreover, the aspects of constructivism extracted from this research are identical to the outcomes shared by Cohen and Ezra (2018) who were of the view that learners through collaboration, social and mutual interaction develop and construct their own meaning and concept of knowledge.

The overall results of this study validate that MALL is a concept that has a phenomenal impact on the achievements of the learners and as if offers room for learning with latest methods so it keeps the learners focused, motivated, energetic, efficient and confident during the process of learning. In this study it was felt that MALL decreases anxiety and problems of learner. Yanguas and Flores (2014) also supported this view that MALL helps learners to decrease levels of anxiety and hindrances in learning process and develops a positive attitude towards language learning especially in ESL contexts.

## Recommendations

- MALL should be properly introduced in modern ESL classrooms
- Pakistani curriculum designers should design some activates related to MALL
- Administration should be given training to implement MALL

- ❖ Practical training regarding MALL tools should be given to the teachers
- ❖ Teacher should be given support by the administration to integrate MALL
- ❖ Incentives should be provided to the teacher who integrate MALL
- ❖ Internet and mobile devices should be common in ESL classrooms.
- ❖ Learners should be encouraged to use MALL inside their learning contexts.

## CONCLUSION

The current section of the study focused upon finding out the opinions and perspectives of the teachers regarding the integration of MALL in their classrooms as a new teaching methodology. ESL teaching is always an important aspect and medium of learning and etching especially in countries where English is considered an official language. In Pakistan English as a language has a lot of value and appreciation amongst the masses. In the educational context; precisely in ESL learning situations, the educators have been trying to find out ways that can facilitate the teaching process and importantly facilitate the learners to have impactful learning channels and processes. As teaching and learning reciprocate each other so for better learning the teaching methods should be impactful and effective to have maximum involvement of the learners. These teaching methods should also have the quality of being interesting to develop an attractive learning ambiance for the learners. MALL being a new method of teaching as well as learning is an interesting, latest, innovative and impactful method proved by many studies earlier. In the Pakistani context this concept is in its earlier phase and there are only a few studies that are conducted on this area. So, in order to have MALL as an effective tool, the teachers are of primary importance. Unfortunately, they are not appreciated to use latest methods for learning there is a strong need to introduce MALL initially in big cities which can gradually broaden up to other areas too. The opinions of the teachers collected clearly show that Pakistani ESL teachers have shown positivity in using methods that are unconventional and they have taken this new mode of technology with vigor and appreciation. The teachers here do not follow the old mindset rather they have preferred to focus upon the latest role of the teacher which is a facilitator and mentor. Another major aspect that can be taken from this study is that the Pakistani ESL teachers have clearly shown that they do not have any issue to lose the so-called dominance of the teacher rather they are eager to learn, improve and use modern gadgets and tools of learning to make their teaching more impactful and effective. Thus, it can be concluded that MALL has been welcomed by Pakistani teachers and they have positive views regarding its implementation.

## REFERENCES


Abbasi, M., & Hashemi, M. (2013). The impacts of using mobile phone on English language vocabulary retention. *International Research Journal of Applied and Basic Sciences, 4*(3), 541–547.

Ahmed, R., Ahmad, N., Mujeeb, M., & Vishnu, P. (2014). Factors that motivate the mobile phone users to switch from 2G to 3G technologies in Karachi. *Research Journal of Recent Sciences, 3*(8), 18–21.

Ali, M. M., Bashir, A., Ikram Anjum, M. A., & Mahmood, M. A. (2020). Impact of Mobile Assisted Language Learning on the Young ESL Learners' Vocabulary in Pakistan. *Journal of Research & Reflections in Education, 14*(1).

Ali, M. M., Mahmood, M. A., Anjum, M. A. I., & Shahid, A. (2020). The acceptance of mobile assisted language learning as primary learning tool for learners in COVID 19 situations. *PalArch's Journal of Archaeology of Egypt/Egyptology, 17*(12), 382-398.

Ali, M. M., Mahmood, M. A., Anwar, M. N., Khan, L. A., & Hussain, A. (2019). Pakistani learners' perceptions regarding mobile assisted language learning in ESL classroom. *International Journal of English Linguistics, 9*(4), 386–398. doi:10.5539/ijel.v9n4p386

Ali, M. M., Malik, N. A., & Rehman, A. (2016). Mobile assisted language learning (MALL) an emerging technology in English language class rooms of Lahore (Pakistan). *Science International (Lahore), 28*(2).

Ali, M. M., Yasmin, T., & Ahmed, K. (2021). Using Whatsapp as MALL Tool to Enhance ESL Learners' Performance in Pakistan. *Ilkogretim Online, 20*(5).

Angelo, T. A., & Cross, K. P. (2012). *Classroom assessment techniques.* Jossey Bass Wiley.

Attar, M., & Chopra, S. S. (2010). Task-based language teaching in India. *Modern Journal of Applied Linguistics, 2*(4).

Balla, E. (2018). *English Language and its importance of learning it in Albanian schools.* Academic Press.

Beatty, K. (2003). *Teaching and researching computer assisted language learning.* Pearson Education Limited.

Bentley, M. L., Ebert, S. E., & Ebert, C. (2007). *Teaching constructivist science.* SAGE Publications.

Berry, T. (2008). Pre-test assessment. *American Journal of Business Education, 1*(1), 19–22. doi:10.19030/ajbe.v1i1.4633

Bhatti, T. M. (2013). Teaching reading through computer-assisted language learning. *TESL-EJ, 17*(2), 1–11.

Bonk, C. J., & King, K. S. (2012). Searching for learner-centered, constructivist and sociocultural components of collaborative educational learning tools. In *Electronic collaborators* (pp. 61–86). Routledge. doi:10.4324/9780203053805-10

Burston, J. (2013). Mobile-assisted language learning: A selected annotated bibliography of implementation studies 1994-2012. *Language Learning & Technology, 17*(3), 157–225.

Çakmak, F. (2022). Review of Mobile assisted language learning across educational contexts. *Language Learning & Technology, 26*(1), 1–4.

Candy, P.C. (1991). *Self-direction for life-long learning*. Jossey-Bass.

Carrier, M., & Pashler, H. (1992). The influence of retrieval on retention. *Memory & Cognition, 20*(6), 633–642. doi:10.3758/BF03202713 PMID:1435266

Cogo, A. (2012). English as a lingua franca: Concepts, use and implications. *ELT Journal, 66*(1), 97–105. doi:10.1093/elt/ccr069

Corbetta, P. (2003). *Social Research: Theory Methods and Techniques*. SAGE Publications Ltd. doi:10.4135/9781849209922

Creswell, J. W., & Poth, C. N. (2017). *Qualitative inquiry and research design: Choosing among five approaches*. Sage publications.

Crompton, H. (2013). A historical overview of mobile learning: toward learner-centered education. In Z. L. Berge & L. Y. Muilenburg (Eds.), *Handbook of Mobile Learning* (pp. 3–14). Routledge.

Dağdeler, K. O., Konca, M. Y., & Demiröz, H. (2020). The effect of mobile-assisted language learning (MALL) on EFL learners' collocation learning. *Journal of Language and Linguistic Studies, 16*(1), 489–509. doi:10.17263/jlls.712891

Darmawati, D. (2018). Improving Speaking Skill Through Mobile-Assisted Language Learning (MALL). *Jurnal Teknologi Sistem Informasi dan Aplikasi, 1*(1), 24-30.

Dudwick, N., Kuehnast, K., Jones, V., & Woolcock, M. (2006). *Analyzing social capital in context: A Guide to using qualitative methods and data. World Bank.* The International Bank for Reconstruction and Development/the World Bank.

Ertmer, P. A., & Newby, T. J. (2013). Behaviorism, cognitivism, constructivism: Comparing critical features from an instructional design perspective. *Performance Improvement Quarterly*, *26*(2), 43–71. doi:10.1002/piq.21143

Ertmer, P. A., & Newby, T. J. (2013). Behaviorism, cognitivism, constructivism: Comparing critical features from an instructional design perspective. *Performance Improvement Quarterly*, *26*(2), 43–71. doi:10.1002/piq.21143

Eysenck, M. W. (2004). *Psychology: An international perspective*. Taylor & Francis.

Farooq, L., Ali, A., Mahmood, S., Farzand, M., Masood, H., & Mujahid, S. (2019). Association between excessive use of mobile phone and insomnia among pakistani teenagers cross sectional study. *American International Journal of Multidisciplinary Scientific Research*, *5*(4), 10–15. doi:10.46281/aijmsr.v5i4.406

Felix, U. (2005). E-learning pedagogy in the third millennium: The need for combining social and cognitive constructivist approaches. *ReCALL, 17*(1), 85–100. doi:10.1017/S0958344005000716

Fernandez, S. (2008). *Teaching and learning languages other than English (LOTE) in Victorian schools*. Office for Policy, Research and Innovation, Department of Education and Early Childhood *Development.*

Fithriani, R. (2021). The utilization of mobile-assisted gamification for vocabulary learning: Its efficacy and perceived benefits. *Computer Assisted Language Learning Electronic Journal (CALL-EJ), 22*(3), 146-163.

Friesen, S. (2008). *Effective teaching practices – A framework*. Canadian Education Association.

García Botero, G., Nguyet Diep, A., García Botero, J., Zhu, C., & Questier, F. (2022). Acceptance and Use of Mobile-Assisted Language Learning by Higher Education Language Teachers. *Lenguaje*, *50*(1), 66–92. doi:10.25100/lenguaje.v50i1.11006

Gharehblagh, N. M., & Nasri, N. (2020). Developing EFL elementary learners' writing skills through mobile-assisted language learning (MALL). *Teaching English with Technology*, *20*(1), 104–121.

Ghorbani, N., & Ebadi, S. (2020). Exploring learners' grammatical development in mobile assisted language learning. *Cogent Education*, *7*(1), 1704599. doi:10.1080/2331186X.2019.1704599

Hanlon, B., & Larget, B. (2011). *Analysis of variance*. Department of Statistic, University of Wisconsin-Madison.

Hassan, W. U., Nawaz, M. T., Syed, T. H., Arfeen, M. I., Naseem, A., & Noor, S. (2015). Investigating students' behavioral intention towards adoption of mobile learning in higher education institutions of Pakistan. *University of Engineering and Technology Taxila Technical Journal, 20*(3), 34.

Holla, S., & Katti, M. M. (2012). Android based mobile application development and its security. *International Journal of Computer Trends and Technology, 3*(3), 486–490.

Hymes, D. H. (1972). On communicative competence. In J. B. Pride & J. Holmes (Eds.), *Sociolinguistics. Selected Readings*. Penguin.

Irshad, S., & Ghani, M. (2015). Benefits of CALL in ESL pedagogy in Pakistan: A case study. *ELF Annual Research Journal, 17*, 1–22.

Islam, R., Islam, R., & Mazumder, T. (2010). Mobile application and its global impact. *IACSIT International Journal of Engineering and Technology, 10*(6), 72–78.

Jahanzaib, R., & Zeeshan, M. (2017). University Teachers' and Students' Beliefs about Grammar Translation Method and Communicative Language Teaching in Quetta, Balochistan, Pakistan. *International Journal of English Linguistics, 7*(2), 151. doi:10.5539/ijel.v7n2p151

Jones, A., & Issroff, K. (2007). Motivation and mobile devices: Exploring the role of appropriation and coping strategies. *Association for Learning Technology, 15*(3), 247–258. doi:10.3402/rlt.v15i3.10934

Keskin, N. O., & Metcalf, D. (2011). The current perspectives, theories and practices of mobile learning. *Turkish Online Journal of Educational Technology-TOJET, 10*(2), 202–208.

Khan, M. Y., & Tufail, H. (2020). *An Investigation into the Effectiveness of MALL during COVID-19 at the Higher*. Academic Press.

Kroeze, J. H. (2012). Postmodernism, interpretivism and formal ontologies. In Research methodologies, innovations and philosophies in software systems engineering and information systems. Information Science Reference. doi:10.4018/978-1-4666-0179-6.ch003

Kuimova, M., Burleigh, D., Uzunboylu, H., & Bazhenov, R. (2018). Positive effects of mobile learning on foreign language learning. *TEM Journal, 7*(4), 837-841.

Kukulska-Hulme, A. (2009). Will mobile learning change language learning? *ReCALL, 21*(2), 157–165. doi:10.1017/S0958344009000202

Kukulska-Hulme, A. (2013). Mobile-assisted language learning. In C. Chapelle (Ed.), *The encyclopedia of applied linguistics*. Wiley.

Kukulska-Hulme, A., Arús-Hita, J., Hou, Z., & Aryadoust, V. (2021). García Laborda, J. (2021). Mobile, Open and Social Language Learning Designs and Architectures. *Journal of Universal Computer Science*, *27*(5), 413–424. doi:10.3897/jucs.68852

Lei, X., Fathi, J., Noorbakhsh, S., & Rahimi, M. (2022). The Impact of Mobile-Assisted Language Learning on English as a Foreign Language Learners' Vocabulary Learning Attitudes and Self-Regulatory Capacity. *Frontiers in Psychology*, *13*, 13. doi:10.3389/fpsyg.2022.872922 PMID:35800918

Lei, X., Fathi, J., Noorbakhsh, S., & Rahimi, M. (2022). The Impact of Mobile-Assisted Language Learning on English as a Foreign Language Learners' Vocabulary Learning Attitudes and Self-Regulatory Capacity. *Frontiers in Psychology*, *13*, 13. doi:10.3389/fpsyg.2022.872922 PMID:35800918

Leonard, D. C. (2002). *Learning theories, A-Z*. Greenwood Press.

Li, F., Fan, S., & Wang, Y. (2022). Mobile-assisted language learning in Chinese higher education context: A systematic review from the perspective of the situated learning theory. *Education and Information Technologies*, *27*(7), 1–24. doi:10.100710639-022-11025-4

Li, R. (2022). Effects of mobile-assisted language learning on EFL/ESL reading comprehension. *Journal of Educational Technology & Society*, *25*(3), 15–29.

Maqsood, L. (2015). *Use of mobile technology among rural women in Pakistan for agricultural extension information*. Michigan State University.

Marcon, T., & Gopal, A. (2005). *Uncertain knowledge, uncertain time*. ASAC.

Mattew, Joro & Manasseh. (2015). The role of information and communication technology in Nigeria educational system. *International Journal of Research in Humanities and Social Studies*, *2*(2), 64–68.

Mohsen, M. A., & Mahdi, H. S. (2021). Partial versus full captioning mode to improve L2 vocabulary acquisition in a mobile-assisted language learning setting: Words pronunciation domain. *Journal of Computing in Higher Education*, *33*(2), 524–543. doi:10.100712528-021-09276-0

Morgana, V., & Kukulska-Hulme, A. (Eds.). (2021). *Mobile assisted language learning across educational contexts*. Routledge. doi:10.4324/9781003087984

Mvududu, N., & Burgess, J. T. (2012). Constructivism in practice: The case for English language learners. *International Journal of Education*, *4*(4), 3. doi:10.5296/ije.v4i3.2223

Ogunlade, O. O. (2014) Information and Communication Technology (ICT). In M. O. Yusuf & S. A. Onasanya (Eds.), Critical Issues in educational technology (pp. 98-104). Department of Education Technology, University of Ilorin.

Ozan, O., Yamamoto, G. T., & Demiray, U. (2015). Mobile learning technologies and educational applications. *Mobile Learning Technologies and Educational Applications*, *9*(3-4), 97–109.

Paris, T. N. S. T., Manap, N. A., Abas, H., & Ling, L. M. (2021). Mobile-Assisted Language Learning (MALL) in Language Learning. *Journal of ASIAN Behavioural Studies*, *6*(19), 61–73. doi:10.21834/jabs.v6i19.391

Parsa, N., & Fatehi Rad, N. (2021). Impact of a Mobile-Assisted Language Learning (MALL) on EFL Learners' Grammar Achievement and Self-Efficacy. *International Journal of Language and Translation Research*, *1*(4), 71–94.

Peng, S. (2019). A Study of the differences between EFL and ESL for English Classroom teaching in China. *IRA International Journal of Education and Multidisciplinary Studies*, *15*(1), 32–35. doi:10.21013/jems.v15.n1.p4

Pingping, G., Qiuyao, W., & Linyan, B. (2021). Enhancing Students' Mobile-Assisted Language Learning through Self-Assessment in a Chinese College EFL Context. *Journal of Education and e-Learning Research, 8*(2), 238-248.

Puangrimaggalatung, S. T. I. A., Yusriadi, Y., & Tahir, S. Z. B. (2022). MALL in Learning English through Social Networking Tools: Students' Perceptions on Instagram Feed-based Task and Peer Feedback. *Computer Assisted Language Learning*, *23*(2), 198–216.

Puebla, C., Fievet, T., Tsopanidi, M., & Clahsen, H. (2022). Mobile-assisted language learning in older adults: Chances and challenges. *ReCALL*, *34*(2), 169–184. doi:10.1017/S0958344021000276

Puebla, C., & Garcia, J. (2022). Advocating the inclusion of older adults in digital language learning technology and research: Some considerations. *Bilingualism: Language and Cognition*, *25*(3), 398–399. doi:10.1017/S1366728921000742

Rashid, S. (2018). *The effect of training in Mobile Assisted Language Learning on attitude, beliefs and practices of tertiary students in Pakistan*. Academic Press.

Reddy, M. S., Mahavidyalaya, P., & Hyderabad, K. (2016). Importance of English language in today's world. *International Journal of Academic Research, 3*(4), 179–184.

Renau-Renau, M. L. (2016). A review of the traditional and current language teaching methods. *International Journal of Innovation and Research in Educational Sciences, 3*(2), 82–88.

Richards, J. C. (2008). *Communicative Language Teaching Today*. Paper Design Internationals.

Salih, A. H. (2019). Effects of mobile assisted language learning on developing listening skill to the department of English students in college of education for women at Al Iraqia University. *European Journal of Language and Literature, 5*(1), 31-38.

Saran, M., Seferoglu, G., & Cagiltay, K. (2009). Mobile assisted language learning: English pronunciation at learners' fingertips. *Eurasian Journal of Educational Research, 34*, 97–114.

Schunk, D. H. (2012). *Learning theories an educational perspective*. Pearson.

Shortt, M., Tilak, S., Kuznetcova, I., Martens, B., & Akinkuolie, B. (2021). Gamification in mobile-assisted language learning: A systematic review of Duolingo literature from public release of 2012 to early 2020. *Computer Assisted Language Learning*, 1–38. doi:10.1080/09588221.2021.1933540

Stockwell, G. (2008). Investigating learner preparedness for and usage patterns of mobile learning. *ReCALL, 20*(3), 253–270. doi:10.1017/S0958344008000232

Strydom, H., Steyn, M. M., & Strydom, C. (2007). An adapted intervention research model: Suggestions for research and practice. *Social Work/Maatskaplike Werk, 43*(4).

Sturm, M., Kennel, T., McBride, R., & Kelly, M. (2009). The pedagogical implications of Web 2.0. In T. Michael (Ed.), *Handbook of research on web 2.0 and second language learning* (pp. 367–384). IGI Global. doi:10.4018/978-1-60566-190-2.ch020

Sweller, J. (2003). Evolution of human cognitive architecture. In B. Ross (Ed.), *The Psychology of learning and motivation*. Academic Press.

Thornton, P., & Houser, C. (2005). Using mobile phones in English education in Japan. *Journal of Computer Assisted Learning, 21*(3), 217–228. doi:10.1111/j.1365-2729.2005.00129.x

Tryphon, A., & Vonèche, J. (1996). *Piaget-Vygotsky: The social genesis of thought*. Psychology Press.

Viberg, O., Wasson, B., & Kukulska-Hulme, A. (2020). Mobile-assisted language learning through learning analytics for self-regulated learning (MALLAS): A conceptual framework. *Australasian Journal of Educational Technology, 36*(6), 34–52. doi:10.14742/ajet.6494

Vygotsky, L. (1962). *Thought and language*. The M.I.T Press. (Original work published 1934) doi:10.1037/11193-000

Wardak, M. (2020). *Mobile Assisted Language Learning (MALL): Teacher Uses of Smartphone Applications (Apps) to Support Undergraduate Students' English as a Foreign Language (EFL) Vocabulary Development*. Lancaster University.

Wong, H. W. L., Jhaveri, A. D., & Wong, L. T. (2015). *The dilemma of matching learning styles and teaching styles in English language classrooms. In English language education in a global world: Practices, issues and challenges*. Nova Science Publishers, Inc.

Xiaolong, T., & Qian, K. (2022). Researching Into the Use of Real-Life Materials in Language Learning Apps: A Case Study of the HANZI App for Learning Chinese Characters. In Applying Mobile Technologies to Chinese Language Learning (pp. 91-122). IGI Global.

Zhang, D., & Perez-Paredes, P. (2021). Chinese postgraduate EFL learners' self-directed use of mobile English learning resources. *Computer Assisted Language Learning, 34*(8), 1128–1153. doi:10.1080/09588221.2019.1662455

## ADDITIONAL READING

Ali, M. M., Gulzar, M. A., & Anwar, M. N. (2018). Impact of MALL on grammar of EFL learners in Pakistan. *ELF Annual Research Journal, 20*, 39–55.

Ali, M. M., Khizar, N. U., Yaqub, H., Afzaal, J., & Shahid, A. (2020). Investigating speaking skills problems of Pakistani learners in ESL context. *International Journal of Applied Linguistics and English Literature, 9*(4), 62–70. doi:10.7575/aiac.ijalel.v.9n.4p.62

Ali, M. M., Mahmood, M. A., Anjum, M. A. I., & Shahid, A. (2020). The acceptance of mobile assisted language learning as primary learning tool for learners in COVID 19 situations. *PalArch's Journal of Archaeology of Egypt/Egyptology, 17*(12), 382-398.

Ali, M. M., Mahmood, M. A., Anwar, M. N., Khan, L. A., & Hussain, A. (2019). Pakistani learners' perceptions regarding mobile assisted language learning in ESL classroom. *International Journal of English Linguistics*, *9*(4), 386–398. doi:10.5539/ijel.v9n4p386

## KEY TERMS AND DEFINITIONS

**CALL:** Computerized-assisted language learning.
**ESL:** English as second language.
**MALL:** Mobile-assisted language learning.

# Chapter 4
# Methods of Evaluation and Assessment in Digital Learning

**Hameed Khan**
https://orcid.org/0000-0002-6801-4711
*Guru Ramdas Khalsa Institute of Science and Technology, Jabalpur, India*

**Kamal Kumar Kushwah**
*Jabalpur Engineering College, India*

**Kanchan Khare**
*Jabalpur Engineering College, India*

**Sujeet Kumar Mahobia**
*Jabalpur Engineering College, India*

**Jitendra Singh Thakur**
*Jabalpur Engineering College, India*

## ABSTRACT

*Assessment techniques are essential for utilization in both digital and online classrooms. The online evaluation must be viewed to evaluate a student's academic performance. Educational institutions are being held to a greater standard of accountability, and learning about online assessment is critical. Perhaps the information presented here can assist teachers in selecting assessment approaches that are appropriate for the pedagogy of online courses. Technology, delivery, pedagogy, learning styles, and learning outcomes must all be balanced in online assessment efficiently and comprehensively assess student learning, while meeting the problems of accountability, reform, and students' learning requirements, a diverse set of online components, methods, assessment criteria, and tools are required. Educators should continue to investigate various types of digital tools and methods for evaluating students in higher education in order to develop novel, efficient, and effective evaluation procedures that will hold institutions accountable for student outcomes in the online environment.*

DOI: 10.4018/978-1-6684-5400-8.ch004

## INTRODUCTION

COVID-19 forced schools and colleges worldwide to close, forcing them to adopt a remote learning approach (García-Peñalvo et al., 2021). Teachers had little time to adjust to online learning, allowing students to continue their studies. Although technology has advanced swiftly, making many daily tasks easier for us, the transition to online education has not gone as smoothly as we would have wanted. Online exams provide innovative and exciting options for students to demonstrate their learning that we may use in our classrooms. Online students will have access to one of the most powerful tools for knowledge gathering and creation: A computer. Consider how you might construct assessments that include technology while still meeting your learning objectives. For instance, you may encourage students to use Web-based resources to find, evaluate, and synthesize information to answer questions or solve problems. It is most likely one of our species' most important features that has allowed us to survive for hundreds of thousands of years. We don't always do an excellent job of assessing or evaluating, despite our nearly instinctive desire to do so. Several examples of incorrect questions, incorrect data being collected, wrong analysis being performed, and inaccurate conclusions being reached. "Don't judge a book by its cover," says a proverb that may be incredibly familiar to readers of this literature. It implies that aspects other than those on the surface should be considered when making judgments regarding something—or someone. When students and instructors think about assessment, they usually think of a long, difficult test. On the other hand, an evaluation can be any work or hobby that assesses students' progress toward learning course objectives. Papers, projects, reflective diaries, teamwork, quizzes, and other typical examples are only a few of the many options. Online learning has expedited evaluation possibilities even further since it provides you, the instructor, with a broad range of instruments to enable college students to connect with academic material in new and attractive ways. When we think of assessments, we usually think of summative assessments, such as assignments and examinations, which are high-stakes, graded evaluations. Formative assessments, which are low-stakes or ungraded evaluations, often used to monitor student knowledge, are just as essential. Formative evaluations help you better understand your students' instructional requirements while also knowing which areas they should concentrate on. Consider how you may add formative assessments into your online course regularly.

Student assessment has changed in the twenty-first century. Though there is much to be said for traditional paper-and-pencil methods, new technologies are always being created to assist educators. The study to comprehend the variety of technologies that are used to assess student learning is the objective of this chapter. Here are a few online evaluation tools that may help you improve your training, engage your audience, and give teachers insight into the growth of their pupils. But first, let us analyze the process of evaluation. This chapter examines how to evaluate and assess online learning in general, as well as how to do so systematically and comprehensively. It also discusses the methodologies and tools used to measure e-learning, as well as how to do so in an online context.

## Definition of Assessment

Assessment is the evaluation process of collecting data on what students know as a consequence of their educational experiences. The reverberations are usually used to highlight areas that need to be hastened and ensure that the superintendence supports the students' preferences.

## Evaluation Objectives

According to the definition, the evaluation of the objectives is the goal of assessment is to evaluate and improve students' learning; however, the goals may alter slightly depending on the type of assessment used (Huber & Helm, 2020).

### Categories of evaluation

1. Formative evaluations: - It determines how well a student understands the information in an online path or session. They're at their best when they're ongoing, constant, and give valuable feedback to students.
2. Summative assessments: - It is often known as final examinations that determine what a student has learned after they have completed a course. They can assess how well your content contributes to the course's standard mastery objectives.

An assessment is about much more than just grades. They help students to prepare for success by challenging them to think, engage, and apply what they have learned to answer questions, solve problems, and convey knowledge when it's relevant and well-constructed (Huber & Helm, 2020).

There are a few different ways to assess students:

- Discussions on the forums
- Online interviews
- Peer review and evaluation
- Online quizzes
- Drag-and-drop activities
- Comprehensions

- Game activities
- Dialogue simulations
- Online polls

The appropriate latest trends to adopt may differ depending on learning goals and objectives (Lara et al., 2020). If you want to assess knowledge to increases swiftly, an online quiz, for example, will suffice (Lara et al., 2014). On the other hand, a conversation simulation is an ideal way to test your students' interviewing abilities.

## Various Online Methods for Evaluating Student e Learning

Few methods to assess the systematic evaluations of students on digital platforms includes: (Darius et al., 2021).

- *Online Tests*

Quizzes are a common kind of traditional evaluation. Combined with technology, they are also an excellent way to keep children engaged in their studies. Quiz questions include multiple-choice, fill-in-the-blanks, and hotspot questions. Quizzes have the benefit of being quick and easy to assess. Another advantage is that the inquiry sequence and preferences may be randomized, resulting in a unique exam for each student.

An online quiz is a useful methodology for assessing learning outcomes for large participants. As every student takes the same exam, you may compare and contrast effects across various courses, schools, or communities. A non-graded online exam can be given before a class's graduation to establish a baseline measure of a student's modern-day knowledge. You might also include a knowledge test in a module to reinforce concepts learned in class or build a final graded quiz at the end of the course to validate students' overall performance (Giray, 2021).

## The Best Way to Make an Online Quiz

You can develop online quizzes using an eLearning authoring toolkit like iSpring Suite. A quiz builder tool is included with the iSpring Suite. Select the relevant templates to quickly and easily create a quiz for your pupils. Depending on how well each employee does on the quiz, you may improve the exam by offering specific response feedback, adding information slides, and building personalized learning pathways.

*Figure 1. Creating Online Quiz using iSpring tool*

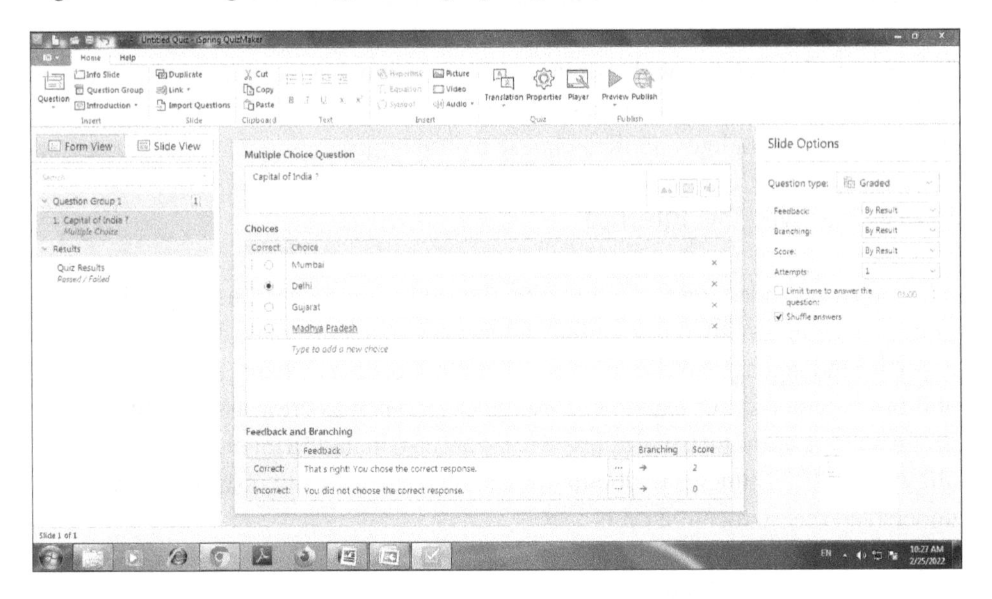


## Essay/Open-Ended Questions

Open-ended or essay-style questions are one of the most used qualitative evaluation approaches. They help students examine their feelings, thoughts, and points of view while evaluating their regular close examination of a subject. This method of inquiry encourages critical thinking and is a fun way to think about higher-level information. Essay questions encourage students to think about, organize, and write their replies over a longer period.

## How can I Make an Open-Ended Evaluation?

One of the question kinds accessible in the iSpring Suite is open-ended evaluations. They cannot be auto-scored in online courses, unlike many other questions; therefore, teachers will have to evaluate them one by one.

## Activities that can be Dragged and Dropped

Drag-and-drop exams demonstrate a learner's ability to link facts and use knowledge to solve a problem. Pictures and text may be used in a drag-and-drop workout, giving it the appearance of being challenging and entertaining. If you want novices to practice their data in a real-life scenario, you must use this assessment technique.

## What is the Best Way to Make a Drag-and-Drop Activity?

The iSpring Suite comes with a drag-and-drop design that lets you move text boxes, pictures, and objects around the page. To make an evaluation, upload the photographs into a question template and then choose a drop target.

## Interviews over the Internet

You may use a video conference to give the study a more personal touch into your online teaching. With quick online interviews, students may demonstrate their expertise in language, music, nursing, and other courses where mastery of certain abilities is required, for example. In some cases, such as crew assignment reports, group interviews might benefit. Interviews can also include a mentoring component, allowing college students to obtain immediate feedback from instructors and better understand their education costs.

## What is the Best Way to do an Online Interview?

Web conferencing like Zoom is used to share online interviews. Take the time to lay out your interview before it starts for the most significant results. Prepare your questions ahead of time and choose a time for the meeting. Allow your online students to give comments or participate in the interviews.

## Simulations of dialog

A dialog simulation prepares students for real-world conversations with customers, employees, and others. When creating a discussion exercise modeled on a student's situation on the job, be sure to let them know what to expect and establish a safe atmosphere for them to practice their reactions and responses.

## How Can I Create a Simulation of Dialogue?

Manually creating activities comparable to conversation simulations using essential slides is possible, but creating a branching scenario in PowerPoint would take time and work. Some particular technologies, such as iSpring, TalkMaster make it simple to create a conversation simulation.

Begin by sketching out the situation you wish to develop. Consider the situation and script, select an appropriate character and place from the built-in collection or submit your own, then use iSpring to build a dialog by giving learner's options and

*Figure 2. Online Simulation tool*

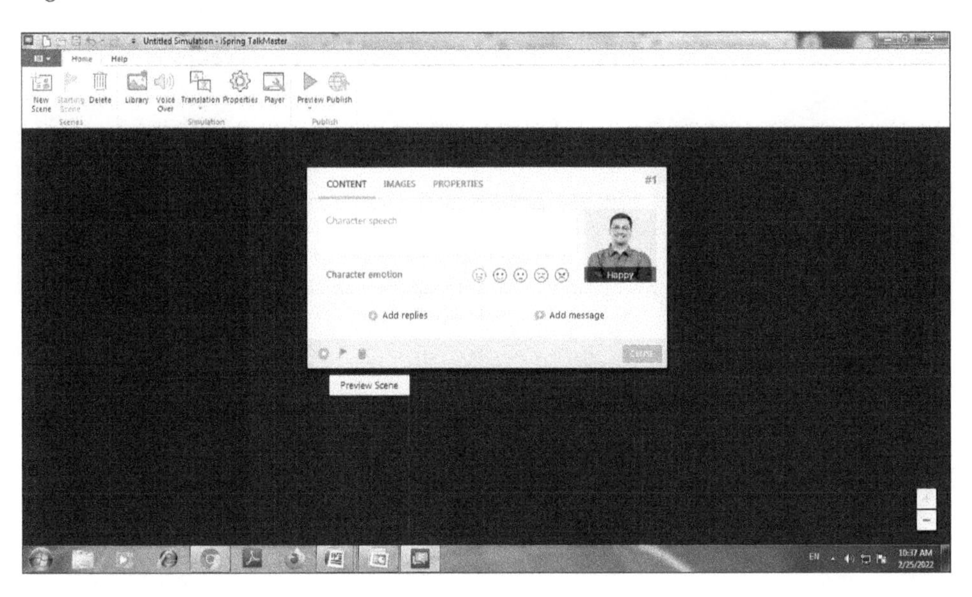


providing feedback. As with a regular quiz, learners will get correct answers and lose points for the wrong ones.

## Online polls

You may also utilize polls to gather feedback from your audience on their study experience. They evaluated everything from gaining knowledge of pleasure to why a student picked a certain option during a lecture. Learners enjoy online surveys because they can categorize themselves, express themselves, and finish them quickly.

You may use poll questions to immediately draw and listen to your students' attention on something vital or break the ice during an online crew interview session. For the latter, you may also conduct a mood survey.

## How Can I Make a Question for an Online Poll?

Using web conferencing providers, you can utilize built-in polling tools if you hold webinars. SurveyMonkey, for example, is a dedicated online platform that allows you to develop, send, and evaluate surveys—using e-Learning content authoring tools like iSpring Suite to create a survey.

*Figure 3. Creating Online Survey using iSpring tool*

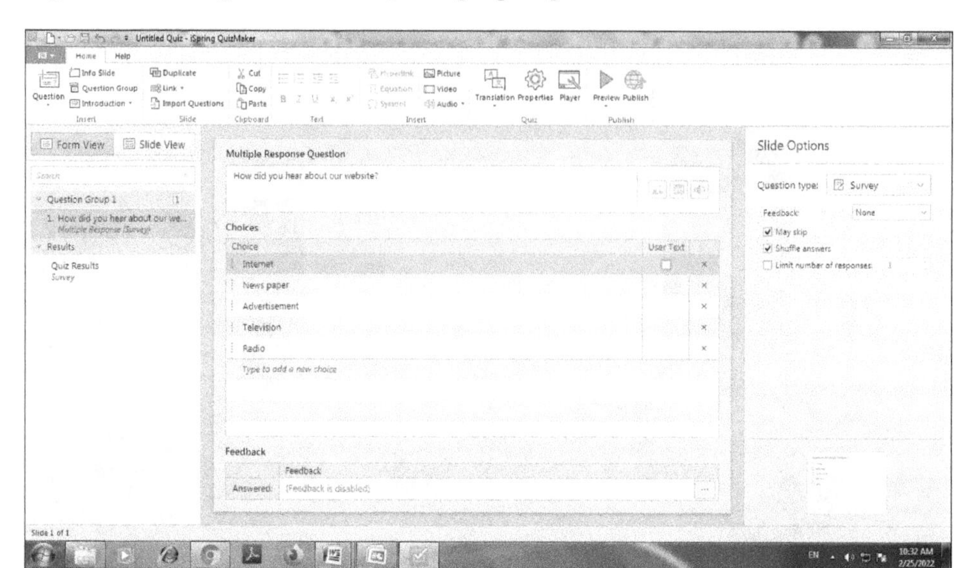


## Game-Type Activities

A series of test questions are converted into a sport with game-like activities. For example, in a minutiae game, beginners could be asked to answer multiple questions in a certain period, with points granted based on the broad variety of correct responses.

Because game-based opinions are no longer considered "tests," they are a good predictor of real-world talents and knowledge. They've also been shown to help in studying by encouraging the development of non-cognitive attributes such as discipline, risk-taking, collaboration, and problem-solving.

Use game-type activities to engage and challenge your pupils in non-traditional ways. Organizations have learned that game-style activities are extremely effective in teacher training, and institutions have recognized that high-achieving students competing in the classroom with their peers (Cipriano et al., 2019).

## Peer Review and Evaluation

By allowing students to analyze and modify each other's work, peer evaluation puts them in the position of the teacher. Participants will be able to reflect on their knowledge and then express their opinions in an organized and consistent manner due to these exercises.

## What is the Best Way to Make a Peer Review Assessment?

Students can read, examine, and evaluate one or more papers provided by their peers using rubrics or prescribed assessment questions utilizing third-party systems like TurnItIn's Feedback Studio. Teachers may log in and track their students' involvement in the activity and monitor comments and peer assessment feedback (Mahapatra, 2021). Before starting the course, the teachers should layout and clearly describe the processes of the peer review and evaluation process. To guarantee that assessments are completed consistently, present each participant with a rubric or set of instructions.

## Discussion board posts

A forum is a type of online discussion board focused on a single topic. Students responding to a forum post are a fantastic way to check their understanding, pique their interest, and motivate them to continue learning.

In this project, students are given a critical thinking subject based on a lesson book and reflect on both. Their replies are then posted on a discussion board for their peers to comment on. Use this strategy when you want learners to participate, discuss, and contribute as part of the learning process while simultaneously being tested on their knowledge of the subject.

## Distance/Online Learning Assessment Tools

Some assessment methods that are ideal for online evaluation have already been highlighted. Let's have a look at what software you could require for different tasks, as well as some additional options.

- *iSpring Suite*

The iSpring Suite is an all-in-one partly eLearning authoring solution. You may also create PowerPoint-based courses, video lessons, interactions, and flipbooks, as well as interactive quizzes, surveys, and dialog simulations for student assessment. Despite its extensive capabilities, the toolkit is simple to use and ideal for those who have never created eLearning content before (Guangul et al., 2020).

- *Socrative*

Socrative is an online quiz creator that allows you to create multiple-choice, true/false, and short-answer questions. A compelling Space Race replica in which

*Figure 4. iSpring Tool Interface*

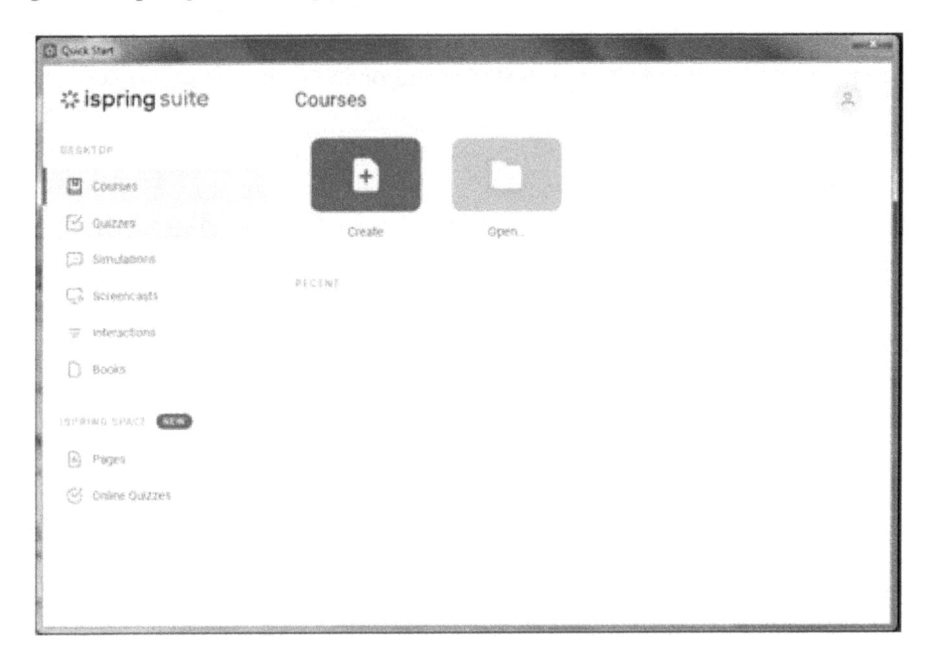


college students "race" to the finish line and exit tickets that allow students to submit feedback on the lecture are two notable components.

- *Spiral*

Spiral is a series of five apps for formative assessment. You can also provide real-time feedback and hear from all of your students by converting slides to a discussion thread, allowing college students to create and share collaborative presentations, and converting videos to a live chat with questions and quizzes.

- *Peergrade*

Peergrade is a web-based tool that allows students to participate in peer-review sessions. After you've set up your project, learners begin working on and then submitting their output - text, files, videos, links, and even Google docs. Students may also comment on each other's work and take action due to their comments. There's also a peek at what's going on with the assignment from the teacher's perspective.

- *EdPuzzle*

EdPuzzle is a video-based tool. Voice-overs, resources, comments, and quizzes may be added to videos by both teachers and students. Instructors may also see if students are viewing videos, how many times they have seen each part, and whether or not they understand the material.

- *Mentimeter*

Mentimeter allows you to create interactive presentations with 13 different interactive questions, such as word clouds and quizzes, and track how students vote on/respond to queries and interact with the display in real-time. You may export results to a PDF or Excel file and examine learners' results using this tool.

- *Google Forms*

Google Forms is a well-known tool for producing surveys and quizzes that can be graded. You may also ask students to complete multiple-choice or short-answer questions in their entirety, specify suitable responses and points, and provide feedback on correct and incorrect answers.

- *Quizalize*

Kahoot has a lot in common with Quizalize. It allows you to choose from over 12,000 official evaluations as well as teacher-created materials, or you may build your own. You may also get real-time statistics on each student's progress and automatically provide them with unique resources based on their quiz results.

- *Nearpod*

Nearpod is a web-based platform for creating engaging, interactive classrooms, including virtual reality, simulations, and gamified quizzes. It allows you to keep track of your student's progress using formative assessments such as surveys, open-ended questions, and more. You may also get real-time student feedback as well as post-session reports (Mahapatra, 2021).

- *Fluency Tutor*

Fluency Tutor is a program that assists college students in measuring and evaluating their oral analyzing progress. You can exchange reading passages with your class and receive recordings of the portions you've been assigned to read. The program includes over 500 ready-to-use reading fluency passages.

## Observing and Evaluating Learning in Online Environments

You may believe that only multiple-choice quizzes are used to assess online learning experiences. Other evaluation approaches to successfully measure how well learners achieve learning outcomes in an online environment can be found via thoughtful design and technology.

## What does 'Good' Formative Assessment Entail in the Digital World (Chen et al., 2020)?

- Ongoing throughout the learning experience
- Promote or Time regulated
- User-friendly
- Clear and specific
- Broken down into manageable pieces of information, then built back up over time
- Balanced: confirms what learners assessment stating areas for improvement
- Provides very specific and targeted user-friendly feedback
- Provides helpful advice, based on feedback

## Assessing Student Learning Authentically Online

In the online world, it is critical to design authentic assessment activities. It is vital, as usual, that your courses begin with a set of clearly stated learning outcomes. If appropriately planned, assessments may promote active learning and foster community among students and instructors.

**Can aid in the learning of students.**

1. Written Assignments: short essays, research article, case study responses.

    - Assignments Tool
    - Can assign students to small groups to provide peer feedback and build community.
    - Students submit written work for assessment electronically.
    - Turnitin software

2. Online Discussion Forum: Asynchronous discussion activities (i.e., discussion board, blog, or wiki).

- Wiki Tool

- Discussions
- Instructor can initiate class discussions with a set of questions.
- Forums Tool
- Opportunity for community building through student moderation.

3. Concept Maps:

- Give pupils a visual depiction of the relationships between the ideas they've learned in college. Relationships between concepts are shown by labeled hyperlinks.
- Lucidchart
- Coggle
- Useful tool for formative assessment of students' understanding at various stages throughout the course.
- Brainstorming/Mindmapping

4. Presentations: Student presentations can be adapted for use in an online classroom.

- Collaborate on Blackboard
- Students build online presentations (i.e., a slide deck or a poster) to show to the teacher and classmates and receive comments from the instructor and peers.
- These presentations can be facilitated via synchronous web-conferencing capabilities.

5. Test/quiz/exam: OWL may give traditional multiple-choice, short- or long-answer questions (Barana & Marchisio, 2016).

- Face-to-face proctored testing can include higher-stakes exams.
- Tests and Quizzes
- OWL can be used to take unproctored exams. These are usually low-stakes, formative examinations that are used to gauge student comprehension of course material.
- Tips for Evaluating Online Student Learning
- Provide specific and thorough rubrics to students to effectively express performance objectives.
- If the course topic is very technical, consider utilizing ungraded, self-check quizzes as a formative evaluation to monitor student learning and see if teaching tactics need to be changed.
- Use synchronous technologies to connect with students in real-time when appropriate. Because online college students have such diverse schedules, it is suggested that synchronous sessions be recorded so that students who cannot attend in person can watch them later.
- Instructors can also use self-and peer assessments to cut down on effort, improve student mastery experiences, and promote community.

- Consider using an announcement or an e-mail to bring notes to the entire class, such as summarizing trends observed in student assignments.
- Common student queries can be answered via Q&A discussion forums.
- In an online course, it's a good idea to use a range of evaluation tools.
- Make use of the surroundings and experiences of your pupils.

One of the most significant advantages of online classes is bringing students from all backgrounds together to learn from one another. Depending on your teaching circumstances, you may have pupils from all across your nation or from other countries. Consider how you may create evaluations that use their different settings and experiences to help them and one another learn more effectively.

## Incorporate Collaboration

Building a feeling of community and connection is especially crucial in online courses (Admiraal et al., 2015). Assigning group duties and projects is one approach to doing this. Group well-designed group projects enable students to interact with one another; understand course subjects more thoroughly via discussion and debate, and develop essential teamwork skills. The group projects have their level of complexity, so be careful to arrange them with specified tasks for group members or have students review each other's work to ensure that everyone contributes equally.

## Make Use of Both Summative and Formative Evaluations

Assessments enable us to measure pupils' understanding and mastery of a material and highlight areas for development. Formative and summative exams can be employed in both face-to-face and online courses (Admiraal et al., 2015). The latter provides more appealing forms for inventive evaluation, allowing students to perform, apply what they've learned, and demonstrate their knowledge in ways that a typical multiple-choice test cannot.

Instructional designers and education professionals can build online course evaluations in minutes using authoring tools like iSpring Suite Max. It's simple to customize courses with your chosen material using predesigned templates and evaluation techniques.

## Distance and Hybrid Learning Assessment Strategies

As the education sector grapples with the implications of Covid-19, we're all pushed to deliver meaningful education experiences at a distance, whether we employ synchronous or asynchronous online sessions, whether we term it distance or virtual

*Figure 5. Distance learning assessment methodology*

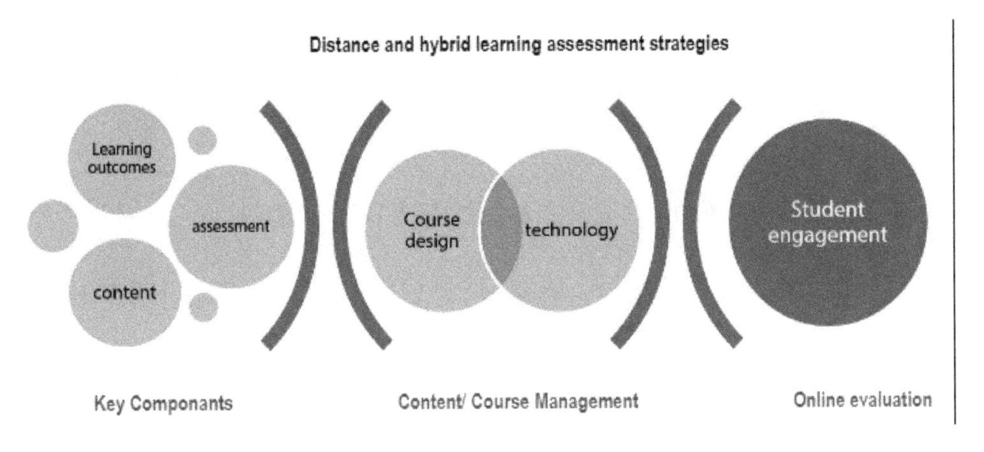


learning. This form of learning isn't new, but it's new to many of us, and it's pushed us to change our habits rapidly.

Formative evaluation from afar is difficult but not impossible, and we must still check for understanding and offer useful comments. The tactics we employ will differ from those used in the classroom in terms of appearance and sound.

The following are four evaluation methods that we have utilized in my digital/ physical classroom. Even though each subject has its own evaluation needs, most instructors will find something useful on this list, whether they teach in person, online, or through a hybrid approach.

## PERSONAL CONFERENCES

Conferencing as amost popular technique for evaluation in both online and offline class. A conference is a pre-arranged meeting with a scholar or students to discuss a topic you want to analyze. Holding one-on-one and small-group conferences is an excellent way to build relationships, and it allows for quick error correction if college students require it. Conferencing can also raise an early red signal about student development, enabling you to respond to a problem sooner rather than later at the end of a unit.

The main difference between hybrid and remote studying conferences is that you can obtain a good picture of what college students know and can do. There's always the internet or a parent to provide advice, so you can get a clear image of what they're up to.

It would be best if you had a purpose in mind to make conferencing work. What skills are most important right now? What abilities are your pupils having the most significant difficulty with? Your conferences will be more productive if you and the students have a clear goal in mind.

## ASSIGNMENTS FOR HIGHER-ORDER THINKING

Authors have found that forcing students to employ Bloom's higher-order thinking talents, such as analyzing, evaluating, or creating, boosts student engagement and allows for more authentic evaluation of both in-class and distance learners. Analyzing and generating media products using persuasive principles, practicing self-evaluation of literacy abilities, and goal setting. Using metacognition and making digital tales using WeVideo are all assessments that have worked successfully in my language classroom for both types of learners. These successful evaluation problems pushed students to use higher-order questioning skills while also allowing me to conduct multi-dimensional assessments. The interdisciplinary character of the tasks allowed for a fair review across several areas, so it wasn't only focused on one skill. This saved me time by allowing me to examine one final work rather than many minor initiatives. It allowed me to communicate with pupils as they were working on a project. It enabled me to employ a variety of assessment techniques.

## QUIZZES ON THE INTERNET

For both formative and summative evaluations, we utilize Google Forms. You can also utilize the quiz function to change how the questions are displayed, and you may establish a lock screen to start once an exam begins so that students cannot access or connect to any other windows. Another useful feature of Google Forms is that it can check multiple-choice replies and provide students grades through email once you've examined their written responses. We utilize Google Forms in conjunction with Google Meets with distance learning students (Agustina & Purnawarman, 2020). Creating a Google Meet for each distance learning student and then ask them to share their display screen and turn on their camera for the comparison duration.

Using Google Forms and Meets, we can identify all of my pupils simultaneously. Open a window for each of my distance learning college students and minimize it to have several windows open on my screen at once and monitor them during the test. We picked this method of assessing distant novices for final exams since it has been shown to be beneficial in several courses at our university.

## DISCUSSIONS ON DIGITAL WRITING

You may use Google Docs to expose and observe the evolution of student-written exams in real-time or asynchronously: Version records allow you to understand prior versions of a report better and determine who contributed to it. We use these features for written assignments, watching evaluations while college students work on them, and using the comment option to provide feedback as necessary (Allagui, 2014). This feature allows me to check in on students in the classroom or the internet and make real-time contributions by using the remark or improving the tool, as long as they have shared their work with me and granted me enhancing permission.

### The Impact of Technology on Digital Learning and Assessment

In several ways, technology may assist us in imagining and redefining evaluation. Learners who create and build goods, perform experiments with mobile devices, and adjust parameters in simulations might benefit from these technologies since they give unobtrusive measurements. Problems can be set in real-world settings with students doing activities, or multi-stage situations that imitate genuine, progressive involvement with the subject matter. Teachers may obtain information on students' progress and learning throughout the school day, allowing them to alter lessons, customize learning, or intervene to address specific learning gaps.

Technology-based exams allow for a range of question formats beyond the restricted multiple-choice, true, or-false, or fill-in-the-blank alternatives that have typified traditional assessments (Daşkın & Hatipoğlu, 2019). The following are some examples of upgraded question types:

- Graphic response refers to any activity in which students reply by drawing, moving, arranging, or choosing graphic areas.
- Students pick or rearrange sentences or phrases within a passage using hot text.
- Equation response, in which students submit an equation as a response.
- Assessments based on performance, in which students complete a sequence of challenging activities.

Students may display more complicated thinking and express their grasp of content using technology-enhanced questions, previously impossible to assess using traditional methods.

Performance-based assessments, in the example, are meant to require students to complete a sequence of sophisticated tasks that require them to synthesize data from numerous sources, evaluate it, and defend their conclusions. Reading excerpts from original texts, assessing the set of passages, and composing an essay in response to a prompt are examples of performance tasks in English language arts. A performance assignment in a mathematics class can challenge students to examine a graph based on accurate data and define the linear connection between the variables.

Performance-based exams can test students' cognitive thinking abilities and use their knowledge to solve actual, relevant situations. They allow students to develop an initial response rather than picking the correct answer from a list. Students can input their replies in the web interface using the technologies available in performance-based exams. Manual-scored items can be combined with machine-scored items in the same system to provide complete test results for activities that require hand scoring. In addition to more standard machine-scored prompts, the Partnership for Assessment of Readiness for College and Careers and the Smarter Balanced Assessment Consortium assess students' ability to thrive in classroom speaking and listening tasks (Bogdanović et al., 2014).

**Teachers may employ various digital tools and applications to help real-time formative assessment in the classroom (Haddad & Youakim, 2014).**

Teachers that employ formative instructional practice in their classrooms have a plethora of constructive assessment methodologies, approaches, and instruments at their disposal (Aljawarneh, 2019). Here is a comprehensive collection of digital tools, applications, and platforms that can assist you and your students in eliciting evidence of learning through formative assessment (Black & Wiliam, 2009).

**Take audio and video recordings (Johnson & Cooke, 2016).**

1. Animoto- Allows students to create a 30-second film demonstrating what they learned in a class.
2. AudioNote-It is a hybrid of a voice recorder and a notepad that records audio and notes for student participation.
3. Edpuzzle- Allows you to track student knowledge using video (your own or from Khan Academy, YouTube, and other sources).
4. Flipgrid- Allows pupils to reply to instructions with 15-second to 5-minute films. Feedback might come from teachers and classmates.
5. QuickVoice- Recorder You may use it to record lessons, meetings, or audio for projects. Easily sync your recordings to your computer for presenting purposes.
6. Vocaroo- It's possible to make audio recordings without using the software. Slideshows, presentations, and websites can all benefit from the recording.
7. WeVideo- enables you to use video to creatively engage students in their studies. Both teachers and students may make videos.

**Create quizzes, polls, and surveys to test your knowledge.**

8. Crowdsignal- Create online polls, quizzes, and questions using this tool. Students can answer questions using cell phones, tablets, and laptops, and information can be filtered for reports.
9. Edulastic allows you to create exams connected to standards and receive immediate feedback.
10. FreeOnlineSurveys is a website that allows you to create surveys, quizzes, forms, and polls.
11. Gimkit- Allows you to create in-the-moment quizzes. And it was created by a student in high school!
12. Kahoot- A game-based classroom response system that allows you to build quizzes with information from the internet.
13. MicroPoll- Creates polls, embeds them in webpages, and analyzes the results.
14. Naiku- Allows you to create quizzes that students may complete on their mobile devices.
15. Obsurvey- Create surveys, polls, and questionnaires using this program.
16. Poll Everyone and Everywhere – It allows you to create a poll or ask a question and view the results in real-time. Allows pupils to express themselves in a variety of ways. You may collect data and create tag clouds to aggregate replies using open-ended questions.
17. Pollster- It has specific unique characteristics, such as enabling multiple responses to a single question.
18. ProProfs-Itis a tool that allows you to create quizzes, polls, and surveys.
19. Quia tool-It allows you to build games, quizzes, and surveys, among other things. Use a database of existing quizzes created by other teachers.
20. Quizalize- is a tool that allows you to design quizzes and assignments.
21. Quizizz- walks you through creating quizzes and allows you to engage students in the process.
22. Quizlet- allows you to create mobile-friendly flashcards, exams, quizzes, and learning activities.
23. Survey- Hero Designed to build questionnaires and surveys.
24. SurveyMonkey- It is a valuable tool for conducting online polls and surveys.
25. SurveyPlanet-This site is also helpful for conducting online polls and surveys.
26. Triventy- Allows you to build quizzes that students may take in real-time on their own devices.
27. Yacapaca- Aids in the creation and distribution of quizzes.
28. Zoho- Survey enables you to create mobile-friendly surveys and view real-time results.

    Create a mind map, brainstorm ideas, and collaborate.
29. AnswerGarden- A tool for online cooperation and brainstorming.

30. Coggle- Mind-mapping applications that can help you comprehend your students' thinking.
31. Conceptboard- Software is similar to mind mapping but uses visual and text inputs to promote team communication visually.
32. Dotstorming-A whiteboard software allows users to publish and vote on digital sticky notes. This tool is ideal for sparking class debate and brainstorming on various subjects and concerns.
33. Educreations- Whiteboard A whiteboard software that allows students to share their knowledge.
34. iBrainstorm- uses a stylus or a finger to allow pupils to collaborate on projects.
35. Miro- Allows for real-time collaboration among the whole class.
36. Padlet- Students can use this blank canvas to build and design collaborative projects.
37. ShowMe-Interactive Whiteboard Another whiteboard technique for ensuring comprehension.
38. XMind Mind-mapping program for desktop and laptop computers.

**Present, engage and inspire your audience.**

39. BrainPOP- Allows you to design your lesson plan using prerecorded videos on various topics, then utilize quizzes to assess what stuck.
40. Buncee- Visualizes, communicates and engages students and instructors with educational content.
41. Five-Card Draw Flickr- To encourage visual thinking, it uses Flickr's tag function.
42. PlayPosit- Allows you to survey what pupils know about a topic by adding formative assessment elements to a library video or popular sites like YouTube and Vimeo.
43. RabbleBrowser- Enables a leader to conduct a group browsing session.
44. Random Name/Word Picker Aids in selecting random names. You can also add a list of keywords to the tool and ask students to guess terms by offering definitions.
45. Socrative- Engages pupils in a topic through exercises and games.
46. Spark- Allows you to customize exit tickets with designs and pictures.
47. Typeform- Helps you add graphical elements to polls.

**Make a word cloud or tag cloud.**

48. EdWordle- Creates word clouds from any text input to aid in collecting comments and debate.

**Word clouds are images made up of many tiny words that together offer a clue to the topic.**

49. Tagxedo- Allows you to assess student agreement and stimulate discussions.
50. Wordables- Aids in eliciting evidence of learning or the determination of background knowledge on a subject.
51. WordArt has a function that allows the user to turn each word into an active link to websites such as YouTube.

**Get instant feedback.**

52. Formative- Allows you to assign tasks, obtain real-time outcomes, and offer rapid feedback.
53. GoSoapBox- It's compatible with the BYOD concept and has a unique feature: a confusion meter.
54. IXL- Options are broken down by grade level and topic area.
55. Kaizena- Gives pupils immediate feedback on their uploaded work. You can provide verbal feedback or use a highlighter. You may also include resources in your message.
56. Mentimeter- Allows you to vote on any issue posed by a teacher using your phone or tablet, improving student involvement.
57. Pear Deck- Allows you to create interactive presentations that students may use on their mobile devices. It also includes a variety of unusual question kinds.
58. Plickers- Without using student devices, you may gather real-time formative assessment data.
59. Quick Key- Assists you in inaccurately marking, grading, and receiving rapid feedback (Blank et al., 2019).
60. Remind- Allows you to text pupils and maintain contact with their families.
61. Seesaw- Improves family communication and facilitates formative evaluation, while kids may utilize the platform to keep track of their progress.
62. Voxer- allows you to send recordings to families to hear how their children are doing; pupils may discuss their work, and you can give feedback.

**Improve student-to-student or teacher-to-student communication.**

63. Biblionasium- Allows you to see what books your pupils have read, set up reading challenges, and keep track of their progress. Students can also write book reviews and provide book recommendations to their classmates.

64. Classkick- Allows you to publish assignments for students and receive comments from both you and your student's classmates. Students can also keep track of their progress and projects.
65. ForAllRubrics-You may import, generate, and score rubrics on your tablet or smartphone.

**Data may be collected offline, scores can be computed automatically, and rubrics can be printed or saved as a PDF or spreadsheet.**

66. Lino- It's a virtual corkboard with sticky notes that students may use to ask questions and make comments on their learning.
67. Stopwatch on the Internet Hundreds of themed digital classroom clocks are available to use during small and large group conversations.
68. Peergrade- Aids in creating assignments and the uploading of rubrics. You may also assign peer-review assignments anonymously. Students can upload and assess their work using the header provided.
69. Spiral- Gives you access to feedback from formative assessments.
70. Verso-Allows you to create a learning plan based on a URL. There is enough room for directions. Students can submit their work, provide comments, and react to those remarks. You may sort through the replies and see how engaged they are.
71. VoiceThread- Allows you to create and share conversations on papers, diagrams, movies, and photos, among other things.

**With live chats, you can keep the conversation continuing.**

72. Chat in the backchannel A Twitter version that teachers control.
73. Chatzy- Supports private internet discussions in real-time.

**Documents or tasks can be created and saved.**

74. Google Forms- A Google Drive tool that helps you create real-time, collaborative documents with students using smartphones, tablets, and PCs.
75. Piazza- You may post lectures, assignments, and homework poses; reply to student queries, and poll students on class topics. Because it mirrors post-secondary class educational forms, this technology is better suitable for older pupils.

*Figure 6. Methods Online Learners' Progress Using Qualitative eLearning Assessment*

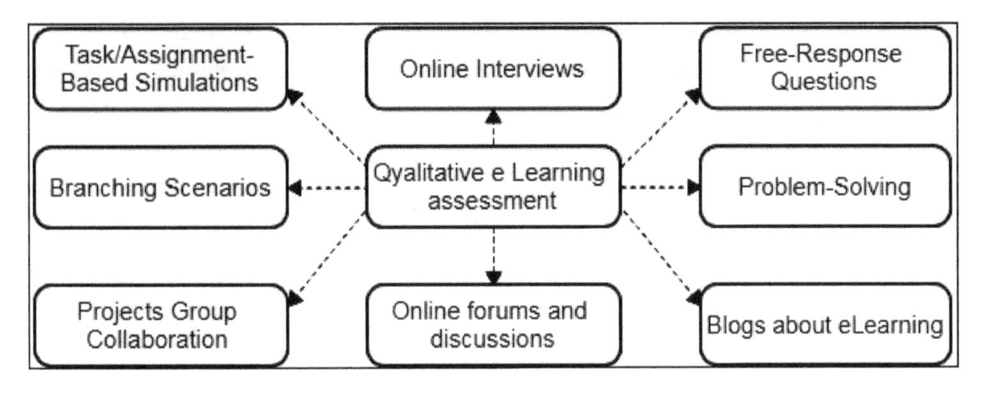


## Methods for Tracking Online Learners' Progress Using Qualitative eLearning Assessment

There are eight Qualitative eLearning Assessment/evaluation Methods for Tracking Online Learners' Progress (Curaj et al., 2015; Khan & Khan, 2019).

As the name indicates, qualitative eLearning assessment prioritizes quality over quantity (Curaj et al., 2015). It helps you assess the depth of an online learner's knowledge rather than just scraping the surface of eLearning course comprehension. Consequently, by identifying areas for development, you may increase your competence and productivity.

- Task/Assignment-Based Simulations

Simulators put students' practical and experiential knowledge to the test. To finish the assignment in a safe virtual environment, online learners must use all their resources and talents (Milligan & Buckenmeyer, 2008). As a result, you can measure competency without incurring any risks in the actual world. Produce reliable results; the simulation must be as realistic as feasible. Background sounds, pertinent pictures, and immersive eLearning characters are examples of this. If the work necessitates software or equipment, they should be included. To assess their performance in context, you must imitate every part of the eLearning experience (Çakıroğlu, 2014). For instance, how well they would function under duress.

- Branching scenarios

Multiple choice points in branching situations take online learners down alternative pathways (Bulut, 2019). Every decision they make moves them closer to the result, emphasizing their activities' bad or positive consequences. To navigate the circumstances and overcome typical barriers, they must use their abilities and talents. Because there are so many branches to consider, it's a good idea to plan and construct a complete eLearning storyboard. It enables to keep track of all decision pathways and ensures consistency.

- Projects for Online Group Collaboration with Feedback

You may also use peer-based eLearning feedback to acquire qualitative data. Make groups of your online students and assign them a topic or stimulus to work on. They must work together to address the problem or create a finished result, such as an online presentation or an eLearning video. The peer observations set this distinct from other online group cooperation initiatives. Provide a checklist or questionnaire for online learners to complete throughout the eLearning assignment.

- Free-response questions

One of the most basic and easiest qualitative eLearning assessment tools is open-ended questions. They do, however, provide the most creative flexibility. There are no correct or incorrect replies. Instead, online students must think about the subject and come to their own conclusions. They may even learn that their existing thoughts or preconceptions prevent them from progressing. The only limitation is that open-ended grading questions are difficult. You may, however, create a rubric ahead of time to speed the process and collect reliable data.

- Case Studies for Problem-Solving

As a qualitative eLearning assessment approach, problem-solving transforms online learners into detectives who must solve the challenge and demonstrate their expertise. It all begins with a case study or a real-life scenario. Remove the conclusion to leave it on a cliffhanger, then encourage online students to come up with answers. They must also describe how they came to their decision and why they believe it is the best course of action. It's not so much about the result as it is about the process of thinking. What abilities did they employ in their strategy? What did they do with their newfound knowledge?

- Blogs about eLearning

Encourage your online students to start an eLearning blog and post once or twice a week. Make a posting schedule that includes prompts or questions, a minimum word count, and upload deadlines. Examine the blogs regularly to track online student progress and identify areas for improvement. You may select from several free blogging platforms. As a result, you should establish certain ground rules and present a list of appropriate tools. To reduce the learning curve for new bloggers, you may provide online lessons or walkthroughs.

## CONCLUSION

An online assessment is a vital part of e-learning and should be given the same level of care and consideration as the learning content you supply. The good news is that you do not have to be a whiz at programming to make them. Many online assessment tools are available to assist you in developing engaging tasks for online evaluation. Choose your technique of measuring student learning and related software to connect your demands with the outcomes you want to achieve. Evaluation is an important part of the learning process since it demonstrates if students have grasped the material and whether the educational objectives have been reached. Online evaluations include:

- Real-time surveys.
- Drag-and-drop interactions.
- Dialog simulations with implications allow students to explore numerous ways through dialogue.
- Other approaches that may be used in the classroom.

Quick authoring tools simplify creating online surveys in minutes by just uploading and copying text. For most sorts of assessments, grading is simple and saves hours of manual grading. The future of the innovative evaluation systems that enables online learning coupled with the classical system opens ways to successful possibilities.

## REFERENCES

Admiraal, W., Huisman, B., & Pilli, O. (2015). Assessment in massive open online courses. *Electronic Journal of E-learning*, *13*(4), 207–216.

Agustina, M., & Purnawarman, P. (2020). Investigating learners' satisfaction utilizing google classroom as online formative feedback tool. *2020 6th International conference on education and technology (ICET)*, 26–31. 10.1109/ICET51153.2020.9276616

Aljawarneh, S. A. (2019). Reviewing and exploring innovative ubiquitous learning tools in higher education. *Journal of Computing in Higher Education*. Advance online publication. doi:10.100712528-019-09207-0

Allagui, B. (2014). Writing through Whatsapp: An evaluation of students writing performance. *International Journal of Mobile Learning and Organisation, 8*(3), 216–231. doi:10.1504/IJMLO.2014.067022

Barana, A., & Marchisio, M. (2016). Ten good reasons to adopt an automated formative assessment model for learning and teaching mathematics and scientific disciplines. *Procedia: Social and Behavioral Sciences, 228*, 608–613. doi:10.1016/j.sbspro.2016.07.093

Black, P., &Wiliam, D. (2009). Developing the theory of formative assessment. *Educational Assessment Evaluation and Accountability, 21*(1), 5.

Blank, D. S., Bourgin, D., Brown, A., Bussonnier, M., Frederic, J., Granger, B., ... Willing, C. (2019). nbgrader: A tool for creating and grading assignments in the Jupyter Notebook. *The Journal of Open Source Education, 2*(11), 32. doi:10.21105/jose.00032

Bogdanović, Z., Barać, D., Jovanić, B., Popović, S., & Radenković, B. (2014). Evaluation of mobile assessment in a learning management system. *British Journal of Educational Technology, 45*(2), 231–244. doi:10.1111/bjet.12015

BulutS. (2019). Assessing online learners' academic self-efficacy in a symbiotic learning environment. doi:10.2139/ssrn.3370615

Çakıroğlu, U. (2014). Analyzing the effect of learning styles and study habits of distance learners on learning performances: A case of an introductory programming course. *The International Review of Research in Open and Distributed Learning, 15*(4). Advance online publication. doi:10.19173/irrodl.v15i4.1840

Charlier, B., Cosnefroy, L., Jézégou, A., & Lameul, G. (2015). Understanding Quality of Learning in Digital Learning Environments: State of the Art and Research Needed. In A. Curaj, L. Matei, R. Pricopie, J. Salmi, & P. Scott (Eds.), *The European Higher Education Area*. Springer. doi:10.1007/978-3-319-20877-0_25

Chen, I. H., Gamble, J. H., Lee, Z. H., & Fu, Q. L. (2020). Formative assessment with interactive whiteboards: A one-year longitudinal study of primary students' mathematical performance. *Computers & Education, 150*, 103833. doi:10.1016/j.compedu.2020.103833

Cipriano, C., Barnes, T. N., Pieloch, K. A., Rivers, S. E., & Brackett, M. (2019). A multilevel approach to understanding student and teacher perceptions of classroom support during early adolescence. *Learning Environments Research*, *22*(2), 209–228. doi:10.100710984-018-9274-0

Darius, P. S. H., Gundabattini, E., & Solomon, D. G. (2021). A Survey on the Effectiveness of Online Teaching–Learning Methods for University and College Students. *J. Inst. Eng. India Ser. B*, *102*(6), 1325–1334. doi:10.100740031-021-00581-x

Daşkın, N., & Hatipoğlu, Ç. (2019). Reference to a past learning event as a practice of informal formative assessment in L2 classroom interaction. *Language Testing*, *36*(4), 527–551. doi:10.1177/0265532219857066

García-Peñalvo, F. J., Corell, A., Abella-García, V., & Grande-de-Prado, M. (2021). Recommendations for mandatory online assessment in higher education during the COVID-19 pandemic. In D. Burgos, A. Tlili, & A. Tabacco (Eds.), Radical solutions for education in a crisis context. Lecture Notes in Educational Technology. Springer. doi:10.1007/978-981-15-7869-4_6

Giray, G. (2021). An assessment of student satisfaction with e-learning: An empirical study with computer and software engineering undergraduate students in Turkey under pandemic conditions. *Education and Information Technologies*, *26*(6), 6651–6673. doi:10.100710639-021-10454-x PMID:33686329

Guangul, F. M., Suhail, A. H., Khalit, M. I., & Khidhir, B. A. (2020). Challenges of remote assessment in higher education in the context of COVID-19: A case study of Middle East College. *EducAsseEvalAcc*, *32*(4), 519–535. doi:10.100711092-020-09340-w PMID:33101539

Haddad, R. J., & Youakim, K. (2014). Google forms: A real-time formative assessment approach for adaptive learning. *Proceedings of the 2014 American society for engineering education, ASEE annual conference and exposition*, 24.649.1–24.649.14. 10.18260/1-2--20540

Huber, S. G., & Helm, C. (2020). COVID-19 and schooling: Evaluation, assessment and accountability in times of crises—reacting quickly to explore key issues for policy, practice and research with the school barometer. *EducAsseEvalAcc*, *32*(2), 237–270. doi:10.100711092-020-09322-y PMID:32837626

Johnson, G. M., & Cooke, A. (2016). Self-regulation of learning and preference for written versus audio-recorded feedback by distance education students. *Distance Education*, *37*(1), 107–120. doi:10.1080/01587919.2015.1081737

Khan, S., & Khan, R. A. (2019). Online assessments: Exploring perspectives of university students. *Education and Information Technologies, 24*(1), 661–677. doi:10.100710639-018-9797-0

Lara, J. A., Aljawarneh, S., & Pamplona, S. (2020). Special issue on the current trends in E-learning Assessment. *Journal of Computing in Higher Education, 32*(1), 1–8. doi:10.100712528-019-09235-w

Lara, J. A., Lizcano, D., Martínez, M. A., Pazos, J., & Riera, T. (2014). A system for knowledge discovery in e-learning environments within the European Higher Education Area—Application to student data from Open University of Madrid, UDIMA. *Computers & Education, 72*, 23–36. doi:10.1016/j.compedu.2013.10.009

Mahapatra, S. K. (2021). Online Formative Assessment and Feedback Practices of ESL Teachers in India, Bangladesh and Nepal: A Multiple Case Study. *The Asia-Pacific Education Researcher, 30*(6), 519–530. doi:10.100740299-021-00603-8

Milligan, A. T., & Buckenmeyer, J. A. (2008). Assessing students for online learning. *International Journal on E-Learning, 7*(3), 449–461.

# Chapter 5
# Emergency Remote Teaching in Language Education:
## Opportunities and Challenges

**Nurdan Atamturk**
*University of Kyrenia, Cyprus*

## ABSTRACT

*This chapter reviews research studies conducted on emergency remote teaching in foreign language education in higher education and presents the results of the qualitative study which evaluates the effectiveness of emergency remote teaching in English as a foreign language instruction. The data were elicited from 15 undergraduate students studying at the English language teaching departments in North Cyprus. The textual data gathered through self-reports revealed that a great majority of the participants were in favor of hybrid instruction after the pandemic. The rationale behind this result was found to be the fact that both in-person and online education had their own merits and demerits in their own way and that hybrid education had a potential to exploit the merits while avoiding the demerits. It was an unexpected result to find that the participants were in favor of the digitalization of language education.*

## INTRODUCTION

Emergency remote teaching came to fore due to the COVID-19 pandemic which is an unexpected and unprecedented crisis worldwide. This crisis has had destructive forces in all fields ranging from economy to industry. Education has been no exception. Despite closures prevalent in most fields and areas, the continuation of education

DOI: 10.4018/978-1-6684-5400-8.ch005

has been sustained through emergency remote teaching in the field of education. Emergency remote teaching entails a temporary change in terms of the delivery of instruction. In the case of the COVID-19 pandemic, the change is from in-person to online delivery mode. As this change was sudden and unprecedented, the transition to emergency remote teaching was troublesome for most higher education institutions. For this reason, it is imperative to design empirical studies evaluating the merits and demerits of emergency remote teaching conducted in a variety of disciplines. In the field of foreign language education, there are only a handful of research studies evaluating emergency remote teaching practices. Language teaching and learning differs from other disciplines in terms of technology use. While in the field of engineering or medicine, for example, the role of textbooks already became obsolete, physical course books were still used as primary sources in English language teaching classes prior to the pandemic. In this respect, online instructional materials were used as supplementary sources in language classes. The characteristics of students studying at English language departments are also different from those who study science. Owing to these reasons, it is imperative to elicit the views of prospective English language teachers of the emergency remote teaching. In order to fulfill this purpose, this study was designed to elicit the perceptions of fifteen undergraduate students studying at the English Language Teaching Departments in universities in north Cyprus. The aim of the study was to evaluate the effectiveness of emergency remote teaching in English as a foreign language instruction.

## BACKGROUND

When a group of 27 pneumonia cases were reported by Wuhan Health Authority in December 2019, many things changed worldwide (Committee W.C.H., 2019). First these cases were defined as novel Coronavirus, then World Health Organization announced COVID-19 " public health emergency of international concern" and then as "pandemic" (Liguori & Winkler, 2020). The pandemic soon affected all nations. Owing to the fact that it was a novel virus and that there was no specific treatment, confinement seemed to be the only option at the time. However, this closure could affect industries very negatively. For this reason, a solution had to be found. Especially in the case of higher education sector closures were unacceptable because there were millions of students pursuing their degrees. This crisis could endanger the higher education institutions which invested in international education (Wang et al., 2020). For this reason, to confront COVID-19, higher education institutions searched for ways to continue education. One of the reasons behind discontinuing traditional education system was that COVID-19 was an infectious disease and that human contact transmitted this disease. Hence, social distancing was imperative.

Traditional classes were held with many students in indoor classrooms, which could make way to the transmission of the disease. The other reason was that large gatherings were forbidden through the measures taken by the governments. The adoption of digitalized education came to the fore as it was impossible to continue with traditional classes, which altered the mode of teaching and brought in substantial challenges regarding unpreparedness.

Before the pandemic, education provided by higher education institutions was predominantly face-to-face, albeit distance education and online education offered by open universities (Erlam et al., 2021). Online education emerged as the best option during the lockdown (Dong et al., 2020; Hodges et al., 2020; Martinez, 2020). Hence, digitalization in education was accelerated. In a very short time after the lockdown millions of tertiary education students underwent a transition from face-to face to emergency remote teaching experience (Karakose, 2021; Trzcioska-Król, 2020 & Vlachopoulos, 2020). This rapid transition from face-to-face to online education introduced opportunities as well as challenges. Rather than online teaching and learning, this paper focuses on emergency remote teaching and learning. Differing from online teaching and learning, emergency remote teaching is a temporary situation which emerges during such a crisis as the COVID-19 pandemic. Emergency remote teaching differs from online learning:

*In contrast to experiences that are planned from the beginning and designed to be online, emergency remote teaching (ERT) is a temporary shift of instructional delivery to an alternate delivery mode due to crisis circumstances. It involves the use of fully remote teaching solutions for instruction or education that would otherwise be delivered face-to-face or as blended or hybrid courses and that will return to that format once the crisis or emergency has abated. The primary objective in these circumstances is not to recreate a robust educational ecosystem but rather to provide temporary access to instruction and instructional support in a manner that is quick to set up and is reliably available during an emergency or crisis. (Hodges et al., 2020)*

As posed by Hodges et al. (2020), the main aim of emergency remote teaching in crisis situations is to provide temporary access to learning and instruction which is reliable during the crisis. In this respect, the main objective of emergency remote teaching is not to create a novel education system but to set up a temporary digital solution to the education problems resulting from the shortcomings of a crisis. Moser et al. (2021) outline the frame of advancing digital instruction developed by Online Learning Consortium and Quality Matters through the Continuity Planning and Emergency Preparedness and the Emergency Remote Instruction Checklist for educators in order to guide and aid them in the transition to remote learning during the crisis. The three phases outlined are as follows:

1. Getting started (including the need for teachers to clarify expectations, provide *clear directions, offer information related to technological assistance, elucidate policy adjustments, and identify best mechanisms for communication between the students and the teacher)*
2. Guiding students and their learning (connecting assignments to learning objectives and providing timely feedback)
3. Teaching effectively in a new environment (focusing on course organization, using short multimedia files, and integrating content that supports a safe and equitable environment). (Moser et al., 2021)

Although this guide was a great help, the fast transition and the exhausting workload set drawbacks for academics especially during the beginning of the lockdown. The relevant literature is replete with negative perceptions of online language learning (Blake, 2015; Doughty, 2015 & Moser et al., 2021). As noted by Moser et al. (2021), 'perceptions about online language learning must be explored in pre-service teacher preparation and in-service teacher professional development'.

## Tertiary Education and Emergency Remote Teaching

Tertiary education is identified as one of the instrumental keys in reducing poverty, fostering growth and shared prosperity since it is believed that well educated people have better employment opportunities and that they are more productive and skilled in dealing with economic shocks better (The World Bank, 2020). According to the World Bank report (2020), there are around 220 million tertiary education students worldwide. This massive number of higher education students illustrates how important the tertiary education industry is. Due to the unprecedented pandemic, higher education sector was at risk of closure.

A great majority of higher education institutions viewed and adopted emergency remote teaching as a kind of life saver during the pandemic. Reporting on the research studies during the first six months of the Covid-19 pandemic Butler-Henderson et al. (2020) found that early studies were about how students and academic staff were responding to rapid adaptation, how institutions were dealing with their new commitments as well as how the responses differed. Both academics and students felt stressed out and unsure at the beginning of this period. Obviously, these negative feelings were reflected on the students, too. Frustration was prevalent in both parties. They were struggling to continue education amid concerns about the deadly Covid-19.

Access to the Internet posed a number of challenges (Verawardina et al., 2020). It was discovered that some academics and students do not have laptops or the Internet connection in their homes. According to NortonLifeLock (2020), in a study conducted with a thousand parents, one thirds of the parents have bought tablets for their children as a result of the pandemic in the USA. Popyk (2020), on the other hand, found that many households were unable to afford any computers for their kids.

It was also discovered that students who lived in underdeveloped areas did not have a reliable Internet connection which is essential for quality online classes (Flack et al., 2020). Information communication technology skills (ICT) of academics was another challenge. As found by Bond (2020) in her review of studies during the pandemic, teacher ICT skills and knowledge was the most frequently cited theme. Bond (2020) acknowledged that teachers with effective ICT skills before the pandemic had fewer problems concerning emergency remote teaching. In a similar vein, Peterson et al. (2020) found that teachers with a range of digital competencies prior to the pandemic were less stressed out than their counterparts who had problems with ICT skills. Nonetheless, this did not mean that teachers with effective ICT skills were lighthearted concerning adaptation to emergency remote teaching at all (Putri et al., 2020). Since emergency remote teaching required different pedagogies, they had to adapt to these pedagogies and find ways to use such pedagogies effectively (Trust & Whalon, 2020) and even the ICT skilled teachers found it difficult to adapt and use the different digital platforms and applications used in emergency remote teaching (Rap et al., 2020).

Most higher education institutions were not equipped with the necessary infrastructure to support the emergency remote teaching platforms. For this reason, they just picked one platform randomly to fasten the start of the online education process but had to change it for several reasons. This also put extra pressure for both academics and students due to adaptation problems.

## Research on Opportunities and Challenges of Emergency Remote Teaching

Advantages of online learning in the relevant literature consists of studying from anywhere, at any time; possibility of saving significant amounts of money; no commuting on crowded buses or local trains; flexibility to choose; and saving time (Bijees, 2017; Nagrale, 2013). Additionally, the flexibility students experience in remote learning is highly valued (Alexander et al., 2012). Comfortable learning environment, time utilization, smooth interaction, social distancing, data utilization, academic achievement, psychological stability and transportation cost reduction (Shim & Lee, 2020) are also found to be the merits of emergency remote teaching.

One of the foremost challenges of emergence of remote teaching emerges as the inequalities in terms of diverse socio-economic situations (Montacuta, 2020). Ferri et al., (2020) specify these challenges resulting from socio-economic inequalities as:

1. lack of resources, including access to educational technologies and the Internet

2. lack of physical spaces to carry out home-based learning among families from poorer backgrounds, who lack the basic skills to support their children, especially regarding secondary education. (Doyle, 2020; Outhwaite, 2020)

Ferri et al. (2020) classify the challenges posed by emergency remote teaching as technological, pedagogical and social challenges. Technological challenges result from the lack of or poor quality Internet connectivity and electronic devices. This problem is prevalent among disadvantaged families with more than one children. To a varying degree insufficient bandwidth or connection failures during classes are observed. Pedagogical challenges include the adoption of new approaches which align with online teaching modalities. Not all teachers' digital literacy is at a desirable level. For this reason, teachers' ICT skills appear to be one of the criticalities. In terms of social challenges, the loss of human interaction between teachers and students is considered one of the major limitations of the emergency remote teaching since students complain about the lack of face-to-face interactions with their instructors reporting that they need to feel emotions during interactions. Network instability, unilateral interactions, reduced concentration, constraints on practice or experiments, insufficient data provision, dissatisfaction with substitution of assignments, constraints on team projects, reduced academic achievement, unprepared class design, reduced understanding of classes, dissatisfaction with assessment, administrative dissatisfaction, dissatisfaction with relationship formation, dissatisfaction with educational environments (Shim & Lee, 2020) are listed as the shortcomings of emergency remote teaching environments.

## Emergency Remote Teaching in Language Education

Online instruction was not prevalent before the pandemic in the field of language education. As noted by Russell (2020) most language teachers lack knowledge and experience of online language design development and delivery before the pandemic. In a similar vein, most language learners may not be good at instructional technologies or they may have adaptation problems and other challenges concerning technology use. The results of Russel's (2020) study indicate that language learners experience language anxiety in online learning environments as well as in traditional classes and that while anxiety levels do not diminish over time among face-to-face learners, it decreases in online learning environments.

In terms of language education, research does not indicate a statistically significant difference between students' learning in face-to face and online environments (Peterson, 2021; Russell & Murphy-Judy, 2020). Moser et al. (2021) mention the best practices for planned online instruction through eight standards and sub-standards developed by Quality Matters:

1. course overview and introduction,
2. learning objectives,
3. assessment and measurement,
4. instructional materials,
5. learning activities and learner interaction,
6. course technology,
7. learner support,
8. accessibility and usability

However, during the time of such a crisis some extrinsic factors may intervene. To illustrate, Moser et al. (2021) found that although all language educators engaged in practices that aligned with the standards of online language learning, the perceived outcomes related to remote teaching during COVID-19 were less than desirable. Computer-assisted language instruction, blended and hybrid teaching as well as web-facilitated classes are amongst the recent trends in language education worldwide. Such trends are also fostered owing to the pandemic and there has been a growing interest in online learning as a trend since then. In the field of language education there are also software programs which teach grammar, pronunciation and vocabulary. There are also many commercially available language teaching software programs employing artificial intelligence to improve users' pronunciation and vocabulary development.

## CONTEXT OF THE STUDY

The internationalized education system in north Cyprus has a crucial role in its small economy. Prior to the pandemic all higher education institutions in north Cyprus conducted face-to-face classes. Hence, distance education or synchronous online classes were not prevalent albeit the limited use of Moodle. Some secondary schools and universities used Moodle but most of them were in the form of asynchronous classes. For this reason, it is not possible to state that academics were familiar with online teaching platforms prior to the pandemic. Owing to this fact, it was difficult for most academics to adapt to the new modalities of teaching and learning in online platforms.

That all Turkish Cypriot universities favored campus based programs before the pandemic could be acknowledged by the fact that diplomas received from distance programs are not as valued as the ones acquired through face-to-face programs neither in Turkey nor in north Cyprus. Once they get their diplomas, Turkish higher education students need to apply to the Turkish Higher Education Council for equivalence of their diplomas granted by the universities in north Cyprus. Recognition and equivalence of diplomas acquired through distance education programs might be problematic. Resulting from the bad reputation of distance education, none of the universities in north Cyprus indulged in distance education.

All universities in north Cyprus are under the governance of the Turkish Higher Education Council and this council took some measures for safety issues during the pandemic and decided to take up online instruction and learning starting from March 2020. All courses were delivered online up until 2021-22 fall semester when it was decided to deliver %60 of all the offered courses face-to-face and the remaining %40 online due to the precautions to reduce student density on campus. Like all universities which moved to online instruction in March 2020, Turkish Cypriot universities changed from on campus to online rapidly as well.

Most universities in the world were unprepared for online instruction in terms of resources and academic capabilities (Treve, 2021) and many academics held negative perceptions of online instruction prior to 2020 (Johnson et al., 2021). The universities in north Cyprus were no exception. The transition to online delivery mode posed too many challenges. Dealing with all these challenges at one time was hard for all academics and learners. In addition to the lack of previously prepared online pedagogies, the lack of desirable ICT skills were the major challenges. Academics started working from home for the first time in their lives and they had to work very long hours because the distinction between working hours and domestic life was blurred. Lecturers had to work long hours answering students' queries to ease their students' anxiety and stress. Students, on the other hand, were stressed out due to the pandemic and worried about the continuation of their education.

As the transition to online mode was fast, academics did not find the time to get ready but jumped in without any training during the initial stage of the emergency remote teaching. Despite the instructional videos on how to use the online platforms, their initial experience with the online mode was mostly like on a trial and error basis. BigBlue Button, Google Meet and Zoom were used as the main online platforms in north Cyprus. During this transition, the main challenge was to design the courses for lecturers and to be able to follow the online courses for students.

During the early days of the pandemic, all stakeholders in education in north Cyprus were of the view that this was a temporary situation and that they had to work hard to find ways to avoid disruption of education. Online education was a kind of savior for them during these lockdown times and it would be ditched as soon as the pandemic was over. Many academics voiced their yearnings for face-to face classes on social media. They never thought at the beginning of the pandemic that online education which became a part of their lives during the pandemic might be a favorable learning and instruction mode during the post COVID-19 times. It never occurred to them that online education would be an integral component of higher education in the post pandemic time.

# METHODOLOGY

## Research Method

This study utilized an in-depth qualitative epistemological thematic analysis method to determine participants' views of emergency remote teaching during the time of the Covid-19 pandemic. As grounded theory informed the current study, the researcher discovered the common themes from the qualitative data which were collected via self-reports. On the self-reports the participants were required to write about how emergency remote teaching affected their learning by giving specific examples. They were also asked to evaluate the advantages and disadvantages of their online learning experience depending on their experience. The qualitative nature of the study was expected to provide deeper insights into the issue. The collected data were coded initially for general categories. Next, categories were identified more specifically in relation to the merits and demerits of emergency remote teaching.

## Participants

The participants of the study were fifteen prospective English language teachers studying at three different private universities in North Cyprus. The age range of the participants was 19-21 and they were all non-native speakers of English. Since the aim of the study was to evaluate the merits and demerits of language classes during the emergency remote teaching during the pandemic, purposeful sampling technique was adopted. Following the ethical approval of a higher education institution, English Language Teaching Departments in North Cyprus were e-mailed to recruit voluntary participants for the study. Seventeen volunteers replied to the e-mail. However, two of them failed to complete the study. An informed consent form was sent to the participants to be signed and returned. The data were collected in January 15 in 2022. By this time the participants had an experience of four academic terms of emergency remote teaching. Before the pandemic all their classes were held face-to-face. Therefore, none of them had an online learning experience prior to the pandemic. All participants took part in the study with pseudonyms.

## Results

The textual data gathered through the self-reports revealed that a great majority of the participants were quite satisfied with their emergency remote teaching experience and that they were in favor of hybrid instruction after the pandemic. The rationale behind this result was found to be the fact that both in-person and online education had their own merits and demerits in their own way and that hybrid education had a potential to exploit the merits while avoiding the demerits. It was an unexpected result to find that the participants who praised face-to-face classes before the pandemic were in favor of the digitalization of language education. In this respect, this study has useful implications for higher education students, prospective teachers as well as in-service English as a Foreign language teachers. Contrary to the results of the research studies which held a negative view of online teaching (Johnson et al., 2020) this study found that overall most participants were highly content with emergency remote teaching practices. While the merits of emergency remote teaching were found to be efficient solution, comfortable learning environment, ease of access to a variety of instructional materials and rapid digitalization of language education, the demerits were identified as the lack of interpersonal communication, attrition and persistent technical challenges.

## Merits of Emergency Remote Teaching in Language Classes

Online classes were perceived as a kind of savior by all of the participants of the study. Since the participants were young, they never had such a crisis in their lives. As the pandemic was unprecedented, at first they were really worried about the discontinuation of their education. As reported by Ali:

*At first I did not know what pandemic meant and how it would change my life. My friends were talking about a lockdown and school closures but it did not occur to me at the time. Besides, I was not worried about getting Covid. We were talking about what we would do when they closed schools....as if education was more important than our health.*

Maureen noted:

*When they closed the university I was very annoyed because I would not be able to graduate on time. When the university announced that they would offer online classes, I was worried but also happy that at least they can offer a solution to this problem at least it was better than school closures.*

The participants of this study perceived online classes as a kind of solution to their problem which is school closures. More than half of the participants noted 'online classes saved my life'. This could be the main reason for valuing emergency remote teaching. As they viewed emergency remote teaching as a savior, they must have developed positive perceptions of emergency remote teaching.

Comfortable learning environment was raised by all participants. As put by Nelly:

*Of course being at home and studying from home is more comfortable than being in*

*a classroom. You have to get dressed in the morning and take the bus to school, spend at least half an hour on the bus....worried about being late to the class was not an issue*

*anymore.*

Similarly, Cansu expressed her views:

*During online education at first I felt as if I were not a student at all. I mean I was not a proper student at all. Later on I enjoyed the comfort that the online classes offered. I didn't have to travel to school and sometimes the school bus is late we are sometimes late to our classes and public transport is not very good in Cyprus. That's why we have to wait for the school bus to come and pick us but during online education we stayed at home... we didn't have to rush.*

Ease of access to a variety of instructional materials during class was found to be an advantage of emergency remote teaching. As asserted by Kaan:

*During online education while the teacher is teaching he can easily log into YouTube and we can all watch the video without spending time. During face-to-face classes we usually followed the course book and there's no Internet connection in most of our classes. During face-to-face classes we also used online materials when the instructor brought his laptop to the class. We watched or used fewer online materials in face-to face classes than we did during our online classes.*

Alp noted:

*Online classes helped us discover millions of instructional materials. I think when I become a teacher I will use online materials in my class because I think it's a very good way to engage students.*

Aisha reported:

*When the class gets boring instructors can use relevant online materials to attract students' attention during online classes. For example, when teaching English culture you can use a reading text but if you use a video on English culture it is more effective.*

Rapid digitalization of language education emerged as the other merit of emergency remote teaching. Casey reported:

*Before emergency remote teaching I was content with my face-to-face classes... I still like and sometimes prefer face-to-face classes but before the pandemic it never occurred to me that language teaching was possible in online classes. I would definitely say face-to-face classes were better but this experience with emergency remote teaching changed my negative opinion about online classes... now I believe that both online instruction and face-to-face classes with traditional ones have their own advantages and disadvantages.*

Sam wrote:

*I'm not a technophobe but I was not really into technology before the pandemic. Of course I have a laptop and I do I use it to do my homework but for example I never remember searching for instructional videos on the Internet. Thanks to the pandemic our habits changed. Now for example I believe that technology must definitely be a part of our classes.*

Seval noted:

*Of course a computer student is expected to use computers in his classes but we as future language teachers are more familiar with books and you know such people are not good at using technology. Before the pandemic if you asked me I would definitely say that without books language teaching is not possible I mean physical books. But now I believe that by the time I graduate all primary and secondary schools will teach both online and face to face English classes because online classes have great advantages for students and teachers and also for schools.*

Through remote teaching the participants who are all prospective language teachers had the opportunity to conduct their classes online and also had an experience of how to use instructional online materials in language classes. Seeing how they benefited from online classes regarding a variety of instructional materials they were all in the view that they would use online materials in their classes in the future.

## Demerits of Emergency Remote Teaching in Language Classes

Lack of interpersonal interaction was found to be one of the demerits of emergency remote teaching. It was discovered that the prospective English language teachers of the current study highly valued their relationship with their instructors. It was revealed that the participants failed to establish such a relationship with their instructors during emergency remote teaching. It was also found that there was a lack of a healthy and effective relationship between the instructors and students during the online mode since interaction barriers with the instructors were raised frequently. Ali noted:

*Interaction with the instructor and also with my classmates is a little different from interaction in face-to-face environment. When conducting a dialogue for example to have a meaningful conversation you need to see people's eyes. look at their facial expressions ...however we lack such details in online classes it was a little bit frustrating.*

Tom responded:

*When the instructor asked questions and if we did not respond quickly he just answered the question that he asked by himself because obviously the instructor was also tired of waiting for students' responses. It was like a monologue.*

Nina wrote:

*During online instruction the gap between the instructors and the students is quite big. In face-to-face classes some instructors were closer to us.*

Student attrition was one of the demerits of emergency remote teaching.
Nalan explained:

*Although I really appreciate staying at home and logging in online classes at a very comfortable environment I don't think it is effective because there's always a distracting thing at home, for example my phone rang.*

Sena commented that the online classes were boring because the instructor went on and on without paying attention to students' pace of learning and it was impossible for them to fully concentrate on their courses. She added that during face-to-face classes their instructors sometimes made jokes and they all laughed and enjoyed themselves but during online instruction they were more formal and not enjoyable at all.

Kaan wrote that online classes were less enjoyable and he did not feel that he belonged to that class. Kaan wrote:

*The instructor was always in a rush to keep up with the syllabus and when we were doing presentations for example if someone was not ready he was not pleased with this because he complained that he didn't have time to arrange extra online hours for missing presentations. I find it very stressful and frustrating.*

Cansu wrote:

*It was a depressing period and I did not feel well. Among many problems I need to continue my education. At first I was happy that it was not suspended but never thought that it would bring too much work. There was a time I felt helpless because it was too demanding and I did not have the strength.*

Persistent technical challenges were found to be the other demerit of emergency remote teaching. Low quality Internet speed was the major problem. Most participants reported that from time to time they did not have a reliable Internet connection to be able to follow their online classes. Frequent network disconnections diminished their willingness to communicate with their instructors and their classmates. Instructors' lack of experience in using technology was also frustrating. The participants complained that some instructors did not have a reliable Internet connection and they suffered from frequent interruptions so the instructor had to start the class several times which frustrated the students and deliberately decreased the quality of their learning experience. Aisha complained that when she was giving a presentation she could not open one of the videos that she needed to show and Alp noted that when he was giving his presentation some of his classmates couldn't hear him. Sena, on the other hand, wrote about the constant buzz coming from the microphones complaining that this buzz gave her headaches.

## Discussion

Despite the demerits, it was found in the study that emergency remote teaching was viewed a kind of savior by all the participants of the study. Hence, they had positive perceptions of emergency remote teaching. This can be acknowledged by the fact that the participants of the study were worried about school closures and emergency remote teaching was used to avoid this undesirable situation. In this respect, this result of the study that the participants had positive perceptions of emergency remote teaching did not go in line with previous studies (Blake, 2015; Doughty, 2015; Johnson et al., 2020; Moser et al., 2021) who reported negative perceptions of online instruction.

Comfortable educational environment was found to be one of the merits of emergency remote teaching. The participants found studying from home more comfortable than their classrooms which was supported by the result of Shim and Lee (2020). The current study revealed that a variety of instructional materials used during online classes was highly valued by the participants who used relatively limited sources, mainly course books, during face to face instruction. The lack of Internet connection in their classrooms could be the main reason for sticking to course books. This result could not be endorsed due to the lack of studies reporting this result. Rapid digitalization of language education was also found to be a novel result. Although the participants were not into computers in language education prior to their emergency remote teaching experience, their views changed in the light of the benefits of online classes. Most of them admitted that they would be using online sources when they start working as a teacher. In this respect, emergency remote teaching created opportunities for them.

As well as merits, the results revealed perceived demerits of emergency remote teaching, too. The lack of interpersonal communication was found to be one of the demerits. Moore (1989) identified three types of sender–receiver interaction, namely learner–content, learner–learner and learner–teacher in the field of communication. Learner–content interaction refers to PowerPoint presentations, instructional videos and e-books in the context of this study. Learner-content interaction has a potential to enhance students' problem-solving and critical thinking skills (Moore, 1989). Zhang and Lin (2020) examined the effect of certain variables on learner satisfaction in online settings to find that learner–content interaction was the sole interaction type that significantly predicted learner satisfaction. Although the participants of the study did not complain about the materials used during emergency remote teaching, they complained about the interruptions during their presentations which could harm learner-content interaction. Obviously, as this study suggested learner-learner interaction in comparison to that of conventional classes was less in online environments. Learner-learner interaction is as important as learner–teacher interaction in foreign language classes. Language learners engage in meaningful conversations with their peers in the target language, learn from each other and practise newly acquired knowledge over each other. While the teacher models the language most of the time, sometimes a classmate can model the language use. Given that learner-learner interaction is highly valued in language classes, the lack of such interaction may affect learning achievement negatively. Additionally, language learning is a social process. The absence of learner-learner interaction could make way to feelings of isolation and stress (Weiner, 2003). As suggested by one of the participants that online classes were boring because the instructor went on and on without paying attention to students' pace of learning, the online classes were more like traditional lecture courses lacking effective online instruction pedagogies. If teachers incorporated more group work activities to foster collaborative working, learners would have more levels of learner–learner interaction, which would affect students' satisfaction during online classes, albeit the fact that Zhang and Lin (2020) revealed a non-significant relationship between learner-learner interaction and satisfaction. Dumford and Miller (2018) acknowledged that students cannot participate in online classes that require cooperation as well as they do in face-to-face classes. It was also revealed that there was less learner-teacher interaction during online mode and that students' participation rate in discussions with diverse groups of students was low (Dumford & Miller, 2018). Borup et al. (2013) found that among these three types of interaction, virtual high school students perceived learner–teacher interaction as the greatest benefit to their learning motivation.

The results revealed students' attrition during emergency remote teaching. A number of studies reported academics being stressed out. As shown by the results of this study prospective language teachers were also tired and weakened during the emergency remote teaching experience. The results revealed persistent technical challenges which corroborated those of Ferri (2020), Flack et al. (2020), Shim and Lee (2020) and Verawardina et al. (2020).

## Implications

This study has a few implications for higher education institutions and academics. First, higher education institutions should immediately incorporate hybrid learning addressing students' learning needs. For this purpose, higher education institutions need to improve their technology infrastructure and set up centers for academics' professional development concerning online instruction. Additionally, the syllabus of teacher training programs need to incorporate courses on how to prepare educational videos in order to equip language teachers with effective technology use in their classes. Since technology has become an integrated part of language learning due to the pandemic such courses are thought to be of great help for future language teachers. Academics need to incorporate more enjoyable activities such as gamification into their online classes so as to stimulate students' focus and motivation. They also need to have online office hours which they can dedicate to diminish students' anxiety, worries and challenges experienced during online modes. Supervisors need to organize sessions with students to teach or to aid them in becoming more autonomous learners. They should also teach how to develop effective strategies to cope with the challenges of online learning mode. Lomicka (2020) suggests that language instructors need to be present, authentic, and available for interaction with their language learners. Teachers were caught unprepared regarding ICT skills. For this reason, teachers should develop their ICT skills and the relevant institutions need to provide in-service training on the issue (Hartshorn & McMurry, 2020). Teachers need to learn online teaching pedagogies as well (Russell & Murphy-Judy, 2020).

## FUTURE RESEARCH DIRECTIONS

Despite the fact that this study provides a number of useful insights into the effects of the Covid-19 pandemic on language learners, there are also a number of limitations that should be addressed in future studies. First of all, this is a small scale study and the participants were recruited from three higher education institutions failing to cover all higher education institutions, which makes making generalizations difficult. The scope of the study covers only a few higher education institutions in north Cyprus. Future studies can be designed as large scale studies with a number of higher education institutions. Future studies can employ a broad sample to make generalizations. Secondly, this study relies on self-reported data from a volunteer sample which may not accurately represent the realities of language learner classes. Future research can employ a variety of instruments or multiple instruments in collecting data. Another limitation is that the data were elicited through a single data source, which is the self-report in this context. Future studies can employ multiple data sources.

## CONCLUSION

In the discipline of English language teaching, emergency remote teaching was initially viewed as a temporary situation. Lessons learned from the emergency remote teaching experience are that online instruction benefit language learners and that if the demerits are avoided or diminished, it has a potential to foster students' academic gains.

Given that emergency remote teaching was a great savior which provided flexibility in terms of education, the rapid transition from face-to-face to online classes brought problems as well. Prior to the Covid-19 pandemic, most language classes were classroom-based. Neither academics nor language learners was familiar with online modes before the pandemic. Adaptation to online instruction and learning posed challenges as well as opportunities. The merits of emergency remote teaching included being an efficient solution to school closures during crises, comfortable environment for learning, ease of access to a variety of instructional materials and rapid digitalization of language education. Amongst these merits, rapid digitalization of language instruction has a potential to offer numerous opportunities. Academics and language learners have been familiar with online instruction and learning in a very short time, which would take many years if it was a planned action. The lack of interpersonal communication, attrition and persistent technical challenges consist in the demerits of emergency remote teaching. Given the student satisfaction and the merits of online instruction, it seems that online instruction will be a part of language classes during the post-pandemic time, which makes way to hybrid language instruction. Efficiency in hybrid instruction can be ensured by diminishing the identified demerits.

This research received no specific grant from any funding agency in the public, commercial, or not-for-profit sectors.

## REFERENCES

Alexander, M. W., Truell, A. D., & Zhao, J. J. (2012). Expected advantages and disadvantages of online learning: Perceptions from college students who have not taken online courses. *Issues in Information Systems, 13*(2), 193–200.

Bijeesh, N. A. (2017). *Advantages and disadvantages of distance learning*. Retrieved May 13, 2022, from http://www. indiaeducation.net/online-education/articles/advantages-and-disadvantages-of-distancelearning.html

Blake, R. (2015). The messy task of evaluating proficiency in online language courses. *Modern Language Journal, 99*(2), 408–412. doi:10.1111/modl.12234_5

Bond, M. (2020). Schools and emergency remote education during the COVID-19 pandemic: A living rapid systematic review. *Asian Journal of Distance Education, 15*(2), 191–247.

Borup, J., Graham, C. R., & Davies, R. S. (2013). The nature of adolescent learner interaction in a virtual high school setting. *Journal of Computer Assisted Learning, 29*(2), 153–167. doi:10.1111/j.1365-2729.2012.00479.x

Butler-Henderson, K., Crawford, J., Rudolph, J., Lalani, K., & Sabu, K. M. (2020). COVID-19 in higher education literature database (CHELD V1): An open access systematic literature review database with coding rules. *Journal of Applied Learning & Teaching, 3*(2), 1–6.

Committee W.C.H. (2019). *Wuhan Municipal Health and Health Commission's briefing on the current pneumonia epidemic situation*. Author.

Dong, C., Cao, S., & Li, H. (2020). Young children's online learning during COVID-19 pandemic: Chinese parents' beliefs and attitudes. *Children and Youth Services Review, 118*, 118. doi:10.1016/j.childyouth.2020.105440 PMID:32921857

Doughty, C. (2015). Accountability of foreign language programs. *Modern Language Journal, 99*(2), 412–415. doi:10.1111/modl.12234_6

Doyle, O. (2020). *COVID-19: Exacerbating educational inequalities?* Retrieved April 5, 2022, from http://publicpolicy.ie/ papers/covid-19-exacerbating-educational-inequalities/

Dumford, A. D., & Miller, A. L. (2018). Online learning in higher education: Exploring advantages and disadvantages for engagement. *Journal of Computing in Higher Education, 30*(3), 452–465. doi:10.100712528-018-9179-z

Erlam, G., Garrett, N., Gasteiger, N., Lau, K., Hoare, K., Agarwal, S., & Haxell, A. (2021). What really matters: Experiences of emergency remote teaching in university teaching and learning during the COVID-19 pandemic. *Frontiers in Education, 6*, 639842. doi:10.3389/feduc.2021.639842

Ferri, F., Grifoni, P., & Guzzo, T. (2020). Online learning and emergency remote teaching: Opportunities and challenges in emergency situations. *Societies (Basel, Switzerland), 10*(4), 86. doi:10.3390oc10040086

Flack, C. B., Walker, L., Bickerstaff, A., Earle, H., & Margetts, C. (2020). *Educator perspectives on the impact of COVID-19 on teaching and learning in Australia and New Zealand.* Retrieved April 4, 2022, from https://www.pivotpl.com/wpcontent/uploads/2020/04/Pivot_StateofEducation_2020_White-Paper-1.pdf

Hartshorn, K. J., & McMurry, B. L. (2020). The Effects of the COVID-19 pandemic on ESL learners and TESOL practitioners in the United States. *International Journal of TESOL Studies, 2*(2), 140–156.

Hodges, C., Moore, S., Lockee, B., Trust, T., & Bond, A. (2020). The difference between emergency remote teaching and online learning. *EDUCAUSE Review.*

Johnson, N., Seaman, J., & Veletsianos, G. (2021). Teaching during a pandemic: Spring transition, fall continuation, winter evaluation. *Bayview Analytics.* Retrieved May 17, 2022, from https://www.bayviewanalytics.com/reports/teaching-duringapandemic.pdf

Karakose, T. (2021). The impact of the COVID-19 epidemic on higher education: Opportunities and implications for policy and practice. *Educational Process: International Journal, 10*(1), 7–12. doi:10.22521/edupij.2021.101.1

Liguori, E., & Winkler, C. (2020). *From offline to online: Challenges and opportunities for entrepreneurship education following the COVID-19 pandemic.* Sage.

Lomicka, L. L. (2020). Creating and sustaining virtual language communities. *Foreign Language Annals, 53*(2), 306–313. doi:10.1111/flan.12456

Martinez, J. (2020). Take this pandemic moment to improve education. *EduSource*. Retrieved May 17, 2022, from https://edsource.org/2020/take-this-pandemic-moment-to-improveeducation/633500

Montacute, R. (2020). *Social mobility and COVID-19*. Retrieved May 17, 2022, from https://www.suttontrust.com/wpcontent/ uploads/2020/04/COVID-19-and-Social-Mobility-1.pdf

Moore, M. G. (1989). Three types of interaction. *American Journal of Distance Education, 3*(2), 1–6. doi:10.1080/08923648909526659

Moser, K., Wei, T., & Brenner, D. (2021). Remote teaching during COVID-19: Impli-cations from a national survey of language educators. *System, 97*, 1–15. doi:10.1016/j.system.2020.102431

Nagrale, P. (2013). *Advantages and disadvantages of distance education*. Retrieved May 17, 2022, from https://surejob.in/ advantages-anddisadvantages-of-distance-education.html

NortonLifeLock. (2020). *NortonLifeLock study: Majority of parents say their kids' screen time has skyrocketed during the COVID-19 pandemic*. NortonLifeLock. Retrieved May 17, 2022, from https://www.businesswire.com/news/home/20200831005132/en/

Outhwaite, L. (2020). *Inequalities in resources in the home learning environment (No. 2)*. Centre for Education Policy and Equalising Opportunities, UCL Institute of Education.

Peterson, L., Scharber, C., Thuesen, A., & Baskin, K. (2020). A rapid response to COVID-19: One district's pivot from technology integration to distance learning. *Information and Learning Sciences, 121*(5/6), 461–469. doi:10.1108/ILS-04-2020-0131

Popyk, A. (2020). The impact of distance learning on the social practices of schoolchildren during the COVID-19 pandemic: Reconstructing values of migrant children in Poland. *European Societies*, 1–15.

Putri, R., Purwanto, A., Pramono, R., Asbari, M., Wijayanti, L., & Hyun, C. (2020). Impact of the COVID19 pandemic on online home learning: An explorative study of primary schools in Indonesia. *International Journal of Advanced Science and Technology, 29*(5), 4809–4818.

Rap, S., Feldman-Maggor, Y., Aviran, E., Shvarts-Serebro, I., Easa, E., Yonai, E., Waldman, R., & Blonder, R. (2020). An applied research-based approach to support Chemistry teachers during the COVID-19 pandemic. *Journal of Chemical Education, 97*(9), 3278–3284. doi:10.1021/acs.jchemed.0c00687 PMID:32952213

Russell, V. (2020). Language anxiety and the online learner. *Foreign Language Annals, 53*(2), 338–352. doi:10.1111/flan.12461

Russell, V., & Murphy-Judy, K. (2020). *Teaching language online: A guide to designing, developing, and delivering online, blended, and flipped language courses.* Routledge. doi:10.4324/9780429426483

Shim, T. E., & Lee, S. Y. (2020). College students' experience of emergency remote teaching due to COVID-19. *Children and Youth Services Review, 119*, 105578. doi:10.1016/j.childyouth.2020.105578 PMID:33071405

The World Bank. (2020). *The World Bank Report.* Retrieved May 17, 2022, from https://www.worldbank.org/en/topic/tertiaryeducation#1

Treve, M. (2021). What COVID-19 has introduced into education: Challenges facing higher education institutions. *Higher Education Pedagogies, 6*(1), 212–227. doi:10.1080/23752696.2021.1951616

Trust, T., & Whalen, J. (2020). Should teachers be trained in Emergency Remote Teaching? Lessons learned from the COVID-19 pandemic. *Journal of Technology and Teacher Education, 28*(2), 189–199.

Trzcioska-Król, M. (2020). Students with special educational needs in distance learning during the COVID-19 pandemic–parents' opinions. *Interdisciplinary Context of Special Pedagogy, 29*(1), 173–191. doi:10.14746/ikps.2020.29.08

Verawardina, U., Asnur, L., Lubis, A. L., Hendriyani, Y., Ramadhani, D., Dewi, I. P., & Sriwahyuni, T. (2020). Reviewing online learning facing the Covid-19 outbreak. *Journal of Talent Development and Excellence, 12*(3s), 385–392.

Vlachopoulos, D. (2020). COVID-19: Threat or opportunity for online education? *Higher Learning Research Communications, 10*(1), 16–19.

Wang, C., Cheng, Z., Yue, X.-G., & McAleer, M. (2020). Risk management of COVID-19 by universities in China. *Journal of Risk and Financial Management, 13*(2), 36. doi:10.3390/jrfm13020036

Weiner, C. (2003). Key ingredients to online learning: Adolescent students study in cyberspace – The nature of the study. *International Journal on E-Learning, 2*(3), 44–50.

Zhang, Y., & Lin, C. H. (2020). Student interaction and the role of the teacher in a state virtual high school: What predicts online learning satisfaction? *Technology, Pedagogy and Education*, *29*(1), 57–71. doi:10.1080/1475939X.2019.1694061

## KEY TERMS AND DEFINITIONS

**Attrition:** Reducing students' strength or endurance through sustained attack or pressure.

**EFL:** English as a foreign language.

**ELT:** English language teaching.

**ESL:** English as a second language.

**Higher Education:** University education.

**Hybrid Education:** A combination of conventional classroom experiences and online courses.

**Tertiary Education:** Higher education.

**TESOL:** Teaching English to speakers of other languages.

# Chapter 6
# Evaluation of the Impact of Technology and Human Resources on Quality in Higher Education

**Meryem Baştaş**
*University of Kyrenia, Cyprus*

## ABSTRACT

*One of the most important problems of our age is the lack of effective and efficient use of human resources. In this context, it is important to establish the human resources profile of the education sector, which has the highest human resources in the public sector, and to investigate whether this resource is used efficiently and effectively. In terms of the quality of education, it is important to evaluate the correct employment, motivation studies, and performance of school employees. However, in the evaluation of the performance of teachers and school staff, who will be involved, according to which criteria and how to evaluate, and the way of using the results of the evaluation are among the answers required. The aim of this research is to meet the expectations and needs of the education system by suggesting the importance, functioning, and applications of human resources in educational practices and by proposing a human resources employment strategy model.*

## INTRODUCTION

The most important resource of the society in the survival and development of the society is the manpower that is properly trained for its purposes. The school is a

DOI: 10.4018/978-1-6684-5400-8.ch006

productive sub-system in the education system and has an important place in the society in terms of constantly creating the desired manpower by equipping the members of the society with the desired behaviors and habits, ensuring the development of the social structure and functioning (Yalçın, 2002, p.24).

Teachers and school employees need a structure that will maximize their contribution in uncovering their potential power and achieving the goals of the school (Altundepe, 1999). Revealing and evaluating the talents of individuals is possible in a democratic environment, with a human-sensitive management approach. The tasks assigned to the employees should be planned in line with their competencies and interests and those who have experience in the field of participation in decisions should be particularly utilized.

In an increasingly competitive environment, managers can establish dominance when they implement performance management processes to achieve their goals and ensure that "the right job is done successfully by the right people". In order to gain a constructive and supportive perspective on the performance measurement and evaluation process, it is important to share the information obtained and make it learnable. In fact, the success of professional managers is highly dependent on others. Human Resources managers have to move away from only dealing with the personnel rights of the personnel and have a strategic perspective that accepts the employees as the most valuable resources of the organization, instead of seeing them as a cost element.

Teachers with certain qualifications and skills should be at the forefront in order for the school administration to use the employees towards the determined goals and objectives effectively, dynamically and efficiently. School administrations, which ensure team work together with the teachers working in their schools, create more solid foundations for the future. Within educational organizations, the way the members of the organization interact with each other and the perception of communication and relations has a significant impact on organizational efficiency and performance (Yaman, 2007, p.11). Even people with a high level of creativity lose their self-confidence in environments where they are not appreciated and valued.

In terms of quality education, the right employment of school staff, motivational studies and evaluation of their performance are important; however, who will take charge, according to which criteria and how the evaluation will be made, and the way of using the obtained evaluation results are among the answers sought in the evaluation of the performance of teachers and school staff. In addition, teachers' opinions on how they evaluate their performance, by whom the evaluation should be made and how the obtained evaluation results will be used are important. When people who work in education are mentioned, the first thing that comes to mind is teachers. Indeed, it is the teachers who ensure the production of educational services in schools (Basaran, 1996, p.123).

In this research, it is aimed to evaluate the impact of human resources on quality in educational practices. With this study, it is also aimed to meet the expectations and needs of the education system by revealing the importance, functioning and applications of human resources in education practices and proposing a human resources employment strategy model.

## CONCEPTUAL FRAMEWORK

### Career Planning and Management

Career is a concept that came into the scope of management late and it started to be considered as a whole only in the seventies. It can be defined as "development processes in parallel with the work done by the employees in the same or different businesses and the experiences they have gained". As it can be understood from the definition, the concept of career and the management of career require responsibility at the individual level, and organizations also participate in this process. In terms of businesses, career management can be defined as estimating the wishes of the employee, planning what is necessary to achieve career goals, determining and implementing strategies (Deniz and Ünal, 2007: 105).

The reason why career planning and management are considered important in businesses is based on the motivation of the employee, job satisfaction and attachment to the business. If employees believe that the business will help them achieve their goals, they cooperate with the business. For this reason, career management is an area of occupation that requires continuity and special effort (Deniz and Ünal, 2007: 106).

Tortop et al. (2013: 221), in their research, define the career system as executing public duties and responsibilities by rising in the hierarchy of management, and also working and raising in line with the statuses determined by the objective rules of the rights, guarantees, obligations, security and all service conditions of the public personnel.

Changes and developments in technology, changes in the characteristics of jobs, and future needs of businesses have led businesses to give importance to career planning and development. Career planning serves the following purposes:

- Effective use of human resources: Employees will be evaluated in positions that suit their own skills and desires.
- Satisfaction of employees' promotion needs: The productivity of employees who work in the same position for a long time will of course be lower, so the company will not be able to fully benefit from the abilities of the employees.

- Evaluation of the employee in a new and different field: Career management activities should be used to ensure that both the employee and the business are not adversely affected by this process.
- Increasing business success: An employee who has just started at the workplace is expected to receive job-related trainings, but both personnel and business need to be provided in-organization training and self-development opportunities so that employees in the same institution can adapt to new situations and follow developments.
- Ensuring employees' sense of belonging to the institution: One of the important factors for the employee to experience this feeling is that the employee's position needs to be a status that is respected and considered important in society.
- Better determination of individual training and development needs: It is important for the employee to benefit from the necessary training opportunities and the necessary needs for personal development to be identified in terms of the organization-individual relationship (Bilgin et al., 2004: 123-124).

## Quality in Education

Although the structure, culture and traditions of educational organizations are different from other organizations, quality management is an important issue that should be applied in education as it is applied in every sector. While there are elements that determine, measure and control quality in the sector, this situation works in the opposite way in educational institutions. Only teachers and what they do cannot determine the quality of the product in the classroom. In fact, students (customers) may not know what the elements of quality are and may not want this quality. It is undoubtedly helpful to try to compare or integrate educational techniques, traditions and practices with quality management techniques. However, if a sincere and voluntary approach to quality management is not accepted at school, it is inevitable that results, which reduce experience and quality, will emerge. Quality in education is defined as an approach that constantly develops, in which administrators, teachers and students actively participate, enjoy this participation, and prioritize school and especially student success. This approach is determined by the commitment and consistency of management, the focus of students and teachers, seeing the facts, continuous improvement, participation of all, and effective learning strategies. An effective learning strategy includes the following items (Aksu, 2002:149):

- Understanding why and how an individual learns,
- Creating a healthy learning environment,
- Recognizing and meeting personal learning needs,

- Preparation of the learning plan in line with the agreed objectives,
- Developing learning opportunities,
- Evaluation of learning products

Being aware of the school goals of the individuals in the education process, the correct interpretation of these goals is important in terms of obtaining qualified outputs in education. Creating a healthy learning and teaching environment for the internal stakeholders of the school where the education service is produced is indispensable in terms of meeting the needs of the students.

The power of the society is limited by the abilities of the people living in the society. The higher the education quality of the current individual is in the society, the higher the organizational capacity in that society is as well. The aim and purpose of educational institutions that provide service to individuals also cause to increase in the quality of service (Keskin and Keskin, 2005). The ideal goal of quality education is not to switch to another learning if what needs to be learned in a certain time is not learned well (Yıldırım, 2001, p. 109). The main element of quality in education is the learning process. Important elements in learning in quality care are listed as follows (Doğan, 2006, p. 26):

- The level required by the education program for the purposes of education and training,
- The quality of the learning environment, the training employee, effective cooperation method,
- Functional system that directs education and training and sufficient economic resources,
- Independent evaluation of the production results of education and training by including learning.

The characteristics of quality education are expressed by Arcano and Langford (cited in Tosun, 2002) as follows;

- The truth of the teacher is that the student conveys the same facts in the tests, and it is far from being a knowledge store. It is the expectation of the best from all students in the class, not just successful students.
- Continuous improvement; to do all the big and small jobs better, to set and achieve high standards, to work together and gain a long-term perspective.
- Collaboration without competition; It means focusing on education in a certain process. It means focusing on learning for the sake of learning, not just implementing the curriculum.

- It is important to recognize that the learner is the recipient of education and is the center of all that happens in the classroom.
- Quality is the understanding that the power that drives quality in the classroom is the teacher.
- Learning of quality is unlimited with concepts since it does not require a specific program.
- Quality is the way of seeing education in all its aspects.

## Planning of Human Resources in Educational Organizations

Human resource planning includes the development of a comprehensive and detailed strategy to meet the future human resource needs of the organization. It is the work carried out by the management to find the right number of employees with the desired skills and abilities in the right place in the required time frame. Human resources planning includes a process that regulates and evaluates the entry, exit and intra-organizational mobility of the individual. The main goal of human resources planning is to ensure the effective and efficient use of human resources (Barutçugil, 2004).

It provides human resources planning, recognizing employees, analyzing, making estimations and arranging the changing needs and requirements in human resources according to the conditions in the organization. Human resource management predicts employee turnover, transfer, retirement, or promotion of human resources within the organization. Human resources planning helps to determine the positions in which employees with certain characteristics will work and take charge in the organization. Training can also be used in increasing the current responsibilities of employees determined by human resources planning, promotion, horizontal transfer, transfer and downward job opportunities (Noe, 1999).

The planning of human resources is the estimation of the employee needs of the organization and the classification of the activities necessary to address these needs. At the end of this process, it aims to establish a movement program that will ensure the necessary number of labor forces with the necessary qualifications and characteristics that enable the organization to achieve its objectives are provided in the required time (Schuler, 1995, cited in Sabuncuoğlu, 2000).

The planning of human resources in educational institutions is the process of assessing the situation of the current employees of the organization, determining the needs that will arise in the future and planning the programs to be implemented to meet these needs. It covers the planning of future years by estimating or determining in advance the retirement time of teachers, the time of appointment to the executive staff, or the time of leaving the job. In schools with more than one branch, it is possible to plan human resources which teacher will be appropriate to be assigned to which school in cases where it is necessary to relocate teachers between schools.

Planning is defined as the process of making decisions that facilitate the achievement of the goals, expectations and wishes of the organization. In addition to these, it includes the steps necessary and to be taken in order to achieve these goals. Planning, which is also defined as determining the path to be followed by looking at the future time or choosing the most ideal and correct behavior for the realization of the goals, provides guidance to the members of the organization working together to write down the things to be done in detail and to reach the common goals (Bayraktaroğlu, 2003).

The aims of human resources planning are to complete the staff, adapt to organizational changes, help the realization of these plans if there are future development or growth plans, and ensure the professional and personal development of current teachers. Moreover, the aim of human resources planning is the process of identifying the path to be used and foreseeing the obstacles and problems that may arise and taking precautions in the way as it moves towards the point that the organization wants to reach. Furthermore, it is to evaluate these obstacles and eliminate these problems and obstacles in the coming years.

## Career Management and Development in Educational Organizations

Self-development of the employees, increasing their capacity and working with the necessary equipment contribute to the increase in their self-confidence to achieve their professional purpose. The most important condition for career development is development. An individual's professional experience is a career. In addition, gaining these experiences is beneficial for organizations as much as individuals. In fact, career is the process that the individual and the organization go through to reach their goals.

Today, employees are programmed in line with the objectives so that the employee assumes full responsibility for productivity. Constantly innovating is becoming part of the duties and responsibilities of employees in the information age (Balkin, Cardy, Gomez-Mejla, 1998).

It turns out that one of the most important factors that cause the success or failure of the organization in the contemporary management approach is the importance given to the development of the human element, skills and abilities. One of the most important ways to use human resources effectively and increase the motivation of employees is to benefit from career development. For this reason, the responsibilities undertaken by the individual and the organization are important in career development.

The concept of career is defined as a series of lifelong jobs endowed with human behavior motifs. Progress in business life and consequently earning more money, taking more responsibility, having more status, power and prestige. In short, career is a process that covers behaviors and attitudes related to the career steps and the position where the work is done, which is located throughout the person's business life (Aytaç, 2006).

Career development includes the efforts of the personnel in educational institutions as in other organizations to achieve the goals and objectives they have set themselves personally and professionally.

The contribution of organizations to these studies is to allow organizational development. The development of individuals and the development of organizations are also the subject. Planning to develop its employees in a long and short time, supporting them to increase their skills and knowledge, actually contributes directly to the development of the organization. The main purpose of career development activities and facilities is to support the orientation and development of the employee's careers. Other objectives in addition to the efforts made in this direction are as follows;

- Reducing the inefficiency caused by the lack of clarity of the target and low motivation,
- Helping employees overcome the problems and obstacles they encounter in the process of promotion,
- Training staff for new tasks that the organization will need in the future,
- Developing a positive organizational culture with high career prospects,
- It is stated as the development of creativity in the organization.

## CONLUSION

This planning was mostly done for the needs of workforce planning. Job analysis and planning are important in terms of determining the minimum qualifications that the employee should have in order to do the job well (Karaca, 2009). On the subject of personnel recruitment, the participants expressed two different views, and one group stated that personnel recruitment was carried out by vacant and examination methods, while the other group stated that it was realized through resource transfer. It is predicted that the state assurance response that stands out on health and safety issues is due to the fact that these participants work in state-affiliated institutions. Other than these, the participants did not express a negative opinion at this point.

It is seen that the results obtained from the answers given by the participants define the basic duties of the human resources unit. However, it has been concluded that there were deficiencies in the fulfillment and competence of these tasks.

In the question in which the research participants put forward the approaches of the human resources unit towards the employee, two important elements that are essential in terms of human resources management and approach formed the themes. In line with the answers given by the participants, the two prominent themes that stood out are "Conflict and resolution strategies" and "Perception and image management". Conflict management is a process that every organization should manage well. In particular, the top managers of the organization and human resources units must have knowledge about how to benefit from the conflict environment for the benefit of the organization. Apart from conflict situations that directly affect the motivation and performance levels of the employees of the organization, the perception and image management of the organization is important.

The opinions expressed by the research participants in line with these two important factors are in the direction of further development. Almost all of the participants expressed the opinion that conflict and resolution strategies should be developed. In this respect, regardless of the field of expertise of the research participants, it was concluded that if the conflict cannot be managed correctly and adversely affects the employees. Büyükses (2010) concluded in his study that teachers' relationships with colleagues affect their work motivation. Also, his views on perception and image management are not very different. In fact, the majority of the participants stated that an active role should be taken in perception and image management and that it was not implemented.

In this respect, it was concluded that the human resources unit is not very effective in the issues of conflict and resolution strategies and perception and image management.

Seminars and training programs expressed the common views of the participants on the level of employee support of the human resources unit. All of the research participants evaluated the support given by the human resources unit at the point of supporting the employee in terms of seminars and training programs.

The participants stated that the seminars and training programs organized to support the employees were not sufficient and that they were organized on demand and only during certain periods. Therefore, in line with the results obtained in the research, it was concluded that seminars and training programs could be organized to support the development of the employees, but according to the expressions of the participants, it was revealed that they are not sufficient and providing enough support.

## REFERENCES

Açıkalın, A. (1999). İnsan Kaynağının Yönetimi Geliştirilmesi. Ankara: Pegem A Yayınları.

Açıkalın, A. (2002). *İnsan Kaynağının Geliştirilmesi.* Pegem A Yayıncılık.

Akalın, A. (2004). Eğitim ve Okul Yöneticiliği El Kitabı. Ankara: Pegem Yayıncılık.

Akdağ, M. (2007). Örgütlerde İnsan Kaynakları ve Halkla İlişkiler Birimleri Örgüt Yapılarının İncelenmesi Üzerine Karsılaştırılmalı Bir Çalışma (Yayımlanmamış Doktora Tezi). Selçuk Üniversitesi, Konya.

Akın A, (2002). İşletmelerde İnsan Kaynakları Performansını Değerleme Sürecinde Coaching. *C.Ü. İktisadi ve İdari Bilimler Dergisi, 3*(1).

Aksoy B, (2005). Bilgi Teknolojilerinin Yarattığı Örgütsel Değişim: Nasıl Bir İnsan Kaynakları Yönetimi? *Bilgi Dünyası, 6*(1), 58-77.

Aksu, G., Acuner, A., & Tabak, R. (2002). Sağlık Bakanlığı Merkez ve Taşra Teşkilatı Yöneticilerinin İş Doyumuna Yönelik Bir Araştırma (Ankara Örneği). Ankara Üniversitesi Tıp Fakültesi Mecmuası, 55(4).

Akyol, B. (2008). Eğitim Örgütlerinde İnsan Kaynakları Uygulamalarının Öğretmen Performansına Etkisi (Yayımlanmamış Yüksek Lisans Tezi). Yeditepe Üniversitesi/ Sosyal Bilimler Enstitüsü, İstanbul.

Akyüz, Y. (2010). *Türk Eğitim Tarihi. M.Ö. 1000- M.S.* Pegem A Yayınları.

Aldemir, C., & Ataol, A. (2001). İnsan Kaynakları Yönetimi. İzmir: Barış Yayınları.

Atılgan, M. (2005). İnsan Kaynakları Yönetiminde Eğitim ve Bir İnceleme: Kaymakam Adaylarının Eğitimi. *Turk İdare Dergisi, 20,* 131–148.

Aytaç, S. (2006). *Çalışma Yaşamında Kariyer Yönetimi Planlaması Gelişimi ve Sorunları.* Ezgi Kitabevi.

Aytaç, S. (2010). İş Yaşamında Kariyer Yönetimi. Yönetimde İnsan Kaynakları Çalışmaları. Ankara: Turhan Kitabevi Yayınları.

Balkın, D., Cardy, R., & Gomez-Mejla, L. (1998). *Managing Human Resources.* Prentice Hall.

Barutçugil, İ. (2004). *Stratejik İnsan Kaynakları Yönetimi.* Kariyer Yayıncılık.

Baş, T., & Akturan, U. (2008). Nitel Araştırma Yöntemleri: NVivo İle Nitel Veri Analizi. Ankara: Seçkin Yayıncılık.

Başaran, İ. E. (1996). *Eğitim Yönetimi*. Yargıcı Matbaası.

Baştaş, M., & Altinay, Z. (2019, November 2). Employment for Disability: Human Resources Management in Higher Education for Quality. *International Journal of Disability Development and Education*, *66*(6), 610–615. Advance online publication. doi:10.1080/1034912X.2019.1643456

Bayraktaroğlu, S. (2003). *İnsan Kaynakları Yönetimi*. Sakarya Kitabevi.

Bek, H. (2006). *İnsan Kaynakları Yönetiminde Eğitim ve Geliştirme Etkinliği*. Sosyal Bilimler Enstitüsü Dergisi.

Bilgin, L., Taşcı, D., & Kağnıcıoğlu, D. V. (2004). İnsan Kaynakları Yönetimi. Eskişehir: Açık Öğretim Fakültesi Yayınları.

Bingöl, D. (1998). *İnsan Kaynakları Yönetimi*. Beta Basım Yayım Dağıtım A.Ş.

Bulut, Y., Duruel, M., Kara, M., & Bilbay, Ö. F. (2016). Yerel Yönetimlerde İnsan Kaynaklarının Etkin Yönetimi: Hatay'da Bir Uygulama. *Strategic Public Management Journal*, *3*(3), 1–24. doi:10.25069pmj.290497

Çalık, C., & Şehitoğlu, E.T. (2006). Okul müdürlerinin insan kaynakları yönetimi işlevlerini yerine getirebilme yeterlikleri. *Millî Eğitim Üç Aylık Eğitim ve Sosyal Bilimler Dergisi*, 170.

Can, H. (2002). *Organizasyon ve Yönetim*. Siyasal Kitabevi.

Can, H., Akgün, A., & Kavuncubaşı, Ş. (2001). Kamu ve Özel Kesimde İnsan Kaynakları Yönetimi. Ankara: Siyasal Kitapevi.

Çelik, V. (2003). *Eğitimsel Liderlik*. Pegem A Yayınları.

Cengiz, E. (2010). Taşımalı İnsan Kaynakları Yönetiminde Öğretmenlerin Örgütlenme Hakkı (Yüksek Lisans Tezi). Beykent Üniversitesi, Sosyal Bilimleri Enstitüsü, İstanbul.

Cent, H. (2007). Özel Okullarda İnsan Kaynakları Yönetimi Uygulamalarının İncelenmesi (Yüksek Lisans Tezi). Yıldız Teknik Üniversitesi / Sosyal Bilimler Enstitüsü, İstanbul.

Clevaland, J. N., Murphy, K. R., & Williams, R. E. (1989). Multiple Uses of Performance Appraisal: Prevelance and Correlates. *The Journal of Applied Psychology*, *74*(1), 20. doi:10.1037/0021-9010.74.1.130

Constance, M. F. (1984). An Examination of Teachers Attitudes Toward Women in Education Administration (Yayımlanmamış Doktora Tezi). University of Massachusetts.

Danışman, A. (2008). *Türkiye'de İnsan Kaynakları Yönetimi Uygulamaları*. Nobel Yayınevi.

David, M., & Sutton, C.D. (2004) Social Research: the basics. London: Sage Publications.

Deniz, M., & Ünal, A. (2007). İnsan Kaynaklarının Bir Fonksiyonu Olarak Örgütsel Kariyer Yönetimi ve Bir Uygulama. *E-Journal of New World Sciences Academy*.

Doğan, E., Apaydın, Ç., & Önen, Ö. (2006). Eğitim hizmetlerinde toplam kalite yönetimi ve kalite politikası. *Mehmet Akif Ersoy Üniversitesi Eğitim Bilimleri Dergisi, 11*, 59–79.

Erdoğan, İ. (1991). *İşletmelerde Personel Seçimi ve Başarı Değerleme Teknikleri*. İ.Ü. İşletme Fakültesi Yayınları.

Erdoğan, İ. (2002). *Okul Yönetimi Öğretim Liderliği*. Sistem Yayıncılık.

Eren, E. (2001). *Örgütsel Davranış ve Yönetim Psikolojisi*. Beta Basım Yayım.

Ergin, C. (2002). *İnsan Kaynakları Yönetimi*. Academyplus Yayınevi.

Filizöz, B. (2003). İnsan Kaynakları Yönetiminde Uluslar Arası Yaklaşım Gerekliliği. *Cumhuriyet Üniversitesi İktisadi ve İdari Bilimler Dergisi, 4*(1).

Fındıkçı, İ. (2000). *İnsan Kaynakları Yönetimi*. Alfa Yayınları.

Fındıkçı, İ. (2009). *İnsan Kaynakları Yönetimi*. Alfa Yayınları.

Genç, Y., & Çat, G. (2013). Engellilerin İstihdamı ve Sosyal İçerme İlişkisi. *Akademik İncelemeler Dergisi, 8*(1).

Gök, S. (2006). *21. Yüzyılda İnsan Kaynakları Yönetimi*. Beta Yayıncılık.

Gürüz, D., & Yaylacı, G. Ö. (2004). *İletişimci Gözüyle İnsan Kaynakları Yönetimi*. Kapital.

İnce, M. (2000). Değişim Olgusu ve Örgütlerde İnsan Kaynakları Yönetiminin Değişen Fonksiyonları. *Selçuk Üniversitesi Sosyal Bilimler Dergisi, 11*, 319–340.

Karaca, D. 2009. İlköğretim Okullarında Yöneticilerin İnsan Kaynakları Yönetimi İşlevlerini Yerine Getirebilme Yeterlikleri ile Öğretmenlerin Örgütsel Bağlılıkları Arasındaki İlişki (Yüksek Lisans Tezi). Akdeniz Üniversitesi/Sosyal Bilimler Enstitüsü, Antalya.

Karasar, N. (2008). Bilimsel araştırma yöntemi. Ankara: Nobel Yayın Dağıtım.

Karcıoğlu, H., & Öztürk, Ü. (2009). İşletmelerde Performans Değerleme İle İnsan Kaynakları Bilgi Sistemleri (İKBS) Arasındaki İlişkisi, İstanbul İlinde Bir Araştırma. *Atatürk Üniversitesi Sosyal Bilimler Enstitüsü Dergisi, 13*(1), 343–366.

Kaya, E. N., & Taş, İ.E. (2015). Personel Yönetimi-İnsan Kaynakları Yönetimi Ayrımı. *KSÜ İİBF Dergisi, 5*(1). 21-28.

Kayıkçı, K. (2001). Yönetici yetiştirme sorunu. *Millî Eğitim Dergisi*, 150.

Keskin, A., & Keskin, B. (2005). *Eğitimde toplam kalite- okul yönetiminin kalite arayışı*. Samsun: Deniz Kültür Yayınları.

Küçükkaya, G. (2006). İnsan Kaynakları Yönetiminde Personel Seçimi ve Bir Uygulama (Yüksek Lisans Tezi). Marmara Üniversitesi, Sosyal Bilimler Enstitüsü, İstanbul.

Kuş, E. (2009). Nicel-nitel araştırma teknikleri: Sosyal bilimlerde araştırma teknikleri nicel mi? Nitel mi? Ankara: Anı Yayıncılık.

Küsmen, B. (2010). Kurumsal İletişim Ve İnsan Kaynakları Yönetimi İlişkisi (Yüksek Lisans Tezi). Marmara Üniversitesi, Sosyal Bilimler Enstitüsü, İstanbul.

Legard, R., Keegan, J., & Ward, K. (2003). In-depth interviews. In Qualitative Research Practice (pp. 139-168). London: Sage.

Liou, S. (2008). An Analysis of the Concept of Organizational Commitment. *Nursing ForumNo., 43*(3), 116–125. doi:10.1111/j.1744-6198.2008.00103.x PMID:18715344

Medya, A. Ş., & Fındıkçı, İ. (1999). *İnsan Kaynakları Yönetimi*. Alfa Yayınları.

Mercin, L. (2005). İnsan Kaynakları Yönetimi'nin Eğitim Kurumları Açısından Gerekliliği ve Geliştirme Etkinliği. *Elektronik Sosyal Bilimler Dergisi, 4*(14), 128–144.

Miles, M. B., & Huberman, A. M. (1994). Qualitative data analysis: An expanded sourcebook. Sage.

Noe, A. R. (1999). İnsan Kaynaklarının Eğitim ve Gelişimi. İstanbul: Beta Yayıncılık.

Orhan, K. (2010). Amerika Birleşik Devletleri'nde ve Avrupa'da insan kaynakları yönetimi yaklaşımlarının bir karşılaştırılması: Avrupalı insan kaynakları yaklaşımı mümkün müdür? [A comparison of human resources management approches' in the United States and European Union: Is actually European approches of the human resources management possible?]. *Ege Academic Review, 10*(1), 271–301.

Özbayram, E. (2014). Türk Çalışma Hayatında Korumalı İşyerleri ve Engelli İstihdamı. Gazi Üniversitesi Sosyal Bilimler Enstitüsü Çalışma Ekonomisi Ve Endüstri İlişkileri Anabilim Dali Yüksek Lisans Tezi, Ankara, Özen, Şükrü (2002). Bağlam, Aktör, Söylem ve Kurumsal Değişim: Türkiye'de Toplam Kalite Yönetiminin Yayılım Süreci. *Yönetim Araştırmaları Dergisi, 1/2*, 47–90.

Özdemir, E., & Akpınar A. T. (2002). Konaklama İşletmelerinde İnsan Kaynakları Yönetimi Çerçevesinde Alanya'daki Otel ve Tatil Köylerinde İnsan Kaynakları Profili. *Kocaeli Üniversitesi Sosyal Bilimler Enstitüsü Dergisi, 2*(3), 85–105.

Özgen, H., Öztürk, A., & Yalçın, A. (Eds.). (2002). İnsan Kaynakları Yönetimi. Adana: Nobel Kitabevi.

Özmen, İ. (2003). Bilgi Sistemleri İş Stratejisi ve Ticari Avantaj Sağlamak İçin Kullanılması. *İstanbul Üniversitesi İşletme Fakültesi, İşletme İktisadı Enstitüsü Dergisi, 13*(45), 51.

Öztay, F. E. (2006). Eğitim Örgütlerinde İnsan Kaynakları Yönetimi İle Oluşturulmuş Kurum Kültürünün Öğretmen Motivasyonuna Etkisi (Yüksek Lisans Tezi). Yeditepe Üniversitesi/Sosyal Bilimler Enstitüsü, İstanbul.

Patton, M. Q. (1987). *How to Use Qualitative Methods in Evaluation.* Sage Publications, Inc.

Raymond, N. A. (2009). İnsan Kaynaklarının Eğitimi Ve Geliştirilmesi. İstanbul: Beta Yayınları.

Sabuncuoğlu, Z. (2000). *İnsan Kaynakları Yönetimi.* Ezgi Kitabevi.

Sadullah, Ö. (2008). İnsan Kaynakları Yönetimine Giriş; İnsan Kaynakları Yönetiminin Tanımı, Önemi ve Çevresel Faktörler. In İnsan Kaynakları Yönetimi. İstanbul: Beta Basım Yayım.

Saylan, N. (2013). Özel İlköğretim Ve Ortaöğretim Okullarında İnsan Kaynakları Yönetimi İşlevlerinin Gerçekleşme Derecesi (Yüksek Lisans Tezi). Hacettepe Üniversitesi/Sosyal Bilimleri Enstitüsü, Ankara.

Schuler, S. R. (1995). *Managing Human Resources.* West Pub.

Şen, M. (2018). Türkiye'de Engellilere Yönelik İstihdam Politikaları: Sorunlar ve Öneriler. *Sosyal Güvenlik Dergisi*, 129-152. . doi:10.32331/sgd.493016

Tanova, C., & Karadal, H. (2004). Kurumsal Strateji İle İnsan Kaynakları Politikaları Arasındaki İlişkinin Analizi. *Dokuz Eylül Üniversitesi İktisadi İdari Bilimler Fakültesi Dergisi*, *19*(2), 123–136.

Taymaz, H. (2009). *Okul Yönetimi*. Pegem A.

Tortop, N., Aykaç, B., Yayman, H., & Özer, M. A. (2013). İnsan Kaynakları Yönetimi. Ankara: Nobel Yayınları.

Tosun, Ü. (2002). *Onurlu disiplin*. Beyaz.

Türkel, A. (1984). *İşletme Yönetimi*. Okan Yayıncılık.

Türkmen, H. (2008). İlköğretim Okul Müdürlerinin Ġnsan Kaynaklarını Yönetme Yeterlilikleri (Yayımlanmamış Yüksek Lisans Tezi). Yeditepe Üniversitesi/Sosyal Bilimler Enstitüsü, İstanbul.

Tutar, H. (2003). *Örgütsel İletişim*. Seçkin Yayınları.

Uğur, A. (2008). *İnsan kaynakları yönetimi*. Sakarya: Sakarya Kitabevi.

Ülsever, C. (2005). *21. Yüzyılda İnsan Yönetimi*. Alfa.

Ünal, S. (2000). Okulda İnsan Kaynakları Yönetimi. *Milli Eğitim Dergisi*, 146.

Yalçın, S. A. (2002). *Personel Yönetimi*. Beta Yayınları.

Yaman, E. (2007). Üniversitelerde Bir Eğitim Sorunu Olarak Öğretim Elemanının Maruz Kaldığı İnformal Cezalar (Doktora Tezi). T.C Marmara Üniversitesi Eğitim Bilimleri Enstitüsü, İstanbul.

Yaman, H. (2010). Türk öğrencilerinin yazma kaygısı: Ölçek geliştirme ve çeşitli değişkenler açısından yordama çalışması. *International Online Journal of Educational Sciences*, *2*(1), 267–289.

Yıldırım, A., & Şimşek, H. (1999), Sosyal Bilimlerde Nitel Araştırma Yöntemleri. Ankara: Seçkin Yayıncılık.

Yıldırım, A., & Şimşek, H. (2008). Sosyal Bilimlerde Nitel Araştırma Yöntemleri. Ankara: Seçkin Yayıncılık.

Yıldırım, A., & Şimşek, H. (2011). Sosyal bilimlerde nitel araştırma yöntemleri. Ankara: Seçkin Yayıncılık.

Yıldırım, İ. (2001). *Öğretmen yetiştirme ve eğitimde kalite paneli*. MEB Öğretmen Yetiştirme ve Eğitimi Genel Müdürlüğü.

Yılmaz, G. (2006). Örgüt Kültürü ve İnsan Kaynakları Yönetimi (Yayınlanmamış Yüksek Lisans Tezi). Marmara Üniversitesi, İstanbul.

Yüksel, Ö. (2000). *İnsan Kaynaklan Yönetimi*. Gazi Kitapevi.

Zaim, H. (2005). *Bilginin Artan önemi ve Bilgi Yönetimi*. İşaret.

# Chapter 7
# Inclusive Education Practice

**Halil Ercan**
https://orcid.org/0000-0001-5154-8234
*University of City Island, Cyprus*

**Razge Sıla Zorba**
*Final International University, Cyprus*

## ABSTRACT

*This chapter provides a variety of different perspectives regarding inclusive education practice in higher education settings. It provides an introduction into learning in the field of higher education. Then, the background information about the field of inclusive education practice follows. Furthermore, it emphasizes the needs that should be met and suggests some ways for inclusion practice to better provide students with different approaches and methods. The chapter also provides a wide explanation in terms of building an appropriate curriculum in higher education for both students with and without disabilities. Finally, it points out the necessary acts to be taken and provides implications in terms of e-learning and inclusion for those to succeed in the field. The chapter will provide insight for educators in the field of inclusive education.*

## INTRODUCTION

Today's schools as a learning environment are rapidly changing and continue to change. Considering the diversity such as learning styles, culture, language, gender, and different family structures, it is not possible to think of students as a homogeneous group today. It is strongly claimed changes that come with all this diversity have emerged as a significant challenge for education (Dovigo, 2017; Kivirand, Leijen,

DOI: 10.4018/978-1-6684-5400-8.ch007

Lepp, & Tammemäe, 2021). Furthermore, each individual in the classroom brings valuable resources and experiences to the classroom, with characteristics such as talents, strengths, skills, personal experiences, knowledge, and beliefs (Gudjonsdottir & Óskarsdóttir, 2016; Sharma, Sokal, Wang & Loreman 2021). On the other hand, regarding the Covid-19 Pandemic and the developments in today's technology world, it is believed that the educational needs of each learner should be reorganized based on his/her needs. Moreover, since the beginning Covid-19 Pandemic case, educators and learners have encountered many different challenges such as lack of regular internet access to join their courses during distance education, actively participating on different platforms, spending so much time in front of a computer, and completing their tasks through on-line learning.

## BACKGROUND

Regarding inclusive practices, education systems and schools undertake the responsibility of arranging and teaching the curriculum for various student groups in accordance with all these characteristics of students. Teachers who are eager to understand the resources their students bring to the classroom environment are able to tailor their teaching to meet their needs (Jackson, Ryndak, & Wehmeyer, 2008; Meijer, Soriano, & Watkins, 2007). At this point, the teachers are considered to be flexible, loyal to her/his students, to be sensitive to students' needs, to use various teaching approaches that provide students with more opportunities, to offer an effective education to various student groups in terms of resources they bring into the classroom.

Considering a teacher who accumulates detailed information about each of her/his students, it could clearly be stated that s/he can regulate how s/he may differentiate learning among her/his students effectively. Inclusive practices differ in the way teachers respond to diversity, the decisions they make about group work, and the way they use their expertise (Alexander, Sperl, Buehl, Fives, & Chiu, 2004; Florian, & Linklater, 2010; Galkiene, & Monkoviciene, 2021). Considering the important features of teaching approaches that allow all students to be successful, it is seen that these teaching approaches focus on comprehensive and systematic ways of collecting information about students, what connections exist between learning and students' lives, and how flexible and open-ended the curriculum can be (Rose, & Parsons, 1998). A flexible curriculum with alternatives allows teachers to support differences in each classroom. In this way the classroom and teaching can offer students alternative ways of learning, ways of working, multiple opportunities for success, and teaching for mixed abilities (Galkiene, & Monkoviciene, 2021).

A teacher who wants to respond to the diversity of her/his students and supports them organizes their teaching from the very beginning of planning, uses flexible and alternative approaches, and creates an environment that provides students with plenty of different learning opportunities. In doing so, the teacher elaborates the instruction according to the depth of each student's knowledge, co-creates challenging and enjoyable learning activities, distinguishes students in integrated curricula and programs, uses the physical and social environment to support learning, and supports students to develop an increased sense of responsibility for their own responsibilities, learning, works collaboratively with students to monitor, evaluate, and adapt teaching (Gudjonsdottir, 2003).

## Building Inclusive Practice in Education

Undoubtedly, it is necessary to make adaptations in the standard curriculum to be able to teach in mainstream classrooms to students with special needs. Individuals with special educational needs in the school environment may need more teaching time, other learning methods, and professional knowledge. This seems possible to be achieved by allocating more time to teachers and using available time in an alternative way. Increasing the necessary resources for inclusive education is possible by increasing the available time through the use of lecturers. This can also allow for the development of inclusive education by enhancing teachers' professional knowledge through experienced colleagues and training sessions (Birhanu, 2015; Okongo, Ngao, Rop, & Wesonga, 2015).

## Peer Teaching

By using peer teaching, teachers can encourage students who are above average in their classes to work more independently and collaboratively with one another. Thus, the teaching time allocated to students in need of special education can be increased. Therefore, cooperative and collaborative learning can lead to a more positive classroom environment when carefully and strategically planned based on clear goals and rules. As for one of the most important points to be mentioned about the teacher and the classroom in inclusive education is their sensitivity and skills in developing social interactions among students. It is particularly important for students with special educational needs to engage in meaningful interactions with their typically developing peers. While the teacher needs to have the right attitude, s/he needs to understand how to develop these relationships and interactions. It should be realized that the organizational structure of the school is a determining factor in the type and the number of resources that teachers prefer to use when building inclusive practice in education at the point of students who need special education (Collins, Azmat, & Rentschler, 2018). In this regard, there seems to be a need for flexible support from within the school, which can be provided by other teachers, school principals, or specialist teachers when necessary. Such support may also be provided through other support services such as dedicated visiting support staff. Furthermore, the ability of schools to cooperate may be necessary to provide additional resources to individuals with special educational needs. Thus, these individuals can be integrated into mainstream schools (Puri, & Abraham, 2004; Disabled Students Sector Leadership Group (DSSLG), 2017)

## Leadership & Teamwork

Regarding the inclusive education practice, the leadership of senior administrators such as the school principal and her assistants is of great importance in the inclusive education practice, as they are decisive in this education practice (Riehl, 2000). The school principal should be considered the only person who can initiate and implement changes in the school, new developments, and processes. Additionally, this is not the only important point as the support given to teachers is another important point. The most important point to be emphasized in this context is to be able to manage to work in an organized manner as a team and to continue working by focusing on important issues hindered in inclusive schools. Working in cooperation with families has great importance to address their needs. In addition, the team members they will work in cooperation with should be people that they can trust (DSSLG, 2017; Paccaud, Keller, Luder, Pastore, & Kunz, 2021).

## Policy

Inclusion in schools can be promoted much more effectively when the state has an inclusion policy. In order for the implementation process of inclusive education to continue in a complete and trouble-free manner, it is necessary for the state to support inclusion very firmly and the goals for education must be clearly defined. Furthermore, states should create all the necessary conditions for mainstreaming education. In particular, they should facilitate and not hinder inclusive education with the necessary financial arrangements. In this regard, leadership is also very important. Policymakers have a key role in terms of implementing government policy not only at the national level, but also at the community, school district, and school cluster levels. Inclusion also needs support outside of schools. At this point, introducing and demonstrating good practices in the early stages of development can dispel fears, unknowns, and doubts that may arise from the unknown (DSSLG, 2017; Salmi, 2018; Salmi, & D'Addio, 2020)

## Dealing with Difficulties, Differences and Diversity

Regarding the recent literature in the field of inclusion, it is clearly seen that behavioral, social, and/or emotional problems of individuals who need special education for the most difficult special needs are the potential difficulties. Moreover, this creates issues for students who find it difficult to stay motivated. Dealing with differences or diversity is one of the biggest challenges in the classroom. Inclusion can be organized in various ways and at different levels. At this point, the teacher is expected to deal with greater diversity in the classroom, to prepare and adapt the curriculum to adequately meet the needs of students with special needs, gifted students, and their peers. On the other hand, addressing diversity should be treated as the most important key issue at the grade level. Teachers need extra help and support from colleagues, special education teachers, and other professionals when dealing with differences in the classroom. Students with special educational needs may sometimes need more specialized help and guidance in their daily classroom routines that cannot be provided by their teachers. In this case, although other teachers and support personnel gain importance, problems such as flexibility, good planning, working, and teaching in cooperation may arise (DSSLG, 2017; Ahmad, & Parween, 2021; Kiel, & Muckenthaler, & Weiß, 2020)

## Cooperative Teaching

The cooperative teaching situation is closely related not only to the class level but also to the school level. In such cases, experts from different support services are needed to increase and expand flexibility, good planning, cooperation, and coordination. Consequently, it could be stated that inclusive education means much more than dealing with diversity. On the other hand, while inclusive education brings challenges in co-teaching and team teaching at the classroom level, it requires good cooperation between teachers at the school level and coordination with experts from other support services. When the effective practices within the scope of inclusive education are examined in the literature, it is seen that some approaches have emerged. The first of these approaches is the cooperative teaching approach. Teachers may need cooperation as well as diverse and flexible support from their colleagues. At this point, cooperative education is seen as an effective way to improve the academic and social skills of individuals in need of special education. As it is obvious, it is of great importance that additional assistance and support be flexible, well-coordinated, and planned (Paulsrud, & Nilholm, 2020; Klang, Olsson, Wilder, Lindqvist, Fohlin, & Nilholm, 2020).

## Cooperative Learning Peer-Teaching Approach

Another effective practice approach in inclusive education is known as cooperative learning. The cooperative learning or peer teaching approach is an effective point for students to learn and develop in both cognitive and social-emotional contexts. A group of students, who are in a flexible and well-thought-out system, can benefit from learning together as they help each other. In this case, it is considered that there will be no indication that more talented students suffer from this situation by missing new challenges or opportunities. The literature on the cooperative learning approach emphasizes that students have made progress in this approach both academically and socially. Moreover, cooperative learning is seen as possible even with students who need special education if the student is let to be put in the position of a teacher. Even students with very serious behavioral problems may pretend to be teachers of younger students. Thus, students with very serious behavioral problems can fully assume these roles, contrary to expectations, when they are in the position of teachers (Sharan, 2010). Since the role of the teacher is assumed, it is the teacher's responsibility to choose the task, to enable the group to start working on the given tasks, to cope with the difficulties encountered, and to produce the necessary solutions. At first glance, the student who takes on the role of the teacher may seem like he is not doing anything due to the responsibility of his role and the students in his group. He may work and continue somewhere in the school. His education may be in disarray. However, this student can be provided with a little guidance to fulfill his responsibilities as a teacher and be encouraged to engage in a good job.

## Collaborative Problem-Solving

Collaborative problem solving is one of the other important approaches we encounter in inclusive education practices. Especially at the point of including students with social/behavioral problems, it is an effective approach for teachers to systematically approach undesirable behaviors in the classroom and to reduce the amount and intensity of the discomfort that such behaviors will cause during the lesson. In such cases, it is stated that clear classroom rules with boundaries such as a set of appropriate incentive approaches and deterrents accepted by the students are effective (Thomson, Brown, Jones, Walker, Moore, Anderson, Davies, Medcalf, Glynn, & Koegel, 2003).

## Heterogeneous Grouping

As the cooperative problem-solving approach, the heterogeneous grouping has also taken its place as an effective approach in inclusive education practices. When dealing with student diversity in the classroom, the heterogeneous grouping and a more differentiated approach to education are not only necessary but effective. Within the scope of this approach, the targeted goals, alternative learning ways, flexible teaching, and the excess of homogeneous grouping ways are at a point that develops inclusive education. This approach is therefore of paramount importance in managing diversity in classrooms. Another important point to remember is that heterogeneous grouping is a prerequisite in cooperative learning (Singletary Walker, Ruggs, Botsford Morgan, & DeGrassi, 2019).

## Effective Teaching, Curriculum, and Individual Education Plan

The effective teaching approach is one of the other important approaches within the scope of inclusive education practices. Given the high expectations for effective education, goal setting, assessment-based education, the creation of effective schools, and effective teaching, direct guidance and feedback approaches can be applied to inclusive education. Another important point is the use of a standard curriculum framework. However, in this context, it should not be forgotten that the curriculum should be compatible not only for individuals with special education needs at the lower level of the process but also for all students and gifted ones. The fact that the curriculum is compatible with both gifted and gifted students in need of special education reveals the Individual Education Plan, which is created specifically for the individual, considering each individual's strengths and needs that need to be developed (Savolainen, Malinen, & Schwab, 2020).

Another point to be particularly noted regarding the individual education plan is the importance of following the normal curriculum framework for good and effective implementation. Furthermore, the risk of over-focusing on individualization in inclusive school should be highlighted. In addition, while heterogeneous grouping expresses the differentiation styles of students, it also allows these students to reach different goals with alternative learning ways. On the other hand, while making heterogeneous grouping, care should be taken to make the necessary arrangements with an effective and target-oriented approach (Jachova, Kovačević, & Hasanbegović, 2018).

## Inclusive Education in Higher Education Settings

University participation in higher education, such as different nationalities, ages, cultures, socioeconomic statuses, and abilities that are often outside the norm, is broader due to the gradual incorporation of collectives. It is seen that the number of students with disabilities in higher education is increasing year by year. Besides, the arrangements made to include and promote inclusiveness in higher education and the developments in these arrangements have been effective in the increase of these students. At this point, the Convention on the Rights of Persons with Disabilities is of great importance in terms of providing access to higher education, vocational education, adult education, and lifelong learning as well as equal access to other individuals without discrimination. Furthermore, the European Union is committed to inclusive education within the scope of higher education. Therefore, the European Strategy 2010-2020 recommends and highlights plans, services that support access and participation in education for non-traditional students (Biscop, 2018).

Necessary measures have been taken against the right of disabled students to study at universities in countries such as Australia, the United States, and the United Kingdom. Further, these rights are protected. A significant number of countries that support mainstreaming in the development of the mainstreaming process have implemented the necessary regulations and practices to make university education accessible to individuals with disabilities. Under laws and policies, many universities have established offices to support the educational needs of students with disabilities, created an environment for the use of new technologies, and implemented them based on inclusive education practices. In addition to all these improvements and developments, recent studies have revealed that there are deficiencies in quality education, education without discrimination, and education based on the principles of inclusive education. This situation reveals that students with disabilities have a higher risk of dropping out of university compared to students without disabilities (Quirke, McCarthy, Treanor, & McGuckin, 2019; Florian, & Spratt, 2013).

In this case, it is of great importance to make the necessary policies and regulations for students not to leave the university and complete their education successfully at the same time. In order to facilitate inclusive education for disabled students and to provide equal opportunities, inclusive education and universal learning design principles should be combined with university policies and practices based on the social model of disability. Inclusive education includes the right to full participation and quality education for all students. Diversity is given great importance in the content of inclusive education. With the importance given to diversity, it is possible to design accessible educational projects by considering different situations. On the other hand, different learning paths can be considered, and foresight can be created for possible needs that may arise in this process. In addition, the social model, society, and universities in this context are at a point where barriers to the integration of disabled university students are removed. Therefore, practices, policies, and attitudes in the social context based on the social model have an impact on access and participation. However, this also prevents and supports any obstacles that may occur. In short, disability according to the social model is a state of abnormality, not a personal tragedy. Finally, it is not a disease that should be treated (Lawrie, Marquis, Fuller, Newman, Qui, Nomikoudis, Roelofs, & Van Dam, 2017).

## Development and the Use of E-Learning in Inclusive Higher Education Practices

Along with the modern development of the digital environment, the development of e-learning has also taken its share with the addition of new technologies and methods. The advantages of e-learning have created a great demand for solving the problems of students with significant social problems or especially physical disabilities. In this context, e-learning is mostly used in the education of individuals with special health and education needs in inclusive education. Of course, in this context, inclusive education has certain requirements in general, not only for its functioning and learning principles in its unique structure but also for e-learning in particular. Moreover, the development of e-learning in inclusive education has been significantly influenced by the systemic changes in the global digital environment as well as the national strategy for improving education. At this point, national institutional conditions should be taken into account in order to evaluate the possibilities and determine the limits of e-learning applications in inclusive education (Bong, & Chen, 2021).

The education system always seeks progressive teaching methods to adapt to and meet social demands. In connection with this, e-learning systems have developed as an alternative learning way with the help of the internet and multimedia towards the end of the 20th century. The development of e-learning is linked to the development of information and communication technologies. In addition, the evolution of e-learning can be better understood by monitoring the development, design changes, structure, and content of the internet environment. When the development stages of e-learning are examined, it is seen that at first, it is read-only or in the form of a web static information network (Ismailov, & Chiu, 2022).

It was more like an instructor-led class providing content only. The second stage, unlike the first stage, has the features of informing, examining, and to some extent connecting people. To give an example at this point, in the second stage, apart from LMS and LC-MS, there are e-portfolios and social networks such as Facebook. While e-learning is based on mobile internet and mobile learning created on the platform in the third development phase, it consists of virtual reality technologies created and added in the cloud. The final stage of development is e-learning; however, it is built on the web or NuroNet. The web is mainly based on the principle of neuro communication in its late development stage. The late-stage web development, which is a late stage of development, is mainly based on the idea of enhancing human intelligence by amplification of physical strength, based on the principle of neuro communication. The basic principles of e-learning consist of self-learning and self-organization (Abbott, 2007).

## The Advantages and Limitations of E-Learning in Inclusive Higher Education

Considering all the development stages of e-learning from the end of the 20th century to the present, it is seen that the use of e-learning is quite common all over the world. Besides, e-learning has many advantages for learning. It has a flexible and accessible teaching format that saves time and money. It also provides the opportunity to realize teaching materials, makes the teaching process transparent, and provides fast statistical results. Non-linear teaching based on the use of special methods shapes the student's ability to receive the necessary information at the right time and in the right place. On the other side, regarding the development and transformation of the web-based on informational and social relations, developments in information technologies and social relations have played an important role in the emergence and development of e-learning. The basis for the successful development of e-learning is the accessibility of information technologies, the ability to focus on social cooperation, and the ability to perceive the current social environment (Meskhi, Ponomareva, & Ugnich, 2019).

E-learning has the features of flexibility and increased information security. In this context, e-learning forms the basis of its own development and transformation. Education for people with disabilities, and especially higher education, is a valuable resource of great importance to them. Moreover, higher education is both effective and permanent in reducing the isolation of people with disabilities and is of great importance for them to gain economic independence. In this case, the duties of universities do not end with creating a special social and cultural infrastructure in education. Universities' mission continues by improving teaching techniques and methods and reassuring students that limited health skills will not be an obstacle to their professional life. Based on the idea of inclusion in education, it is not the student who should be ready to be integrated into the education system. On the contrary, on the basis of the idea of inclusion, the education system should be ready to integrate the student. It is seen that the first ideas for the implementation of inclusive education emerged in the 1970s. It is seen that it started to be applied with more systematic outlines in the United States of America in the 1980s, and it was applied in this way in European countries in the 1990s. Today, inclusive education attracts attention in many countries (Abbott, 2007; Meskhi, Ponomareva, & Ugnich, 2019).

These countries include Southern European countries, Scandinavian countries, the United States, Canada, and countries such as Japan, Australia, and New Zealand. Various models exist to support inclusive education in universities. To give an example of these models, the model in Great Britain selects targeted support for students with disabilities. Besides that, looking at the other model example in Sweden, support is received from universities and educational institutions that provide education to students with disabilities. When the ratios of disabled students among their disabled peers in various countries are examined, it is seen that these ratios differ according to each country. In addition, it is seen that the rate of students with disabilities has increased. In this context, all approaches to inclusive education are based on the social integration model that integrates and adapts the social relations of the disabled (Abbott, 2007; Meskhi, Ponomareva, & Ugnich, 2019; Ramberg, & Watkins, 2020).

Regarding the basic features of inclusion, it is seen that it has features compatible with the social integration model. These characteristics include promoting social diversity, resisting the practices of social exclusion, breaking down social and cultural barriers to the interaction of all unique groups of people, and including people with disabilities. To summarize, e-learning is a way of removing all kinds of obstacles that will enable people with disabilities to integrate into society and to enable these individuals to participate more effectively in social life. At this point, e-learning in inclusive education focuses on evaluating the change in the role of the teacher and the change of other factors in the context of its change (Lakhal, Mukamurera, Bédard, Heilporn, Chauret, 2020).

The flexibility of e-learning makes education accessible to different groups of people. Depending on this situation, e-learning has a very important social function. Further, the advantages of e-learning in the education systems of many countries are at a point that will solve the problems that arise in individuals receiving private health services, especially in the development of inclusion. Inclusive education emerges as both a new and important stage in the development of education. It is noteworthy that it is adaptable and accessible to meet the various needs of individuals with special health needs. Today, the development of inclusive education has depended on the increase in the number of individuals with special health needs (Moriña, 2017).

The inclusion of students with special health needs in society and the fact that students with special health needs do not experience any obstacles in the social and cultural context constitute the important building blocks of inclusion in higher education. In addition to professional skills, people with disabilities who want to have a certain profession and get higher education in this way need both support and certain learning and conditions. Besides, education for individuals with disabilities may be much more important than for individuals without any special health problems. Digital technologies such as e-learning tools make a great contribution to the development of inclusive education. Exercises and repetitions can also be done to assist learning and use digital technologies to expand learning opportunities and make them more effective. Thus, digital technologies give the educator the opportunity to actively engage in the educational process without permission. For instance, the educator can facilitate the training process, actively create opportunities for cooperation in the process, and at the same time contribute to the development of this cooperation (Petretto, Carta, Cataudella, Masala, Mascia, Penna, Piras, Pistis, & Masala, 2021).

Within the scope of inclusive education, people with disabilities have various needs. To meet these needs, there is a variety of help that e-learning can offer. At the beginning of these needs is integration with society, acquiring professional and general cultural information on the way to active life, and overcoming social and cultural obstacles. It is of great importance to understand how e-learning is at a key point in the formation of knowledge in individuals with disabilities. It is of great importance to understand how e-learning is at a key point in the formation of knowledge in individuals with disabilities. Therefore, unformalized information can emerge as formalized and informal to us. Besides, formalized information is the information conveyed using official language (Meskhi, Ponomareva, & Ugnich, 2019).

Informal information is personal information that is circumstantial and does not require to be formatted about the situation and distribution. The way to reach unformatted, that is, personal and informal information, is through personal experiences. However, such information can only be transferred to another person by another person. Unlike the formalized, explicit and formal transfer of information, the transfer of implicit and informal personal information requires close interaction, a common understanding, and the establishment of trust between the subjects of this information. Further, nonverbal information, which is personal, is scattered. However, it cannot easily be combined. In order to fully realize the potential of tacit knowledge, knowledge of the subject, participation, and cooperation is of great importance. In this case, although it seems possible to distinguish explicit and implicit knowledge on the basis of concept, both types of knowledge are integrated with each other on the basis of application. Implicit knowledge, which we call implicit personal knowledge, provides a foundation for sensitive skills that are difficult to implement in the profession. Moreover, skills that are considered sensitive are those that help people socialize. Therefore, both difficult and sensitive skills are considered important for people with disabilities (Blasco, 2014; Meskhi, Ponomareva, & Ugnich, 2019).

However, when the e-learning mechanism is evaluated, it is seen that it is based on formalization. Thus, formalization becomes important for open knowledge transfer. E-learning tools can be partially used at the point of transferring tacit knowledge. E-learning tools are mainly integrated within the scope of transforming tacit knowledge into explicit knowledge. People with disabilities need help to acquire implicit and explicit knowledge in the development of learning and opportunities. Furthermore, for them to integrate these types of knowledge into their social life, they need to overcome or remove social and cultural barriers. Overcoming social and cultural barriers is one of the most important components of high-inclusive education. This is where e-learning can step in and play an important role (Blasco, 2014; Meskhi, Ponomareva, & Ugnich, 2019).

Read-only web-based e-learning software platforms for web static pages are essentially online training courses. These tools are based on formalization. Since they are based on formalization, they can be used in explicit knowledge transfer. In such a case, data support should be provided as well as special software for students with disabilities. Jaws, ZoomText, Fusion, and Digital Accessible Information System are a few of the examples that can be provided. While teamwork-based e-learning tools for the education of the disabled make it possible to inform people, collaborate, and socialize with them to some extent, the web is much more suitable for static pages than read-only web-based e-learning tools (Meskhi, Ponomareva, & Ugnich, 2019; Bong & Chen, 2021).

As e-learning tools make it possible to inform and socialize with people through interaction, it builds the foundation of the personal learning environment. On the other hand, social networks and blogs, which form the basis of e-learning through these e-learning tools, contribute more to socialization, but cannot always provide the necessary communication with the student. Learning tools based on the mobile internet and mobile learning enable people to create quality content and services and meet the needs of individuals with disabilities at the highest level. However, these learning tools cannot provide full socialization and transfer of tacit knowledge. One of the tools used in e-learning is virtual reality. Virtual reality applications are also a technology that can be used for space transformation. At this point, the use of virtual reality applications is an important tool to overcome existing inequalities such as physical limitations caused by human abilities. Furthermore, they are a tool that can be used to create a model of a particular external environment. Thus, people can share their experiences not by creating texts or narratives but also by creating a field of experiences that aim to take an action. Although virtual reality applications can help us overcome inequalities such as physical limitations, they are insufficient to solve this problem (Kent, 2015; Ponomareva, & Ugnich, 2018).

In addition, there are some limitations regarding the use of e-learning in mainstreaming higher education. It is not always possible to observe an increase in students' use of the latest information and communication technologies, the development of e-learning tools, and students' perceptions of information in the quality of education. In most cases, students find an easier way to learn to use information and communication technologies. Therefore, students should be taught how to manage their knowledge and improve their communication skills. One of the other e-learning challenges faced in higher education is the continuous adaptation and renewal of the university environment to a permanent e-learning environment. Confidence in e-learning can be emphasized at the point of gaining professional knowledge and skills as one of the important problems (Kent, 2015; Ponomareva, & Ugnich, 2018).

## CONCLUSION

As it is known, the success of the education of students with disabilities is shaped by the conditions created by the educational institutions of inclusive education. Therefore, besides modern education systems, special techniques, software use, teacher support, and e-learning use should be developed in higher education programs. Thus, students with or without disabilities will be provided with a variety of different opportunities to improve themselves. At this point, the development of e-learning receives importance since the trends in higher education keep increasing day by day. Therefore, educators in higher education are expected to follow or develop new approaches in order to meet their students' needs. Further, while e-learning addresses the learning demands of students with disabilities, it supports the integration of these students into educational environments from various aspects.

## ACKNOWLEDGMENT

We would like to thank IGI GLOBAL for giving us the opportunity to reflect and share our research on this subject with readers.

We would also like to thank our family members for their endless support, motivation, and support during this process.

## REFERENCES

Abbott, C. (2007). E-inclusion: Learning difficulties and digital technologies. Future lab. *Education.*

Ahmad, W., & Parween, S. (2021). Managing behavioral/emotional problems in inclusive classrooms and understanding the best practices. In A. Singh, C. J. Yeh, S. Blanchard, & L. Anunciação (Eds.), *Handbook of research on critical issues in special education for school rehabilitation practices* (pp. 443–461). IGI Global.

Alexander, P. A., Sperl, C. T., Buehl, M. M., Fives, H., & Chiu, S. (2004). Modeling domain learning: Profiles from the field of special education. *Journal of Educational Psychology, 96*(3), 545. doi:10.1037/0022-0663.96.3.545

Birhanu, M. (2015). Perception of students and instructors toward students with disabilities: Issues, challenges, and opportunities to implement inclusive education. *Research Journal of Educational Studies and Review, 1*, 30–56. doi:10.4236/oalib.1103174

Biscop, S. (2018). *European strategy in the 21st century: New future for old power.* Routledge.

Blasco. (2014). Making the tacit explicit: Rethinking culturally inclusive pedagogy in international student academic adaptation. *Pedagogy, Culture, 23*(1), 1–22.

Bong, W. K., & Chen, W. (2021). Increasing faculty's competence in digital accessibility for inclusive education: A systematic literature review. *International Journal of Inclusive Education.* Advance online publication. doi:10.1080/13603116.2021.1937344

Collins, A., Azmat, F., & Rentschler, R. (2018). Bringing everyone on the same journey: Revisiting inclusion in higher education. *Studies in Higher Education, 44,* 1475–1487. doi:10.1080/03075079.2018.1450852

Disabled Students Sector Leadership Group (DSSLG). (2017). *Inclusive teaching and learning in higher education as a route to excellence.* London: Department for education. Available Online: https://www.gov.uk/government/uploads/system/uploads/attachment_data/file/58 7221/Inclusive_Teaching_and_Learning_in_Higher_Education_as_a_route_to excellence.pdf

Dovigo, Dovigo, & Janssen. (2017). Special educational needs and inclusive practices. Sense Publishers.

Florian, L., & Linklater, H. (2010). Preparing teachers for inclusive education: Using inclusive pedagogy to enhance teaching and learning for all. *Cambridge Journal of Education, 40*(4), 369–386.

Florian, L., & Spratt, J. (2013). Enacting inclusion: A framework for interrogating inclusive practice. *European Journal of Special Needs Education, 28*(2), 119–135. doi:10.1080/08856257.2013.778111

Galkienė, A., & Monkevičienė, O. (2021). Preconditions of transforming the educational process by applying inclusive education strategies: Theoretical background. In *Improving Inclusive Education Through Universal Design for Learning* (Vol. 5, pp. 1–21). Springer.

Gudjonsdottir, H., & Óskarsdóttir, E. (2016). Inclusive education, pedagogy, and practice. Culturally responsive teaching practices. In S. Markic & S. Abels (Eds.), *Science Education Towards Inclusion* (pp. 7–22). Nova Science Publishers.

Ismailov, M., & Chiu, T. (2022). Catering to Inclusion and diversity with universal design for learning in asynchronous online education: A self-determination theory perspective. *Frontiers in Psychology, 13*, 819–884. doi:10.3389/fpsyg.2022.819884 PMID:35265016

Jachova, Z., Kovačević, J., & Hasanbegović, H. (2018). Individual education plan foundation of a quality inclusive education. *Journal Human Research in Rehabilitation*, *8*(2), 88–93. doi:10.21554/HRR.091811

Jackson, L. B., Ryndak, D. L., & Wehmeyer, M. L. (2008). The dynamic relationship between context, curriculum, and student learning: A case for inclusive education as a research-based practice. *Research and Practice for Persons with Severe Disabilities*, *34*(1), 175–195.

Kent, M. (2015). Disability and e-learning: Opportunities and barriers. *Disability Studies Quarterly*, *35*(1), 1–15. doi:10.18061/dsq.v35i1

Kiel, E., Muckenthaler, M., & Weiß, S. (2020). Students with emotional and behavioral problems in inclusive classes: A critical incident analysis. *Journal of Emotional and Behavioral Disorders, 29*(4), 213-225. doi:https://doi:29.10.1177/1063426620967286

Kivirand, T., Leijen, Ä., Lepp, L., & Tammemäe, T. (2021). Designing and implementing an in-service training course for school teams on inclusive education: Reflections from participants. *Education Sciences*, *11*(4), 166. doi:10.3390/educsci11040166

Klang, N., Olsson, I., Wilder, J., Lindqvist, G., Fohlin, N., & Nilholm, C. (2020). A cooperative learning intervention to promote social inclusion in heterogeneous classrooms. *Frontiers in Psychology, 11*, 586–489. doi:10.3389/fpsyg.2020.586489 PMID:33414744

Lakhal, S., Mukamurera, J., Bédard, M. E., Heilporn, G., & Chauret, M. (2020). Features fostering academic and social integration in blended synchronous courses in graduateprograms. *International Journal of Educational Technology in Higher Education*, *17*(1), 1–22. doi:10.118641239-020-0180-z

Lawrie, G., Marquis, E., Fuller, E., Newman, T., Qui, M., Nomikoudis, M., Roelofs, F., & van Dam, L. (2017). Moving towards inclusive learning and teaching: A synthesis of recent literature. *Teaching & Learning Inquiry*, *5*(1), 9–21. doi:10.20343/teachlearninqu.5.1.3

McLoughlin, C. (2001). Inclusivity and alignment: Principles of pedagogy, task, and assessment design for effective cross-cultural online learning. *Distance Education*, *22*(1), 7–29. doi:10.1080/0158791010220102

Meijer, C., Soriano, V., & Watkins, A. (2007). Inclusive education across Europe: Reflections upon 10 years of work from the European agency for development in special needs education. *Childhood Education*, *83*(6), 361–365. doi:10.1080/00094056.2007.10522951

Meskhi, B., Ponomareva, S., & Ugnich, E. (2019). E-learning in higher inclusive education: Needs, opportunities, and limitations. *International Journal of Educational Management*, *33*(3), 424–437. doi:10.1108/IJEM-09-2018-0282

Moriña, A. (2017). Inclusive education in higher education: Challenges and opportunities. *European Journal of Special Needs Education*, *32*(1), 3–17. doi:10.1080/08856257.2016.1254964

Okongo, R. B., Ngao, G., Rop, N. K., & Wesonga, J. N. (2015). Effect of availability of teaching and learning resources on the implementation of inclusive education in pre-school centers in Nyamira North Sub-County, Nyamira County, Kenya. *Journal of Education and Practice*, *6*(35), 132–141. http://Hdl.Handle.Net/123456789/3198

Paccaud, A., Keller, R., Luder, R., Pastore, G., & Kunz, A. (2021). Satisfaction with the collaboration between families and schools - the parent's view. *Front. Educ.*, *6*, 86. doi:10.3389/feduc.2021.646878

Parsons, C., & Castle, F. (1998). The cost of school exclusion in England. *International Journal of Inclusive Education*, *2*(4), 277–294. doi:10.1080/1360311980020402

Paulsrud, D., & Nilholm, C. (2020). Teaching for inclusion: A review of research on the cooperation between regular teachers and special educators in the work with students in need of special support. *International Journal of Inclusive Education*, *27*, 1–15. doi:10.1080/13603116.2020.1846799

Petretto, D. R., Carta, S. M., Cataudella, S., Masala, I., Mascia, M. L., Penna, M. P., Piras, P., Pistis, I., & Masala, C. (2021). The use of distance learning and e-learning in students with learning disabilities: A review on the effects and some hint of analysis on the use during covid-19 outbreak. Clinical practice and epidemiology in mental health. *Clinical Practice and Epidemiology in Mental Health*, *17*, 92–102. doi:10.2174/1745017902117010092 PMID:34733348

Ponomareva, S., & Ugnich, E. (2018). E-learning opportunities and limitations in inclusive higher education. In *SHS Web of Conferences* (Vol. 50, p. 01138). EDP Sciences. https://10.1051hsconf/20185001138

Puri, M., & Abraham, G. (Eds.). (2004). *Handbook of inclusive education for educators, administrators, and planners: Within walls, without boundaries*. Sage Publishing.

Quirke, M., McCarthy, P., Treanor, D., & McGuckin, C. (2019). Tomorrow's disability officer – a cornerstone on the universal design campus. *The Journal of Inclusive Practice in Further and Higher Education, 11*(1), 29–42.

Ramberg, J., & Watkins, A. (2020). Exploring inclusive education across Europe: Some insights from the European agency statistics on inclusive education. In *FIRE, Forum for International Research in Education* (Vol. 6, pp. 85–101). Stockholm University. doi:10.32865/fire202061172

Riehl, C. J. (2000). The principal's role in creating inclusive schools for diverse students: A review of normative, empirical, and critical literature on the practice of educational administration. *Review of Educational Research, 70*(1), 55–81. doi:10.1177/0022057409189001-213

Rose, R., & Parsons, L. (1998). Supporting the subject coordinator through the process of curriculum monitoring in a special school. *Support for Learning, 13*(1), 21–25. doi:10.1111/1467-9604.00050

Salmi, J. (2018). *All around the world: Higher education equity policies across the globe*. The Lumina Foundation.

Salmi, J., & D'Addio, A. (2020). Policies for achieving inclusion in higher education. *Policy Reviews in Higher Education, 5*(1), 47–72. doi:10.1080/23322969.2020.1835529

Savolainen, H., Malinen, O.-P., & Schwab, S. (2020). Teachers' efficacy predicts teachers' attitudes towards inclusion - a longitudinal cross-lagged analysis. *International Journal of Inclusive Education, 27*, 1–15. doi:10.1080/13603116.2020.1752826

Sharan, Y. (2010). Cooperative learning for academic and social gains: Valued pedagogy, problematic practice. *European Journal of Education, 45*, 300–313. doi:10.1111/j.1465- 3435.2010.01430.x

Sharma, U., Sokal, L., Wang, M., & Loreman, T. (2021). Measuring the use of inclusive practices among preservice educators: A multi-national study. *Teaching and Teacher Education, 107*, 103506. doi:10.1016/j.tate.2021.103506

Thomson, C., Brown, D., Jones, L., Walker, J., Moore, D. W., Anderson, A., Davies, T., Medcalf, J., Glynn, T. L., & Koegel, R. L. (2003). Resource teachers learning and behavior: Collaborative problem-solving to support inclusion. *Journal of Positive Behavior Interventions, 5*(2), 101–111. doi:10.1177/10983007030050020501

Walker, S. S., Ruggs, E. N., Morgan, W. B., & DeGrassi, S. W. (2019). Diverse perspectives on inclusion: Exploring the experiences of individuals in heterogeneous groups. *Equality, Diversity and Inclusion*, *38*(1), 2–19. doi:10.1108/EDI-11-2017-0250

Zakiah, W. G., Karsidi, R., & Yusuf, M. (2021). The implementation of inclusive educational policies in elementary school. *Jurnal Pendidikan dan Pengajaran*, *54*(1), doi:doi:130-140.10.23887/jpp.v54i1.32210

## KEY TERMS AND DEFINITIONS

**Cooperative Learning:** Cooperative learning aims to enable students to work together to maximize learning, both among themselves and among each other. It is used for educational and instructive purposes by forming small groups within the scope of students working together.

**Cooperative Teaching:** Cooperative or co-learning is an educational approach that general and special educators use to teach heterogeneous student groups, both academically and behaviorally.

**Digital Technologies:** Digital technologies are the technologies that are used to support teaching and learning such as laptops, tablets, mobile phones, online resources, digital tools, systems devices, and resources. Digital tools can produce, reserve, and operate the data.

**Diversity:** Diversity is a dimension that makes people different and at the same time unique within the scope of these characteristics such as age, gender, ethnicity, religion, disability, sexual orientation, education, and nationality.

**E-Learning:** E-learning, known as online or electronic learning, obtains information by accessing information through digital technologies and media.

**Education System:** The education system refers to state education, which consists of programs that include everything aimed at educating the population from kindergarten to high school.

**Higher Education:** Higher education is learning that takes place at a university, college, or institute after completion of the upper secondary level.

**Inclusion:** Inclusion is a practice in which different groups and individuals are accepted without any discrimination in the cultural and social context because of their different backgrounds.

**Inclusive Education:** Inclusive education is of great importance for a quality education system, it is the design of schools, classrooms, programs, and activities in such a way that all students can learn by participating, according to the diversity of their needs.

**Information and Communication Technologies:** Information and communication technologies are various technological tools and resources. Through these technological tools and resources, information can be created, transmitted, shared, and stored and used again.

**Special Education:** Special education is education specially designed to meet the unique needs of the individual who differ socially, mentally, or physically from the average.

# Chapter 8
# Aggrandising Education 4.0 for Effective Post-Pandemic Higher Education:
## The Capacity of Industry 4.0 Technologies and Meaningful Hybrid E-Training

**John Kolawole Aderibigbe**
*University of the Western Cape, South Africa*

## ABSTRACT

*The COVID-19 pandemic has forced the higher education sector to move from traditional in-person teaching and learning to hybrid pedagogical practices. Presently, almost all higher education institutions have commenced transiting from the physical classroom space to the online teaching and learning space. Hence, the impact of the fourth industrial revolution (4IR) has started manifesting in higher education, as evident in the modus operandi adopted recently by the service providers. In other words, as the world advances, higher education institutions are incorporating Industry 4.0 (I4.0) technologies. This transition is part of the evolution of higher education for the 21st century, referred to as Education 4.0 (EDUC4). Hence, this chapter presents a discus on promoting EDUC4 for effective post-pandemic higher education, considering the essential role of I4.0 technologies and meaningful hybrid e-training.*

DOI: 10.4018/978-1-6684-5400-8.ch008

## INTRODUCTION

Education is an integral part of society, aiming to impart innovative skills, knowledge, ability and competencies required by the current volatile, uncertain, complex, ambiguous, radical and rapid (VUCA-RR) world. In other words, education imparts individuals' competencies in diverse aspects of human endeavour to successfully navigate through society's rapid and radical changes (Francois, 2015; Suyaprom & Manmee, 2018). The Industrial sector, for instance, started to witness a transition from the Electronic age to the Digital age from the beginning of the 21st-century. Likewise, the Education sector has moved in the same direction by digitalising teaching and learning processes. This progression is the outcome of research and innovation provided by education 4.0 (EDUC4) (Noh & Abdul Karim, 2020).

EDUC4 is a pedagogical method associated with the Fourth Industrial Revolution (4IR). It is rooted in the 4IR to satisfy labour market demands resulting from flexible, skill-based learning, customised and accessible (Costan et al., 2021). EDUC4 inspires learners to acquire the required resources to learn the necessary skills, knowledge, and competencies for effective performance in the evolving digitalised world of work. Its adoption became prominent with the advent of the COVID-19 pandemic restrictions, especially among higher institutions of learning, while the trend continues in the post-pandemic era (Costan et al., 2021). Moreover, the extensive demand and use of the Internet and cyber-physical systems by tertiary education stakeholders during the COVID-19 pandemic and post-pandemic periods has promoted the hybrid approach to teaching, learning, assessment and research (Alakrash & Adul Razak, 2022).

In terms of the learning process, EDUC4 involves the use of a Virtual Learning Environment (VLE) to blend natural and cybernetic educational resources – a hybrid learning approach that includes the Internet of Things (IoT), using wearables and intelligent sensors, and artificial intelligence (AI) for system automation. The EDUC4 learning process is carefully synergised with the normative vision for education in the new economy and society. Education in the 'new normal' is equipping learners with four critical skills: technology, global citizenship, interpersonal, innovation and creativity skills (World Economic Forum, 2020), while the content of EDUC4 learning is designed to build upon and enhance the basic foundational skills, such as reading, numeracy and writing.

Given the above, educational experts and related policymakers are converging to proffer strategies for the regional and global economy. Nonetheless, the higher education sector, especially in the economically impaired countries around the world, is facing the challenge of integrating I4.0 technologies and providing meaningful hybrid e-training. If improperly managed, the identified challenge could hinder the vision of effective e-learning and meeting the required standard of 21st-century education (Mhlanga, 2020; Mhlanga & Moloi, 2020b).

## CHAPTER OBJECTIVE

The overall objective of this chapter is to enhance the potential of EDUC4 for effective post-pandemic higher education, while the chapter theoretically examines the role of I4.0 technologies and meaningful hybrid e-training in EDUC4. The learning objectives are presented in seven phases, as indicated in Figure 1. The first phase describes the theoretical background of EDUC4, I4.0 technologies and meaningful hybrid e-training. The second phase presents empirical literature reports on the relationship between EDUC4, I4.0 technologies and meaningful hybrid e-training. Next is the conceptual model that illustrates the hypothesised relationship between EDUC4, I4.0 technologies and meaningful hybrid e-training. The fourth phase presents the implications of the relationships between the variables above for stakeholders, while the fifth and sixth phases of the diagram indicate the chapter's conclusion and recommendations. Figure 1 below shows the chapter structure.

## CONCEPTUAL BACKGROUND OF EDUCATION 4.0, INDUSTRY 4.0 TECHNOLOGIES AND MEANINGFUL HYBRID E-TRAINING

It is imperative to prepare 21st-century graduates for the current and future world of work. The contemporary world is volatile, uncertain, complex, ambiguous, radical and rapid (VUCA-RR) (Nowacka & Rzemieniak, 2022). Consequently, the higher education sector is bracing up teaching and learning processes with advanced technologies to adequately educate and equip the graduates with necessary competencies that match the challenges of the dynamic world of work, using EDUC4.

EDUC4 is an innovative strategy to learning, which aligns itself with the 4IR (Costan et al., 2021). The 4IR concentrates on robotics, smart technology, artificial intelligence and all that now impacts human endeavours including tertiary education (Alakrash & Adul Razak, 2022). Hence, for the tertiary institutions to remain relevant to the contemporary economy, they must prepare, educate and equip the tertiary education students for the VUCA-RR world where the cyber-physical systems are driving all industries. In other words, the current situations dictate that the educators should teach the tertiary education students about 4IR and transform the traditional pedagogy to learning by utilising technologies to advance the higher education.

Nonetheless, cyber-physical systems are gradually gaining influence in the higher education sector, certainly imparting the skills requirements for the academics and

*Figure 1. Chapter structure*
*Source: Author's own work*

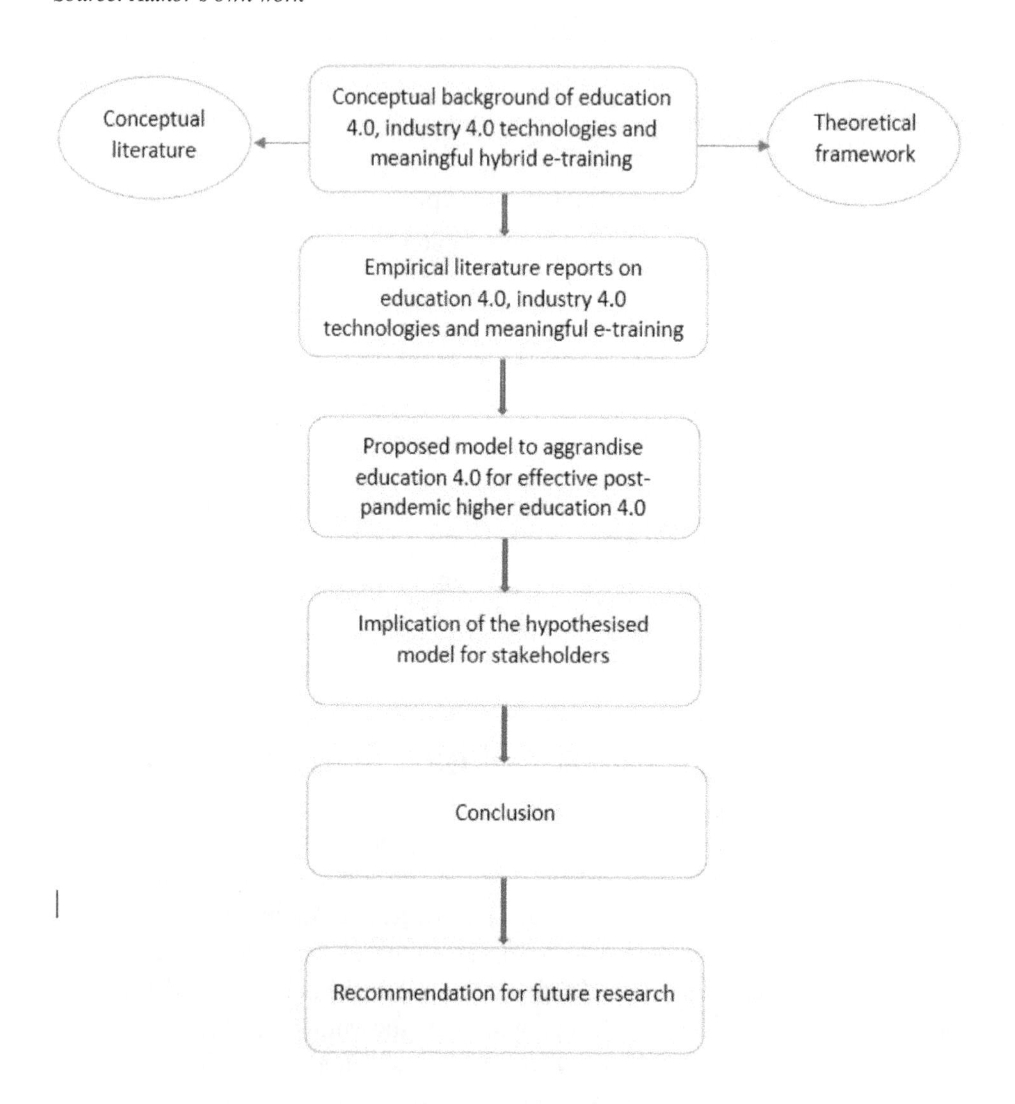


positively contributing to their efforts towards producing graduates with 21st-century attributes (Mäkiö et al., 2021). At least 27% of the activities in higher education such as teaching, learning, data collection and processing have the potential to be automated with the aid of advanced technologies (Chui, Manyika & Miremadi, 2016). It thus helps reduce the growth of the administrative expenses of education, lower its cost and improve its quality.

Moreover, industry 4.0 can potentially impact the soft skills students will need in the future. Soft skills and abilities such as complex problem solving; data analysis;

adaptability and flexibility; complex decision making and sound judgment abilities; team collaboration; creativity and innovation; communication; deductive and inductive reasoning; work analysis and evaluation; and positive psychological development strength are now considered crucial for corporate performance (Haseeb et al., 2019; Mohanta et al., 2019; Prifti et al., 2017). Hence, EDUC4 involves developing with the times, and its implication for higher education institutions means that adopting this approach will help educate and equip students with the essential competencies for influential role players in today's corporate world.

On the other hand, meaningful hybrid e-training is an approach that assures the universities of successfully preparing students for the 21st-century world of work (Rosseni et al., 2010). Life-long training and learning are of immense benefit to the re-skilling and upskilling of the human resource in the 4IR era (Mystakidis, 2021). In the context of post-pandemic higher education, meaningful hybrid e-training is needed to foster learners' readiness for the global economy.

## Conceptual Literature

### The Advent of Education 4.0

According to Awang et al. (2020), EDUC4.0 declares a new approach in the higher education sector as it emphasises innovation and fosters the adoption and use of information, the Internet and technology. Lawrence et al. (2019) explained that human-machine interfaces become universal, enhancing a transformation in innovation through technology. The process of this transformation includes education that correlates with the development of Web services 1.0, 2.0 and 3.0 (Gerstein, 2014). According to Gerstein (2014), educational changes were previously based on Web 1.0, which describes a period in the global network with low ergonomics. Moreover, Awang et al. (2020) reported four different phases of transition in educational technology that comprise education 1.0, education 2.0, education 3.0 and education 4.0.

Specifically, in Miranda et al. (2021), education 1.0 is characterised by systems mechanisation that formed aiding technologies for education such as the paper-making machine, mechanical printing, graphite pencil, ballpoint pen and the typewriter. Education 1.0 is peculiar for its educational ideologies centred on instructivism, essentialism and behaviourism. However, education was a luxury created mainly for the rich during the era of education 1.0 (Intelitek, 2018). According to Salmon (2019), learners were mainly consumers of information resources offered for absorption. Typically, learners participated in activities based on those resources. Occasionally, they engaged in personal reading and research using the local library. Furthermore, Salmon (2019) explained that learners are involved in group discussions and debates.

Under the education 1.0 learning system, learners could develop their hypotheses only when they were researchers. In other words, in the education 1.0 era, the teacher was the centre of education, responsible for determining and circulating the vital information that the students needed.

According to Miranda et al. (2021), education 2.0 overlapped with the second industrial revolution in the early 20th century. It is characterised by massive production, industrialisation and electricity. Similarly, Salmon (2019) reported that, from around 2005, some academicians began to adapt Web 2.0 technologies in the teaching and learning services to enhance the traditional approaches to education. "Even at that time, though, we did not see the key processes of education being transformed significantly. Although some groundwork was done, some cracks and fractures occurred in long-held assumptions of learning and teaching. The hugely dominant and previously largely unconscious models of Education 1.0 were occasionally called into question, usually at ground level" (Salmon, 2019, p. 99).

Likewise, Miranda et al. (2021) acknowledged that technological advancement in education 2.0 paved the way for relevant contributions to the higher education sector. While the first set of electronic devices, such as printers, calculators and computers used in the higher education sector appeared, the educational ideologies during the Education 2.0 period were primarily constructivist and andragogical. "The teacher's role changed from a sage to a reference and information source to help develop the tools for professional implementation, and the student's role continued to be passive. Nevertheless, an active role for students began to emerge, where students became owners of the knowledge. The learning approach was also teacher-centred, but peer assessment was encouraged, with the teacher still being fundamental. Also, practices such as correspondence and broadcast education emerged" (Miranda et al., 2021, p. 3). Thereafter, education 3.0 broke through.

The emergence of education 3.0 towards the end of the 20th century mainly revolved around automation, control and computerisation (Miranda et al., 2021). According to Intelitek (2018), several kinds of courseware were designed to replace teachers, while the introduction of computers into classrooms did not change teaching, learning, assessment or evaluation approaches. In other words, education 3.0 moved the second industrial revolution state of mind to computers without a drastic change (Intelitek, 2018). Moreover, Miranda et al. (2021) explained that the transition from education 2.0 to education 3.0 brought a vision in which students and teachers did not need to be involved in a simultaneous session for teaching and learning to occur. During the dispensation of education 3.0, the teaching and learning approaches more heutagogical and connectivist. Here, teachers were considered as collaborators, orchestrators and curators while students were enabled to develop their knowledge (Miranda et al., 2021).

Salmon (2019) reported that most undergraduates entering universities at that time had developed through a world that was Internet-oriented. By implication, the learners and employers of education 3.0 'live online' daily, with the majority of the people having highly sophisticated smart mobile devices that aid immediate and continual interactions with others. According to Salmon (2019), education 3.0 empowers students to become conscious of their learning. Consequently, learners can relate their knowledge to an outcome upon graduation. It prepares them for the volatile, uncertain, complex, ambiguous, and radical world of work. Nevertheless, higher education currently (in 2022) operates with EDUC4.

EDUC4, according to Velinova-Sokolova (2021), is an institute of beliefs that promotes smart thinking in education. Using EDUC4, "higher education institutions apply new learning methods, innovative didactic and management tools, and smart and sustainable infrastructure mainly complemented by new and emerging ICTs to improve knowledge generation and information transfer processes" (Miranda, et al., 2021, p. 4). Miranda et al. (2021) believe that the combination of the learning management system, innovative didactic, smart infrastructure and new learning methods will enhance the training and producing of graduates with the 21st century competencies. Figure 2 below presents the evolution of higher education, from education 1.0 to education 4.0 and their associated characteristics.

## Industry 4.0 technologies

Ellahi et al. (2019) explained that the German government initially formed the concept of industry 4.0 in 2013 in collaboration with Acatech. By leading the new project, the government regards itself as a pioneer in Industrial IT practices (Ellahi et al., 2019). According to Martinelli et al. (2020), the 4IR and I4.0 are interrelated phenomena. The 4IR is driven by I4.0 and its associated technologies (Costan et al., 2021).

"The first industrial revolution was triggered by water and steam power to move from human labour to mechanical manufacturing; the second was built on electric power to create mass production. The third used electronics and information technology to automate manufacturing. The 4IR is the current automation and data exchange trend in manufacturing technologies. I4.0 is gradually implemented, often with digitalisation as the first important step. Digital technologies allow for new business models and value-producing opportunities, and are attainable for most developing countries" (UNIDO, 2019, p.3). The development in I4.0 technologies now has a significant impact on all fields of human endeavour, including education (Eleyyan, 2021; Syazali et al., 2019).

Martinelli et al. (2020) explained that I4.0 is not a single technology. Instead, it is a collection of diverse technologies brought together by system integrators,

*Figure 2. The evolution of higher education from education 1.0 – education 4.0*
*Source: Author's own work*

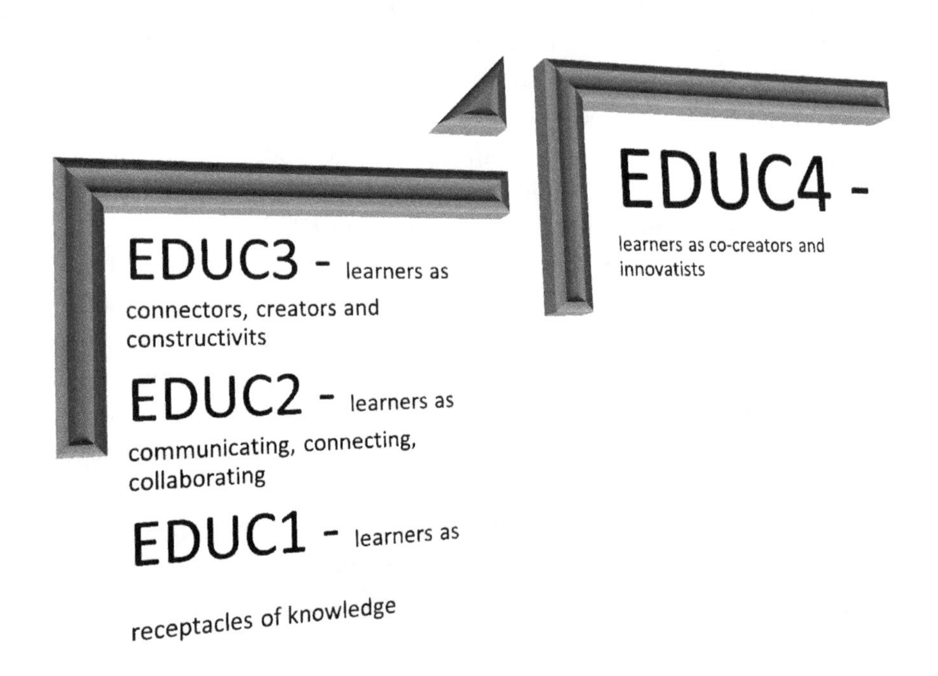


technological leaders, government policymakers, and pivotal users. Similarly, Lichtblau et al. (2015) stated that numerous technologies related to increased connectivity, automation and digitisation are used to implement the elements of I4.0 technologies. Moreover, Bai et al. (2020) and Veile et al. (2018) believe some technologies represent I4.0. In other words, I4.0 technologies are characterised by vertically, horizontally, intelligently connected people, objects, robots, and information and communication technology systems; and combined for industrial value. Thereby, I4.0 is thought to qualify for sustaining and enabling organisations' competitiveness and be a suitable solution to address the shortage of high-quality human resources, especially in the underdeveloped part of the world (Sae-Lim & Jermsittiparsert, 2019; Veile et al., 2018).

Chiarini (2021) reported that I4.0 is based on different technologies. Nevertheless, those technologies have various names that are frequently overlapped, yet there is no agreement concerning their classification. Some of the I4.0 technologies include: Smart sensors, Industrial Internet of Things (IIoT), cloud computing, artificial intelligence and data analytics, collaborative robots, big data. Figure 3 below presents a list of some of the I4.0 technologies and their descriptions.

*Figure 3. Industry 4.0 technologies*
*Source: Author's own work*

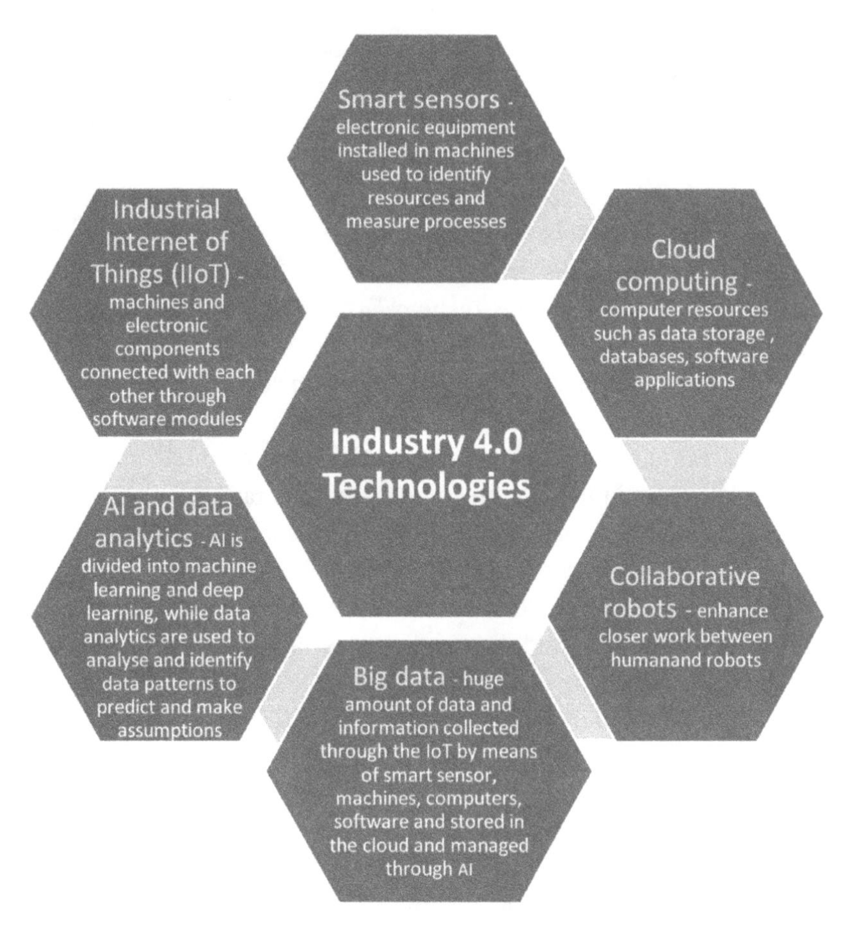


Veile et al. (2018) asserted the I4.0 technologies facilitate communication among people, but they also help humans communicate with robots and objects, and robots communicate with each other. Neaga's (2019) reports showed that the ongoing tertiary education and research activities in the universities around the world are taking the opportunities related to I4.0 technologies. Moreover, professionals are responding swiftly to the challenges of educating the 'Generation Z' (anyone born from 1997 onward) learners to fit the VUCA-RR work environment after graduation from the university (Dimock, 2019). For instance, the Education and Skills 2030 project of the Organisation for Economic Co-operation and Development (OECD) has changed its focus areas recently, from 'Key Competencies' to 'Transformation Competencies' (OECD, 2019).

According to Jadoul (2021), numerous higher institutions and research organisations have activated 4.9G/LTE and 5G initiatives on their campuses. Many of the universities have commenced collaboration research projects with industry and public sector. Indicated below is a few of the institutions where 4.9G/LTE and 5G initiatives are launched in partnership with the business world. "In Australia, the University of Technology Sydney is building and running a state-of-the-art 5G innovation facility at the university's Tech Lab campus. The University for Business and Technology in Kosovo is rolling out 5G private wireless network to enable research and testing use cases driven by immersive, Internet of Things (IoT) and AI technologies. In Germany, the Technical University of Kaiserslautern is also deploying a 5G standalone (SA) campus-wide private wireless network, while the 5G4KMU project, which spans five leading research centres in the state of Baden-Württemberg, is providing small- and medium-sized enterprises with an expert introduction to 5G to help them develop new 5G-based products, applications and business models. And in the UK, the University of Strathclyde has joined forces with Nokia to help utilities prepare power grids for emerging technologies through improved communications capabilities" (Jadoul, 2021).

In light of the above, the OECD Learning Compass 2030 indicates the knowledge, skills, attitudes and values students need not just to weather the changes in our environment and in our daily lives, but to help shape the future we want. Thereby, the Education and Skills 2030 project of the OECD is driven by the aim to meet the tests of the 21st century with the view that learners need to be empowered and have a feeling of self-efficacy so that they can help develop a world where sustainability and well-being are guaranteed (OECD, 2019).

## Meaningful hybrid e-training

According to Din et al. (2012), the advent of e-training is a giant step to the democratisation of higher education for learners with diverse learning preferences. In their statement, Din et al. (2011) reported that infusing technology into conventional teaching creates a meaningful hybrid e-training and competency-based higher education. This suggested that hybrid e-training should incorporate all five elements (content, delivery, service, outcome and structure) of meaningful hybrid e-training to ensure meaningful learning. In another case, Din et al. (2010) stressed that the hybrid e-training programmes have revealed a significant gap between developing technology and comprehensive pedagogical strategies to determine programme standard. Furthermore, Din et al. (2010) believed that meaningful hybrid e-training involvement offers an articulate drive for a planned educational revolution through lifelong education. Consequently, human resources will continually update in terms of required skills and competencies to maintain a competitive advantage in the universal economy.

Cain et al. (2016) explained that hybrid e-learning offers different benefits over using any single learning methods. In other words, it has a competitive edge in terms of learning effectiveness, cost-effectiveness, access to knowledge, pedagogical richness and ease of revision. Moreover, the hybrid e-learning involves coaching by a supervisor; online communities; chat; reference to a manual and participation in seminars; coaching by a supervisor; forums and workshops (Cain et al., 2016). The hybrid e-learning brings a more natural way to learn and work.

In terms of outcome, Sukiman et al. (2022) explained that hybrid e-learning improves the learning process when learners gain new knowledge, skills and competencies. In other words, the learning outcome achieved through the hybrid e-learning is the expected consequences in knowledge, skills, and competencies after engaging in the learning activities to fulfil the 21st century demands – learning autonomy, digital skills, communication and media literacy, critical thinking, collaboration, creativity, teamwork, career competencies, problem-solving skills, adaption skill, cross-cultural understanding, data analysis and research skills, ICT-know-how, innovation and leadership (Sukiman et al., 2022; Alfauzan & Tarchouna, 2017). Moreover, Chu et al. (2017) postulated that the capacity of a long-life learner is necessary to balance the technological evolution.

## Theoretical Framework: *Connectivism Theory*

The connectivism theory of learning developed by George Siemens (2004) underpins the chapter. It explains the relationships between education 4.0, industry 4.0 technologies, and meaningful hybrid e-learning. Connectivism theory of learning considers the trends in learning, use of technology and networks, and the diminishing half-life of knowledge in explaining learning processes in the digital age. It connects essential features of several learning theories, social structures, and technology to establish a theoretical explanation for learning in the digital age. According to Siemens (2004), the "half-life of knowledge" is the period from when knowledge is achieved to when it becomes outdated. Connectivism theory explains that half of what is known now was unknown a decade ago. Thus, the amount of knowledge in the world has doubled what we learned in the last ten years.

Connectivism theory proposed the following eight principles: "Learning and knowledge rest in a diversity of opinions; learning is a process of connecting specialised nodes or information sources; learning may reside in non-human appliances; capacity to know more is more critical than what is currently known; nurturing and maintaining connections is needed to facilitate continual learning; ability to see connections between fields, ideas, and concepts is a core skill; currency (accurate, up-to-date knowledge is the intent of all connectivist learning activities; decision-making is itself a learning process – Choosing what to learn, and the meaning of incoming information is seen through the lens of a shifting reality" (Siemens, 2004). Technology influenced connectivism theory's assumptions with the belief that information is a network continually acquired through the Internet. George Siemens believes learners can acquire new content through the Internet. He further opines that learners identify credible sources of information through technology. Thus, the pre-technology learning theories such as constructivism, behaviourism, and cognitivism are invalid in the Era of EDUC4 (Abik et al., 2012).

Moreover, since connectivism theory is grounded in technology, it encourages the distribution of knowledge across networks, focused on the future and not the past (Siemens, 2012). Hence, educators need to embrace connectivism fully to guarantee that knowledge in the 21st century is delivered appropriately (Abik et al., 2012). According to Fiore (2017), the student-teacher-network-content "tetrahedron" of connectivism theory brings networking into the learning procedure. Thus, whether a learner is learning via e-learning or distance education, teaching and learning are enhanced by including connectivism theory.

## EMPIRICAL LITERATURE: RELATIONSHIPS BETWEEN EDUC4, I4.0 TECHNOLOGIES AND MEANINGFUL E-TRAINING

Little empirical-related research has previously been conducted in this niche. This chapter presents the findings of the related past studies concerning EDUC4, I40 technologies and meaningful e-learning. Moraes et al. (2022) studied the integration of I4.0 technologies with EDUC4 to improve learning using a mixed-method to extract data from 51 published articles in Scopus, Web of Science and ScienceDirect databases. The findings revealed a significant use of the Internet of Things, augmented reality, virtual reality and simulation in higher education from 2011. The study concluded that I4.0 technologies support the 21st-century learning process, especially in higher education. Halili and Sulaiman (2021) reported in their study of students' perception of integration of EDUC4 in a science programme in which university students had positive responses towards integrating EDUC4 to sustainable technological development. Another related research conducted by Srivani et al. (2022) shows a direct relationship between students' perception of EDUC4 and its implementation in learning. The study further shows that respondents expressed confidence in EDUC4 as it improves the learning process.

Mircea et al. (2021) investigated the impact of the IoT on the Romanian higher education environment. The researchers collected data from a study population of 44 teaching staff and 122 university students who expressed average IoT knowledge. The analysed data shows that the adoption of the IoT in higher education has a statistically significant positive influence on excellence in teaching and learning. The findings of the study also reveal that the adoption of the IoT in Romanian universities has a statistically positive impact on intra-and extra-university connectivity.

Another related investigation conducted by Banica et al. (2017), where the authors evaluated the role of IoT in higher education, reported that the blending of I4.0 technologies and education leads to faster and simpler learning. The study's findings show that I4.0 technologies enhance the quality of students and their level of knowledge. Similarly, a study on e-training conducted in a public university in Saudi Arabia by Altwijri and Aldosemani (2022) shows that e-training significantly impacts the university's staff effectiveness and efficiency. Nevertheless, Heriyanto et al. (2019) reported in their investigation that the teachers' lack of understanding of I4.0 negatively impacted their use of the character education approach. Mystakidis et al. (2021) examined deep and meaningful e-learning with social virtual reality environments (SVREs) in higher education and found that SVREs provide authentic, collaborative interactions and personalised learning.

In a study of the impact and effectiveness of e-learning on teaching and learning by Encarnacion et al. (2021), the research participants viewed e-learning as an effective tool to enhance knowledge and skills acquisition. Likewise, Kuimova et al. (2016) reported in their study of e-learning as a means to improve the quality of higher education that e-learning promotes objective assessment, and it is convenient. The relationships between EDUC4, I4.0 technologies and meaningful e-training are showed in Figure 4 below.

## Discussion on the Proposed Model

The proposed model indicates the capacity of I4.0 technologies and meaningful hybrid e-training to promote EDUC4 for effective post-pandemic higher education. The hypotheses stated below illustrate the relationships between EDUCA, I4.0 technologies and meaningful hybrid e-training.

### Statement of hypotheses

$H_1$: Industry 4.0 technologies are significantly positively correlated to education 4.0

$H_2$: Meaningful hybrid e-training is significantly positively correlated to education 4.0

$H_3$: Industry 4.0 technologies and meaningful hybrid e-training are significant joint contributors to education 4.0

In view of knowledge obtained from literature and the theoretical framework, the proposed model in Figure 4 postulates that I4.0 technologies are positively related

*Figure 4. A proposed model to aggrandise education 4.0 for effective post-pandemic higher education*
*Source: Author's own work*

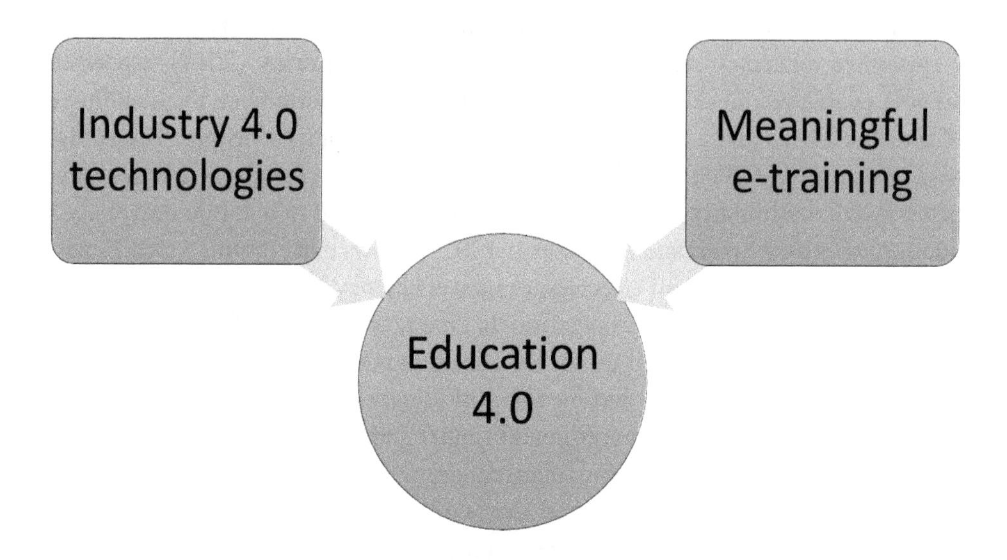


to EDUC4. Thus, the model suggests that post-pandemic higher education applies new learning methods, innovative didactic and management tools, and intelligent and sustainable infrastructure facilitated by new and emerging ICTs to improve knowledge generation and information transfer processes (Velinova-Sokolova, 2021). For instance, the Internet of Things, artificial intelligence, cloud computing and other advanced technology features from I4.0 have drastically imparted teaching and learning processes during and after the COVID-19 pandemic challenges. The COVID-19 pandemic has forced the higher education sector to move from traditional in-person teaching and learning to hybrid pedagogical practices. The higher education institutions are transiting from the physical classroom space to the online teaching and learning space. Hence, the 4IR impact has started manifesting in higher education, as evident in the modus operandi adopted recently by the service providers.

Recent studies support the assumed positive relationship between I4.0 technologies and EDUC4. For instance, Moraes et al. (2022) studied the integration of I4.0 technologies with EDUC4 to improve learning using a mixed-method approach to extract data from 51 published articles in Scopus, Web of Science and ScienceDirect databases. The findings revealed a significant use of the Internet of Things, augmented reality, virtual reality and simulation in higher education from 2011. The study concluded that I4.0 technologies support the 21st-century learning process, especially in higher education. Similarly, Mircea et al. (2021) investigated the impact of the

IoT on the Romanian higher education environment. The researchers collected data from a study population of 44 teaching staff and 122 university students who expressed average IoT knowledge. The analysed data show that the adoption of the IoT in higher education has a statistically significant positive influence on excellence in teaching and learning. The findings of the study also reveal that the adoption of the IoT in Romanian universities has a statistically positive impact on intra-and extra-university connectivity.

Secondly, the proposed model in Figure 4 indicates that meaningful hybrid e-training is positively correlated to EDUC4. Thus, the model suggests that EDUC4 is also driven by hybrid e-training, democratising higher education for learners with diverse learning preferences. The model explains that hybrid e-training is a gap bridging intervention between the developing technologies and comprehensive pedagogical strategies toward educational revolution through lifelong education to update skills and competencies for a competitive advantage in the universal economy. In other words, infusing technology into conventional teaching creates a meaningful hybrid e-training and competency-based higher education.

Recent studies support the assumed positive relationship between meaningful hybrid e-training and EDUC4. For instance, a study on e-training conducted in a public university in Saudi Arabia by Altwijri and Aldosemani (2022) shows that e-training significantly impacts the university's staff effectiveness and efficiency. Nevertheless, Heriyanto et al. (2019) reported in their investigation that the teacher's lack of understanding of I4.0 negatively impacted their use of the character education approach. Mystakidis et al. (2021) examined deep and meaningful e-learning with social virtual reality environments (SVREs) in higher education and found that SVREs provide authentic, collaborative interactions and personalised learning.

Lastly, the proposed model in Figure 4 indicates that I4.0 technologies and meaningful hybrid e-training jointly contribute to EDUC4. The hypothesis explains that EDUC4 is attainable if I4.0 technologies are synergised meaningfully with hybrid e-training with the normative vision for education in the new economy and society. EDUC4 is equipping learners with four critical skills: technology, global citizenship, interpersonal, innovation and creativity skills (World Economic Forum, 2020).

The assumed collective impact of I4.0 technologies and meaningful hybrid e-training on EDUC4 is supported by Mystakidis et al. (2021). They examined deep and meaningful e-learning with social virtual reality environments (SVREs) in higher education and found that SVREs provide authentic, collaborative interactions and personalised and experiential learning. Likewise, Encarnacion et al. (2021) reported that research participants viewed e-learning as an effective tool to enhance knowledge and skills acquisition.

Although the proposed model has explained the direction of relationships between EDUC4, I4.0 technologies and meaningful hybrid e-training, the assumed connections between the three concepts therein are yet to be confirmed empirically. Nevertheless, this chapter's deductions and submissions have set a basis for empirical studies in the niche and contributed to aggrandising EDUC4 for effective post-pandemic higher education.

## Implication for Stakeholders

The following essential suggestions are derived from the review of the capacity of industry 4.0 technologies and meaningful hybrid e-training to enhance education 4.0 for effective post-pandemic higher education. They are for the consideration of all the stakeholders in the higher education sector in their strategic plans:

1. Given the conjectured model in Figure 4, hands-on and innovative faculty development is required to allow the university staff to acquire skills and competencies based on I4.0 technologies. Hence, post-pandemic higher education needs to regularly review and amend the curriculum in collaboration with the policymakers in the corporate world to sustain itself within the space of the VUCA-RR world of work. In other words, the higher education sector needs to fully recognise, adopt and implement EDUC4 to assure its relevance to the global economy through training and producing human resources with required graduate attributes for the VUCA-RR corporate world.
2. Considering the illustrations provided in Figure 4, higher education institutions will have to embrace and implement EDUC4 models that promote academic freedom and enhance the link between the educational institutions, professionals, entrepreneurs and the labour market demands. By implication, academics will henceforth provide training and education with the primary aim to upskill learners' capacities. Professors and lecturers will need to base their teachings on market needs, cultivate entrepreneurial skills, and view enterprises as truly extended arms in the university's training activities.
3. Universities of the post-pandemic era need to foster their synergies with industry and community research and development. By so doing, the 21st century higher education will become an essential sustenance system for the local and universal industrial advancement. Hence, university graduates must be trained academically and professionally using the e-training technique to become flexible and ready to learn from experts with diverse backgrounds – I4.0 work settings require technologically-oriented human resources (Yüceol, 2021).
4. The model in Figure 4 also suggests that employers could cooperate with the higher institutions of learning and research institutes in the hybrid e-training process to ascertain the readiness of a well-trained workforce. Thus, the

cooperation of employers with the higher institutions of learning will facilitate access to market data that helps develop curricula for training and education programmes relevant to the VUCA-RR corporate world.

## CONCLUSION

The chapter examined the capacity of I4.0 technologies and meaningful hybrid e-training to promote EDUC4 for effective post-pandemic higher education. It proposed a conceptual model using information gathered from the relevant literature and connectivism theory, to show the relationships between I4.0 technologies, meaningful hybrid e-training and EDUC4. The chapter concludes that I4.0 technologies can promote EDUC4 towards delivering effective higher education in the post-pandemic era. It also concludes that meaningful hybrid e-training can enhance EDUC4 towards providing effective higher education in the post-pandemic period. Lastly, the chapter reveals that I4.0 technologies and meaningful hybrid e-training jointly drive EDUC4 towards delivering an effective post-pandemic higher education. Given the above submissions, the chapter recommends that the conglomerates cooperate and support the higher institutions of learning and research institutes in the hybrid e-training process to ascertain the availability of a well-trained workforce through intelligent technologies and access to market information.

However, being aware of the information therein, the propositions of the chapter are solely based on a systemic review of the literature. The author of the chapter would recommend that future investigations of the influence of I4.0 technologies and meaningful hybrid e-training on EDUC4 should consider an empirical approach to test the propositions in the hypothesised model to aggrandise education 4.0 for effective post-pandemic higher education.

## REFERENCES

Abik, M., Ajhoun, R., & Ensias, L. (2012). Impact of technological advancement on pedagogy. *Turkish Online Journal of Distance Education, 13*(1), 224-237. https://files.eric.ed.gov/fulltext/EJ976961.pdf

Alakrash, H. M., & Adul Razak, R. (2022). Education and the fourth industrial revolution: Lessons from COVID-19. *Computer. Material & Continua*, *70*(1), 951–962. Advance online publication. doi:10.32604/cmc.2022.014288

Alfauzan, A. A., & Tarchouna, N. (2017). The role of an aligned curriculum design in the achievement of learning outcomes. *Journal of Education and E-Learning Research, 4*(3), 81–91. doi:10.20448/journal.509.2017.43.81.91

Altwijri, A. M., & Aldosemani, T. I. (2022). Employee perceptions of the effectiveness of e-training to meet performance evaluation requirements. *International Journal of Learning, Teaching and Educational Research, 21*(2), 49–71. doi:10.26803/ijlter.21.2.4

Awang, Y., Taib, A., & Muda, N. (2020). Perceived challenges towards education 4.0 implementation among academicians: A preliminary analysis. *e-Academia Journal of UiTM Cawangan Terengganu, 2*(9), 8-17. http://journal-academiauitmt.uitm.edu.my

Bai, C., Dallasega, P., Orzes, G., & Sarkis, J. (2020). Industry 4.0 technologies assessment: A sustainability perspective. *International Journal of Production Economics, 229*, 107776. doi:10.1016/j.ijpe.2020.107776

Banica, L., Burtescu, E., & Enescu, F. (2017). The impact of internet-of-things in higher education. *Scientific Bulletin - Economic Sciences, 16*(1), 53-59. https://ideas.repec.org/a/pts/journl/y2017i1p53-59.html

Cain, W., Bell, J., & Cheng, C. (2016). Implementing robotic telepresence in a synchronous hybrid course. In *Advanced Learning Technologies (ICALT). 2016 IEEE 16th International Conference on*. IEEE. 10.1109/ICALT.2016.79

Chiarini, A. (2021). Industry 4.0 technologies in the manufacturing sector: Are we sure they are all relevant for environmental performance? *Business Strategy and the Environment, 30*(7), 3194–3207. doi:10.1002/bse.2797

Chu, S. K. W., Reynolds, R. B., Tavares, N. J., Notari, M., & Lee, C. W. Y. (2017). *21st century skills development through inquiry-based learning: From theory to practice*. Springer. doi:10.1007/978-981-10-2481-8

Chui, M., Manyika, J., & Miremadi, M. (2016, July). Where machines could replace humans and where they can't (yet): The technical potential for automation differs dramatically across sectors and activities. *McKinsey Quarterly.*

Costan, E., Gonzales, G., Gonzales, R., Enriquez, L., Costan, F., Suladay, D., Atibing, N. M., Aro, J. L., Evangelista, S. S., Maturan, F., Selerio, E. Jr, & Ocampo, L. (2021). Education 4.0 in developing economies: A systematic literature review of implementation barriers and future research agenda. *Sustainability, 13*(22), 12763. doi:10.3390u132212763

Dimock, M. (2019). *Defining generations: Where millennials end and generation z begins*. Pew Research Centre. https://pewrsr.ch/2szqtJz

Din, R., Nordin, M. S., Kassim, N. A., Ahmad, T. B. T., Jusoff, K., Johar, N. A., Zaman, M. F. K., Zakaria, M. S., Ahmad, M., Karim, A. A., & Mastor, K. A. (2010). Development and validation of meaningful hybrid e-training model for computer education. *International Journal of Computer Science and Information Technologies, 1*(3), 179–184. http://www.ijcsit.com/ijcsit-issue3.php

Din, R., Nordin, N., Jusoff, K., Nordin, M. S., Zakaria, M. S., Mastor, K. A., & Embi, M. A. (2011). Hybrid e-training measurement tool: Reliability and validity (2011). *Middle East Journal of Scientific Research*, *7*(2), 184–188. http://www.idosi.org/mejsr/mejsr7(2)11/10.pdf

Din, R., Norman, H., Karim, A., Shah, P., Rahmat, F. R., & Kamarulzaman, F. (2012). Hybrid e-training assessment tool for higher education. *WSEAS Transactions on Advances in Engineering Education, 2*(9), 52-61. https://www.wseas.org/multimedia/journals/education/2012/55-353.pdf

Eleyyan, S. (2021). The future of education according to the fourth industrial revolution. *Journal of Educational Technology & Online Learning*, *4*(1), 23–30. https://dergipark.org.tr/jetol

Ellahi, R. M., Khan, M. U. A., & Shah, A. (2019). Redesigning curriculum in line with Industry 4.0. *Procedia Computer Science*, *151*, 699–708. doi:10.1016/j.procs.2019.04.093

Encarnacion, R. E., Galang, A. D., & Hallar, B. A. (2021). The impact and effectiveness of e-learning on teaching and learning. *International Journal of Computing Sciences Research*, *5*(1), 383–397. doi:10.25147/ijcsr.2017.001.1.47

Fiore, A. (2017). *How can a theory guide or inform practice?* http://annemariefiore.com/connectivism/

Francois, E. J. (2015). *Education and society: Building global education with a local perspective*. Palgrave Macmillan. doi:10.1057/9781137386779_1

Gerstein, J. (2014). Moving from Education 1.0 through education 2.0 towards education 3.0. In L. M. Blaschke, C. Kenyon, & S. Hase (Eds.), *Experiences in self-determined learning* (pp. 83–99). Create Space Independent Publishing Platform.

Halili, S. H., & Sulaiman, S. (2021). Students' perception to integrate education 4.0 in Science program. *Multidisciplinary Journal for Education, Social and Technological Sciences*, *8*(1), 45–57. doi:10.4995/muse.2021.14768

Haseeb, M., Hussain, H., Slusarczyk, B., & Jermsittiparsert, K. (2019). Industry 4.0: A Solution towards Technology Challenges of Sustainable Business Performance. *Social Sciences, 8*(5), 184. doi:10.3390ocsci8050154

Heriyanto, Satori, D., Komariah, A., & Suryana, A. (2019). Character education in the era of industrial revolution 4.0 and its relevance to the high school learning transformation process. *Utopía y Praxis Latinoamericana, 24*(5), 327-339. https://www.redalyc.org/articulo.oa?id=27962050036

Intelitek. (2018). *The education 4.0 revolution: An analysis of industry 4.0 and its effect on education.* https://intelitek.com/2018/05/11/what-is-education-4-0/

Jadoul, M. (2021). How industry 4.0 is transforming higher education. *Education Technology.* https://edtechnology.co.uk/comments/how-industry-4-0-transforming-higher-education/

Kuimova, M., Kiyanitsyna, A., & Truntyagin, A. (2016). E-learning as a means to improve the quality of higher education. *SHS Web of Conferences, 28,* 01129. 10.1051hsconf/20162801129

Lawrence, R., Fung Ching, L., & Haslinda, A. (2019). Strengths and weaknesses of education 4.0 in the higher education institution. *International Journal of Innovative Technology and Exploring Engineering (IJITEE), 9*(2S3), 511 – 519. doi:10.35940/ijitee.B1122.1292S319

Lichtblau, K., Stich, V., Bertenrath, R., Blum, R., Bleider, M., Millack, A., Schmitt, K., Schmitz, E., & Schröter, M. (2015). *Industrie 4.0 Readiness.* Impuls-Stiftung.

Mäkiö, E., Azmat, F., Ahmad, B., Harrison, R., & Colombo, A. W. (2021). T-CHAT educational framework for teaching cyber-physical system engineering. *European Journal of Engineering Education.* Advance online publication. doi:10.1080/03043797.2021.2008879

Martinelli, A., Mina, A., & Moggi, M. (2020). The enabling technologies of industry 4.0: Examining the seeds of the fourth industrial revolution. *Industrial and Corporate Change.*

Mhlanga, D. (2020). Industry 4.0: The challenges associated with the digital transformation of education in South Africa. In Ö. Aydin (Ed.), *The impacts of digital transformation* (pp. 13–26). Efeacademy.

Mhlanga, D., & Moloi, T. (2020b). COVID-19 and the digital transformation of education: What are we learning on 4IR in South Africa? *Education Sciences, 10*(7), 180. doi:10.3390/educsci10070180

Miranda, J., Navarrete, C., Noguez, J., Molina-Espinosa, J., Ramirez-Montoya, M., Navarro-Tuch, S., Bustamante-Bello, M., Rosas-Fernandez, J., & Molina, A. (2021). The core components of education 4.0 in higher education: Three case studies in engineering education. *Computers & Electrical Engineering, 93*(107278), 107278. Advance online publication. doi:10.1016/j.compeleceng.2021.107278

Mircea, M., Stoica, M., & Ghilic-Micu, B. (2021). Investigating the impact of the internet of things in higher education environment. *IEEE Access: Practical Innovations, Open Solutions, 9*, 33396–33409. doi:10.1109/ACCESS.2021.3060964

Mohanta, B., Nanda, P., & Patnaik, S. (2019). *Management of V.U.C.A. (volatility, uncertainty, complexity and ambiguity) using machine learning techniques in industry 4.0 paradigm. Studies in Big Data, 64*. doi:10.1007/978-3-030-25778-1_1

Moraes, E. B., Kipper, L. M., Hackenhaar Kellermann, A. C., Austria, L., Leivas, P., Moraes, J. A. R., & Witczak, M. (2022). Integration of industry 4.0 technologies with education 4.0: Advantages for improvements in learning. Interactive Technology and Smart Education. doi:10.1108/ITSE-11-2021-0201

Mystakidis, S. (2021). Deep meaningful learning. *Encyclopedia, 1*(3), 988–997. doi:10.3390/encyclopedia1030075

Mystakidis, S., Berki, E., & Valtanen, J. P. (2021). Deep and meaningful e-learning with social virtual reality environments in higher education: A systematic literature review. *Applied Sciences (Basel, Switzerland), 11*(5), 2412. doi:10.3390/app11052412

Neaga, I. (2019). Applying industry 4.0 and education 4.0 to engineering education. *Proceedings 2019 Canadian Engineering Education Association (CEEA-ACEG19) Conference*, 1-6. 10.24908/pceea.vi0.13859

Noh, S. C., & Abdul Karim, A. (2020). Design thinking mindset to enhance education 4.0 competitiveness in Malaysia. *International Journal of Evaluation and Research in Education, 2*(2), 490–501. doi:10.11591/ijere.v10i2.20988

Nowacka, A., & Rzemieniak, M. (2022). The impact of the VUCA environment on the digital competences of managers in the Power Industry. *Energies, 15*(1), 185. doi:10.3390/en15010185

OECD. (2019). *OECD future of education and skills 2030*. OECD Publishing.

Prifti, L., Knigge, M., Kienegger, H., & Krcmar, H. (2017). A competency model for “industrie 4.0” Employees. In J. M. Leimeister & W. Brenner (Eds.), Proceedings der 13. Internationalen Tagung Wirtschaftsinformatik (WI 2017) (pp. 46–60). Academic Press.

Rosseni, D., Mohamad, S. N., Norlide, A. K., Tunku, B., Tunku, A., Kamaruzaman, J., Nur, A. J., Muhammad, F. K. Z., Mohamad, S. Z., Mazalah, A., Aidah, A. K., & Khairul, A. M. (2010). Development and validation of meaningful hybrid e-training model for computer education. *International Journal of Computer Science and Information Technologies*, *1*(3), 179–184.

Sae-Lim, P., & Jermsittiparsert, K. (2019). Is the Fourth Industrial Revolution a Panacea? Risks toward the Fourth Industrial Revolution: Evidence in the Thai Economy. *International Journal of Innovation. Creativity and Change*, *5*(2), 732–752.

Salmon, G. (2019). May the fourth be with you: Creating education 4.0. *Journal of Learning for Development*, *6*(1), 95–115. doi:10.56059/jl4d.v6i2.352

Schultz, R. B., & DeMers, M. N. (2020). Transitioning from emergency remote learning to deep online learning experiences in Geography Education. *The Journal of Geography*, *119*(5), 142–146. doi:10.1080/00221341.2020.1813791

Shahini, F. (2021). *Distance education: Challenges and opportunities in a post-pandemic world. Case of Kosovo* [Thesis]. Rochester Institute of Technology. https://scholarworks.rit.edu/theses

Siemens, G. (2004). Connectivism: A learning theory for the digital age. *International Journal of Instructional Technology and Distance Learning, 2*. http://www.itdl.org/Journal/Jan_05/article01.htm

Siemens, G. (2012). *The future of higher education*. http://www.elearnspace.org/blog/2012/06/16/the-future-of-higher-education-and-other imponderables/

Srivani, V., Hariharasudan, A., Nawaz, N., & Ratajczak, S. (2022). Impact of education 4.0 among engineering students for learning English language. *PLoS One*, *17*(2), e0261717. doi:10.1371/journal.pone.0261717 PMID:35108282

Stone, P., Brooks, R., Brynjolfsson, E., Calo, R., Etzioni, O., Hager, G., Hirschberg, J., Kalyanakrishnan, S., Kamar, E., Kraus, S., Leyton-Brown, K., Parkes, D., Press, W., Saxenian, A., Shah, J., Tambe, M., & Teller, A. (2016). *Artificial intelligence and life in 2030: One-hundred-year study on artificial intelligence. Report of the 2015-2016 Study Panel*. Stanford University. https://ai100.stanford.edu/2016-report

Sukiman, H. (2022). The pattern of hybrid learning to maintain learning effectiveness at the higher education level post-COVID-19 pandemic. *European Journal of Educational Research*, *11*(1), 243–257. doi:10.12973/eu-jer.11.1.243

Suyaprom, S., & Manmee, T. (2018). Education Reform in Thailand 4.0: A True Story or a Soap Opera. *Asian Political Science Review*, *2*(2), 88–95.

Syazali, M., Putra, F., Rinaldi, A., Utami, L., Umam, W. R., & Jermsittiparsert, K. (2019). Partial Correlation Analysis Using Multiple Linear Regression: Impact on Business Environment of Digital Marketing Interest in the Era of Industrial Revolution 4.0. *Management Science Letters*, *9*(11), 1875–1886. doi:10.5267/j.msl.2019.6.005

United Nations Industrial Development Organisation. (2016). Industry 4.0: Opportunities and challenges of the new industrial revolution for developing countries and economies in transition. UNIDO.

Veile, J., Kiel, D., Müller, J. M., & Voigt, K. (2018). How to implement Industry 4.0. An empirical analysis of lessons learned from best practices. *International Association for Management of Technology IAMOT 2018 Conference Proceedings*, 1-24.

Velinova-Sokolova, N. (2021). Higher education and COVID-19 in conditions of Education 4.0. *International Scientific Journal "Industry 4.0"*, *5*(4), 165-168.

World Economic Forum. (2020). Schools of the future: Defining new models of education for the fourth industrial revolution. *Platform for Shaping the Future of the New Economy and Society*. https://www.weforum. org/platforms/shaping-the-future-of-the-new-economy-and-society

Yüceol, N. (2021). The steps to be taken in higher education for successful adaptation to industry 4.0. *Yükseköݤretim Dergisi, 11*(3), 563–577. doi:10.2399/yod.21.617715

# Chapter 9
# Merits of Six Hat Metaphors and Station Techniques for Project Management Skills in Online Courses:
## Learner Engagement to Online Courses

**Fahriye Altinay**
*Near East University, Cyprus*

**Mehmet Altinay**
*University of Kyrenia, Cyprus*

**Zehra Altinay**
*Near East University, Cyprus*

**Mutlu Soykurt**
*University of Kyrenia, Cyprus*

**Gokmen Daglı**
*University of Kyrenia, Cyprus*

## ABSTRACT

*Digital transformation has forced higher education institutions to adapt new models of education and learning. In pandemic times, higher education institutions have started to practice online learning experiences. In this respect, the time comes to consider the active learning in higher education by the merits of online learning environments. Experiences of graduate school students were examined on the use of six hats and station methods in online course activities. These experiences and thoughts were gathered through story-based reflections through reflection task. It is revealed that active learning in higher education models is possible by integrating different learning activities in the online context. Learners developed research and project management skills through personalized learning and collaborative learning. They gained the ability to look at topics from different angles and ability to accept criticism.*

DOI: 10.4018/978-1-6684-5400-8.ch009

## INTRODUCTION

World is changing due to health needs and protection. As adaptation requires change, the life styles and learning styles all have changed. Pandemic times have forced us to focus on new ways of learning and teaching at all levels of education. The use of online practices led to strategic innovation at higher education institutions in fostering quality in education services. In this respect, higher education institutions have started to become social agents to diffuse transformation in both social responsibilities for learners and technological innovations (Kaplan, Haenlein, 2016).

Higher education institutions play a great role to create a sense of online community by initiating online education. Online community is important in learning and teaching process by encapsulating motivation, student centered learning, interaction and social presence (Gray, Ulbrich, 2017). Making stories, scenarios in online learning and teaching experiences foster learner driven education based on specific, measurable, attainable, relevant and time based strategies as a smart policy.

Future of learning relies on strategic decisions of higher education with accepting the transformation and becoming social agents in process of adaptation. As a result, future of learning is becoming more active and personalized in online context. Therefore, changing roles of teachers as facilitators are crucial in providing qualified services in online learning. Connecting, informing, engaging, collaborating, contextualizing, personalizing and reflecting through assessment are key elements in order to give support to online learning (Zhao, 2003).

In higher education institutions, online learning requires personalized learning and process evaluation for adding meaningful learning and social involvement to the value of learning. Belonging is important in teaching and institutional support to provide student engagement for the personalized learning. In this respect, cultural, historical activity theory enhances the importance of engagement and personal learning and underlines the importance of activities based on gaining experiences while learning. Designing learning activities to foster skills and competences on online courses is crucial.Based on personalized learning and active learning process, using constructive teaching strategies lead to learning activities that make learners become more engaged to the course. Creating the learning context and activities that learners can explore, collaborate, connect, share and reflect is needed to foster merits of CHAT theory and social theory in online context (Foot, 2001). The open education resources and practices play a great role to internalize project based learning and engaging learning activities. Therefore, it is essential to use valuable assignments for adding value for the next time use. Giving only one assignment without any meaning is not helpful. Making learning meaningful relies on the learning activities and learning processes.

Learner driven education plays an important that active learning is essential to make learners become engaged to learning activities. In this respect, using methods of active learning such as group work, role play, etc in education are the heart of instruction and shows the art of teaching. In this respect, students' active involvement in the course can be enriched by learning activities. In online context, roles of teachers are managerial and also pedagogical. Therefore, creating variations in online learning activities enhance the richness of personalized learning in conducting student centered education in this digitalized active context (Dwivedi, Dwivedi, Bobek, and Sternad Zabukovšek, 2019; Brieger, Arghode, McLean, 2020).

Project management and method is a personalized learning method in education. It is a method that fosters the competences of learners by integrating different fields together. It gives insights on research in a scientific way (Becker, Kehoe, Tennent, 2007). In addition, it provides active learning opportunity within a personalized way and also process which is essential. Giving guidance to learning and voluntarism in selecting of a topic becomes crucial for acquiring collaboration, research within scientific process. It is accepted that projects foster meaningful and certain learning. It makes learners more active and also enhances students to engage more to the course. It can be seen that learners enrich abilities in computer and information management and in research skills (Robinson, Hullinger, 2008). Project management and development course is skills and competence based course that mainly leads to experiences while learning. The course has the nature of sequences and steps to merge with the theory and practice. It requires personalized learning. In this course, variation of learning activities is essential to make social involvement of learners in online context. In this respect, this research study aims to explore the use of six hats methods and station method in project management and development courses while improving project management and development within online learning process.

## Research Questions

*How does six hats method develop skills in online context?*

*How does station method develop skills in online context?*

*How do learners develop skills in project management and development by different learning activities in online context?*

## MATERIALS AND METHODS

This research paper reflects the nature of qualitative research design. Experiences, perceptions and values of context meanings were evaluated in this research study. In this respect, story based reflections through reflection task were used as data collection in order to explore experiences of learners in online context (Yıldırım, Simsek, 2011). Using learning activities and experiences of learners from those learning activities were examined in order to point out the gained experiences, skills and competences in online context while doing the project. Research process aims to determine the experiences based on learning activities. In this research six hats method was used to put learning into deeper thinking in the course content and share reflections within the collaborative learning context. Also, station method was used to increase the creativity in thinking from different angles. These two methods were used in online context and examination of skills and competences development in project management for the development of the course in online context. Purposive sampling was used in this research study and 13 graduate students were chosen as a study group from the project management and development courses. The learners are adult learners who have educational backgrounds and working as teachers at state schools. Collected data were analyzed based on thematic analysis (Miles, Huberman, 1994). Themes were categorized based on collected data that were obtained from the experiences and reflections of leaners in online learning process in relation to the use of six hats and station methods.

## RESULTS

Views on the application of six hat teaching technique under online context: Under this dimension the views of participants are on Table 1.

In online context, *one participant evaluated the views regarding the use of teaching six hat technique as "I think Six hat teaching technique is a method of teaching that enables scholars to look at cases from different angles" (G(2)),* One other participant with regard to this theme., *"Six hat is different from continuing with old habits in fact it leads to escape from old habits and gain different perspectives. That's why six hat technique can look emotional, creative, looking also to cases which are negative.cases, rationally, positive, impartial different and six hat technique contributes to look at things from different angles and is an strong technique'.. " (G:(4))* One other participant with regard to another theme said that this method helps to prevent each other to create obstacles on participants that have different views. Another participant with regard to this theme "With this approach, we can remove the obstacles between people that have different views." *(G:(8))* Another participant in relation to this theme. Six hat teaching technique is important with respect to sharing knowledge, leading us to direct work plan and take us to right knowledge "*six hat teaching technique leads also to division of labor and sharing of knowledge to get suggestions of others to put our studies into right direction. This*

*Table 1. Views on use and application of six hat technique*

| Themes | Frequencies | Percentage |
|---|---|---|
| Importance of six hat technique in labor division and getting access to sharing knowledge and getting suggestions to direct us to right information | 13 | 100% |
| Six hat technique is better, more productive and in our projects its contribution to science is more useful | 6 | 46% |
| It directs to reach all colors and helps us to think | 8 | 61% |
| There is a need in every research for all and all kinds of ideas and thinking for development | 9 | 69% |
| Six hat technique helps to capture and be aware of problems missed and gives room for correction and leads to right result | 10 | 76% |
| Six hat teaching technique is a method that helps to look at cases from different angles | 5 | 38% |
| It helps people to get away from their traditional thinking and gain different angles and ways of thinking. | 6 | 46% |
| One can look at cases more rational, positive, neutral, emotional, with feelings, creative,with negative perspectives,producing solutions using six hat learning technique. | 7 | 53% |
| | 12 | 92% |

*technique and in all others every study needs support. Six hat technique is a very useful technique for all studies.*

Regarding to the contribution to science, six hat teaching technique is important with regard to division of work and knowledge sharing Taking the suggestions of others in this teaching technique enables the scholars to get access to the correct and accurate information to put their studies in the right direction. In every research there is need for support. In order to make our studies better and productive and contribute more to science six hat teaching technique is very helpful as stated by the researcher" (G(9)) .

*One participant expressed his view as "Station management, requires that all class has to work at all stages at the station to contribute to the work done before and take the group a step forward. and complete the semi-finished and teaches to complete the unfinished task" (G(5)).One other participant related with this theme. "Stations in brief enable students to achieve their different learning activities at the same time.* Learning stations develop class discussions and help for independent studies. I want to express that in this approach teachers and students are the determining factors." *(G:(4))* One other participant with regard to this theme said that., *"Students according to their readiness, they became active to share different reflections.*

*Table 2. Views on using station management technique in online context*

| Themes | Frequency | Percentage |
|---|---|---|
| Station technique is very rich and goes to far back to history of literature | 6 | 46% |
| Similar to a study under consideration or discovering the working title and to what extend it had been studied. | 8 | 61% |
| Even the topics which are under study there will be someone at every station who will want to take this information to another station by looking at to the missing information or someone who will want to add more information | 13 | 100% |
| Like a flag competition having the information and contributing to the literature and handing over to the other person coming next. All class | 7 | 53% |
| working at all stages of the station contribute to the work of the group to move one step ahead and complete the unfinished task | 11 | 84% |
| To maintain that all students complete their different learning activities at the same time | 6 | 46% |
| Learning stations help and develop class discussions using independent studies | 9 | 69% |
| Students become ready using station approach according to different learning tasks and activities and prevent loss of time | 5 | 38% |
| Using this approach contributes to students to teach and learn and prepare their projects related with the topic. | 7 | 53% |

*Table 3. Views on under online circumstances: Project management process and skills development*

| Themes | Frequency | Percentage |
|---|---|---|
| Using these approaches, feeling of curiosity develops and lead to a project and this is an important factor to start work | 11 | 84% |
| Before starting a project one can see why this project had not been realized | 10 | 76% |
| These approaches as in project management contribute to take risk and develop new ideas | 8 | 61% |
| The other important point that these approaches contribute in the process of project management is the realization to focus | 6 | 46% |
| In the process of development of new ideas with these approaches fixing, institutional or personal goals and project management can be developed | 7 | 53% |
| With these approaches risk in project management can be reduced to minimum | 13 | 100% |
| Application of these approaches in project management process leads to production of successful projects, sharing of interesting ideas, detecting risks and contribute to acquire different perspectives | 9 | 69% |

Project management and skills development in online context.

One participant expressed views on, project management process and level, skills development, we, the users of these approaches our curiosity and feelings. In fact, this feeling should exist and is essential before starting to work before starting the project. Because, before starting we have to ask why was this project had not been achieved. If it was possible you could start the project with your curiosity" G(6). Another participant with regard to this theme thinks that with these approaches, there should be questioning, freedom to express thoughts, demonstration of creativity and free communication.

In Project management one takes risk and produces new ideas. These approaches, in the process of project management contributed to me to focus. While applying and focusing on approaches, we are learning to focus on project management." G(3). Another participant regarding this theme said that, "Starting with the ideas and approaches submitted by friends I can decide on my institutional and personal goals and I can develop new ideas on this project management process. On the other hand discussion on risk factors on project management helped to find the right way and minimized risk factors (G:(9). Another participant with regard to this theme thinks that "When using these approaches there should be questioning, freedom to express thoughts, demonstration of creativity and existence of free communication in the process which will all lead to total success. Projects can be achieved by applying all these approaches in project management processes that will lead to production of successful projects, sharing of interesting ideas, detecting risks and contribute to learn to look at things from different angles (G(2).

## DISCUSSION AND CONCLUSION

Project management is self-regulated learning which needs collaboration and exchange of ideas in concluding each part of the project. In this respect, facilitating the merits of online learning and learning activities is very crucial to upgrade the skills. Online learning activities foster variations in learning and makes learners more involved to the course contents. With this stance, learners learn how to learn actively (Altınay, Altınay, Dagli, Altınay, 2018)

In this research, graduate students actively participated in project management course and they developed project based learning activities in online context. Exchange of ideas from different angles were gained from six hats method and station method. With these two methods, graduate students discussed deeply their projects and shape their project activities in a collaborative way. In addition, they enhanced their self-learning and they gained the skills of research, time management, task management and knowledge management. Graduate students enhanced their abilities to discuss issues in online context by practicing collegiality as critical friends in online learning.

In online context, participants enhanced the skills of teamwork and collaboration. Participants experienced the common decision making while learning through six hats technique. Also, they learnt to respect the views of others. They studied productively within collaboration and they considered needs of group members in order to explore good research theme for their peers. All of them became innovative and they gained the ability of making constructive criticism based on assigning themselves as leaders. In this learning process, they experienced collaboration learning and supportive learning.

This research study revealed that online learning activities by using alternative teaching methods developed abilities of learners and enhanced their competences in research and motivation for learning in an active manner. In addition, this research sheds a light to put insights on how online learning enhances project management process by using six hats methods and station. Story based reflections and also ideas that were reflected from colors enhanced creativity of learners in an active manner (Sozudogru, Altinay, Dagli, Altinay, 2019). In addition, these online learning experiences developed work based learning experiences of adult learners and enhanced their professional developments (Hoffman, Leafstedt, 2014; Quinn, Shurville, McNamara, Brown, 2009). Research participants reflected that they gained new insights from online learning process and also this way of learning engagement opened ways for their professional area to create new ideas and practices in their working contexts. Time is to consider details by creating own stories as becoming part of smart policy for adding value. The online learning experiences and stories become model of active learning in higher education.

## ACKNOWLEDGMENT

Thanks too much research participants for this good experience.

## REFERENCES

Altınay, F., Altınay, M., Dagli, G., & Altınay, Z. (2018). Being leader in global citizenship at the information technology age". *Quality & Quantity*, *52*(1), 31–42. doi:10.100711135-017-0585-5

Becker, K., Kehoe, J., & Tennent, B. (2007). Impact of personalised learning styles on online delivery and assessment. *Campus-Wide Information Systems, 24*(2), 105–119. doi:10.1108/10650740710742718

Brieger, E., Arghode, V., & McLean, G. (2020). Connecting theory and practice: Reviewing six learning theories to inform online instruction. *European Journal of Training and Development, 27*(5), 1843–1860. doi:10.1108/EJTD-07-2019-0116

Dwivedi, A., Dwivedi, P., Bobek, S., & Sternad Zabukovšek, S. (2019). Factors affecting students' engagement with online content in blended learning. *Kybernetes, 48*(7), 1500–1515. doi:10.1108/K-10-2018-0559

Foot, K. A. (2001). Cultural-historical activity theory as practice theory: Illuminating the development of a conflict-monitoring network. *Communication Theory, 11*(1), 56–83. doi:10.1111/j.1468-2885.2001.tb00233.x

Gray, K., & Ulbrich, F. (2017). Ambiguity acceptance and translation skills in the project management literature. *International Journal of Managing Projects in Business, 10*(2), 423–450. doi:10.1108/IJMPB-05-2016-0044

Hoffman, J., & Leafstedt, J. (2014). Understanding the Use of Technology for Facilitating Inquiry-Based Learning. *Inquiry-based Learning for Faculty and Institutional Development: A Conceptual and Practical Resource for Educators (Innovations in Higher Education Teaching and Learning, 1*, 421-437. doi:10.1108/S2055-364120140000001021

Kaplan, A. M., & Haenlein, M. (2016). Higher education and the digital revolution: About MOOCs, SPOCs, social media, and the Cookie Monster. *Business Horizons, 59*(4), 441–450. doi:10.1016/j.bushor.2016.03.008

Miles, M. B., & Huberman, A. M. (1994). *Qualitative Data Analysis: An Expanded Sourcebook* (2nd ed.). Sage.

Quinn, D., Shurville, S., McNamara, J., & Brown, C. (2009). Assessment of online discussion in work-integrated learning. *Campus-Wide Information Systems, 26*(5), 413–423. doi:10.1108/10650740911004822

Robinson, C. C., & Hullinger, H. (2008). New Benchmarks in Higher Education: Student Engagement in Online Learning. *Journal of Education for Business, 84*(2), 101–109. doi:10.3200/JOEB.84.2.101-109

Sozudogru, O., Altinay, M., Dagli, G., Altinay, F., & Altinay, F. (2019). Examination of connectivist theory in English language learning: The role of online social networking tool. *The International Journal of Information and Learning Technology*, *36*(4), 354–363. Advance online publication. doi:10.1108/IJILT-02-2019-0018

Yıldırım, A., & Şimşek, H. (2011). Sosyal Bilimlerde Nitel Araştirma Yöntemleri. Seçkin Yayınevi.

Zhao, F. (2003). Enhancing the quality of online higher education through measurement. *Quality Assurance in Education*, *11*(4), 214–221. doi:10.1108/09684880310501395

# Chapter 10
# Actual Practicum Course vs. Virtual Living Lab in Tourism Education:
## Alike and Unlike at Once

**Aniesa Samira Bafadhal**
https://orcid.org/0000-0002-5666-0660
*Brawijaya University, Indonesia*

**Muhammad Rosyihan Hendrawan**
https://orcid.org/0000-0003-0438-2571
*Brawijaya University, Indonesia*

## ABSTRACT

*As part of the curriculum at the Department of Tourism, Brawijaya University, Malang City, Indonesia, the authors are conducting a virtual tourism course to understand the interrelation of virtual reality (VR) and augmented reality (AR) in the tourism and hospitality fields. Moreover, this course also included practicums to create and use varied, immersive systems such as Web-VR, 3D VR, Multiplayer 3D VR, Marker-Based AR, and Marker-Less AR content in the context of tourism business etiquette and procedures as a virtual tour guide. In continuation, under the coordination of the tourism laboratory, they initiated a virtual living lab together with students and stakeholders that focus on strengthening Malang's City identity as a heritage city by using AR/VR technologies. Therefore, this chapter aims to define and recognise basic insights of the concept, types, and characteristics of remote practicum methods. Specifically, this review also describes with examples required equipment and best practice software and explains the advantages and limitations that may occur.*

DOI: 10.4018/978-1-6684-5400-8.ch010

## INTRODUCTION

Covid-19 outbreak prevalence has devastated higher education institutions to temporarily suspend conventional in-class lectures and practice-based courses, thus transforming them into online platforms. This most significant and unprecedented disruption of education systems in human history indeed brought numerous challenges (United Nations, 2021). The required sweeping changes in curricula, pedagogy, and the learning space have occurred in this ongoing global uncertainty. Yet new forms of face-to-face learning and practice emerged in this long hiatus. As the virtual world, known as "metaverse," began to be introduced into present life rapidly, a low-cost and convenient virtual equipment, user-friendly metaverse software, is becoming more and more commonly used in education (Kye et al., 2021). Metaverse is a collaborative virtual reality environment facilitated by a persistent computer network where multiple users appear to be present and explore graphical representations, gain immersive experiences with objects, and interact socially in real-time for work, leisure, or education purposes (Bafadhal, 2020).

Based on the wisdom of Confucius, who said, "Not hearing is not as good as hearing, hearing is not as good as seeing, seeing is not as good as knowing, knowing is not as good as acting; true learning continues until it is put into action," that makes the practical part of education must be a priority. The successful adjustment of virtual tools into the tourism curriculum, practicum, and fieldwork project provides better learning of the application of virtual technologies. Students need to be aware of not merely the aspects of knowledge enrichment along with improving digital skills; they also need to use them to get better prepared for their future careers.

The pandemic continues to strike hard on Indonesian tourism, leading to leisure and hospitality workers suffering through inevitable layoffs. Unfortunately, most tourism labor in Indonesia has an inadequately educated and well-trained workforce, and rarely have they graduated from suitable higher education institutions. In turn, this has consequences for tourism post-pandemic recovery. Even more, in this challenging time, the lack of practical application of theory and technologies such as in internship courses (Park & Jones, 2021), field trips (Benckendorff et al., 2019), and practicum (Lieberman et al., 2022) will cause the students not obtain an active learning environment and stagnancy of students' technological literacy which lead to decreased self-efficacy, reduced competitive advantage of graduates in the labor market and tended to prepare-less for this ever-changing industry.

Hence, to cope with such needs for practical and off-site field learning, an interactive virtual learning platform is necessary for transforming the crisis of teaching-learning into an innovative opportunity for tourism education. Increasing ubiquitous technologies allow our bodies to keep at home but cultivate cognitive, technical, and social skills just at the click of the mouse or swipe of the screen, thus making learning contiguous, continuous, and omnipresent at the same time. The value of education cannot be merely measured through the teaching-learning material inside the walls, but anything spread out to bring life to learning by stimulating students to develop lifelong learners anywhere. Hence, practicum learning that was initially in the laboratory can be applied at home (Kirkman et al., 2002) or even everywhere. Bafadhal & Hendrawan (2021a) reviewed the existing and potential exploitation of Virtual Reality (VR) and Augmented Reality (AR) in Serious Game that offers an interactive, entertaining, educational and alternative way to learn different aspects of a destination, thus can be presented as an essential learning space complement or temporary substitution through "learn from home." Moreover, when "learning from home" is becoming unavoidable in a world of uncertainty and fast-changing socio-political circumstances, more of such virtual and online platforms are regarded as sustainable to be applied across disciplines, courses, and over a long period of teaching time (Hales & Jennings, 2017).

Hughes & Moshell (1997) states that graduates are expected to be responsive to the development of metaverse technology; they suggested that metaverse technologies should be included in the curriculum for theoretical and practical courses in school-based education. The teaching concept should be updated constantly, and with VR/AR, educators can effectively improve enthusiasm in learning and make up for the shortages of traditional teaching. Hence, metaverse allows educators to develop a curriculum integrated with cutting-edge technologies such as VR/AR in STEM subjects and social sciences.

Young learners have been studied in immersive virtual environments, such as The Narrative Immersive Constructionist/Collaborative Environments (NICE) project by using CAVE (Roussos et al., 1999) and Virtual Playground (Roussou et al., 2006). An introductory undergraduate VR course is presented by Stansfield (2005) on a Computer Science curriculum. Generally, the virtual reality practical course is designed for students on STEM subjects such as Häfner et al., (2013) in an engineering course, Cliburn (2006) in computer graphics and Bortnik et al., (2017) in a chemistry laboratory, Yen et al., (2013) in astronomy and Izard et al., (2017) in medical education, Akçayır et al., (2016) in science laboratories.

However, in its development, the virtual environment is also used in social science and behavioral subjects such as art courses (Zimmerman & Eber, 2001), linguistics courses (Xie et al., 2022), and business ethics courses (Sholihin et al., 2020). The form of virtual learning is not something new in the tourism and hospitality field, for example, in hospitality education. Interactive games such as Cesim Hospitality, HOTS Hotel, and DECA Virtual Business Hotel are widely utilized by education students of the hotel school (Poulova et al., 2020). Penfold (2009) states that Virtel is a virtual hotel e-simulation developed by The Hong Kong Polytechnic University, an active learning tool that helps students face realistic workplace situations for pre-internship preparation or industrial placement preparation. In addition, a virtual field trip of The Hong Kong Polytechnic University students in a virtual hotel has also been developed using the Second Life metaverse (Penfold, 2009).

As part of our curriculum at the Department of Tourism, Brawijaya University, Malang City, Indonesia, we are conducting a Virtual Tourism course to understand the interrelation of VR/AR in the tourism and hospitality fields. This course is structured as an essential introduction to the study and management of virtual tourism based on VR/AR, starting from the basic concepts of virtual tourism, the introduction of tele-tourists as virtual tourism actors, virtual destinations (such as virtual hotels and virtual museum), the necessary system components and various benefits and challenges in implement virtual tourism. Bafadhal (2020) states that virtual tourism refers to the application of virtual reality technology or its derivatives to tourism and hospitality destinations that form a virtual environment that replicates existing goals or synthetically created imaginations in the form of 360° video/photo spherical or 3D or n-D animation where tele-tourists using graphic representations can appear as if they can explore and interact with each other in it and get a virtual experience before, during, after and with or without visiting the actual destination for planning, business, preservation or tourism education.

Moreover, this Virtual Tourism course also included practicums to create and use various immersive systems such as Web-VR, Mobile VR, 3D VR, Multiplayer 3D VR, Web-AR, Marker-based AR, and Marker-less AR content in the context of the tourism business and also etiquette and procedures as a virtual tour guide. Therefore, this paper aims to define and recognize essential insights into the concept, types, and characteristics of practicum methods through the AR/VR platform in tourism educational applications that have been already implemented in our virtual tourism practicum course based on various immersive system categories namely non-immersive, low-immersive, semi-immersive and fully-immersive virtual tourism derived from Beck et al. (2019). Specifically, this review also describes examples, required equipment, best practice software, and the advantages and limitations that may occur, as shown in Table 1.

Few computer users make a lifestyle (or identity) of being someone who uses computers (Grudin, 1993) and generally, people can "own" or inhabit their virtual bodies (Chalmers, 2022) called "Avatar" (Burdea & Coiffet, 2003), "player" (Dibbell, 1998), "personas" (Cooper & Reimann, 2003), "digital persona" (Kerckhove, 1995), "virtual representatives" (Zhou et al. 2014), embodied virtuality" (Weiser, 1991) or "personal virtual identities" (Munar, 2010). Students always have access to virtual objects such as a phone, fax, a reservation book, computers, and documents internal to the hotel (regulations, menu, price lists, tourist information, etc.). The students interact using Avatars that play different roles (customers, travel agents, taxi drivers, etc.) (Segond et al., 2005).

*Table 1. Virtual Tourism Practicums Course*

| No. | Characteristics | Practicum Types | | | | | | |
|---|---|---|---|---|---|---|---|---|
| | | Virtual Reality (VR) | | | | Augmented Reality (AR) | | |
| | | Web-VR | Mobile-VR | 3D VR | Multiplayer 3D VR | Web-AR | Marker-based AR | Marker-less AR |
| 1 | User Hardware | Computer/Laptop &/ Big Screen | Smartphone & VR devices, | Computer/Laptop | Computer/Laptop & VR devices | Computer/Laptop &/ Tablet | Smart phone | Smart phone &/ AR devices |
| 2 | Software | A-Frame | A-Frame | Millealab | Millealab | Assemblr | Unity | Assemblr |
| 3 | Advantages | Open Source | Open Source | No Coding; Drag and Drop virtual assets; Create virtual classes; quizzes with assessment; | No Coding; Drag and Drop virtual assets; Create virtual classes; quizzes with assessment; | No Coding; Drag and Drop virtual assets; Create virtual classes; no need to download the viewer application, | Open Source; Create a customized virtual item | No Coding; Drag and Drop virtual assets; Create virtual classes; quizzes with assessment. |
| 4 | Limitation | Complex coding | Complex coding | Accessible to Play &/ Freemium; You Need to download the viewer application, | Accessible to Play &/ Freemium; You Need to download the viewer application, | Accessible to Play &/ Freemium | Complex coding | Accessible to Play &/ Freemium; You Need to download the viewer application, |
| 3 | Immersion Level | Semi Immersive | Semi Immersive | Non-Immersive | Fully Immersive | Semi-Immersive | Non-Immersive | Fully Immersive |
| 4 | Simulation Types | Linier | Linier | Open Ended | Massive Online | Linier | Linier | Massive Online |
| 5 | Interaction | One to One | One to One | One to Many | One to Many | One to Many | One to One | One to Many |
| 6 | Content Form | Mostly 360° photos/videos with VR tech | Mostly 360° pictures/videos with VR tech | Primarily 2D/3D/4D with VR tech, 360° photos/videos with VR tech; | Especially 2D/3D/4D with VR tech, 360° pictures/videos with VR tech; | Especially 2D/3D/4D with AR tech | Especially 2D/3D/4D with AR tech | Especially 2D/3D/4D with AR tech |
| 7 | Access | Online | Online | Online | Online | Online or On-site | On-site | Online or On-site |

Virtual Reality (VR) is a technology created to affect the user experience so that it feels as if it enters/blends/exists in the virtual world so that the real world is temporarily forgotten/replaced. Virtual Reality Tourism Practicum is "*a part of education communication channels which can generally be accessed based on website or mobile, that provides a complete picture of the real-life employee task that can be displayed in realistic environment settings to certain the point of interest of the destination or virtual class using visual information formats with a combination of animation 3D/4D-panoramas, 360° photo galleries and videos that allowed the Avatar of the student to navigate and obtain the feeling of being there that offers a more efficient information gathering process, create an immersive user experience, and can potentially implement and planned properly for wide-ranging marketing and new customer service opportunities such as educational tools*". We have introduced materials and conducted remote practicum on VR-based virtual tourism courses for our students, especially in Web-VR, Mobile VR, 3D VR, and Multiplayer 3D VR.

a) Web-Based VR (Web-VR) Practicum is "web technology has enabled many tourism educational institutions to offer VR tours. Students as users of this website can move a mouse to see 360°angle photos or video views of the various parts of the learning environment or destination, including its interior and exterior. Web-VR only can be used online by accessing the institution's website. Users of this VR website can move a mouse to see 360° angle views of the various parts of the destination or virtual class/lab". As shown in Figure 1, student practicum work in Kajoetangan Heritage Village, Malang City, using A-Frame software (https://bit.ly/kajoetangan-kh).

b) Mobile-Basedsed VR Practicum "*is remote access destination or virtual class with 360° angle photos/videos views by using mobile devices such as smartphones, tablets, or smartwatches and downloadable apps that could bring VR to learning environment such as virtual destination/lab/class that can be used both online and on-site as direct downloads or via established digital distribution channels (e.g., Google Play Store, Apple Store)*". As shown in Figure 2, student practicum work in Brawijaya Military Museum, Malang City using A-Frame software (https://museum-brawijaya.glitch.me/)

## Brawijaya Military Museum, Malang City

c) 3D VR Practicum is "*a form of replicating the actual class/lab/destination design and management through a 3D graphical user interface which provides a platform for real-time social interaction and entertainment that can be described as more of an extension of class/destination life-like reality that realizes realistic display of virtual environment, network information, study, services, and simulation*". As shown in Figure 3. We build a 3D replica of the Cor Jesu Heritage Building of Malang City using the Millealab application so that students can explore its architecture, attraction, icons, and history.

d) Multiplayer 3D VR Practicum is "*a 3D virtual simulation of lab/class/destination which can only be accessed via social Metaverse by the student using their Avatar where they can carry out the task, competition, collaboration, attended lecturing, doing homework or quiz and spend time and interact with one another, and using the virtual item so that provides features that can only be used, consumed and have value inside the virtual world*". As shown in Figure 4. We build a 3D replica of the Balekambang Beach with Heritage Temple in

Malang City using the Millealab application so that students can get lecturing and do some tour guide tasks and so on.

*Figure 1. Web VR Practicum: Kajoetangan Heritage Village, Malang City*

*Figure 2. Mobile Based VR Practicum*

*Figure 3. 3D VR Practicum: Cor Jesu Heritage Building, Malang City*

## Heritage Temple, Malang City

Augmented Reality (AR) is adding a virtual layer which can be an image, 2D/3D, textual information, video, or other virtual elements to the real world that already exists in real-time so that it is as if the virtual world objects enter/blend/present into the world real. Azuma (1997) proposed the first definition of AR by identifying the three main elements that characterize it: the combination of natural and virtual elements, real-time interaction, and the reproduction of content/elements in 3D. Augmented Reality Tourism Practicum is "*the use of AR technologies in tourism and hospitality business that can add-on reality experience in which real and virtual elements coexisted in the same place both online or on-site visit, for the purposes to make exploring the class/lab or destination area is more enjoyable and obtaining a wealth of information by using several applications inside the computer, portable devices, mobile devices (e.g., smartphones, tablets, and AR glasses) by permitting an interaction in real-time and displaying elements in 3D both marker-based or marker-less AR"*. We have also introduced materials and conducted remote practicum on AR-based virtual tourism courses for our students, especially in Web-AR, Marker-based AR, and Marker-less AR.

a) Web-Based AR Practicum "permits students at prior visit to have an immersive experience while seated in front of their computer/laptop so via web student can use 3D object form to scan and track present virtual objects to the real world". As seen in Figure 5. Students make the Singosari Temple in Malang City using the AR web by Assemblr application, which is more informative and interactive, such as virtual guide sound and video (http://asblr.com/86dYa).

*Figure 4. Multiplayer 3D VR Practicum: Balekambang Beach*

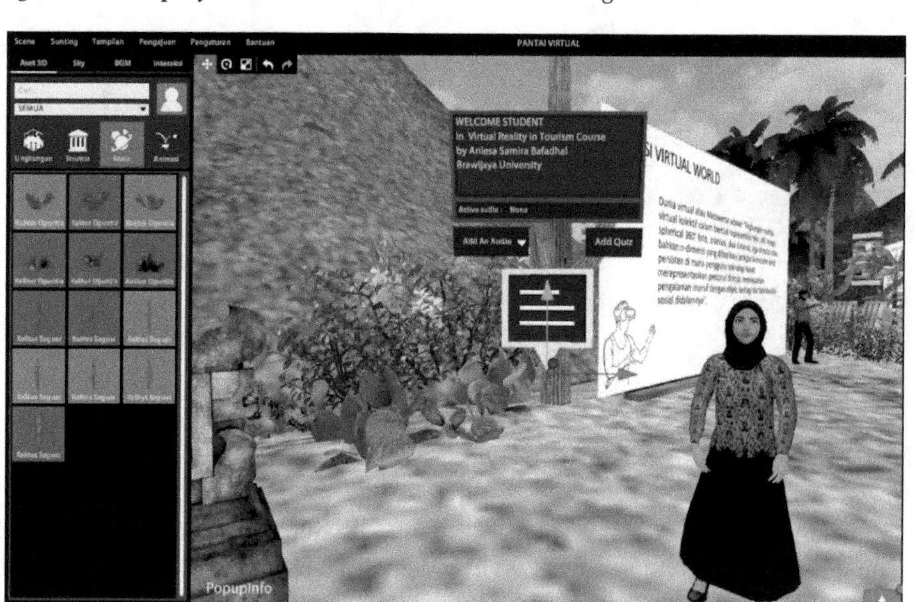


b) Marker-Based AR Practicum is "an AR usage through a handheld device (e.g., smartphone, camera, and tablet), marker AR applications permit students to explore the surrounding area and get an added experience and a richness of information when accessing hotel magazines, restaurant menu books, destination promotion pamphlets embedded with established AR marker and can be accessed in various parts of the on-site class/lab/real destination." As shown in Figure 7, our student-created Bromo Tengger Semeru Mountain destination booklet using embedded marker-based AR by Unity (https://bit.ly/markerbased)

*Figure 5. Web-AR Practicum: Singosari Temple, Malang City*

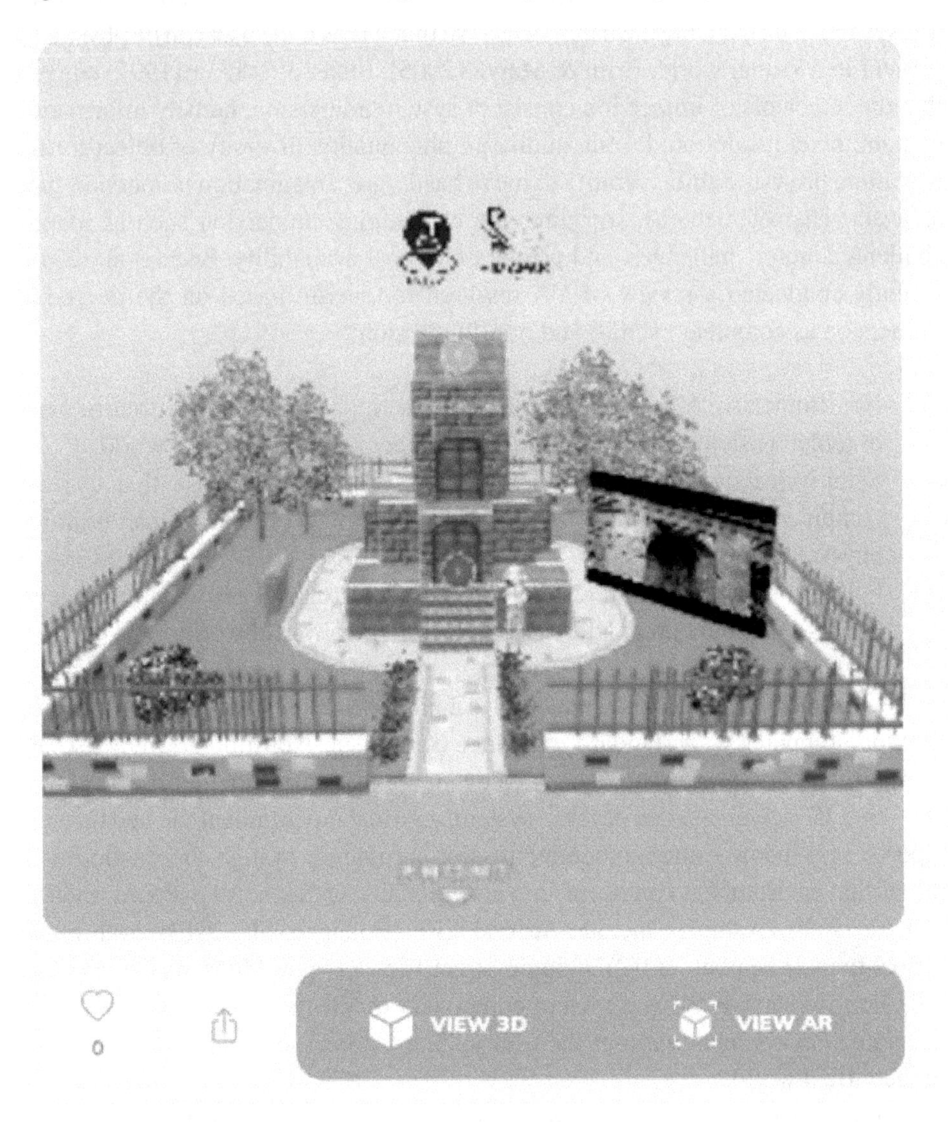


Markerless AR Practicum. "AR that has been increasingly interested in using various AR applications in the in-class learning and experience through markerless AR. Students can use this AR learning material by accessing the online or on-site class/lab/destination/or everywhere to get additional information about the destination or lecturing or as a part of edutainment. As shown in Figure 7. We made a 3D replica of the Brawijaya Military Museum tank collection using the Assemblr application (https://bit.ly/markerless).

Immersion refers to the objective level of sensory performance provided by the VR system in influencing the user's senses so that it is as if the user can be physically present in a virtual world. Ermi & Mäyrä (2005); Slater & Wilbur (1997) suggest that the indicators of immersion consist of system immersion, namely information content, pixel resolution, layout, audio, graphic quality, diversity of object forms, narration, browsing ability, ability to move head/view, Imagination immersion such as avatar character, theme, storyline and challenging immersion such as mental challenge, motor challenges, and primary end goal availability. Beck et al. (2019) recently conducted a review of VR research in tourism based on the degree of immersion as complete-, semi-, and non-immersion:

a) Non-immersive VR tour technological systems (e.g., those use smartphones or tablets) users have a low degree of contact with the physical world,
b) Semi-immersive VR tour technological systems (e.g., those that use big computer screens or projectors) users have some degree of contact with the physical world,
c) Fully-immersive VR tour technological systems (e.g., head-mounted devices, HMDs), users are completely isolated from the physical world.

Non-immersive VR implements VR techniques that only rely on the web on a desktop computer with standard computer equipment. Non-immersive VR (VR) displays content shot at a natural or synthetic (non-existent) destination and displayed 360° on a PC screen using a desktop system, a virtual environment viewed through a portal or window using a moderate resolution monitor to high. Interaction with the virtual environment can occur in conventional ways such as keyboard, mouse, and trackball. Examples include Second Life (Huang et al., 2013), web-based virtual tours (Lee et al., 2012), Google Street View/Google Maps, or Google AR/VR. Non-immersive VR is a system component in VR that provides a computer-generated environment without the user feeling wholly isolated and fully present in the virtual world.

Semi-immersive VR is a relatively new implementation of VR technology and borrows heavily from technology developed in in-flight/military simulation using multiple screens. Semi-immersive VR projecting content displays content that is captured on a natural or synthetic (non-existent) destination and displayed 360° onto a large screen monitor, concave screen, projector or display walls, or multiple projections to produce with a wide field of view, this system enhances the feelings of telepresence and immersion experienced by the user and enables a multi-user virtual travel experience. Example of CAVE (Carrozzino & Bergamasco, 2010). Semi-immersive VR is a type of system component in VR that is more similar to a

*Figure 6. Marker Based AR Practicum: Bromo Tengger Semeru Mountain*

widescreen movie experience so that it is enough to give the feeling of being present in a virtual world.

Fully-immersive VR is the most widely known VR implementation where users use Head-Mounted Displays (HMDs) or Gesture Control Devices to visit virtual destinations. Fully-immersive VR isolates the user entirely from the real world by providing content that is shot at a natural or synthetic (non-existent) destination

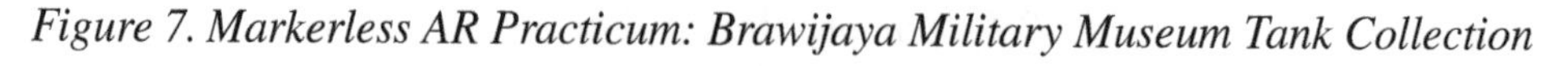

*Figure 7. Markerless AR Practicum: Brawijaya Military Museum Tank Collection*

and rendered 360° using a VR headset gear, facilitating complete visual immersion, and allowing virtual tourism experiences that have the potential to stimulate the visual senses and other senses of users. Tussyadiah et al. (2018) grouped three types of VR headsets: 1). A wired HMD, such as the Oculus Rift or HTC Vive; 2). Wireless HMDs, such as the Samsung Gear VR; and 3). Low Immersion HMD, like Google Cardboard; 4) can also be equipped with Gesture Control Devices such as the Oculus Touch. Fully Immersive VR is a system component in virtual reality technology that allows users to ideally experience an artificial virtual environment as if it were the real world.

Furthermore, the VR/AR functions are established not only to cope with the unavailability of face-to-face teaching, and on-site field experience poses many exciting opportunities. Virtual environments allow collaborative learning space that facilitates and encourages students and other parties to work together about specific issues or problems. In this context, digital technologies that support significant connection and communication among different stakeholders within destination networks and markets should be considered crucial for business accomplishment

(Law et al., 2014). Therefore, they help promote contextual learning and interaction with actual problematic circumstances, actors and conditions.

In continuation, under the coordination of the Tourism Laboratory, we initiated a Virtual Living Lab together with students and stakeholders that focus on strengthening Malang City identity as a Heritage City by using the virtual environment platform. Virtual laboratories are one of the most common aids to overcoming problems encountered in various learning situations by resembling a natural laboratory (Wästber et al., 2019). Unfortunately, the mechanisms in traditional virtual laboratories generally cannot meet the challenge of addressing real-life problems and needs because they "merely" serve as isolated testbeds with restricted access to students and lecturers only. Thus, the living labs network approach attempts to meet that challenge (De Leon et al., 2008). Furthermore, a living lab is a platform for all stakeholders from Public-Private-People Partnership (PPPP), such as practitioners, academicians, and other communities, wherein the initial stage of the innovation process to co-creation for planning, prototyping, validation, and testing of new products, system or concept to generated beneficial innovation (Beutel et al., 2017). This constructive alignment principle ensues from early curriculum design to implementation and aligns graduate attributes with the needs of employers. Moreover, assessments must also be constructively aligned with intended learning outcomes (Stefani, 2009).

In terms of territorial context, the living lab can take the form of a physical area or virtual reality (Westerlund & Leminen, 2011). The continuum of physical, social, and virtual spaces within the living lab also enables us to reach a larger society (Veeckman & Van Der Graaf, 2015). Geography-based activities, such as the living labs in the tourism industry, can provide areas of consultation and cooperation, such as official administrative spaces or meeting rooms, or virtual community spaces where people will be in physical proximity or virtual proximity. The correlation between physical and virtual is often referred to as "two sides of the same coin," whereas they are considered two parts of the same thing, which is "reality" (Hendrawan & Bafadhal, 2022). A virtual learning space should not be viewed as a competitor to a physical learning space. The assimilation of the material and the virtual environment will reinforce each other (Bafadhal & Hendrawan, 2021b). Higher education providers shall make such technological adjustments to encourage many types of practicum ideas that arise (Orr et al., 2018).

Bafadhal (2021b) argues that the virtual tourism living lab is a learning and open innovation space that involves the co-creation of a virtual network for R&D of products, services, systems, technologies, or innovative concepts in the broad sector where local governments can provide policies and have the authority to help formal funding and legal. Communities can provide information on local contexts, and business managers can develop virtual content the coordination with academics;

consumers can engage in content testing and collectively improve through feedback from local communities.

Penfold (2009) suggested there are three types of virtual education simulations – linear, open-ended, and massive online and each has its strengths and weaknesses and a primary purpose or outcome:

a) The linear approach of virtual education is suitable for some basic skills training. For more advanced skills like analytical and interpersonal skills.
b) An open-ended approach would be more effective. Virtual education provides isolated events learning.
c) It can be further improved to allow system thinking with interrelated events and situations in a massive online approach. This is more closely related to a real-world scenario. A vast online environment also facilitates peer learning through knowledge distribution.

Virtual tourism living lab is "*an immersive virtual laboratory/classroom environment in the form of 3D VR or its derivatives which can be accessed in a linear, cyclical or massive online approach that helps lecturers, students or other professionals to provide realistic work-life settings, and provides challenges, illustrations, scenarios that allow or student to practice real-life tourism tasks, including problem-solving, customer relations, interpersonal skills and operational procedures that serve as virtual lab test grounds to build mockups of their new concepts, policies, designs and prototypes as well as ad complements or additional learning experiences in tourism education, planning, management and evaluation of learning outcome*".

Furthermore, the effectiveness of the Virtual Living Lab's mechanism and remote collaboration amid the pandemic as a proxy for face-to-face practicum courses are presented. Living lab in several studies has helped destination managers increase tourists' attractiveness (Cigir, 2018). Malang City in Indonesia is well-known as "Paris van Oost Java" as it has the best colonial city planning in the era of the Dutch East Indies in the early 20th century. Malang City Government has made efforts to bring back the legacy by determining and branding Malang City as a Heritage City (Bafadhal, 2021a). This claim must be proven before it can be said to be a success. Our initiative prototyping Malang Heritage City into a virtual living lab setting is expected to increase the value of the tourism experience concretely by encouraging higher interaction between actors, co-creation, and personalization (Neuhofer et al., 2015). This promotes a more structured and meaningful approach to learning for students as they can see the practical relevance of their learning (Benckendorff et al., 2019). The management of tourist destinations that double as cultural heritage sites and residents' homes face several problems that must be addressed together because it is feared that if it is not immediately addressed, the branding of Malang City as a Heritage City will only become a short-lived cultural euphoria.

First, some of the problems that can be identified are the problem of privacy and the dualism of the function of space in the houses of residents. The colonial heritage building in Malang City, a cultural heritage site and a tourist attraction, contains complex problems, mainly if residents still use the house for daily activities. According to Lynch (1981), the "citizen" factor also has a vital role in building an image (in this case, identity as a tourist destination) by giving a sense of the environment through its behavior and creative power. In the background and develop their desires. Tourists need to understand the customs and manners when visiting and taking photos of these attractions. In addition, the issue of privacy and home security also needs to be considered when the number of tourists who incidentally are foreigners to residents increases. On the other hand, tourists, especially notable interest tourists, are not satisfied if they only enjoy colonial heritage architecture on the house's exterior without being allowed to tour its interior. The presence of tourists can interfere with residents' daily lives; especially the researchers found that not all residents understand and agree on the concept of thematic village tourism, so it can potentially miscommunicate.

Second, it is related to the capacity and carrying capacity of cultural heritage tourism destinations which are of concern. The low power and carrying capacity of tourist destinations for residents and tourists can also damage cultural heritage sites (Cimnaghi & Mussini, 2015); especially with the naked eye, it can be seen that Malang City does not have adequate amenities such as road access in the form of narrow alleys and the difficulty of parking spaces. So that popularity, commercialization, mass tourism, and harmful excesses of tourism can disrupt site preservation and reduce tourist satisfaction.

Third, the increasing harmful excess of tourism on the preservation of cultural heritage sites is caused by the popularity of cultural heritage tourism among tourists. Various tourist activities and behaviors can also endanger (bad tourist behavior) cultural sites, such as theft of vital data and cultural properties, vandalism, destruction, landscape changes due to negligence, littering, and pollution. Fourth, increasing public indifference can also cause damage to the site (Nyaupane & Timothy, 2010), of course, today's millennial society prefers information in interactive visuals compared to monotonous text.

Fifth, planning and governance that are less organized by related parties and tend to be ceremonial and episodical can reduce an image, spatial identity, and sustainability. It can be understood that this is because this tourist area has only just been inaugurated, so management has not gone well. Many residents do not understand the concept of tourism, and tourists also do not know how this tourist village should run because of the lack of information. In practice, tourists can only enjoy Malang City if they have booked several days in advance to the manager to get a guide without separating this tourist attraction is only a collection of antique galleries in narrow alleys or old houses. In addition, activities without careful planning, such as the construction of either changing the function of the building, adding the original form or demolition, the impact of population density, or even tourism planning and commercialization that ambitious can also threaten the sustainability of colonial heritage buildings as cultural heritage sites, destinations and at the same time as homes for urban residents.

Cullwick (1975) explains that the marketer's job is to manage demand to match long-term goals rather than trying to increase sales without paying attention to these goals. Managing requests includes managing usage levels, types, expectations, and user behavior. Departing from these problems, one solution that can be used is initiating a living lab-based collaboration to create virtual tourism content by destination managers by considering the information and needs of stakeholders, namely, local government, destination managers, tourists, and residents of heritage cities.

Therefore, virtual tourism is believed to be able to answer the first problem on the Malang Heritage City site by diverting the number of tourist visits directly to virtual visits on virtual tourism content so that it can complement actual visits through the virtual experiences offered (Hu et al., 2012) or used by tourists as an alternative to essential visits (Guttentag, 2010) so that privacy, problems of spatial dualism, limited site access, security of cultural heritage houses from various harmful excesses of tourists can be minimized. Hu et al. (2012) view virtual tourism as an element of tourism activities that are economically safe and safe from modern humans.

Then to answer the second and third problems, virtual tourism offers realistic experiences that can be used for planning individual tourist trips so that they can better consider the carrying capacity and capacity of tourist destinations (Stepaniuk et al., 2014) and reduce harmful excesses of tourism in the Malang City environment. Virtual tourism allows visits to environmentally sensitive areas unsuitable for many visitors without risking and damaging heritage sites. In addition, it is believed that by disseminating the realistic experiences offered by virtual reality applications, the pressure of visitors on cultural heritage areas will be reduced where instead of putting the original cultural heritage at risk of damage, virtual tours can help protect the site by allowing visitors to access the simulation and stay safe while enjoying the area (Cheong, 1995). Virtual tourism can provide an alternative form of access to threatened heritage sitesn and objects that reduce the impact of overcrowding and, at the same time, improve the overall tourist experience. Digital cultural heritage tourism helps preserve cultural heritage and significantly increases its accessibility (Tonta, 2008).

Answering the fourth problem, the ability of virtual reality technology to store and provide exact and accurate data sets can help provide information, monitor degradation, and provide blueprints for the restoration of these sites and objects (Guttentag, 2010). By using a 3D scanning device, cultural heritage sites and things can be converted into digital form or virtual 3D models (Cignoni & Scopigno, 2008), so it is believed that virtual tourism in Malang City can effectively communicate information from cultural heritage sites while at the same time providing users with the latest technology and providing immersive and interactive virtual experiences, especially for disabled travelers, seniors tourist and millennials.

Virtual tourism in the living lab can answer the fifth problem through the joint development of cultural heritage site managers to improve site management's governance, planning, and implementation. Collaboration between regions and related parties such as academics, institutions, companies, and the community (Public. Private, People Partnership) in the form of joint management of Malang City as a virtual living lab can increase the value of the tourist experience concretely by encouraging higher interaction, co-creation, and increased personalization (Neuhofer et al., 2015). In the development of living labs, local governments can provide policies and have the authority to assist funding, establish cultural heritage sites and encourage formally legal communities to cooperatively provide information and willingness to access colonial heritage houses for research and development purposes; destination managers and academics develop virtual tourism content below, and travelers can engage in content testing and collectively improve through feedback from citizens and tourist.

The target group involved in this mentoring activity is the direct manager of heritage tourism destinations in Malang City by inviting local government representatives, tourist community groups, representatives of residents, and tourists. Around ten external participants attended the activity. The place of implementation will be held at the Virtual Living Lab Malang Heritage City because it has representative technology specifications to create virtual tourism content with all actors, as shown in Figure 9. The implementation of activities is planned as follows:

## 1. Initiation of Interactive Dialogue

We are conducting a poll and identifying the problems of the actors involved in the Kampoeng Heritage Kajoetangan virtual tourism living lab model, such as local governments, destination managers, academics, residents, and tourists. The living lab in this community service activity is an initiation in assistance to managers to develop innovation in virtual tourism Malang Heritage City which involves destination managers, tourists, residents, government, and academics.

The activity started with an interactive dialogue starting with asking open questions about the views of the government and management regarding the mentoring model that has been carried out so far and the recognition of managers, tourists, and residents what are the problems, challenges, or obstacles in strengthening the Malang Heritage City branding. The identification of challenges/barriers discussed in the initial session can be developed in the form of other derivative questions, and conclusions are drawn together to create alternative models through the model of living lab assistance. This stage is expected to produce a Cooperation Agreement related to the joint development of the Malang Heritage City's virtual living lab model.

2. **Process of Remote Practicum**

Academics in creating virtual tourism content based on the living lab model of heritage destinations in Malang City. This stage is expected to produce virtual tourism content based on 360° gallery images and 3D AR/VR from Malang Heritage City which is immersive and interactive. Content creation is divided into two stages, firstly taking 360° photos and videos as the main ingredient for virtual tourism content in 10 main heritage site locations by each of the destination managers and then academics process 360° photos into virtual tourism content utilizing Millelab software (VR platform) and Assemblr (AR platform) in remote practicums.

3. **Evaluation with FGD**

Conduct evaluation and feedback from the living lab model and virtual tourism content developed to assess the extent to which the model can be applied and the effectiveness and efficiency of the proposed empowerment model. The assessment was carried out by filling out FGDs by academics, residents, and tourists after seeing the virtual tourism content of Malang Heritage City. As shown in Figure 8 below:

4. **Habituation with Application in the Field**

The final stage is habituation through direct implementation in the field of the living lab model in a synergistic, simultaneous and continuous manner, as well as habituation to the preparation and improvement of virtual tourism content so that it can continue to adapt to developments and technology and harmonize the various needs of the actors involved, especially tourists and the community. This stage also includes installing the technology and determining the display and storage media for virtual tourism content in several locations to promote heritage tourism in Malang City.

In the new practical teaching method of virtual reality, the traditional listening and speaking relationship of filling duck is completely changed through simulation drills, role-playing, and student's actual participation so that students are familiar with the relevant professional skill of tourism specialty, effectively training their

*Figure 8. FGD Malang Heritage City in Virtual Living Lab*

on-the-spot language expression, flexibility, good psychological quality and other abilities (Xu & Li, 2018).

With the virtual reality of scene reproduction, various evaluation criteria are used to carry out multiple evaluation scores, thereby establishing a tangible, real-time, and visible competition scene among the students to stimulate the students' competitive psychology and further activate the classroom atmosphere, making the practical teaching curriculum project are-oriented a task-driven evaluation way with a focus on the cultivation of students' ability of subjective independent thinking.

Students learn to search materials independently, which reduces the intervention of lecturers and exercises students' ability to solve problems in practical ways; the tasks and contents of the optional courses are used for group discussions, on-site practice exercises, and defense to improve students' self-confidence, steady speech ability as well as their non-stage-fright defense ability and psychological quality, thus gradually improving the comprehensive practical ability of tourism professionals. With this examination and evaluation method, students' participation in the curriculum and effective interaction among team members are fully mobilized to obtain multi-angle and multi-dimensional thinking to deal with problems and increase cohesion and cooperation among team members (Xu & Li, 2018).

## Virtual Living Lab Framework

While offering VR/AR services to the student base may still feel very sci-fi for now, anyone working in education needs to be aware of the waves it's already making in the industry. The current review has demonstrated that the virtual environment could play a role in higher education; it needs not just be considered a "gimmick" but also contains "hidden gems" that are important to know in making future education. Using proper instructional strategies, VR/AR may provide students with numerous benefits and lead to practical learning experiences. The VR/AR technology also gives the opportunities to create an educational experience that is more engaging and attractive.

The collaborative tasks in education allow lecturers and students to communicate with each other and learn through play and exploration (Bistaman et al., 2018). The enjoyment quality factor of the virtual environment had a more substantial impact on student satisfaction than the quality of the teaching material. This does not mean that the quality of the teaching material is less important, but the ease of access and navigation, as well as being a fun system, are the first steps in providing a pleasant learning environment for students using the virtual environment tools (Kao et al., 2008). Achuthan et al. (2017) showed that learning was improved when students could use virtual labs before physical ones. Studies also show that students' learning outcome is equal to or higher, in non-traditional laboratories, such as virtual laboratories, compared to traditional laboratory environments (Brinson, 2015). Research shows that using the virtual environment can provide an excellent online learning context and present activities and assessments authentic (Herrington et al., 2003).

This new scenario has exposed many shortcomings and inefficiencies in the training system, from computer facilities and the supportive environment needed for online training to resources and behavior change (Cinar et al., 2020). The development of a virtual laboratory, as well as implementing it as a laboratory exercise for learning, requires knowledge in the three domains outlined by the TPACK model (Mishra & Koehler, 2009), i.e., technology, pedagogy, and content knowledge. Building a virtual laboratory for teaching and learning is complex, incorporating diverse areas such as interaction design, visualization, and pedagogy (Wästberg et al., 2019). The expected demand for the virtual lab is that they should function as efficiently as self-instructive learning materials. There are difficulties in making students achieve their learning goals without lecturer guidance. It cannot be taken for granted that a virtual laboratory can function without a lecturer-lead debriefing (Wästberg et al., 2019). Accordingly, lecturers in this province are increasingly expected to provide synchronous instruction and learning modules in traditional classrooms. Furthermore, there is a lack of understanding regarding how to best involve the user throughout the co-creative innovation process, both in the conventional and virtual setting, and how it affects the innovation process (Ståhlbröst, 2008). To ensure the "sustainability" of Living Lab, Mastelic et al. (2015) argue that a robust model is needed, particularly in considering the Living Lab through the business model perspective, based on a long-term strategy that considers funding structure, target audience, and revenue streams, in among other essential factors in routine processes.

*Figure 9. Malang City Heritage Tourism*

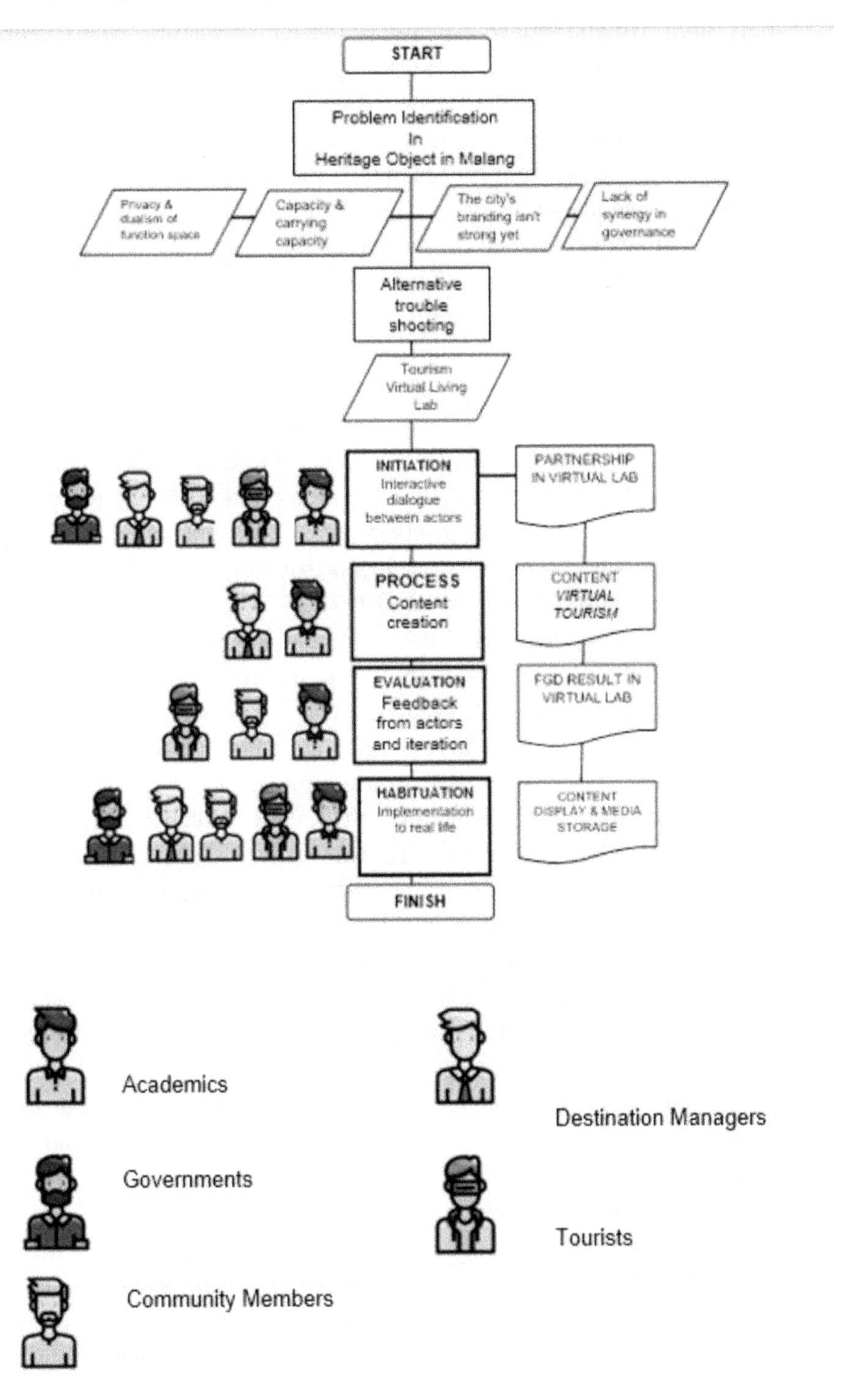

In the past, virtual reality (VR) has been relatively under-emphasized in education due to its' high cost and limited availability (Checa & Bustillo, 2019). Creating a virtual destination takes a long time to be convincing and realistic, so the more hyperreality and complexity the resolution and graphics of a virtual destination are, the more expensive it will be to manufacture. In addition to stimulating the sense of sight, other equipment is needed to create a virtual destination that is able to stimulate the overall senses of its users, and equipment to get a multisensory experience is still expensive and difficult to obtain. Creating a virtual site takes a long time to be convincing and realistic, so the more hyperreal and complex the resolution and graphics of the virtual site, the more expensive it will be. Besides, stimulating the sight sense, other equipment is needed to make virtual sites, and getting a multisensory experience is still expensive and hard to come by. The fast development of image technologies let the university anxious that their projects may become obsolete. Therefore, the emulator is needed to transfer the databases to the latest media. Price issues may occur, and the prohibitive costs of VR technologies and concomitant staff development, operations, and maintenance would find no place in dwindling school or university budgets that are overwhelmingly dominated by human resource costs (Roussos et al., 1999).

At the present time, the digital entertainment industry renewal has fostered the development of low-cost devices for virtual reality laboratories. A set of low-cost devices coupled to a versatile academic space, allows us to develop a VR lab targeted to make VR technology accessible to a greater number of undergraduate and graduate students (Rodriguez, 2016). Furthermore, AR/VR technology will help provide more effective visual information than the conventional media for promotion or a "try before you buy" experience (Tussyadiah et al. 2017). It obviously eases people to access edutainment resources, particularly for those who have limited travel capabilities in terms of either time, health, physical, or money. A virtual visit does not only function as an alternative yet provides more informative, varied, and interactive than the physical one, so it can become a complementary attraction to the actual visit. Methods such as private donations, sponsorships, or voluntary payments can allow the virtual living lab to gain income based on the visitors' willingness and ability to pay. The increasing property visibility through a mix of media, such as in-house and virtual tours, results in higher selling prices online, and a virtual living lab is no exception.

Eventually, *simulacra* provide tremendous promise for digital resilience education; nevertheless, they trigger the educators to encounter new constraints. When "learn from home" is becoming unavoidable in current uncertain circumstances, this review has identified some plot twists that are foreshadowed to prepare the education providers in the case to shift from the veridical physical learning space to verisimilitude virtual realm space. Metaverse, is this panacea or placebo to higher education misery amid the pandemic?

## REFERENCES

Achuthan, K., Francis, S. P., & Diwakar, S. (2017). Augmented reflective learning and knowledge retention perceived among students in classrooms involving virtual laboratories. *Education and Information Technologies*, *22*(6), 2825–2855. doi:10.100710639-017-9626-x

Akçayır, M., Akçayır, G., Pektaş, H. M., & Ocak, M. A. (2016). Augmented reality in science laboratories: The effects of augmented reality on university students' laboratory skills and attitudes toward science laboratories. *Computers in Human Behavior*, *57*, 334–342. doi:10.1016/j.chb.2015.12.054

Azuma, R. T. (1997). A survey of augmented reality. *Presence (Cambridge, Mass.)*, *6*(4), 355–385. doi:10.1162/pres.1997.6.4.355

Bafadhal, A. S. (2020). Pariwisata Virtual (Virtual Tourism). In M. A. Sutiarso (Ed.), *Manajemen Pariwisata: Sebuah Tinjauan Teori dan Praktis*. Widina Bhakti Persada.

Bafadhal, A. S. (2021a). Staycation During Covid-19 Pandemic with Virtual Tourism: Tele-Tourist Attitude Toward Experience in Cultural Heritage Destination. *Journal of Indonesian Tourism and Development Studies*, *9*(2), 87.

Bafadhal, A. S. (2021b). Pendampingan Pembuatan Konten Virtual Tourism sebagai Inisiasi Living Lab. Cagar Budaya Kampoeng Heritage Kajoetangan. *Jurnal Abdimas Pariwisata*, *1*(2), 66–73. doi:10.36276/jap.v1i2.20

Bafadhal, A. S., & Hendrawan, M. R. (2021a). Research and Development Web-Based Virtual Military Museum as a Tool for Edu-Tourism from Home During the Covid-19 Pandemic. In *International Conference on Innovation and Technology (ICIT 2021)* (pp. 75-85). Atlantis Press. 10.2991/aer.k.211221.010

Bafadhal, A. S., & Hendrawan, M. R. (2021b), Towards Infinity and Beyond Reality: A Cutting-Edge Virtual Museum. In Globalisation of Cultural Heritage: Issues, Impacts, and Challenges. Trengganu: Penerbit Universiti Malaysia Trengganu (UMT).

Beck, J., Rainoldi, M., & Egger, R. (2019). Virtual Reality in Tourism: A State of the Art Review. *Tourism Review*, *74*(3), 586–612. doi:10.1108/TR-03-2017-0049

Benckendorff, P. J., Xiang, Z., & Sheldon, P. J. (2019). *Tourism Information Technology*. Cabi. doi:10.1079/9781786393432.0000

Beutel, T., Jonas, J. M., & Moeslein, K. M. (2017). Co-creation and User Involvement in a Living Lab.: an Evaluation of Applied Methods. In Proceedings der (Vol. 13, pp. 1453-1464). Academic Press.

Bistaman, I. N. M., Idrus, S. Z. S., & Abd Rashid, S. (2018). Augmented reality technology for primary school education in Perlis, Malaysia. *Journal of Physics: Conference Series, 1019*(1), 012064. doi:10.1088/1742-6596/1019/1/012064

Bortnik, B., Stozhko, N., Pervukhina, I., Tchernysheva, A., & Belysheva, G. (2017). Effect of virtual analytical chemistry laboratory on enhancing student research skills and practices. *Research in Learning Technology, 25*(0). Advance online publication. doi:10.25304/rlt.v25.1968

Brinson, J. R. (2015). Learning outcome achievement in non-traditional (virtual and remote) versus traditional (hands-on) laboratories: A review of the empirical research. *Computers & Education, 87*, 218–237. doi:10.1016/j.compedu.2015.07.003

Burdea, G. C., & Coiffet, P. (2003). *Virtual reality technology*. Wiley & Sons. doi:10.1162/105474603322955950

Carrozzino, M., & Bergamasco, M. (2010). Beyond virtual museums: Experiencing immersive virtual reality in real museums. *Journal of Cultural Heritage, 11*(4), 452–458. doi:10.1016/j.culher.2010.04.001

Chalmers, D. J. (2022). *Reality+: Virtual Worlds and the Problems of Philosophy*. W. W. Norton.

Checa, D., & Bustillo, A. (2019). A review of immersive virtual reality serious games to enhance learning and training. *Multimedia Tools and Applications, 79*(9-10), 5501–5527. doi:10.100711042-019-08348-9

Cheong, R. (1995). The virtual threat to travel and tourism. *Tourism Management, 16*(6), 417–422. doi:10.1016/0261-5177(95)00049-T

Cigir, K. (2018). Creating a Living Lab. Model for Tourism and Hospitality Businesses to Stimulate CSR and Sustainability Innovations. *WIT Transactions on Ecology and the Environment, 217*, 569–583. doi:10.2495/SDP180491

Cignoni, P., & Scopigno, R. (2008). Sampled 3D models for CH applications: A viable and enabling new medium or just a technological exercise? *Journal on Computing and Cultural Heritage, 1*(1), 1–23. doi:10.1145/1367080.1367082

Cimnaghi, E., & Mussini, P. (2015). An application of tourism carrying capacity assessment at two Italian cultural heritage sites. *Journal of Heritage Tourism, 10*(3), 302–313. doi:10.1080/1743873X.2014.988158

Çınar, M., Doğan, D., & Tüzün, H. (2020). The effect of design tasks on the cognitive load level of instructional designers in 3D MUVEs. *International Journal of Technology and Design Education*, 1–18.

Cliburn, D. (n.d.). Incorporating Virtual Reality Concepts into the Introductory Computer Graphics Course. In *Proceedings of the SIGCSE*. ACM.

Cooper, A., & Reimann, R. (2003). *About-face 2.0: the essentials of interaction design*. Wiley Publishing, Inc.

Cullwick, D. (1975). Positioning Demarketing Strategy: Marketers must integrate the changes in the business environment into effective new product, pricing, distribution, and promotion strategies. *Journal of Marketing*, *39*(2), 51–57. doi:10.1177/002224297503900209

De Leon, M. P., Hribernik, K. A., & Eriksson, M. (2008). The Living Labs Approach to a Virtual Lab. Environment. In *Encyclopedia of Networked and Virtual Organizations* (pp. 818–821). IGI Global. doi:10.4018/978-1-59904-885-7.ch108

Dibbell, J. (1998). *My tiny life: Crime and passion in a virtual world. New York*. Holt.

Ermi, L., & Mäyrä, F. (2005). Fundamental Components of the Gameplay Experience: Analysing Immersion. *Proceedings of the DiGRA Conference on Changing Views: Worlds in Play*.

Grudin, J. (1993). Interface: An evolving concept. *Communications of the ACM*, *36*(4), 110–119. doi:10.1145/255950.153585

Guttentag, D. A. (2010). Virtual reality: Applications and implications for tourism. *Tourism Management*, *31*(5), 637–651. doi:10.1016/j.tourman.2009.07.003

Häfner, P., Häfner, V., & Ovtcharova, J. (2013). Teaching methodology for virtual reality practical course in engineering education. *Procedia Computer Science*, *25*, 251–260.

Hales, R., & Jennings, G. (2017). Transformation for sustainability: The role of complexity in tourism students' understanding of sustainable tourism. *Journal of Hospitality, Leisure, Sport and Tourism Education*, *21*, 185–194. doi:10.1016/j.jhlste.2017.08.001

Hendrawan, M. R., & Bafadhal, A. S. (2022). Virtual Museum. In D. Buhalis (Ed.), *Encyclopedia of Tourism Management and Marketing*. Edward Elgar Publishing.

Herrington, J., Oliver, R., & Reeves, T. C. (2003). Patterns of engagement in authentic online learning environments. *Australasian Journal of Educational Technology, 19*(1). Advance online publication. doi:10.14742/ajet.1701

Hu, W., Liu, G. P., & Zhou, H. (2012). Web-based 3-D control laboratory for remote real-time experimentation. *IEEE Transactions on Industrial Electronics, 60*(10), 4673–4682. doi:10.1109/TIE.2012.2208440

Huang, Y. C., Backman, S. J., Backman, K. F., & Moore, D. (2013). Exploring user acceptance of 3D virtual worlds in travel and tourism marketing. *Tourism Management, 36*, 490–501. doi:10.1016/j.tourman.2012.09.009

Hughes, C. E., & Moshell, J. M. (1997). Shared Virtual Worlds for Education: The Explore Net Experiment. *Multimedia Systems, 5*(2), 145–154. doi:10.1007005300050050

Izard, S. G., Juanes, M. J. A., & Palomera, P. R. (2017). Virtual Reality Educational Tool for Human Anatomy. *Journal of Medical Systems, 41*(5), 76. doi:10.100710916-017-0723-6 PMID:28326490

Kao, F. C., Tung, Y. L., & Chang, W. Y. (2008). *183 The Design of 3D Virtual Collaborative Learning System with Circuit-Measuring Function*. Academic Press.

Kerckhove, D. (1995). *The Skin of Culture: Investigating the new electronic reality*. Kogan Page.

Kirkman, B. L., Rosen, B., Gibson, C. B., Tesluk, P. E., & McPherson, S. O. (2002). Five challenges to virtual team success: Lessons from Sabre, Inc. *The Academy of Management Perspectives, 16*(3), 67–79. doi:10.5465/ame.2002.8540322

Kye, B., Han, N., Kim, E., Park, Y., & Jo, S. (2021). Educational Applications of Metaverse: Possibilities and Limitations. *Journal of Educational Evaluation for Health Professions, 18*, 18. doi:10.3352/jeehp.2021.18.32 PMID:34897242

Law, R., Buhalis, D., & Cobanoğlu, C. (2014). Progress on Information and Communication Technologies in Hospitality and Tourism. *International Journal of Contemporary Hospitality Management, 26*(5), 727–750. doi:10.1108/IJCHM-08-2013-0367

Lee, J., Kim, Y., Ahn, E., & Kim, G. J. (2012). Applying "out of the body" funneling and saltation to interaction with virtual and augmented objects. In *2012 IEEE VR Workshop on Perceptual Illusions in Virtual Environments* (pp. 7-9). IEEE. 10.1109/PIVE.2012.6229793

Lieberman, L. J., Ball, L., Beach, P., & Perreault, M. (2022). A Qualitative Inquiry of a Three-Month Virtual Practicum Program on Youth with Visual Impairments and Their Coaches. *International Journal of Environmental Research and Public Health, 19*(2), 841. doi:10.3390/ijerph19020841 PMID:35055663

Lynch, K. (1981). *A Theory of Good City Form.* MIT Press.

Mastelic, J., Sahakian, M., & Bonazzi, R. (2015). How to keep a living lab alive? *Info, 17*(4), 12–25. doi:10.1108/info-01-2015-0012

Mishra, P., & Koehler, M. (2009). Too cool for school? No way! Using the TPACK framework: You can have your hot tools and teach with them, too. *Learning and Leading with Technology, 36*(7), 14–18.

Munar, A. M. (2010). Digital exhibitionism: The age of exposure. *Culture Unbound, 2*(3), 401–422. doi:10.3384/cu.2000.1525.10223401

Neuhofer, B., Buhalis, D., & Ladkin, A. (2015). Smart Technologies for Personalized Experiences: A Case Study in the Hospitality Domain. *Electronic Markets, 25*(3), 243–254. doi:10.100712525-015-0182-1

Nyaupane, G. P., & Timothy, D. J. (2010). Heritage awareness and appreciation among community residents: Perspectives from Arizona, USA. *International Journal of Heritage Studies, 16*(3), 225–239. doi:10.1080/13527251003620776

Orr, D., Weller, M., & Farrow, R. (2018). *Models for Online, Open, Flexible and Technology Enhanced Higher Education Across the Globe: A Comparative Analysis.* International Council for Open and Distance Education.

Park, M., & Jones, T. (2021). Going Virtual: The Impact of Covid-19 on Internships in Tourism, Events, and Hospitality Education. *Journal of Hospitality & Tourism Education, 33*(3), 176–193. doi:10.1080/10963758.2021.1907198

Penfold, P. (2009). Learning through the world of second life—A hospitality and tourism experience. *Journal of Teaching in Travel & Tourism, 8*(2-3), 139–160. doi:10.1080/15313220802634224

Poulova, P., Cerna, M., Hamtilova, J., Malý, F., Kozel, T., Kriz, P., & Ulrych, Z. (2020). Virtual hotel–gamification in the management of tourism education. In *International Conference on Remote Engineering and Virtual Instrumentation* (pp. 773-781). Springer.

Rodriguez, N. (2016). Teaching virtual reality with affordable technologies. In *International Conference on Human-Computer Interaction* (pp. 89-97). Springer.

Roussos, M., Johnson, A., Moher, T., Leigh, J., Vasilakis, C., & Barnes, C. (1999). Learning and building together in an immersive virtual world. *Presence (Cambridge, Mass.)*, *8*(3), 247–263. doi:10.1162/105474699566215

Roussou, M., Oliver, M., & Slater, M. (2006). The Virtual Playground: An educational virtual reality environment for evaluating interactivity and conceptual learning. *Virtual Reality (Waltham Cross)*, *10*(3-4), 227–240. doi:10.100710055-006-0035-5

Segond, F., Parmentier, T., Stock, R., Rosner, R., & Muela, M. U. (2005). Situational language training for hotel receptionists. In *Proceedings of the Second Workshop on Building Educational Applications Using NLP* (pp. 85-92). Academic Press.

Sholihin, M., Sari, R. C., Yuniarti, N., & Ilyana, S. (2020). A new way of teaching business ethics: The evaluation of virtual reality-based learning media. *International Journal of Management Education*, *18*(3), 100428. doi:10.1016/j.ijme.2020.100428

Slater, M., & Wilbur, S. (1997). A Framework for Immersive Virtual Environments (FIVE): Speculations on the Role of Presence in Virtual Environments. *Presence (Cambridge, Mass.)*, *6*(6), 603–616. doi:10.1162/pres.1997.6.6.603

Ståhlbröst, A. (2008). *Forming future IT: the living lab way of user involvement* (Doctoral dissertation). Luleå tekniska universitet.

Stansfield, S. (2005). An introductory VR course for undergraduates incorporating foundation, experience and capstone. In *Proceedings of the SIGCSE*. ACM. 10.1145/1047344.1047417

Stefani, L. (2009). Planning, Teaching and Learning: Curriculum design and development. In H. Fry, S. Ketteridge, & S. Marshall (Eds.), *A Handbook for teaching in learning in higher education: enhancing academic practices* (pp. 40–57). Routledge.

Stepaniuk, K., Bałakier, U., & Januszewska, A. (2014). Virtual tours in the opinion of the users of social networking sites in Poland and Belarus. *Ekonomia i Zarządzanie*, *6*(1).

Tonta, Y. (2008). Libraries and museums in the flat world: Are they becoming virtual destinations? *Library Collections, Acquisitions & Technical Services*, *32*(1), 1–9. doi:10.1080/14649055.2008.10766187

Tussyadiah, I. P., Wang, D., Jung, T. H., & Tom Dieck, M. C. (2018). Virtual reality, presence, and attitude change: Empirical evidence from tourism. *Tourism Management*, *66*, 140–154. doi:10.1016/j.tourman.2017.12.003

United Nation. (2021). *Policy Brief: Education During Covid-19 and Beyond*. United Nation.

Veeckman, C., & Van Der Graaf, S. (2015). The City as Living Laboratory: Empowering Citizens with the Citadel Toolkit. *Technology Innovation Management Review*, *5*(3), 6–17. doi:10.22215/timreview/877

Wästberg, S. B., Eriksson, T., Karlsson, G., Sunnerstam, M., Axelsson, M., & Billger, M. (2019). Design Considerations for Virtual Laboratories: A Comparative Study of Two Virtual Laboratories for Learning about Gas Solubility and Colour Appearance. *Education and Information Technologies*, *24*(3), 2059–2080. doi:10.100710639-018-09857-0

Weiser, M. (1991). The Computer for the 21 st Century. *Scientific American*, *265*(3), 94–105. doi:10.1038cientificamerican0991-94 PMID:1675486

Westerlund, M., & Leminen, S. (2011). Managing the Challenges of Becoming an Open Innovation Company: Experiences from Living Labs. *Technology Innovation Management Review*, *1*(1), 19–25. doi:10.22215/timreview/489

Xie, Y., Liu, Y., Zhang, F., & Zhou, P. (2022). Virtual Reality-Integrated Immersion-Based Teaching to English Language Learning Outcome. *Frontiers in Psychology*, *12*, 767363. doi:10.3389/fpsyg.2021.767363 PMID:35211053

Xu, X., & Li, Y. (2018). Teaching method of tourism curriculum design based on practical teaching method. *Educational Sciences: Theory and Practice*, *18*(6).

Yen, J.-C., Tsai, C.-H., & Wu, M. (2013). Augmented reality in the higher education: Students' science concept learning and academic achievement in astronomy. *Procedia: Social and Behavioral Sciences*, *103*, 165–173. doi:10.1016/j.sbspro.2013.10.322

Zarzuela, M. M., Pernas, F. J. D., Calzón, S. M., Ortega, D. G., & Rodríguez, M. A. (2013). Educational tourism through a virtual reality platform. *Procedia Computer Science*, *25*, 382–388. doi:10.1016/j.procs.2013.11.047

Zhou, J., Zuo, M., Yu, Y., & Chai, W. (2014). How fundamental and supplemental interactions affect users' knowledge sharing in virtual communities? A social cognitive perspective. *Internet Research*, *24*(5), 566–586. doi:10.1108/IntR-07-2013-0143

Zimmerman, G. W., & Eber, D. E. (2001). When worlds collide!: an interdisciplinary course in virtual-reality art. In *Proceedings of SIGCSE*. ACM. 10.1145/364447.364545

# Chapter 11
# Coronavirus Impact on Digital Technology Use in University Student Software Engineering Project Management

**Kamalendu Pal**
https://orcid.org/0000-0001-7158-6481
*City, University of London, UK*

## ABSTRACT

*This chapter discusses the challenges for the higher education sector during the coronavirus pandemic. It examines the advantages of information and communication technology (ICT) tools in advancing higher education and students' changing communication practices during the recent pandemic. The chapter identifies research gaps, highlighting the consequential effect on lesser-developed countries, the psychological effect on the student community, and the vital role of management in handling distributed software development practice. It also presents that the main objective should be to develop more resilient higher education teaching and learning provisions that are responsive and adaptive to future crises. For example, an undergraduate software development case study describes a group of computer science students' views on digital communication channel utilization behaviour during the coronavirus pandemic. Finally, a multiple-choice questions and answers method provides the students' views regarding the relevant research issues and a view of university students' communication channel utilization patterns.*

DOI: 10.4018/978-1-6684-5400-8.ch011

## INTRODUCTION

Humanity resides on Earth with ambitious goals to mitigate unprecedented social, economic, health, well-being, and environmental challenges. Education, science, technology, and innovation play their role in managing these unthinkable challenges. Higher educations are essential to improving the quality of life of people, given their great relevance in making economic and social decisions, their capacity to increase employment opportunities and their contribution to social exclusion (Lipka, ForkoshBaruch, & Meer, 2019). In addition, some other issues dominating strategic thinking in higher education institutions operational activities. These issues need to include (i) inclusion of lesbian, gay, bisexual, transgender, and queer (LGBTQ) students in higher education, (ii) providing the opportunity for disabled students for higher education, (iii) removing barriers for low-income family's student to get the opportunity of higher education, and (iv) the many meanings of quality education (Unterhalter, 2019).

Higher education can usher in economic changes and improve living conditions by increasing productivity, reducing social inequality (Unterhalter et al., 2022), and helping to improve living standards. For example, people with disabilities and students in low-income families, despite the efforts that educational institutions are making (e.g., making policies, disability support offices, staff training) to achieve success. However, despite the commitment to ensure higher education access for students with disabilities, the dropout rate in this group is still high (Veitch, Strehlow, & Boyd, 2018). Several studies, such as that by Cotton, Nash, and Kneale (2017), have reported differences between countries and institutions in this dropout rate.

In this way, higher education institutions continually look for student-centered effective teaching and learning methods to enhance students' satisfaction and improve the global performance criteria to gain a competitive advantage. It is worth to remember that technology can be a tool to enable teachers to support learners with a diverse range of backgrounds, skills, capabilities, languages, and impairments. However, the use of technology in higher education institutions is based on the interrelationships amongst at least three areas: technology, theories of learning and educational teaching and learning practice issues. This interrelatedness implies dynamic relationships where the changes in one area make other areas change. For example, technological developments call for the reconceptualization of learning theories and changes in the designs of educational practices. The challenge for teaching in higher education is ensuring that the learning environment institutions provide best helps the learners to learn.

Recent technological developments have produced a new generation of computer, information, and communication technology-based learning environments. There are, to a significant extent, characterized and conditioned by such mobile and portable devices as smartphones, laptops, and desktop computers with wireless broadband access. As a result, there is a need for educational approaches to teaching and learning in higher education that consider this technological development. With developments in mobile technology, an increasing proportion of learning activities may take place outside the confines of a controlled classroom, and the teacher role may be challenged accordingly. For example, in an environmentalist view of education, education is seen as a type of communication where the teacher facilitates student learning. To facilitate student learning when mobile technology is used for learning purposes, teachers need knowledge of how students maneuver and study within these environments. One crucial concern is understanding how students interact with their surroundings to create learning sites. Such insights may allow teachers to rearrange and redesign educational practices to address their students.

In order to design educational practices, one needs to clarify what characterizes mobile learning. There are varied, overlapping, and still evolving definitions of mobile learning. Many see mobile-learning as a natural evolution of e-learning or as a new stage of distance learning and e-learning (Georgiev et al., 2004) (Rajasingham, 2011). Some define mobile learning in the context of devices, emphasizing the mobility aspects of the devices used. Many academics and practitioners use the term mobile as a synonym for mobile phone. This amounts to an oversimplification that misses the whole concept because viewing a telephone as a device which operates wirelessly reveals only a fragile aspect of what today's mobile technologies can offer. Indeed, the researchers proposed the thesis that the appearance of the mobile phone had signalled a significant innovation in human evolution. While the computer creates the initial human effort, which inspired to highlight of mental rather than physical human powers (in comparison to all previous human constructs; for an elaboration of this argument – please refer (Laouris & Laouri, 2006), the mobile phone goes one step further.

Many authors, for example (Mostakhdemin-Hosseini & Tuimala, 2005), view mobile learning simply as the natural evolution of e-learning that completes a missing component of the solution (i.e., adding the wireless operational ability) or as a new platform of distance and e-learning (e.g., Georgiev et al., 2004), one that describes it as occupying a sub-space within the e-learning space (which in its turn occupies a sub-space within the d-learning space). A terminology change also characterizes the transition from e-learning to the m-learning revolution. However, the detailed classification of these learning methods and any debates regarding their effectiveness is beyond the scope of this chapter.

Quinn (2000), for example, defines mobile learning as learning that takes place with the help of mobile devices. On the other hand, Laouris and Eteokleous (2005) suggest a broader view that involves a shift of focus from device to human, thus defining mobile learning in the context of the learning environment and learning experiences. Within the m-learning field, such terms as mobile, spontaneous, intimate, situated, connected, informal, realistic situation and collaboration are used to characterize these learning environments (Laouris & Eteokleous, 2005). Mobile learning also envisions learners who are continually on the move and learn across space and time, moving from topic to topic and in and out of interaction with technology (Sharples, 2000) (Sharples et al., 2007). An environment-independent and time-independent pedagogy may thus be needed.

Nowadays, digital technology has expanded rapidly, covering many aspects of everyday life, such as game playing. The latter has evolved to a new era, as motion sensing technologies have been integrated into game consoles, allowing more realistic and immersive gameplay. Motion sensors are devices which provide a natural user interface, allowing users to interact without any intermediary device. They can capture gestures and/or detect voices.

Playing can be a powerful learning approach through which students can develop new skills, participate in new social environments, and undertake new social roles (Vygotsky, 1978) (Pal, 2022). Gee (2003) argues that games allow players to be knowledge producers rather than in the educational scenario where students too often consume but do not produce. Playing games requires deep thinking (Squire, 2008), which is crucial for learning since students participate in active experiences and do not simply receive information passively (Whitton & Moseley, 2012). Researchers (Parsons et al., 2000) (Charitos et al., 2000) support that through Virtual Environments, users can practice skills safely, avoiding potentially dangerous real-world consequences. For instance, users with special needs (e.g., students with autism spectrum disorders) could practice social skills while reducing the impact of a possible social failure. Moreover, sensor-based technology could enhance their abilities and help them to cultivate their skills by putting them in situations in which they probably could not respond in real life. Additionally, they can support the development of logical thinking and critical thinking skills (Inkpen et al., 1995) (Higgins, 2014).

In addition, computers and video games could be used as innovative tools for constructive teaching approaches in classrooms. Constructivism state that people construct their understanding and knowledge of the world through practical activities which allow them to gain experiences and reflection upon those experiences (Vygotsky, 1978). MacFarland et al. (2002), based on how learning is achieved, distinguish games as those in which: (a) learning is achieved because of tasks stimulated by the games' content, (b) knowledge is developed through the game content, and (c) skills arise because of playing the game. The educational use of the game depends on the teacher's creativity. For example, Kandroudi & Bratitsis (2012) support those games could not teach anything on their own; the educator is responsible for finding creative ways of incorporating the simulated worlds of the games into exciting learning activities. Furthermore, MacFarland et al. (2002) indicate the crucial relationship between games and the associated learning, which teachers should consider. Oblinger (2006) states that pupils should be involved, through technology, in the learning process to (a) be engaged with the theories, (b) acquire knowledge through autonomous and discovering learning, (c) cultivate thinking skills, (d) learn how to learn (metacognition), (e) interact and communicate, and (f) operate as active knowledge producers.

Practitioners highlighted their research findings for students' experience in higher education with virtual reality (VR) and augmented reality (AR) (DePape et al., 2019). The popularity of AR and VR were used in real-world applications and justified by costs (Maloney et al., 2012) (Wu et al., 2013). A great deal of enthusiasms was expressed in regarding mobile app-based teaching and learning practice in higher education in recent years (Pechenkina et al., 2017). Moreover, rapid growing signaled-based wireless sensors with smart devices motivate the development of many learning methodologies for intellectual disabilities in recent decades. Some of the recent mobile applications in teaching and student engagement research are present in APPENDIX-1.

In this way, digital technologies can provide appropriate channels for higher educational institutions on the context of delivery. For example, the epidemic of coronavirus (known as COVID-19) at the end of 2019 forced governments to take invasive measures to prevent the spread of the disease, including closures of educational institutions. The international health pandemic (i.e., coronavirus) has casted a bitter light on the susceptibility and challenges humanity faces in recent decades. It has highlighted an analysis of current inequalities and a picture of what steps forward requires taking, primarily among them appreciation the education of billions of students whose daily life and learning has been affected due to academic institutions closures wholly or delivered online teaching to provide moderately the students require.

The coronavirus pandemic has adversely affected higher education daily activities worldwide, with face-to-face teaching and learning practices and student assessment styles being changed or cancelled due to the lockdown imposed by governments. Most educational institutions have also struggled with digital teaching delivery challenges (Talidong & Toquero, 2020). Higher education institutions were asked to formulate crisis management strategies to continue teaching and learning activities. For example, the United Kingdom government requested fellow citizens to minimize social contact as much as possible and went on to advise that "you can still work, but we are asking as many as possible to work from home" (BBC, 2020). Subsequently, face-to-face teaching was stopped for higher education institutions worldwide, with academics and teachers asked to formulate alternative student-support activities as replacements for attendance at lectures, tutorials, laboratory sessions, workshops, and seminars. In addition, the teaching and learning activities were altered due to an overhaul of planned assessment processes. As the coronavirus pandemic threat has developed further, the rapidly changing nature of communication provided to students and educators (e.g., academic, teacher) may have added additional sources of anxiety and pressure. In addition, mental, psychological, and emotional pressures became part of student and educator life. Finally, an early study highlights that the students were at risk of being left behind the health and wellbeing during a formative stage of learning, the opportunity for appropriate education, personal development, and economic benefits (United Nations, 2020).

The switch to digital learning has had consequences for education's accessibility, quality, and equity. It revealed gaps in the preparedness of both formal and non-formal education providers. Some institutions were unable to adjust well or fast enough, and, as a result, some students were entirely shut out of education. Students from disadvantaged backgrounds were particularly affected, while others, the most privileged and affluent, continued their studies through alternative learning methods, predominantly distance and online learning. However, it soon became apparent that online educational activities were often not inclusive and of lesser quality without uniform access. These shortcomings generated learning gaps, of which the consequences are yet to be assessed.

Countries and education sectors were affected differently due to a variety of factors. Some of the factors are students' age, ability to learn independently, the nature of pedagogies used at each level, and the extent of integrating distance and online learning into usual education provision. In addition, no uniform or consistent formal support was provided to educators and parents; the support that emerged was non-formal, self-organized or unrehearsed training arranged as a bottom-up support network.

To a greater extent, none of the countries was prepared for a swift transition of their higher educational system, eliminating all engagements requiring the personal presence and maintaining the programs. Despite numerous examples of quick inspirational solutions, countries lacked preparedness in terms of digital education infrastructure, service provisions, and digital skills shortage. For example, only fifty-eight per cent of the European Union (EU) citizens in 2019 possessed basic digital skills, ranging from almost eighty per cent in Finland to just over thirty per cent in Italy. Within countries, similar discrepancies exist based on geographical location (i.e., rural areas and regions with lower digital connectivity) (Dutta & Lanvin, 2020). Therefore, the switch to online education and reliance on information and communication technology (ICT) during the current pandemic outbreak exacerbated the existing inequality and digital divide in the world.

Academics and practitioners in international publications have highlighted the current pandemic impact on educational institutions. These research articles address some burning issues (e.g., the impact of technology in changing distance learning practice, post-lockdown analysis of some individual educational institutions). However, the present societal challenges due to the current pandemic problems on higher educational institutions have yet to be determined entirely to understand the initial interventions to transform digital learning to manage the pandemic's effect. Hence, this chapter aims to assess emerging evidence on the impact of the current pandemic on higher educational institutions and analyze the prevalence of digital learning changes in the educational sector. In addition, the World Health Organization (WHO) advocates for rapid reviews to be carried out to understand better the challenges (Roy et al., 2020).

In order to mitigate the above guidance, the following aims have been established for the review process of this chapter: (i) to summarize the impact of the current pandemic as reported from a selection of available studies on educational institutions; (ii) to analyze the measures that were put in place following the COVID-19 lockdown of educational institutions; and (iii) to appraise gaps in knowledge and understanding and revealing possible future research directions regarding the effect of the current pandemic on the educational institutions. Also, this review provides guidelines to educators and institutions regarding the transition from traditional education to an online learning world.

The remaining structure of this chapter is as follows. The following section presents an overview of the methods used for this research. Next, it provides the descriptive results, the themes identified from academic literature, and a case study to apply an undergraduate software engineering team-based project teaching and learning practice. Finally, the chapter provides future research directions and concludes with concluding remarks.

## BACKGROUND OF THE METHOD ADOPTED FOR THE RESEARCH

Reviewing existing academic literature within a particular area of research is challenging and interdisciplinary. It is ambitious to keep up with the state-of-the-art, be at the forefront of research, and assess the collective evidence in a particular study area. Therefore, the literature review as a research method is more relevant than ever. Traditional literature reviews often lack thoroughness and rigor and are conducted ad hoc rather than a specific methodology. Therefore, there can be questions about the quality and trustworthiness of these types of reviews. The answer to quality and trustworthiness issues is beyond this chapter's scope.

There are diverse ways researchers gather relevant academic literature. In the current work, research articles gathered from standard academic databases (e.g.,

*Table 1. Exclusion and inclusion guidance rules*

| Exclusion Rules | Inclusion Rules |
|---|---|
| Commentaries, editorial comments, news articles, and individual opinions are excluded. | Research articles deal with coronavirus pandemic (i.e., COVID-19). |
| Publications that discuss general educational settings only; and do not relate to the current pandemic are excluded. | The research discusses the current pandemic impact on how that may have impacted educational institutions. |
| Presenting relevant issues with another pandemic (e.g., EBOLA virus-related crisis). | |

Science Direct, Emerald, Pro-quest, Wiley online Library, Springer Link, and Taylor & Francis) search. These academic reference databases are valuable sources for researching the phenomena under investigation. Used Google Scholar to double-check the search and find any missing relevant studies during the initial database search (Li et al., 2020).

Using the keyword-based search strategy to retrieve the relevant research articles is one of the most common search strategies (Rodiguez-Hernandez et al., 2020). The keyword search used terms including coronavirus pandemic and education, COVID-19 and teaching, higher education, or university education; these were searched for within the title, abstract, and keyword sections, a technique used in previous research projects (Plockinger et al., 2016). Analyzed the research publications of relevant context for inclusion and exclusion based on the guidance rules as shown in Table 1.

As mentioned earlier in the initial search process, only 126 research articles related to the recent pandemic and general education were selected from the publication. During the selection activity, sixty-two research articles related to non-higher education institutions were rejected, leaving only ninety-four eligible research contributions that presented current pandemic effects in the higher education sector. Some of these research articles were then excluded due to duplication of issues discussed. Also, thirty-seven published research articles were rejected in the selection process since they did not fully match the inclusion and exclusion criteria set out in Table 1. These included research articles, individual or group opinions, editorial that did not offer original data, and studies that presented business cases without sufficient information. Finally, the current research reviewed only the title and abstract section of research articles for the selection process.

## Descriptive Results

This review selected thirty-six research studies that focused on the impact of the coronavirus pandemic on educational institutions. The initial analysis found that most research in the publication searching period was published in the United States of America's educational institutions. The spread of research findings shows that the selected articles were concentrated primarily on specific countries, as shown in Figure 1. Some of these are developing countries with diverse cultural, economic, and social profiles to those of developed nations that seem to deal with pandemic and radical changes in educational institutions more effectively.

The current research collected relevant issues from a sample academic article that reflect the coronavirus pandemic situations for only a few countries, which includes the United States of America, United Kingdom, China, India, Indonesia, Ireland, Italy, Philippines, Australia, Spain, Germany, Kuwait, and other countries (e.g., Brazil, Canada, South Africa). Besides, most of the collected research articles were written and published in the lockdown period; and the presented research primarily used online questionnaires targeted at educational institutions' educators and students.

The individual research article analyzed student feedback in the current pandemic, individual subject performance, subject content, academic institutions correspondence, and other official documents. After initial analysis, some of the themes emerged: (i) suggestion to adopt a fully online learning (e-learning) environment, (ii) measures that can support educational institutions' future strategies for teaching and learning activities during and after the pandemic. However, it is problematic to ascertain the generality of these studies used in the review process, as simple textual analysis on its own might not produce generalized views.

## Thematic Analysis

At the time of review, different themes started to emerge. It is worth breaking these themes down into the following key areas: digital learning, e-learning challenges, the digital transformation to virtual emergency assessment, the psychological impact of the coronavirus pandemic, and creating collaborative cultures. The thematic analysis will highlight the crucial findings after the initial analysis of collected academic articles below.

## Digital Learning

The term digital learning is increasingly used but often fails to provide a clear understanding of what the term means. Moreover, it is sometimes used interchangeably with technology-enhanced learning (TEL) and with e-learning or online learning; however, each of these terms reflects a different stage in the evolution of the discipline. Digital provides many opportunities to engage learners, personalize learning experiences and widen access. It can make it easier for learners and educators to

*Figure 1. Geographic coverage of literature*

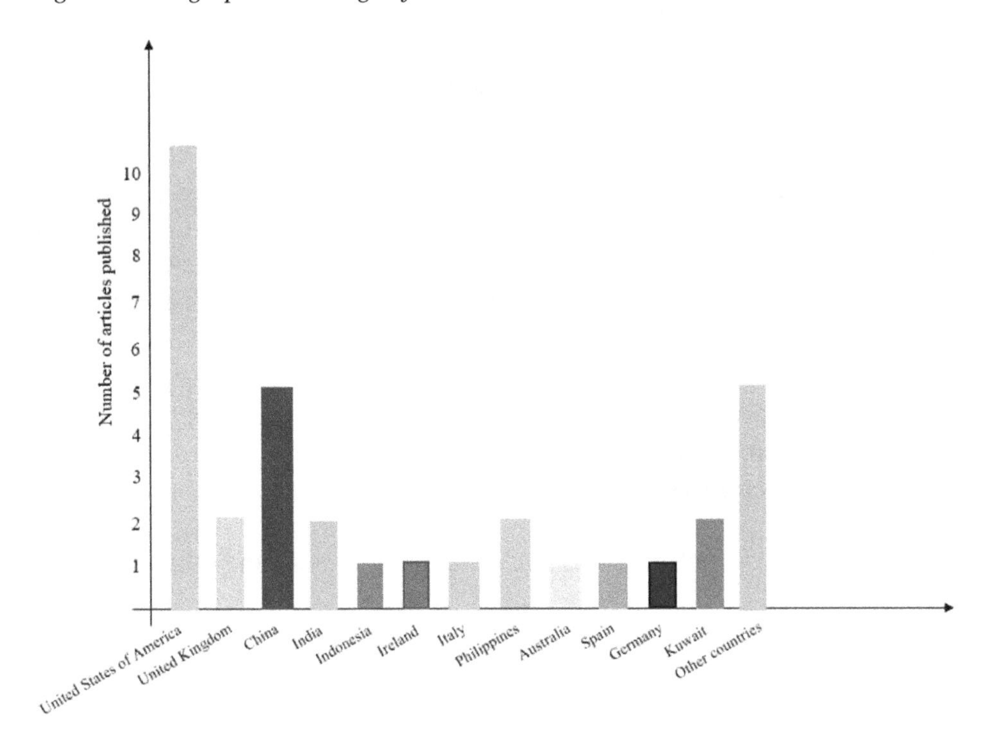


engage with each other actively (e.g., through email, IM (instant messages), video chat, online forums, social media) and with learning materials.

Some researchers expressed that the coronavirus pandemic has forced academic institutions to pursue digital learning (Majanja, 2020). A few researchers highlighted that digital learning has a beneficial influence in combating COVID-19 problems, including educator technical skills enhancement (Abdulrahim & Mabrouk, 2020); teaching and learning delivery systems have been better restructured (Rajhans et al., 2020); and courses have been rapidly transformed (Skulmowski & Rey, 2020). Besides, there has been a rise in multifaceted digital learning techniques (Zainuddin et al., 2020); and it facilitates better feedback to students (Jayathirtha et al., 2020).

However, several educators expressed concerns about the overall efficacy of online teaching techniques, and many doubts are being highlighted regarding the future viability of education institutions if only digital learning infrastructures provide post-pandemic education (Code et al., 2020).

## E-Learning Challenges

'E-learning' is a conjugate term that is a hybrid by construction. The two elements have joined together to form a new hybrid term like other conjugate terms. Moreover, this hybrid term consists of two elements: 'e' and ' learning'. The element 'e' of e-learning has a more extended history than many assume, including long-term efforts to capture voice and images and store and then transmit those recordings. With each capture – from records to compact disks (CDs), converted to text chat – there are trade-offs in quality, interactivity, and transferability: trade-offs that mark both the advantages and disadvantages of technological mediation.

Typical of the problems facing researchers in e-learning is the case of electronic interactive whiteboards – touch-sensitive screens, which work in conjunction with a computer and projector – and their efficacy in learning. The detailed discussions about e-learning origin and related issues are beyond the scope of this chapter.

## Digital Transformation to Emerging Virtual Assessment

Moving from campus-based face-to-face learning to remote teaching and learning has featured heavily in the academic literature on the coronavirus pandemic and its impact on educational institutions. The findings and recommendations by academics and practitioners who have reported the COVID-19 related issues have tended to concentrate on three areas: methodological, pedagogical, and tactical.

A group of researchers highlighted the importance of methodological approaches, technical difficulties, considering how these may be resolved, and the importance of always having a second strategy ready in case the first strategy fails to deliver the outcome (Dhawan, 2020). An essential technological infrastructure solution to provide a virtual environment is 'cloud technology' (Zhou et al., 2020), and it can act as a part of contingency planning for such factors as traffic overload on online platforms (Dhawan, 2020). Besides, a critical requirement to ensure that academics' ability to change reflects students' needs in online learning behaviour.

The academic articles that focus on pedagogy stress the importance of adopting strategies for designing online courses that make building relationships between students and educators more effectively whilst continuing to meet the goals of the teaching curriculum (Itow, 2020) (Kessler et al., 2020). Besides, the same academics advocate the appropriate uses of pedagogy to prepare teaching materials. Another research suggests a pedagogical approach that may help educators design and provide an e-learning facility where learning takes place in a student-centered self-determined environment (Majanja, 2020). However, few other researchers suggest that educators should be encouraged to use flipped classroom approaches and that higher education institutions should become adept at setting teaching and learning policies about these approaches (Yen, 2020).

## Psychological Impact of Coronavirus Pandemic

The sudden closure of academic institutions due to pandemic and the subsequent lockdown has left ordinary students and staff bewildered and dealing with diverse types of problems that can contribute to increased anxiety and stress due to its side effects (e.g., job instability, financial concerns, home-based or hall of residence-based education, loneliness, despair, trauma, and sickness).

Several researchers highlight the mental health-related issues of students and staff. For example, a few published articles commented that the move to online learning had harmed both student and staff mental health-related issues. However, one research finding highlights that those students displayed significant mental health issues when faced with a public health emergency (Cao et al., 2020).

An important finding comes from research of the online migration that followed COVID-19, highlighting the major problem caused to pedagogical roles within the higher education sector, creating problems from an educational perspective and educators' personal lives (Watermeyer et al., 2020). They also report that online learning migration creates extra challenges in academic life, particularly in the academic labour market. In addition, a total change in teaching and learning practice in an online environment and alteration of assessment methods has required rapid and often tricky adaptation.

## Creating Collaborative Culture

Changes in teaching and learning service have needed people to communicate and collaborate at various levels of practice in educational institutions. For example, many academic articles discuss that good collaborative culture can often be recognized by traits such as straightforward and flexible structures, prioritizing tasks, challenging work, communication within the professional communities, and relying on goodwill (Talidong & Toquero, 2020) (Regehr & Goel, 2020). Other researchers (Justis et al., 2020) (Krishnamurthy, 2020) suggest that the means of achieving an excellent collaborative culture may be to ensure that an academic institution establishes itself as a community service and does so to find new income streams, respond to cultural shifts, and establish clear opportunities for academics at all levels within the academic institution to collaborate at, and with, higher levels within the industry. Some other studies reflect the future of education post-coronavirus pandemic with a view to digital delivery of teaching and learning activities continuing within the educational institutions. A research study suggests that the current situation could drive innovative, new, and elegant technological resources and closer collaboration between academic institutions (Longhurst et al., 2020).

Moreover, a group of researchers recommended that local communities form part of future educational decisions made within the communities in which they reside (Aguliera et al., 2020). Furthermore, a study identifies that academic have a pivotal role in developing sustainable and quality student support. In addition, student support networks are significant in ensuring that online delivery not only works but continues to serve successfully (Raaper & Brown, 2020). Going forward, academic institutions need to ensure that this pivotal contract is maintained through better dialogue and collaboration.

Recommendations from academic literature provide some tactical recommendations (please see Table 2) for handling crucial issues in meeting the current crisis. The different suggestions provided by the researchers usher several themed approaches to online delivery, some of which appear apparent. However, some provide innovative and novel methods that can hugely enhance online teaching services and the students' experience. For example, since the outbreak of the recent pandemic and the subsequent lockdown, such as Microsoft Teams, Google Meets, and Google Classroom, the rise of online teaching platforms has been increasing. So too has the ability of both academic institution educators and students to adapt rapidly to these alternative online support facilities. These platforms' success in supporting everyday life for individuals and families is also true. However, recent research has highlighted the adaptability of the human being to changing circumstances and surroundings. As one study suggests, the educational institution may be about to move into an age of the algorithm as the professor, where educational practitioners and learners collaborate in regular teaching and learning practices (Krishnamurthy, 2020).

It is also apparent that with diminished scopes to spend time together in person come new challenges to remain socially connected. For example, during the first few months of the current coronavirus pandemic, industry reports highlighted that digital media use heavily increased as people spent more time at home due to lockdowns (Kemp, 2020). Such increases were especially prevalent for social media and information technology-based messaging applications, but specifically remarkable was the unprecedented uptake in video conferencing applications. This further bears assessment, given educators' and students' extensive reliance on information and communications technologies (ICTs) for social interaction under such stay-at-home circumstances. The other important aspect of higher education teaching and learning delivery is an appropriate collaborative culture within the digital learning environment. However, there is research gap of students view regarding communication channels used in the current pandemic. The following

*Figure 2. Few communication channels in global software development*

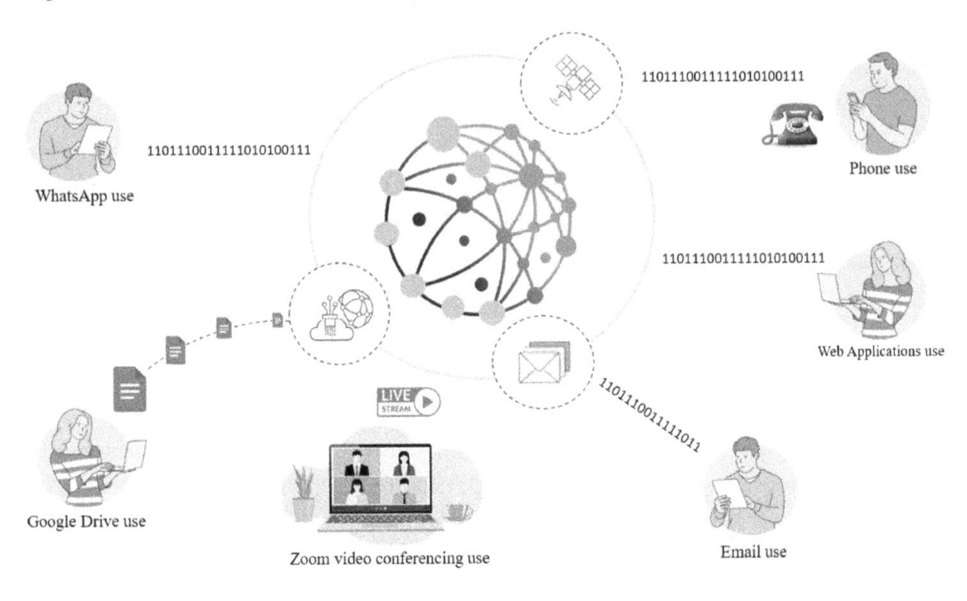


section describes a students' reflective experience of information technology use in an undergraduate software engineering team project.

## BEHAVIOR CHANGE CASE STUDIES

### Case of Collaborative Software Development

Software systems design and development have changed from an individual activity of designing standalone applications to a primarily distributed and collaborative approach that depends on or contributes to large and complicated software ecosystems (Pal, 2020) (Pal, 2019). Thus, software systems designers need to collaborate with, learn from and co-design with many other team members, creating a participatory culture within distributed software development work practice (Pal & Karakostas, 2020).

Promising distributed and collaborative software system design and development needs proper communication mechanisms. Thus, encouraging software developers' collaboration and communication need new technology-supported techniques (e.g., telephone, web-based applications, WhatsApp, email, and Zoom video conferencing system) are adopted. An essential diagrammatic representation of a few of the communication channels is depicted in Figure 2. The affluence and capability of these tools are improving current global software design and development activities. Subsequently, software developers require to learn new skills to use these tools. Moreover, these communication tools permit creativity in work activity, usher engagement, and help software design and development participation. This commitment is also advocated for cultural issues of the global software design team.

Appreciating global software design and development team-based culture is the basis to understanding what goes on in software development teams, coordinating them, and enhancing their work practice (Schein, 1992). Team-based software design and development culture is defined as the shared assumptions, beliefs, and expected behaviours (norms) present in a global team.

Within these new initiatives of software development regular activities, software design includes externalized knowledge (e.g., project-related document exchange, technical guidelines, programming instructions to manage software development) and the tacit knowledge that resides in developers' heads (e.g., design constraints, hardware constraints, operational practices). In reality, communication and software development tools (e.g., Computer-Aided Software Design Environment) provide guidance to generate and share (i.e., externalize) tacit knowledge in a highly collaborative environment.

Knowledge management is a crucial mechanism to foster improvements in software development processes. Organizational culture is an integral factor in knowledge management's success since it influences how software developers learn and share knowledge within a team. A research-based justification is that organizational culture affects how staff learn, acquire, and share knowledge (Knapp & Yu, 1999). Finally, the chapter provides a case study of an undergraduate software development team project to assess KM and organizational culture practices. This case study for software design and development duration was around three months. Twenty-one students expressed their views regarding team project communication channel uses and KM-related issues.

## Relevance of Knowledge Management in Software Development

As software development is an abstract engineering discipline, knowledge management is essential. When developing software, a high degree of coordination (Kraut & Streeter, 1995) and management (Sommerville, 2001; Pressman, 2000) become vital tasks. Because the focus is to solve specific problems, software projects' organization often differs enormously from one to the other. A research work (Sveiby, 1997) points out that most companies face similar problems in administrating their intellectual capital. For example, he explains that employees are usually highly educated and qualified professionals whose regular job is using their competence to develop software. Their primary resource is their knowledge; therefore, they are called knowledge workers.

The core activities of software engineering contain the management of documents or competencies and software re-use. With product and project memory, the authors refer to the evolution of software, e.g., with the help of systems for version control, change management or design documentation. Finally, the learning and improvement include a recording of results and experiences. The reason is to learn from that and improve future decisions or activities. The desire to improve in these three areas of concern motivates knowledge management in software development (Pal & Williams, 2021). In order to conduct knowledge management successfully, many different approaches are possible and documented. For example, information systems applied to manage a company's knowledge or support managing a company's knowledge are referred to as knowledge management systems.

## COORDINATION AND COMMUNICATION IN SOFTWARE DEVELOPMENT

Coordination between software development team members is one of the most challenging ways to improve software systems design and development. For example, a group of researchers (Kraut & Streeter, 1995) argue that the software design and development industry has been in difficulties mode for its entire existence, and an important reason is a difficulty coordinating work between team members. Academics and practitioners have empirically studied professional software development teams to understand by analyzing software development processes, techniques, CASE tools, and human factors in the coordination process. Inter-team coordination is an essential concern as software development increasingly becomes globally distributed and remains a persistent industry challenge.

Simple coordination can be viewed as decision-making and action-taking *collaboration,* communication, and *cooperation.* These three components of work practices are necessary but insufficient for coordination. Collaboration is an essential part of group work. Communication is necessary because member A needs to communicate with person B, in some form, what needs to be done needed for the group. Cooperation is essential because B requires being willing to do what is required for the group. If any of the three mandatory components are lacking, the outcome will be less than ideal.

Viewing coordination through this framework leads one to ask several research questions:

1. What kinds of behaviours are associated with being helpful or unhelpful to others?
2. How do members of a software team communicate to get work done?

3. How do software teams handle dependencies on a personal level?

This chapter presents a survey-based data analysis to understand inter-team dependencies in software development.

## Background of Survey-Based Data Analysis

The experimental work was conducted in an undergraduate team-based student software design and development project. Multiple choice questionaries were used to survey students. The study was based on three individual groups, and each group consisted of pre-assigned team members. The rationale behind students' pre-assignment to teams is to ensure that teams balance talent, skills, and expertise and become aware that one must learn to establish good working relations with "*strangers*" and acquaintances in their future career's friends.

Each team worked independently of others on the same case study. The team members ' joint responsibilities were each team's internal organization, planning the project, defining a management structure, and carrying out the work (technical or organizational). In addition, each team member was expected to adopt two roles in a software development project, associated job titles, and responsibility for those tasks falling within their remit.

Each team member adopts two roles (e.g., project manager, deputy project manager, system analyst, designer, programmer or coding specialist, software tester) described in the policy document. Project manager responsible for team planning, coordination, and risk management. The team manager was the central contact point to the team consultant and the client, and the role must contribute to technical work. The Deputy project manager was second in command and responsible for documentation, reports, and standards, including technical work. A system analyst was responsible for the elicitation of customer requirements; the system designer oversaw the system design process. The programmer was dedicated to implementing the system. The software tester was responsible for writing a test plan, testing the system and its components, and recording the outcomes. Each team member had one primary role and a secondary role, e.g., project manager/systems analyst or designer/programmer. The roles were appropriately spread. Finally, it ensured that essential roles within the team were covered when members were absent.

The survey revealed that the most helpful behaviours between all the teams are related to cooperation and availability. The unhelpful behaviours are related to location (primarily felt by the distributed team members), ownership and awareness, and availability. This research finds that coordination problems in the distributed teams can be considered a superset of collocated teams' problems; distributed development adds additional difficulties caused by location (i.e., time zone), culture, and meetings mode.

## EXPERIMENTAL STUDY METHOD

The online survey consisted of one-hour; semi-structured, open-ended multiple-choice questions based on the 'echo' method designed by Bavelas (Bavelas, 1942). The method is used in studies of organizations to examine task interactions in new product development (Duimering et al., 2006) and task structures of a group of professionals (Bjorn et al., 2014).

### Student Survey Results

In this step, participating students' opinions were gathered through discussions and questionnaires. The contextual information of communication and collaboration information, channel preference, and the relationship between the knowledge management cycle and organizational culture through the CVF was discussed at length. Then a multiple-choice opinion survey questionnaire was used in the opinion collection process.

In a team-based software design and development practice, groups of people are connected by the similarity of their project activities. Group members do not have to be spatially or socially connected, but they solve similar problems and learn from each other through processes like group discussion or one-to-one subject-specific matter. Members advance through a process called team-based or group-based learning and provide value to the software development community.

For example, a software designer may start acquiring knowledge by reading discussions and reporting bugs (or errors). Over time, the software designer learns from community discussions and collaborations. This way, software designers or developers may start fixing bugs and enhance their skills to the point where they can use the acquired knowledge to help other group members.

Due to the globalization of the software industry, software design and development can take place in a distributed setting, where contributors need not be in the same office or town. These global software developers often communicate on a scale and are mostly interconnected via information and communication technology (ICT) based application tools. These global communication tools can help software project management issues (e.g., sharing technological knowledge, collaboration with project members or clients). In addition, the participating students provided their opinions on the following categories: (i) coordinate with others, (ii) communicate

*Figure 3. Communication channels used by the respondents*

| | Face-to-Face | Books | Web Search | Dedicated Websites | Video Conferencing | Private Discussion | Group Discussion | Electronic mail | Telephone Conversation | Online Collaboration |
|---|---|---|---|---|---|---|---|---|---|---|
| | Analog | | Digital | | | | | | | |
| Communicate with Others | 65% | | | | 35% | 11% | 22% | 38% | 77% | |
| Coordinate with Others | 12% | | | | 27% | | | | | |
| Learn | 63% | | | | 21% | | | | | |
| Find Answers | | 52% | 37% | 29% | 5% | | | | | |
| Learn with Other Team Members | 45% | | | | | | | | | |
| Watch Activities | | | | 24% | 31% | | | | | |

with other members, (iii) learn with other members, (iv) learn by watching, and (v) stay up to date.

The student opinion survey also used different communication channels and resources, such as video conferencing, textbook, google search, private discussion, group discussion, and private chat facility, for project collaboration and knowledge management. This section presents more detailed information on why specific channels were considered vital to the team project management. For example, in the student team project context, the current survey on KM practice belongs to more than one quadrant of the SECI model. Figure 3 presents some participating students' opinions in a two-dimensional visual representation.

Most of the team members (65%) expressed their preference for face-to-face communication for software system design. Their primary justification is that they can receive quick feedback from the team members, facilitate talking through complex problems, discuss ideas, and make software design decisions. Thus, the team uses its efforts to make explicit knowledge tacit, supporting the learning process. One example of the internalization practice identified is team members integration, which occurs after a project member learns about the team's software development process. Therefore, knowledge internalization occurs when the team's explicit knowledge (stored on Google Drive) is presented to help project team members to learn it.

The success of a software development team is the ability to coordinate successfully with one another. Private discussion (e.g., Zoom video conferencing, Email, Telephone) is essential for supporting team collaboration through single or multiple channels. Besides, effective teams contain team members who appreciate each other's ideas. If team members are ignored or belittled after providing input, they will probably stop engaging in team activities (e.g., team meetings, discussions). When this disengaging attitude prevails, collaboration is complicated. Also, some team members are not naturally driven to start communication and discussion. Taking the time to assess who is driven to talk things through compared to those who are not allowed a team member ensures everyone is given appropriate airtime.

Electronic mail (or email) is identified as a virtual channel (38%) to support discussion across virtually every platform and among different stakeholders (e.g., client, team member). It is a convenient channel for disseminating information to large groups while keeping conversations private and persistent for later retrieval. This is how one can communicate privately and have proof later.

Team members were introduced with technologies, practices, and tools for software development (e.g., software documentation, technical articles, formal lecture handouts) using different channels (e.g., virtual learning environment – Moodle, Email, Forum, Blogs, and Dedicated websites). Within a team-based software development project, tasks consist of activities that require to be carried out by one or multiple team members. For example, the project manager can allocate a task to multiple team members or leave it unassigned for anyone to carry out the work. Tasks need to have start dates and due dates or be left without dates to be completed anytime. Software project management tools are handy to keep the team members up to date with the progress.

Learning with other team members is an important activity in software development projects. It is part of developing a team, whether a new team leader or an experienced manager. People need training and support throughout their working life, both as individuals and as teams, to develop their skills and work effectively. A substantial number of survey participants (45%) expressed their view positively on team learning.

In addition, team members learn by watching others or finding answers to a problem from books, web searches, or dedicated websites. For example, it can be watching a video on a YouTube channel or watching a recording in a teaching and learning environment (e.g., Moodle). Web search can be a valuable tool for learners, and a bit of instruction in how to search for learning sources will help the learners become critical thinkers and independent learners. More than half of the student participants (52%) in the assessment expressed that they find problem solutions using recommended technical books in software development. At the same time, thirty-seven per cent of the participating students agreed that they get a problem solution by using a web search.

Telephone conversations have the advantage of enabling communication among software development team members and clients of a particular project. For example, many participants (77%) expressed their support favoring telephone conversation.

## FUTURE DIRECTIONS FOR RESEARCH

Most of the research included in this analysis has come from the developed or the stronger developing countries, with almost no research published about lesser developed but developing countries or undeveloped countries. Thus far, education is at the heart of all these countries' futures. How those countries have adapted to the coronavirus related crisis and responded to educating citizens is a crucial area of future research that needs to be assessed. It will be alluring to compare the experience of educators, students, and other education business stakeholders in different regions and countries. Given that evidence advocates that people from Black, Asian, and Minority groups (BAME) are more likely to be seriously impacted by coronavirus pandemic, education institutions should concentrate precisely on these groups' impact and contrast the disabled person down the educational activities of BAME staff and students. Other applications may concentrate on, for example, the impact on employment, economic growth, future earning differentials, trade gaps, student recruitment, and digital literacy. The influence of hearing the student voice when decisions are being made in a time of crisis, pandemic, or radical change, may also be a key area to do further investigative research.

## CONCLUSION

This chapter reviews the coronavirus pandemic impact on higher educational institutions. It also highlighted that the current pandemic poses extraordinary challenges to global public health, socioeconomic stability, food security, and other social goods. The inequality (e.g., education, healthcare, social wellbeing) of opportunities, which divide people within and across countries, seem to worsen due to the current pandemic. Public education and public health are very closely interrelated. It is undeniable that education makes a scholarly society. The collective action and collaboration of these common goods (i.e., education, public health) help to defeat future pandemics. It will usher new dawn to build civic trust and understanding, deepen human empathy, create the option of progressing in science and innovation, and appreciate human society's value.

The chapter also presents two case studies to examine changes in student behaviour and their psychological antecedents during the coronavirus pandemic. One of the case studies was specifically interested in student learning related communication and knowledge sharing skills in a group project context.

Although current literature is still relatively scarce about the coronavirus pandemic's impact on academic institutions, there are significant indications of increased disruption in teaching and learning, particularly in the change from face-to-face teaching to virtual teaching and learning. Many studies have proposed ways to achieve such transitions, such as training in digital literacy, using digital flipped classrooms, encouraging students to use peer to peer learning, and building a collaborative community. Also, the pandemic has pressured educators to go beyond their regular working routine; the reviewed academic articles depict the pandemic's negative psychological impact. Finally, the educators must focus on improving student engagement, whether virtually or onsite, during the pandemic and post-pandemic.

## REFERENCES

Abdulrahim, H., & Mabrouk, F. (2020). COVID-19 and the Digital Transformation of Saudi Higher Education. *Asian Journal of Distance Education*, *15*(1), 291–306.

Aguliera, E., & Nightengale-Lee, B. (2020). Emergency Remote Teaching across Urban and Rural Contexts: Perspectives on Educational Equity. *Inf. Learn. Sci.*, *2020*(121), 471–478. doi:10.1108/ILS-04-2020-0100

Alonso-Fernández, C., Caballero Roldán, R., Freire, M., & Martinez-ortiz, I., & FernándezManjón, B. (2019). Predicting students' knowledge after playing a serious game based on learning analytics data. *IEEE Access: Practical Innovations, Open Solutions*.

Baloran, E. T. (2020). Knowledge, Attitudes, Anxiety, and Coping Strategies of Students during COVID-19 Pandemic. *Journal of Loss and Trauma*, *2020*, 1–8.

Bavelas, A. (1942). A method for investigating individual and group ideology. *Sociometry*, *5*(4), 371–377. doi:10.2307/2785286

BBC. (2020). Coronavirus: Only Go to Your Job If You Cannot Work from Home—Hancock. In *Coronavirus Pandemic*. BBC. https://www.bbc.co.uk/news/uk-52022417

Bjorn, P. M., Esbensen, M., Jensen, E., & Matthiesen, S. (2014). Does distance still matter? Revisiting the CSCW fundamentals on distributed collaboration. *ACM Transactions on Computer-Human Interaction*, *21*(5), 27. doi:10.1145/2670534

Cameron, K. S., & Quinn, R. E. (1999). *Diagnosing and Changing Organizational Culture Based on the Competing Values Framework*. Addison-Wesley Publishing Company, Inc.

Cao, W., Fang, Z., Hou, G., Han, M., Xu, X., Dong, J., & Zheng, J. (2020). The Psychological Impact of the COVID-19 Epidemic on College Students in China. *Psychiatry Research, 2020*(287), 112934. doi:10.1016/j.psychres.2020.112934 PMID:32229390

Charitos, D., Lepouras, G., Vassilakis, C., Katifori, V., & Halatsi, L. (2000). An Approach to Designing and Implementing Virtual Museums. *Proceedings of the Seventh UK VR-SIG Conference.*

Code, J., Ralph, R., & Forde, K. (2020). Pandemic Designs for the Future: Perspectives of Technology Education Teachers during COVID-19. *Inf. Learn. Sci., 2020*(121), 419–431. doi:10.1108/ILS-04-2020-0112

Cotton, D. R., Nash, T., & Kneale, P. (2017). Supporting the retention of non-traditional students in higher education using a resilience framework. *European Educational Research Journal, 16*(1), 62–79.

DePape, A., Barnes, M., & Petryschuk, J. (2019). Students' Experiences in Higher Education with Virtual and Augmented Reality: A Qualitative Systematic Review. *Innovative Practice in Higher Education, 3*(3), 22–57.

Dever, D. A., & Azevedo, R. (2019). Autonomy and types of informational text presentations in game-based learning environments. In S. Isotani, E. Millán, A. Ogan, P. Hastings, B. McLaren, & R. Luckin (Eds.), *AIED'19: Proceedings of the 20th International Conference on Artificial Intelligence in Education* (pp. 110-120). Springer.

Dhawan, S. (2020). Online Learning: A Panacea in the Time of COVID-19 Crisis. *Journal of Educational Technology Systems, 2020*(49), 5–22. doi:10.1177/0047239520934018

Duimering, P. R., Ran, B., Derbentseva, N., & Poile, C. (2006). The effects of ambiguity on project task structure in new product development. *Knowledge and Process Management, 13*(4), 239–251. doi:10.1002/kpm.260

Dutta, S., & Lanvin, B. (2020). *The Network Readiness Index 2020: Accelerating Digital Transformation in a post-COVID Global Economy*. Academic Press.

Gee, J. P. (2003). *What video games have to teach us about learning and literacy*. Palgrave Macmillan.

Georgiev, T., Georgieva, E., & Smrikarov, A. (2004). *M-learning – a new stage of e-learning*. Paper presented at the International Conference on Computer Systems and Technologies – CompSysTech' 2004.

Georgiev, T., Georgieva, E., & Smrikarov, A. (2004). M-learning: a new stage of e-learning, *Proceedings of the International Conference on Computer Systems and Technologies (CompSysTech)*, *4*(28), 1–4.

Gouedard, P., Pont, B., & Viennet, R. (2020). *Education responses to COVID-19: Implementing a way forward*. OECD Education Working Paper No. 224.

Higgins, S. (2014). Critical thinking for 21st-century education: A cyber-tooth curriculum? *Prospects*, *44*(4), 559–574.

Inkpen, K., Booth, K., Klawe, M., & Upitis, R. (1995). Playing together beats playing apart, especially for girls. In J. Schnase, & E. Cunnius (Eds.), *Proceedings of CSCL 1995: The First International Conference on Computer Support for Collaborative Learning* (pp. 177– 181). Hillsdale, NJ: Erlbaum.

Itow, R. C. (2020). Fostering Valuable Learning Experiences by Transforming Current Teaching Practices: Practical Pedagogical Approaches from Online Practitioners. *Inf. Learn. Sci.*, *2020*(121), 443–452. doi:10.1108/ILS-04-2020-0106

Jayathirtha, G., Fields, D., Kafai, Y. B., & Chipps, J. (2020). Supporting Making Online: The Role of Artifact, Teacher, and Peer Interactions in Crafting Electronic Textiles. *Inf. Learn. Sci.*, *2020*(121), 381–390. doi:10.1108/ILS-04-2020-0111

Justis, N., Litts, B.K., Reina, L., & Rhodes, S. (2020). Cultivating Staff Culture Online: How Edith Bowen Laboratory School Responded to COVID-19. *Inf. Learn. Sci. 2020.*

Kandroudi, M., & Bratitsis, T. (2012). Exploring the Educational Perspectives of XBOX Kinect Based Video Games. *Proc.ECGBL 2012*, 219-227.

Kemps, S. (2020). *Report: Most important data on digital audience during coronavirus*. Growth Quarter – The Next Web. https://thenextweb.com/growth-quarters/2020/04/24/report-most-important-data-on-digital-audiences-during-coronavirus/

Kessler, A. Barnes, S. Rajagopal, K. Rankin, J. Pouchak, L. Silis, M. & Esser, W. (2020). Saving a Semester of Learning: MIT's Emergency Transition to Online Instruction. *Inf. Learn. Sci.*

Knapp, E. & Yu, D. (1999). Understanding organizational culture: how culture helps or hinders the flow of knowledge. *Knowledge Management Review*, 16-21.

Kraut, R. E., & Streeter, L. A. (1995). Coordination in Software Development. *Communications of the ACM, 38*(3), 69–81.

Krishnamurthy, S. (2020). The Future of Business Education: A Commentary in the Shadow of the Covid-19 Pandemic. *Journal of Business Research, 2020*(117), 1–5.

Laine, T. H., & Joy, M. (2009). Survey on Context-Aware Pervasive Learning Environments. *International Journal of Interactive Mobile Technology, 3*(1), 70–76.

Lane, H. C., & D'Mello, S. K. (2019). Uses of physiological monitoring in intelligent learning environments: A review of research, evidence, and technologies. In T. Parsons, L. Lin, & D. Cockerham (Eds.), *Mind, brain and technology. Educational Communications and Technology: Issues and Innovations*. Springer.

Laouris, Y., & Eteokleous, N. (2005). *We need an educational relevant definition of mobile learning*. Academic Press.

Laouris, Y., & Laouri, R. (2006).Can Information and Mobile Technologies serve to close the gap and accelerate development? *Proceedings of MLearn 2006*.

Li, W., Liao, J., Li, Q., Baskota, M., Wang, X., Tang, Y., Zhou, Q., Wang, X., Luo, X., Ma, Y., Fukuoka, T., Ahn, H. S., Lee, M. S., Chen, Y., Luo, Z., & Liu, E. (2020). Public Health Education for Parents during the Outbreak of COVID-19: A Rapid Review. *Annals of Translational Medicine, 2020*(8), 628. doi:10.21037/atm-20-3312 PMID:32566565

Lipka, O., Forkosh-Baruch, A., & Meer, Y. (2019). Academic support model for post-secondary school students with learning disabilities: Student and instructor perceptions. *International Journal of Inclusive Education, 23*(2), 142–157.

Longhurst, G. J., Stone, D. M., Dulohery, K., Scully, D., Campbell, T., & Smith, C. F. (2020). Strength, Weakness, Opportunity, Threat (SWOT) Analysis of the Adaptations to Anatomical Education in the United Kingdom and Republic of Ireland in Response to the Covid-19 Pandemic. *Anatomical Sciences Education, 2020*(13), 301–311. doi:10.1002/ase.1967 PMID:32306550

Majanja, M. K. (2020). The Status of Electronic Teaching within South African LIS Education. *Library Management, 2020*(41), 317–337. doi:10.1108/LM-05-2020-0084

Majanja, M.K. (2020). The status of electronic teaching within South African LIS education. *Library Management, 41*(6/7), 317-337. doi:10.1108/LM-05-2020-0084

Maloney, S., Hass, R., Keating, J. L., Molloy, E., Jolly, B., Sims, J., Morgan, P., & Haines, T. (2012). Breakeven, Cost Benefit, Cost Effectiveness, and Willingness to Pay for Web-Based Versus Face-to-Face Education Delivery for Health Professionals. *Journal of Medical Internet Research, 14*(2), 1–16.

McFarlane, A., Sparrowhawk, A., & Heald, Y. (2002). *Report on the Educational Use of Games. TEEM.* Teachers Evaluating Educational Multimedia.

McFarlane, A., Sparrowhawk, A., & Heald, Y. (2002) Report on the educational use of games: an exploration by TEEM of the contribution which games can make to the education process in Cambridge. *U.K. TEEM (Teachers Evaluating Educational Multimedia), 27.*

Mcmahon, C.J., Heying, R., & Budts, W. (2022). Paediatric and adult congenital cardiology education and training in Europe. *Cardiol Young*, 1-18.

Mostakhdemin-Hosseini, A., & Najafabadi, N. (2006). *The Mobile Phone Constitutive Effect on Student Life in Finland.* IEEE-IMCL, Interactive Mobile.

Nesenbergs, K., Abolins, V., Ormanis, J., & Mednis, A. (2021). Use of Augmented and Virtual Reality in Remote Higher Education: A Systematic Umbrella Review. *Education in Science, 11*(8), 1–12.

Oblinger, D. G. (2006). *Learning Spaces, Washington.* EDUCAUSE.

Pal, K. (2019). Markov Decision Theory Based Crowdsourcing Software Process Model. In Crowdsourcing and Probabilistic Decision-Making in Software Engineering: Emerging Research and Opportunities. IGI Global.

Pal, K. (2020). Framework for Reusable Test Case Generation in Software Systems Testing. In Software Engineering for Agile Application Development. IGI Global.

Pal, K. (2022). Reflection on Teaching Practice for Agile Methodology Based Product Development Management. In Teaching Innovation in University Education: Case Studies and Main Practices. IGI Global.

Pal, K., & Karakostas, B. (2020). Software Testing Under Agile, Scrum, and DevOps. In Agile Scrum Implementation and Its Long-Term Impact on Organizations. IGI Publication.

Pal, K., & Williams, I. (2021). Software Development Knowledge Management System Using Web Portal. In Digital Technology Advancement in Knowledge Management. IGI Publication.

Parsons, S., Beardon, L., Neale, H. R., Reynard, G., Eastgate, R., Wilson, J. R., Cobb, S. V., Benford, S. D., Mitchell, P., & Hopkins, E. (2000). Development of social skills amongst adults with Asperger's Syndrome using virtual environments: the 'AS Interactive' project. In *Proc. The 3rd International Conference on Disability, Virtual Reality and Associated Technologies, ICDVRAT 2000*, 163-170.

Pechenkina, E., Laurence, D., Oates, G., Eldridge, D., & Hunter, D. (2017). Using a gamification mobile app to increase student engagement, retention and academic achievement. *International Journal of Educational Technology in Higher Education, 14*(13), 1–13.

Plöckinger, M., Aschauer, E., Hiebl, M. R. W., & Rohatschek, R. (2016). The Influence of Individual Executives on Corporate Financial Reporting: A Review and Outlook from the Perspective of Upper Echelons Theory. *Journal of Accounting Literature, 2016*(37), 55–75. doi:10.1016/j.acclit.2016.09.002

Pressman, R. S. (2000). *Software engineering: A Practitioner's Approach (European Adaption)* (5th ed.). McGraw-Hill International.

Quinn, C. (2000). *mLearning: mobile, wireless, in-your-pocket learning*. LineZine. www.linezine.com/2.1/features/cqmmwiyp.htm

Raaper, R., & Brown, C. (2020). The Covid-19 Pandemic and the Dissolution of the University Campus: Implications for Student Support Practice. *Journal of Professional Capital and Community*, 2020.

Rajasingham, L. (2011). *Will mobile learning bring a paradigm shift in higher education?* Education Research International.

Rajhans, V., Memon, U., Patil, V., & Goyal, A. (2020). Impact of COVID-19 on Academic Activities and Way Forward in Indian Optometry. *Journal of Optometry, 2020*(13), 216–226. doi:10.1016/j.optom.2020.06.002 PMID:32703749

Regehr, C., & Goel, V. (2020). Managing COVID-19 in a Large Urban Research-Intensive University. *Journal of Loss and Trauma, 2020*(6-7), 1–17. doi:10.1080/15325024.2020.1771846

Rodríguez-Hernández, C. F., Cascallar, E., & Kyndt, E. (2020). Socio-Economic Status and Academic Performance in Higher Education: A Systematic Review. *Educational Research Review, 2020*(29), 100305. doi:10.1016/j.edurev.2019.100305

Roy, D., Tripathy, S., Kar, S. K., Sharma, N., Verma, S. K., & Kaushal, V. (2020). Study of Knowledge, Attitude, Anxiety & Perceived Mental Healthcare Need in Indian Population during COVID-19 Pandemic. *Asian Journal of Psychiatry, 2020*, 51. doi:10.1016/j.ajp.2020.102083 PMID:32283510

Rus, I., & Lindvall, M. (2002, June). Knowledge Management in Software Engineering. *IEEE Software, 19*(3), 26–38. doi:10.1109/MS.2002.1003450

Schein, E. H. (1992). *Organizational Culture and Leadership* (2nd ed.). Jossey Bass.

Sharples, M. (2000). The design of personal mobile technologies for lifelong learning. *Computer Education.*

Sharples, M., Taylor, J., & Vavoula, G. (2007). *A Theory of Learning for the Mobile Age. The Sage Handbook of E-learning Research.* Sage.

Sjostrom, M., Lindholm, L., & Samuelsson, E. (2017). Mobile App for Treatment of Stress Urinary Incontinence: A Cost-Effectiveness Analysis. *Journal of Medical Internet Research, 19*(5), 1–12.

Skulmowski, A., & Rey, G. D. (2020). COVID-19 as an Accelerator for Digitalization at a German University: Establishing Hybrid Campuses in Times of Crisis. *Human Behavior and Emerging Technologies, 2020*(2), 212–216. doi:10.1002/hbe2.201 PMID:32838228

Sommerville, I. (2001). *Software Engineering* (6th ed.). Addison-Wesley.

Squire, K. D. (2008). Video games and education: Designing learning systems for an interactive age. *Educational Technology, 48*(2), 17–26.

Sveiby, K. E. (1997). *The New Organizational Wealth: Managing & Measuring Knowledge-Based Assets.* Berrett-Koehler Publishers, Inc.

Talidong, K. J. B., & Toquero, C. M. D. (2020). Philippine Teachers' Practices to Deal with Anxiety amid COVID-19. *Journal of Loss and Trauma, 2020*(6-7), 1–7. doi:10.1080/15325024.2020.1759225

United Nations. (2020). Policy Brief: Education during COVID-19 and beyond. United Nations.

Unterhalter, E. (2019). The Many Meaning of Quality Education: Politics of Targets and Indicators in SDG4. *Global Policy, 10*(1), 39–51.

Unterhalter, E., Longlands, H., & Vaughan, R. P. (2022). Article. *Journal of Human Development and Capabilities*, 1–30.

Veitch, S., Strehlow, K., & Boyd, J. (2018). Supporting university students with socially challenging behaviours through professional development for teaching staff. *Journal of Academic Language and Learning*, *12*(1), 156–167.

Vygotsky, L. S. (1978). *Mind in society*. Harvard University Press.

Watermeyer, R., Crick, T., Knight, C., & Goodall, J. (2020). COVID-19 and Digital Disruption in UK Universities: Afflictions and Affordances of Emergency Online Migration. *Higher Education*, *2020*(81), 623–641. PMID:32836334

Whitton, N. & Moseley, A. (2012). *Using games to enhance learning and teaching: A beginner's guide*. London: Taylor and Francis.

Wu, H. K., Lee, S. W. Y., Chang, H. Y., & Liang, J. C. (2013). Current status, opportunities and challenges of augmented reality in education. *Computer Education*, *62*, 41–49.

Yen, T. T. F. (2020). The Performance of Online Teaching for Flipped Classroom Based on COVID-19 Aspect. *Asian J. Educ. Soc. Studies*, *2020*(8), 57–64. doi:10.9734/ajess/2020/v8i330229

Zainuddin, Z., Perera, C. J., Haruna, H., & Habiburrahim, H. (2020). Literacy in the New Norm: Stay-Home Game Plan for Parents. *Inf. Learn. Sci.*, *2020*(121), 645–653. doi:10.1108/ILS-04-2020-0069

Zhou, L., Wu, S., Zhou, M., & Li, F. (2020). 'School's Out, But Class' On,' The Largest Online Education in the World Today: Taking China's Practical Exploration During The COVID-19 Epidemic Prevention and Control as an Example. *Best Evid. Chin. Edu.*, *2020*(4), 501–519. doi:10.15354/bece.20.ar023

## ADDITIONAL READING

United Nations. (2020). *Policy Brief: The World of Work and Covid-19*. https://un.org/sites/un2.un.org/files/ the_world_of_work_andcovid-19.pdf

United Nations Development. (2021). *Program Responding to the COVID-19 Pandemic: Leaving No Country Behind*. https://www.undp.org/tag/report?type=publications

## APPENDIX

In recent decades, mobile and ubiquitous learning is getting importance from higher education teaching and learning professionals. Like no previous technology, mobile technology (e.g., cell phones, pads, smartphones) has spread at an unprecedented pace in the last few years. For example, in 2021, mobile phone subscriptions reached 8.3 billion (Thales, 2021). Mobile devices are considered '*social innovation cockpits*', changing socio-cultural practices and structures in all spheres of life (Pachler et al., 2010). This transformation is considered an important milestone from an evolutionary perspective because it helps people on this earth to use different communication channels free from the constraints of '*physical proximity* and '*spatial immobility*' related issues (Geser, 2004). In addition, mobile technologies are increasingly providing a means to engage with learning for higher education students at the time of their desperate needs. This way, higher education students can use mobile devices to play subject-related games, watch videos and listen to lecture materials while doing their secondary jobs. Besides, some digital technologies (e.g., virtual and augmented reality) provide higher education students with a better learning experience.

Different research works have been conducted to discover and provide insights into the growing body of academic literature on mobile computing-based learning. Some of these reviews are based on teaching material design purposes, and others deal with students' interaction and engagement with mobile devices. For example, in 2004, Naismith and fellow researchers reviewed mobile learning and learners' activity-focused case studies on using mobile technologies for teaching and learning purposes (Naismith et al., 2004). Another research group (Cheung & Hew, 2009) reviewed research methodologies used in mobile learning for different educational institutions (e.g., schools and higher education institutions). This research group reviewed 44 academic publications and highlighted that descriptive research was a dominating methodology in their collected samples. In addition, most of these research groups used questionnaires as a data collection method. Frohberg and research colleagues (Frohberg et al., 2009) reviewed a sample of 109 mobile learning projects to assess and evaluate the outcome. They also used a classification method to categorize them against a mobile learning task model. Hwang and Tasi (2011) reviewed research trends in mobile and ubiquitous learning by assessing 154 research publications from six major technology-enhanced learning publications from 2001 to 2010. This particular research group found that the number of studies increased significantly over time. They also highlighted that higher education students were the most frequent learning population, and most publications did not consider a specific learning domain.

*Table 2. Relative comparison of existing digital learning for academic institutions*

| Reference | Description | Objective |
|---|---|---|
| (Alonso-Fernandez et al., 2019)<br>(Alonso-Fernandez et al., 2020)<br>(Lane & D'Mello, 2019)<br>(Dever et al., 2019) | Several studies have examined knowledge acquisition with game-based learning environments using a range of data channels. | Channel such as gameplay behaviour traces.<br>Channel such as facial expressions.<br>Channel such as eye gaze |
| (Sjostrom et al., 2017) | Malin Sjostrom and fellow researchers presented a '*mobile app*' to treat stress urinary incontinence. It facilitates self-management and improves adherence to medical treatment. The researchers investigated the cost-effectiveness of the app. | The software-based app for treating stress urinary incontinence is a new, cost-effective, first-line treatment with the potential to increase healthcare access sustainably for patients. |
| (Pechenkina et al., 2017) | This study investigated whether a gamified mobile learning app influences students' academic performance and boosts their engagement in the subject. | This research concluded that in the context of the broader scholarship of the mobile app, enhanced learning and applied game principles in higher education. |
| (Maloney et al., 2012) | Stephen Maloney and colleagues try to present a comparison of web-based and face-to-face education delivery for healthcare professionals. | Break-even analysis identified the web-based educational approach as robustly superior to face-to-face education. |
| (Wu et al., 2013) | A group of researchers discussed the overview of augmented reality (AR) that can support mobile environments to generate student learning engagement. | Researchers recommend that mobile or smartphones enhance their technology empowerment to be more affordable in executing any application in the learning process. |
| (Nesenbergs et al., 2021) | Krisjanis Nesenbergs and fellow researchers presented a systematic review on AR / VR use in remote higher education. | The results show that most of the reviewed experiments pertain to organizing laboratory or practical exercises within virtual or augmented reality in cases when physical presence is not feasible, Some of the reviewed research experiments were very encouraging, especially in medicine related education. |
| (Laine & Joy, 2009) | T. H. Laine and M. Joy presented their observations on most common sensor technology in teaching and learning environment. | Context-aware Learning arises from the inclusion of context-awareness in the learning process. Thus, the educational process takes advantage of the flexibility provided by the use of real-time environmental information within the process. |

# Chapter 12
# COVID-19 Reactions, Responses, and Ramifications for the Future of Education

**Oindrila Chakraborty**
*J.D. Birla Institute, India*

## ABSTRACT

*In this chapter an endeavour has been established to capture the pre-COVID-19 and COVID-19-related educational transformation and adaptability of the teaching-learning community to embrace the exigency-based changes along with the exploration of the community of inquiry model (CoI) with its three basic elements: social presence, cognitive presence, and teaching presence. The chapter also delves into the learners' and teachers' reactions and adaptability towards the change to acquire it as a permanent solution to the traditional teaching procedure. There would be a discourse on the use of ICT (information and communications technology) to address the issues of coping mechanism with the virtual platform, making it a seamless process. In this chapter, the target audience gets a fair cognitive familiarity with the present state and future prediction of the COVID-19-driven pandemic and ramification of it in the future for academic discourse and referencing.*

## INTRODUCTION

The Covid 19 introduced a havoc transformation in the global educational scenario by creating huge disturbances, alienation and almost collapse of the existing teaching-learning process. The precautionary measures incorporated several social distancing, shielding and cleaning norms, culminating in Government declaration for closing of

DOI: 10.4018/978-1-6684-5400-8.ch012

Schools, Colleges and other educational Institutions. (Pokhrel and Chhetri,2021) as the instantaneous impact of tremendously contagious Novel Corona virus (Dhawan, 2020) divulging the world to a never before dilemma. The Government of most of the countries led to a strategic paradigm shift overnight to deal with the concurrence and potential danger (Chaturvedi et al., 2020). Following the protocol of several first world countries, Bhutan was the first to shut down the educational Institutes among SAARC countries, which later intensified as national lock down policy (Kuensel, 2020, (Palden, 2020). Under such pressure of home bound situation, teaching-learning process stranded a need for blended learning with both Flex and Enriched Virtual Model through 'online pivot' (George, 2020). An instant shift of education from 'Brick and Mortar' to 'Phygital' Mode compelled both the teachers' and Learners' community to adapt to the newness and speed of change (Zimmerman, 2020; Huarcaya-Victoria, 2020). This brought a psychological collision to the already lifestyle compromised teaching-learning community, compressing the entire educational system to digital interface of e-learning (Chaturvedi et al, 2019; Govindarajan et al, 2020). The teaching Community initiated adapting to infrastructural development to equip themselves (Bao, 2020) to deliver the lectures in streaming platform or in recorded version of it to acclimatize ameliorating the procedure (Acharya, 2017), (Ajzen, I. 1991). The academic seniors experimented with virtual classrooms like 'Virtual Interactive Case-Based Education' They deliberately chose platforms like Zoom, MS-Teams, Google Meet, Google Classroom, Google with screen sharing and virtual breakout group capability (eg, Zoom) and included text-based audience response to capitalize on learner engagement and encourage camaraderie (Redinger et al, 2020). A virtual learning Environment (VLE) is created to enable a perfect teaching-learning experience with an integration and amalgamation of e-learning method (Al-Fraihat, 2020). Studies revealed that teachers can foster perceived control over the scholars and offer direction on most excellent avenues for teaching-learning amid pandemic.

## BACKGROUND

The onset of Covid 19 introduced an unprecedented and challenging scenario all over the world; not only due to the perilous disease outcome but also because of the grave, comparatively unfamiliar, novel initiatives in all walks of life. The educational section could not be any exception. Within a short tenure of the pandemic, many research initiatives got precipitate recognition on the teaching and learning methods just to avoid the face-to-face interaction. The anxiety of losing productive academic years from 19-22 was quite obvious, since none of the new and alternative educational techniques (like hybrid classroom or Flex and Enriched Virtual Model through 'online pivot' (George, 2020), e-learning mode) were well established and time-tested.

## AIM OF THE STUDY

The study mainly aims to explore the changing educational system during the trying times of Covid-19 and the afterwards experimentation of the Teaching-Learning system to accommodate the underlying needs, under the given constraints. It involves secondary data sources, for most of the parts of the chapter.

## LITERATURE REVIEW OF THE PEDAGOGY DURING THE COVID TIME

In most nations, schools, training facilities, and higher education institutions have been forced to close as a result of lockdown and social isolation measures brought on by the COVID-19 epidemic. The way educators provide great instruction has undergone a fundamental shift. The education system—through a range of online resources. Distance learning, online learning, and Continuous learning has emerged as a cure-all solution for this unparalleled worldwide disaster enduring the challenges faced by both teachers' and students' communities. It might be challenging to go from traditional face-to-face instruction to online instruction as the experience and adaptability are completely different for the students and the teachers (Pokhrel and Chhetri,2021).

In most nations, schools, training facilities, and higher education institutions have been forced to close as a result of lockdown and social isolation measures brought on by the COVID-19 epidemic. The way educators provide great instruction has undergone a fundamental shift. The education system—through a range of online resources. Distance learning, online learning, and Continuous learning has emerged as a cure-all solution for this unparalleled worldwide disaster enduring the challenges faced by both teachers' and students' communities. It might be challenging to go from traditional face-to-face instruction to online instruction as the experience and adaptability are completely different for the students and the teachers (Pokhrel, and Chhetri 2021). In this regards,,e-learning resources has been extremely essential and majorly helpful in facilitating student learning; when schools and colleges have been closed for uncertain period due to the epidemic (Subedi et al., 2020).

Staff and student readiness for the new changes were to be assessed and supported appropriately while being adapted to such difficult situation. While students who have a faster adaptation rate to a new learning environment compared to students who have a fixed mindset find it facile to adapt and modify. For online learning, there has been no one-size-fits-all methodology. There are several topics with various requirements for different learning groups. Different methods of online learning are required for various courses and age groups (Doucet et al., 2020). Online learning has been an additional advantage for students with physical disabilities, as it provides more flexibility to interact in the virtual environment while studying, with less physical movement (Basilaia & Kvavadze, 2020).

Students, parents, and educators all across the world have been affected by the unforeseen ripple effect of the COVID-19 pandemic as schools have been shuttered to deal with the worldwide pandemic. Governments, first responders, and health authorities are working hard to contain the pandemic, and educational systems are doing their best to keep providing high-quality instruction to everyone at this challenging period.

Many students are experiencing psychological and emotional hardship at home or in their living environment, making it difficult for them to work well. The ideal methods for home-schooling children online have not yet been determined (Petrie, 2020).

## TRANSFORMATION AND EXPERIMENTATION OF TEACHING-LEARNING MECHANISM

In the natural course of process, crises beget innovation and rebirth of techniques and Covid disruption reemphasized the need of innovation and disruption, once again. The commotion held by the current Covid-19 pandemic resulted in tremendous change in every sphere of lives including economic and social (Krishnamurthy, 2020). Within weeks, complete but gradual educational shutdown happened from elementary to higher education, leading to transformational changes evolving to an online platform of teaching-learning scenario (Mishra et al., 2020). As per UNESCO, higher education institutions (HEIs) were in full shut down mode in 185 countries by April 2020, concerning more than a thousand million learners across the world (Marinoni et al., 2020).

The new normal era, disarranged and obstructed by COVID 19 impacts, has evolved a radical transformation of academia, incorporating a histrionic dependence on digitisation in higher education (Dwivedi et al., 2020). The sudden forced shutting down of face-to-face teaching has led academia into "unfamiliar terrain" leading to online learning medium (Carolan et al., 2020) in record time.

Following the textbook definition of the disruption, it means a sudden change in the educational system as a makeover from the conventional, models of knowledge transmission, introducing displacement of existing educational policies and thereafter challenging those relatable models through continuous improvement of the methodologies (Carolan et al., 2020; Mishra et al., 2020). Innovations that change the direction of education, also could displace existing models, indicating disruptive transformation, which fulfils the requirements of existing customers along available services (Christensen et al., 2006). There was the apprehension that the success of educational innovation and transformation should lie on sustainability, scope, and scale (Carolan et al., 2020), extending its horizon into participatory culture with better engagement of the learners and reflecting a more tangible outcome-based evaluation process. As a result of transition, the paradigm shift towards e-learning and webinars from traditional classrooms and seminars could be considered as new normal educational practices, induced by Covid disruption (Mishra et al., 2020). This expedited the speed of digitization in the domain of higher education (Krishnamurthy, 2020).

## EXPLORATION OF COMMUNITY OF INQUIRY MODEL IN TRANSFORMATIONAL EDUCATION AND COVID INFLICTED PANDEMIC

Online education being the new burgeoning issue of higher education (Singh and Holt, 2013) has been accepted as pillar of success to hone new skill, knowledge and new avenue of learning (Wood and Shirazi, 2020). With onset of disastrous COVID-19, the conventional and time-tested, face-to-face teaching approach within the boundaries of classroom has been completely substituted by the novel online teaching pedagogy. Albeit extreme limitations, all the stakeholders like teachers, parents, students and higher educational institutes are leaving no stone unturned to make the process seamless. Plethora of academic experiments have been conducted, keeping a base of community of inquiry (COI) framework was proposed and adapted by Garrison et al. (2000), though in psychology the idea was introduced by Dewey (1959) as a primitive model. The three overlapping cohorts represent a holistic structurisation of the social interaction, indicating the coherence of teaching-learning purview. COI assists students to perfectly assimilate their new addition of knowledge to the old domain (Hilliard and Stewart, 2019). The three vital elements of Community of Inquiry model (Garrison, 2003) are Social Presence (the ability of participants to project their individual personalities in order to identify and communicate with the community and develop inter-personal relationships. (Garrison, 2009), Cognitive Presence (the extent to which learners are able to construct and confirm meaning through sustained reflection and discourse. (Garrison, Anderson, & Archer, 2001, 2004) and Teaching Presence (the design, facilitation, and direction of the social and cognitive processes for the purpose of realizing the relevant learning outcomes

(Anderson, Rourke, Garrison, & Archer, 2001). Venkatesh et al. (2003) conceptualized demography based behavioural inclinations towards COI model, while Park et al. (2012) the behavioural discrepancies are more due to online experiences rather than gender-based variation. However, neither Venkatesh et al. (2003) nor Park et al. (2012) used CoI as a core element of the research methodology. Shea and Bidjerano (2009) stated about complication of using other technological platforms like Wikipedia, blogs, streaming video.Garrison and Arbaugh (2007) investigated the generalizability of the COI model for different disciplines, questioning the validity of the model in further years (Garrison et al. 2010). Later Carlon et al. (2012) and Choy and Choon (2016) re-emphasized the cardinal demographical features like gender affects the perceptual abilities of the students under the purview of COI model for e-learning.

*Figure 1. Community of Inquiry model adopted from Garrison and Anderson (2003)*

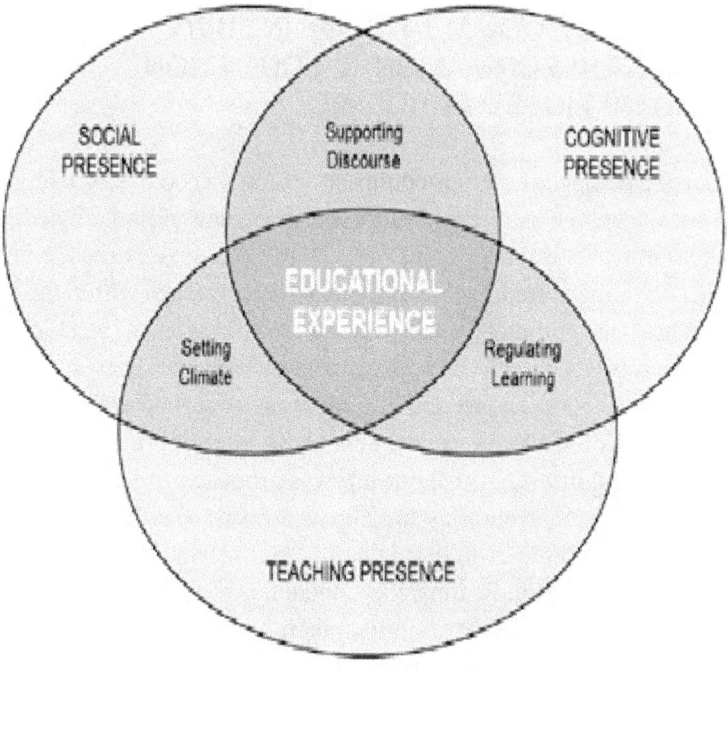

## USE OF ICT DURING EDUCATIONAL PROCESS

Information and communications Technology has been a cardinal component in contemporary education and became more imperative during Covid times due to no direct contact hour was available with the teaching-learning community and only distant learning was permissible with limited virtual access to the students. The online education was greatly dependent on various desktop or mobile based applications like Zoom, Googlemeet, Webex etc., and different interactive platforms like Swayam, Impetus, etc. Nonetheless, with the advent of world wide web, the entire teaching pedagogy has been caressed at the doorstep of the teachers as well as learners. The ICT tools can be used for e-creation, e-courses, reading-writing tools on one side, also as virtual interactive platform creation (Webinar) for experiential positioning of the content (Manisha Mohite,2020).

ITC can have multifarious uses of diverse nature both for, Teaching and Learning community with diversifiable advantages.

The teaching community can benefit from professional progress; knowledge enhancement through e-book, e-journal, participative discussion forum, Training, webinar, workshop; setting curricular boundaries for a chosen subject to make it for lucid to the learners; guiding using virtual platform and e-content (Manisha Mohite,2020).while the learning community can enjoy the flexibility of Time with enhancement of knowledge with 24X7 possibility of interaction with concerned teacher(Manisha Mohite,2020).

The augmentation of network technology in ICT accomplishes comprehensive accessibility and information diffusion and allows physically isolated different students to study and be in touch with each other (Kardan et al., 2013).

## RESPONSE AND REACTION OF TEACHING-LEARNING COMMUNITY

The reaction of Teaching-Learning Community was diverse and completely different for both the communities. The students' community, especially the ones in high schools and mediocre were ecstatic with the examination procedure, since it was relaxed and highly awarding with a lenient checking of the answer scripts but the teaching community apprehended the different pace of learning for slow learners and fast learners (Sintema, 2020). Though it also led to negative impact like students riot and expected job market turbulence in France (Maurin & McNally, 2008).

Teachers were accommodative to all sorts of creative experiment with various teaching pedagogies along the collaborative assistance from the teaching institutes to bring the students, teachers and parents on the same platform as a teaching-learning community cohort (Doucet et al., 2020).

## COMPLICATIONS AND CONSEQUENCES OF COVID DRIVEN ADAPTATIONS IN ACADEMIA-ISSUES, PROBLEMS AND CHALLENGES

The pandemic bought a major psychological change in the teaching-learning community and introduced all sorts of adaptations to ease the transition to housebound academic conditions of the students. Academic Institutions were trying to provide all types of resources to the underprivileged students including instructional supports and study materials and were used to sustain the most wide-spread pandemic inflected teaching method-online teaching (Schleicher and Reimers,2020). Many countries introduced television channels to help the suburban and rural population of students, along the underprivileged (Schleicher and Reimers,2020). For the privileged ones streaming videos, to Microsoft teams, Zoom, Google Meet, Skype, GoToMeeting, WhatsApp, ezTalk, emails, BlueJeans, YouTube. etc. many teaching-learning media were involved in online teaching and experimented to aid the closure of the school and colleges. But the covid driven negative consequents are also quite extensive, many institutes revoked and postponed their co-curricular activities like academic conferences (Panesar et al., 2020).

## CONTEMPORARY ACADEMIC TRENDS DURING COVID INFLICTED CRISES

Apart of the hybrid learning procedure- a flexible teaching- learning system with more student centric approach and openness, this pandemic has introduced most of the noble procedures to explore the best of breed approaches. It is needless to mention, the nationwide initiatives like the different television channels to help in upgrading the educational need, academic institute to go for collaborations with the diverse virtual platforms like zoom and google meet, the initiatives of schools and other educational institutes to raise the social skills and awareness programmes, the continuous educational programmes like webinars, talk shows, etc., these not only supported the academic lacuna of the students, that was created by the closure of the academic institutes but also filled the mental vacuum and psychological monotony of the uncertain time.

## MANAGERIAL SIGNIFICANCE OF THE ACADEMIC TRANSFORMATION

The pandemic has made a permanent paradigm shift in the academic world, which most probably will stay in long run, making it a sustainable development in academia. Though it is questionable, whether it will be prudent for knowledge absorption or not, especially for those domains of knowledge, where hands-on training becomes imperative (like laboratory-based work-bio sciences, medical field etc.). But it is undeniable that the usefulness of online workshop and training sessions will enrich people across the borders and cannot be discarded as important aids in academia.

## SCOPE OF THE FUTURE EDUCATION

With the onset of the new normal, it is becoming arduous to continue with only the conventional physical classroom related teaching pedagogy and it is evidently imperious to continue with the hybrid mode of education despite a questionable outcome of the latter.

## CONCLUSION

It is now quite coherent that the sudden shock of Covid inflicted Pandemic has changed the psychological parameters of the entire academic world permanently with the commencement of a new era, more commonly known as 'New Normal'. The emerging trend of comparatively heavier dependence on virtual world seems to be sustainable due to its flexibility, adaptability, business aspect and pro-students' perspective. This uncalled-for alteration, as a by-product of the peril, has introduced a permanent transformation and ramification, transmuting the overall dynamics of the educational scenario across the world. With the more variants of the disease and the mental insecurity, along the physical boundaries of the triangle- the teacher, Parents and the students will fight back the battle with more initiatives, alternatives, experimentations and cooperations.

## REFERENCES

Acharya, R. (2017). Rapport building in classroom: Strategies and role in learners' performance. *Tribhuvan University Journal*, *31*(1-2), 185–192. doi:10.3126/tuj.v31i1-2.25354

Ajzen, I. (1991). The theory of planned behavior. *Organizational Behavior and Human Decision Processes, 50*(2), 179–211.

Ajzen, I., & Fishbein, M. (1980). *Understanding attitudes and predicting social behavior*. Prentice Hall.

Akyol, Z., Garrison, D. R., & Ozden, M. Y. (2009). Online and blended communities of inquiry: Exploring the developmental and perceptional differences. *The International Review of Research in Open and Distributed Learning, 10*(6), 65–83.

Al-Fraihat, D., Joy, M., Masa'deh, R. E., & Sinclair, J. (2020). Evaluating e-learning systems success: An empirical study. *Computers in Human Behavior, 102*, 67–86.

Arbaugh, J. B. (2013). Does academic discipline moderate CoI -course outcomes relationships in online MBA courses? *Internet and Higher Education., 17*, 16–28.

Arbaugh, J. B., Bangert, A., & Cleveland-Innes, M. (2010). Subject matter effects and the Community of Inquiry (CoI) framework: An exploratory study. *Internet Higher Education., 13*, 37–44.

Ash, S. L., & Clayton, P. H. (2004). The articulated learning: An approach to guided reflection and assessment. *Innovative Higher Education, 29*(2), 137–154.

Bao, W. (2020). COVID-19 and online teaching in higher education: A case study of Peking University. *Human Behaviour and Emerging Technologies, 2*(2), 113–115.

Basilaia, G., & Kvavadze, D. (2020). Transition to online education in schools during a SARS-CoV-2 coronavirus (COVID-19) pandemic in Georgia. *Pedagogical Research, 5*(4), 10.

Carlon, S., Bennett-Woods, D., Berg, B., Claywell, L., LeDuc, K., & Marcisz, N. (2012). The community of inquiry instrument: Validation and results in online health care disciplines. *Computer Education, 59*, 215–221.

Carolan, C., Davies, C. L., Crookes, P., McGhee, S., & Rox-Burgh, M. (2020). COVID 19: Disruptive impacts and transformative opportunities in undergraduate nurse education. *Nurse Education in Practice, 46*, 215–223.

Chaturvedi, S., Rizvi, I. A., & Pasipanodya, E. T. (2019). How Can Leaders Make Their Followers to Commit to the Organization? the Importance of Influence Tactics. *Global Business Review, 20*(6), 1462–1474.

Choy, J. L. F., & Choon, L. Q. (2016). Modelling relationships between students' academic achievement and community of inquiry in an online learning environment for a blended course. *Australasian Journal of Educational Technology, 32*, 106–124.

Dewey, J. (1959). *My pedagogic creed. In Dewey on Education*. Teachers College, Columbia University.

Dhawan, S. (2020). *Online Learning: A Panacea in the Time of COVID-19 Crisis*. Academic Press.

Doucet, A., Netolicky, D., Timmers, K., Tuscano, F. J. (2020). *Thinking about pedagogy in an unfolding pandemic* (An Independent Report on Approaches to Distance Learning during COVID-19 School Closure). Work of Education International and UNESCO.

Dwivedi, Y., Hughes, L., Coombs, C., Constantiou, I., Duan, Y., & Edwards, J. (2020). Impact of COVID-19 pandemic on information management research and practice: Transforming education, work and life. *International Journal of Information Management*, 55.

Garrison, D. R., & Anderson, T. (2003). E-learning in the 21st century: A framework for research and practice. Routledge.

Garrison, D. R., Anderson, T., & Archer, W. (2000). Critical inquiry in a text-based environment: Computer conferencing in higher education. *The Internet and Higher Education*, *2*(2-3), 87–105.

Garrison, D. R., Anderson, T., & Archer, W. (2001). Critical thinking, cognitive presence, and computer conferencing in distance education. *American Journal of Distance Education*, *15*(1), 7–23.

Garrison, D. R., Anderson, T., & Archer, W. (2004). Student Role Adjustment in Online Communities of Inquiry: Model And Instrument Validation. *Journal of Asynchronous Learning Networks*, *8*(2), 61–74.

Garrison, D. R., & Arbaugh, J. B. (2007). Researching the community of inquiry model: Review, issues, and future directions. *The Internet and Higher Education*, *10*, 157–172.

Garrison, D. R., & Archer, W. (2000). *A transactional perspective on teaching and learning: A framework for adult and higher education*. Pergamon.

George, M. L. (2020). Effective Teaching and Examination Strategies for Undergraduate Learning during COVID-19 School Restrictions. *Journal of Educational Technology Systems*, *49*(1), 23–48.

Govindarajan, V., & Srivastava, A. (2020). What the Shift to Virtual Learning Could Mean for the Future of Higher Education. *Harvard Business Review*.

Hilliard, L. P., & Stewart, M. K. (2019). Time well spent: Creating a community of inquiry in blended first-year writing courses. *Internet Higher Education.*, *41*, 11–24.

Huarcaya-Victoria, J. (2020). Mental health considerations about the COVID-19 pandemic. *Revista Peruana de Medicina Experimental y Salud Pública*, *37*, 327–334.

Jensen, T. (2019). Higher Education in the Digital Era: The Current State of Transformation Around the World. International Association of Universities (IAU). *Journal of Educational Technology Systems*, *49*(1), 5–22.

Kardan, A. A., Sadeghi, H., Ghidary, S. S., & Sani, M. R. F. (2013). Prediction of student course selection in online higher education institutes using neural network. *Computer Education*, *65*, 1–11.

Krishnamurthy, S. (2020). The future of business education: A commentary in the shadow of the Covid-19 pandemic. *Journal of Business Research*, *117*, 1–5.

Kuensel. (2020). *First confirmed coronavirus case in Bhutan.* Kuensel. https://kuenselonline.com/first-confirmed-coronavirus-case-in-bhutan

Marinoni, G., Van't Land, H., & Jensen, T. (2020). *The Impact of Covid-19 on Higher Education Around the World.* IAU Global Survey Report.

Maurin, E., & McNally, S. (2008). Vive la révolution! Long-term educational returns of 1968 to the angry students. *Journal of Labor Economics*, *26*(1), 1–33.

Mishra, L., Gupta, T., & Shree, A. (2020). Online teaching-learning in higher education during lockdown period of COVID-19 pandemic. *International Journal of Educational Research*, *1*, 12–34.

Mohite, M. (2020). Covid 19 and use of ICT in education. *Educational Resurgence Journal*, *2*(4), 17–23.

Rippe, Weisfeld-Spolter, & Yurova. (2021). Pandemic Pedagogy for the New Normal: Fostering Perceived Control During COVID-19. *Journal of Marketing Education*, *43*(2), 260–276.

Panesar, K., Dodson, T., Lynch, J., Bryson-Cahn, C., Chew, L., & Dillon, J. (2020). Evolution of COVID-19 guidelines for University of Washington oral and maxillofacial surgery patient care. *Journal of Oral and Maxillofacial Surgery*, *78*(7), 1136–1146.

Park, S. Y., Nam, M. W., & Cha, S. B. (2012). University students' behavioral intention to use mobile learning: Evaluating the technology acceptance model. *British Journal of Educational Technology*, *43*, 592–605.

Petrie, C. (2020). *Spotlight: Quality education for all during COVID-19 crisis* (hundred Research Report #01). United Nations. https://hundred.org/en/collections/qualityeducation-for-all-during-coronavirus

Pokhrel, S., & Chhetri, R. (2021). A Literature Review on Impact of COVID-19 Pandemic on Teaching and Learning. *Higher Education for the Future*, *8*(1), 133–141.

Redinger, Cornia, & Tyler. (2020). Teaching during A Pandemic. *Journal of Graduate Medical Education, 12*(4), 403–405.

Schleicher, A., & Reimers, F. (2020). Schooling Disrupted, Schooling Rethought: How the COVID-19 Pandemic is Changing Education. OECD.

Singh, V., & Holt, L. (2013). Learning and best practices for learning in open-source software communities. *Computer Education*, *63*, 98–108.

Sintema, E. J. (2020). Effect of COVID-19 on the performance of grade 12 students: Implications for STEM education. *Eurasia Journal of Mathematics, Science and Technology Education*, *16*(7), 2–6.

Subedi, S., Nayaju, S., Subedi, S., Shah, S. K., & Shah, J. M. (2020). Impact of e-learning during COVID-19 pandemic among nurshing students and teachers of Nepal. *International Journal of Science and Healthcare Research*, *5*(3), 9.

Venkatesh, V., Morris, M. G., Davis, G. B., & Davis, F. D. (2003). User acceptance of information technology: Toward a unified view. *Management Information Systems Quarterly*, *27*, 425–478.

Wood, R., & Shirazi, S. (2020). A systematic review of audience response systems for teaching and learning in higher education: The student experience. *Computer Education*.

Zimmerman, J. (2020). Coronavirus and the Great Online-Learning Experiment. *The Chronicle of Higher Education*, *6*(2), 122–138.

# Compilation of References


Guangul, F. M., Suhail, A. H., Khalit, M. I., & Khidhir, B. A. (2020). Challenges of remote assessment in higher education in the context of COVID-19: A case study of Middle East College. *EducAsseEvalAcc*, *32*(4), 519–535. doi:10.100711092-020-09340-w PMID:33101539

Chen, I. H., Gamble, J. H., Lee, Z. H., & Fu, Q. L. (2020). Formative assessment with interactive whiteboards: A one-year longitudinal study of primary students' mathematical performance. *Computers & Education*, *150*, 103833. doi:10.1016/j.compedu.2020.103833

Admiraal, W., Huisman, B., & Pilli, O. (2015). Assessment in massive open online courses. *Electronic Journal of E-learning*, *13*(4), 207–216.

Allagui, B. (2014). Writing through Whatsapp: An evaluation of students writing performance. *International Journal of Mobile Learning and Organisation*, *8*(3), 216–231. doi:10.1504/IJMLO.2014.067022

Agustina, M., & Purnawarman, P. (2020). Investigating learners' satisfaction utilizing google classroom as online formative feedback tool. *2020 6th International conference on education and technology (ICET)*, 26–31. 10.1109/ICET51153.2020.9276616

Daşkın, N., & Hatipoğlu, Ç. (2019). Reference to a past learning event as a practice of informal formative assessment in L2 classroom interaction. *Language Testing*, *36*(4), 527–551. doi:10.1177/0265532219857066

Bogdanović, Z., Barać, D., Jovanić, B., Popović, S., & Radenković, B. (2014). Evaluation of mobile assessment in a learning management system. *British Journal of Educational Technology*, *45*(2), 231–244. doi:10.1111/bjet.12015

Haddad, R. J., & Youakim, K. (2014). Google forms: A real-time formative assessment approach for adaptive learning. *Proceedings of the 2014 American society for engineering education, ASEE annual conference and exposition*, 24.649.1–24.649.14. 10.18260/1-2--20540

Aljawarneh, S. A. (2019). Reviewing and exploring innovative ubiquitous learning tools in higher education. *Journal of Computing in Higher Education*. Advance online publication. doi:10.100712528-019-09207-0

Black, P., &Wiliam, D. (2009). Developing the theory of formative assessment. *Educational Assessment Evaluation and Accountability, 21*(1), 5.

García-Peñalvo, F. J., Corell, A., Abella-García, V., & Grande-de-Prado, M. (2021). Recommendations for mandatory online assessment in higher education during the COVID-19 pandemic. In D. Burgos, A. Tlili, & A. Tabacco (Eds.), Radical solutions for education in a crisis context. Lecture Notes in Educational Technology. Springer. doi:10.1007/978-981-15-7869-4_6

Johnson, G. M., & Cooke, A. (2016). Self-regulation of learning and preference for written versus audio-recorded feedback by distance education students. *Distance Education, 37*(1), 107–120. doi:10.1080/01587919.2015.1081737

Blank, D. S., Bourgin, D., Brown, A., Bussonnier, M., Frederic, J., Granger, B., ... Willing, C. (2019). nbgrader: A tool for creating and grading assignments in the Jupyter Notebook. *The Journal of Open Source Education, 2*(11), 32. doi:10.21105/jose.00032

Charlier, B., Cosnefroy, L., Jézégou, A., & Lameul, G. (2015). Understanding Quality of Learning in Digital Learning Environments: State of the Art and Research Needed. In A. Curaj, L. Matei, R. Pricopie, J. Salmi, & P. Scott (Eds.), *The European Higher Education Area*. Springer. doi:10.1007/978-3-319-20877-0_25

Khan, S., & Khan, R. A. (2019). Online assessments: Exploring perspectives of university students. *Education and Information Technologies, 24*(1), 661–677. doi:10.100710639-018-9797-0

Milligan, A. T., & Buckenmeyer, J. A. (2008). Assessing students for online learning. *International Journal on E-Learning, 7*(3), 449–461.

Çakıroğlu, U. (2014). Analyzing the effect of learning styles and study habits of distance learners on learning performances: A case of an introductory programming course. *The International Review of Research in Open and Distributed Learning, 15*(4). Advance online publication. doi:10.19173/irrodl.v15i4.1840

BulutS. (2019). Assessing online learners' academic self-efficacy in a symbiotic learning environment. doi:10.2139/ssrn.3370615

Huber, S. G., & Helm, C. (2020). COVID-19 and schooling: Evaluation, assessment and accountability in times of crises—reacting quickly to explore key issues for policy, practice and research with the school barometer. *EducAsseEvalAcc, 32*(2), 237–270. doi:10.100711092-020-09322-y PMID:32837626

Lara, J. A., Aljawarneh, S., & Pamplona, S. (2020). Special issue on the current trends in E-learning Assessment. *Journal of Computing in Higher Education, 32*(1), 1–8. doi:10.100712528-019-09235-w

Lara, J. A., Lizcano, D., Martínez, M. A., Pazos, J., & Riera, T. (2014). A system for knowledge discovery in e-learning environments within the European Higher Education Area—Application to student data from Open University of Madrid, UDIMA. *Computers & Education, 72*, 23–36. doi:10.1016/j.compedu.2013.10.009

Darius, P. S. H., Gundabattini, E., & Solomon, D. G. (2021). A Survey on the Effectiveness of Online Teaching–Learning Methods for University and College Students. *J. Inst. Eng. India Ser. B, 102*(6), 1325–1334. doi:10.100740031-021-00581-x

Giray, G. (2021). An assessment of student satisfaction with e-learning: An empirical study with computer and software engineering undergraduate students in Turkey under pandemic conditions. *Education and Information Technologies, 26*(6), 6651–6673. doi:10.100710639-021-10454-x PMID:33686329

Cipriano, C., Barnes, T. N., Pieloch, K. A., Rivers, S. E., & Brackett, M. (2019). A multilevel approach to understanding student and teacher perceptions of classroom support during early adolescence. *Learning Environments Research, 22*(2), 209–228. doi:10.100710984-018-9274-0

Mahapatra, S. K. (2021). Online Formative Assessment and Feedback Practices of ESL Teachers in India, Bangladesh and Nepal: A Multiple Case Study. *The Asia-Pacific Education Researcher, 30*(6), 519–530. doi:10.100740299-021-00603-8

Barana, A., & Marchisio, M. (2016). Ten good reasons to adopt an automated formative assessment model for learning and teaching mathematics and scientific disciplines. *Procedia: Social and Behavioral Sciences, 228*, 608–613. doi:10.1016/j.sbspro.2016.07.093

Abbasi, M., & Hashemi, M. (2013). The impacts of using mobile phone on English language vocabulary retention. *International Research Journal of Applied and Basic Sciences, 4*(3), 541–547.

Abbott, C. (2007). E-inclusion: Learning difficulties and digital technologies. Future lab. *Education.*

Abdulrahim, H., & Mabrouk, F. (2020). COVID-19 and the Digital Transformation of Saudi Higher Education. *Asian Journal of Distance Education, 15*(1), 291–306.

Abik, M., Ajhoun, R., & Ensias, L. (2012). Impact of technological advancement on pedagogy. *Turkish Online Journal of Distance Education, 13*(1), 224-237. https://files.eric.ed.gov/fulltext/EJ976961.pdf

Acharya, R. (2017). Rapport building in classroom: Strategies and role in learners' performance. *Tribhuvan University Journal, 31*(1-2), 185–192. doi:10.3126/tuj.v31i1-2.25354

Achuthan, K., Francis, S. P., & Diwakar, S. (2017). Augmented reflective learning and knowledge retention perceived among students in classrooms involving virtual laboratories. *Education and Information Technologies, 22*(6), 2825–2855. doi:10.100710639-017-9626-x

Açıkalın, A. (1999). İnsan Kaynağının Yönetimi Geliştirilmesi. Ankara: Pegem A Yayınları.

Açıkalın, A. (2002). *İnsan Kaynağının Geliştirilmesi*. Pegem A Yayıncılık.

Acikkar, M., & Akay, M. F. (2009). Support vector machines for predicting the admission decision of a candidate to the School of Physical Education and Sports at Cukurova University. *Expert Systems with Applications, 36*(3), 7228–7233. doi:10.1016/j.eswa.2008.09.007

Aguliera, E., & Nightengale-Lee, B. (2020). Emergency Remote Teaching across Urban and Rural Contexts: Perspectives on Educational Equity. *Inf. Learn. Sci., 2020*(121), 471–478. doi:10.1108/ILS-04-2020-0100

Ahmad, W., & Parween, S. (2021). Managing behavioral/emotional problems in inclusive classrooms and understanding the best practices. In A. Singh, C. J. Yeh, S. Blanchard, & L. Anunciação (Eds.), *Handbook of research on critical issues in special education for school rehabilitation practices* (pp. 443–461). IGI Global.

Ahmed, R., Ahmad, N., Mujeeb, M., & Vishnu, P. (2014). Factors that motivate the mobile phone users to switch from 2G to 3G technologies in Karachi. *Research Journal of Recent Sciences, 3*(8), 18–21.

Ainley, M., Hidi, S., & Berndorff, D. (2002). Interest, learning, and the psychological processes that mediate their relationship. *Journal of Educational Psychology, 94*(3), 545–561. doi:10.1037/0022-0663.94.3.545

Ajzen, I. (1991). The theory of planned behavior. *Organizational Behavior and Human Decision Processes, 50*(2), 179–211.

Ajzen, I., & Fishbein, M. (1980). *Understanding attitudes and predicting social behavior.* Prentice Hall.

Akalın, A. (2004). Eğitim ve Okul Yöneticiliği El Kitabı. Ankara: Pegem Yayıncılık.

Akçayır, M., Akçayır, G., Pektaş, H. M., & Ocak, M. A. (2016). Augmented reality in science laboratories: The effects of augmented reality on university students' laboratory skills and attitudes toward science laboratories. *Computers in Human Behavior, 57*, 334–342. doi:10.1016/j.chb.2015.12.054

Akdağ, M. (2007). Örgütlerde İnsan Kaynakları ve Halkla İlişkiler Birimleri Örgüt Yapılarının İncelenmesi Üzerine Karsılaştırılmalı Bir Çalışma (Yayımlanmamış Doktora Tezi). Selçuk Üniversitesi, Konya.

Akın A, (2002). İşletmelerde İnsan Kaynakları Performansını Değerleme Sürecinde Coaching. *C.Ü. İktisadi ve İdari Bilimler Dergisi, 3*(1).

Aksoy B, (2005). Bilgi Teknolojilerinin Yarattığı Örgütsel Değişim: Nasıl Bir İnsan Kaynakları Yönetimi? *Bilgi Dünyası, 6*(1), 58-77.

Aksu, G., Acuner, A., & Tabak, R. (2002). Sağlık Bakanlığı Merkez ve Taşra Teşkilatı Yöneticilerinin İş Doyumuna Yönelik Bir Araştırma (Ankara Örneği). Ankara Üniversitesi Tıp Fakültesi Mecmuası, 55(4).

Akyol, B. (2008). Eğitim Örgütlerinde İnsan Kaynakları Uygulamalarının Öğretmen Performansına Etkisi (Yayımlanmamış Yüksek Lisans Tezi). Yeditepe Üniversitesi/Sosyal Bilimler Enstitüsü, İstanbul.

Akyol, Z., Garrison, D. R., & Ozden, M. Y. (2009). Online and blended communities of inquiry: Exploring the developmental and perceptional differences. *The International Review of Research in Open and Distributed Learning, 10*(6), 65–83.

Akyüz, Y. (2010). *Türk Eğitim Tarihi. M.Ö. 1000- M.S.* Pegem A Yayınları.

Alakrash, H. M., & Adul Razak, R. (2022). Education and the fourth industrial revolution: Lessons from COVID-19. *Computer. Material & Continua, 70*(1), 951–962. Advance online publication. doi:10.32604/cmc.2022.014288

Aldemir, C., & Ataol, A. (2001). İnsan Kaynakları Yönetimi. İzmir: Barış Yayınları.

Alexander, M. W., Truell, A. D., & Zhao, J. J. (2012). Expected advantages and disadvantages of online learning: Perceptions from college students who have not taken online courses. *Issues in Information Systems, 13*(2), 193–200.

Alexander, P. A., Sperl, C. T., Buehl, M. M., Fives, H., & Chiu, S. (2004). Modeling domain learning: Profiles from the field of special education. *Journal of Educational Psychology, 96*(3), 545. doi:10.1037/0022-0663.96.3.545

Alfauzan, A. A., & Tarchouna, N. (2017). The role of an aligned curriculum design in the achievement of learning outcomes. *Journal of Education and E-Learning Research, 4*(3), 81–91. doi:10.20448/journal.509.2017.43.81.91

Al-Fraihat, D., Joy, M., Masa'deh, R. E., & Sinclair, J. (2020). Evaluating e-learning systems success: An empirical study. *Computers in Human Behavior, 102*, 67–86.

Ali, M. M., Mahmood, M. A., Anjum, M. A. I., & Shahid, A. (2020). The acceptance of mobile assisted language learning as primary learning tool for learners in COVID 19 situations. *PalArch's Journal of Archaeology of Egypt/Egyptology, 17*(12), 382-398.

Ali, M. M., Yasmin, T., & Ahmed, K. (2021). Using Whatsapp as MALL Tool to Enhance ESL Learners' Performance in Pakistan. *Ilkogretim Online, 20*(5).

Ali, M. M., Bashir, A., Ikram Anjum, M. A., & Mahmood, M. A. (2020). Impact of Mobile Assisted Language Learning on the Young ESL Learners' Vocabulary in Pakistan. *Journal of Research & Reflections in Education, 14*(1).

Ali, M. M., Mahmood, M. A., Anwar, M. N., Khan, L. A., & Hussain, A. (2019). Pakistani learners' perceptions regarding mobile assisted language learning in ESL classroom. *International Journal of English Linguistics, 9*(4), 386–398. doi:10.5539/ijel.v9n4p386

Ali, M. M., Malik, N. A., & Rehman, A. (2016). Mobile assisted language learning (MALL) an emerging technology in English language class rooms of Lahore (Pakistan). *Science International (Lahore), 28*(2).

Alonso-Fernández, C., Caballero Roldán, R., Freire, M., & Martinez-ortiz, I., & FernándezManjón, B. (2019). Predicting students' knowledge after playing a serious game based on learning analytics data. *IEEE Access: Practical Innovations, Open Solutions.*

Alruwais, N., Wills, G., & Wald, M. (2018). Advantages and challenges of using e-assessment. *International Journal of Information and Education Technology (IJIET)*, *8*(1), 34–37. doi:10.18178/ijiet.2018.8.1.1008

Altınay, F., Altınay, M., Dagli, G., & Altınay, Z. (2018). Being leader in global citizenship at the information technology age". *Quality & Quantity*, *52*(1), 31–42. doi:10.100711135-017-0585-5

Altwijri, A. M., & Aldosemani, T. I. (2022). Employee perceptions of the effectiveness of e-training to meet performance evaluation requirements. *International Journal of Learning, Teaching and Educational Research*, *21*(2), 49–71. doi:10.26803/ijlter.21.2.4

American Association of Higher Education. (n.d.). *Assessment forum: 9 principles of good practice for assessing student learning*. Retrieved from https://www.aahe.org/assessment/principl.htm

Angelo, T. A., & Cross, K. P. (2012). *Classroom assessment techniques*. Jossey Bass Wiley.

Appiah, M., & Van Tonder, F. (2018). E-Assessment in Higher Education: A Review. *International Journal of Business Management and Economic Research*, *9*(6).

Arbaugh, J. B. (2013). Does academic discipline moderate CoI -course outcomes relationships in online MBA courses? *Internet and Higher Education.*, *17*, 16–28.

Arbaugh, J. B., Bangert, A., & Cleveland-Innes, M. (2010). Subject matter effects and the Community of Inquiry (CoI) framework: An exploratory study. *Internet Higher Education.*, *13*, 37–44.

Arnò, S., Galassi, A., Tommasi, M., Saggino, A., & Vittorini, P. (2021). State-of-the-art of commercial proctoring systems and their use in academic online exams. *International Journal of Distance Education Technologies*, *19*(2), 41–60. doi:10.4018/IJDET.20210401.oa3

Ash, S. L., & Clayton, P. H. (2004). The articulated learning: An approach to guided reflection and assessment. *Innovative Higher Education*, *29*(2), 137–154.

Atılgan, M. (2005). İnsan Kaynakları Yönetiminde Eğitim ve Bir İnceleme: Kaymakam Adaylarının Eğitimi. *Turk İdare Dergisi*, *20*, 131–148.

Attar, M., & Chopra, S. S. (2010). Task-based language teaching in India. *Modern Journal of Applied Linguistics*, *2*(4).

Australian Catholic University. (2014). *Assessment and evaluation approaches and methods for the online environment*. Retrieved from https://leocontent.acu.edu.au/file/22207b30-7a02-4e71-8948-7ed523bef6fd/3/html/ddv_3_60.html

Awang, Y., Taib, A., & Muda, N. (2020). Perceived challenges towards education 4.0 implementation among academicians: A preliminary analysis. *e-Academia Journal of UiTM Cawangan Terengganu*, *2*(9), 8-17. http://journal-academiauitmt.uitm.edu.my

Aytaç, S. (2010). İş Yaşamında Kariyer Yönetimi. Yönetimde İnsan Kaynakları Çalışmaları. Ankara: Turhan Kitabevi Yayınları.

Aytaç, S. (2006). *Çalışma Yaşamında Kariyer Yönetimi Planlaması Gelişimi ve Sorunları*. Ezgi Kitabevi.

Azuma, R. T. (1997). A survey of augmented reality. *Presence (Cambridge, Mass.)*, *6*(4), 355–385. doi:10.1162/pres.1997.6.4.355

Bafadhal, A. S., & Hendrawan, M. R. (2021b), Towards Infinity and Beyond Reality: A Cutting-Edge Virtual Museum. In Globalisation of Cultural Heritage: Issues, Impacts, and Challenges. Trengganu: Penerbit Universiti Malaysia Trengganu (UMT).

Bafadhal, A. S. (2020). Pariwisata Virtual (Virtual Tourism). In M. A. Sutiarso (Ed.), *Manajemen Pariwisata: Sebuah Tinjauan Teori dan Praktis*. Widina Bhakti Persada.

Bafadhal, A. S. (2021a). Staycation During Covid-19 Pandemic with Virtual Tourism: Tele-Tourist Attitude Toward Experience in Cultural Heritage Destination. *Journal of Indonesian Tourism and Development Studies*, *9*(2), 87.

Bafadhal, A. S. (2021b). Pendampingan Pembuatan Konten Virtual Tourism sebagai Inisiasi Living Lab. Cagar Budaya Kampoeng Heritage Kajoetangan. *Jurnal Abdimas Pariwisata*, *1*(2), 66–73. doi:10.36276/jap.v1i2.20

Bafadhal, A. S., & Hendrawan, M. R. (2021a). Research and Development Web-Based Virtual Military Museum as a Tool for Edu-Tourism from Home During the Covid-19 Pandemic. In *International Conference on Innovation and Technology (ICIT 2021)* (pp. 75-85). Atlantis Press. 10.2991/aer.k.211221.010

Bahadır, E. (2016). Using Neural Network and Logistic Regression Analysis to Predict Prospective Mathematics Teachers' Academic Success upon Entering Graduate Education. *Educational Sciences: Theory and Practice*. Advance online publication. doi:10.12738/estp.2016.3.0214

Bai, C., Dallasega, P., Orzes, G., & Sarkis, J. (2020). Industry 4.0 technologies assessment: A sustainability perspective. *International Journal of Production Economics, 229*, 107776. doi:10.1016/j.ijpe.2020.107776

Balkın, D., Cardy, R., & Gomez-Mejla, L. (1998). *Managing Human Resources*. Prentice Hall.

Balla, E. (2018). *English Language and its importance of learning it in Albanian schools*. Academic Press.

Baloran, E. T. (2020). Knowledge, Attitudes, Anxiety, and Coping Strategies of Students during COVID-19 Pandemic. *Journal of Loss and Trauma, 2020*, 1–8.

Banica, L., Burtescu, E., & Enescu, F. (2017). The impact of internet-of-things in higher education. *Scientific Bulletin - Economic Sciences, 16*(1), 53-59. https://ideas.repec.org/a/pts/journl/y2017i1p53-59.html

Bao, W. (2020). COVID-19 and online teaching in higher education: A case study of Peking University. *Human Behaviour and Emerging Technologies*, *2*(2), 113–115.

Barutçugil, İ. (2004). *Stratejik İnsan Kaynakları Yönetimi*. Kariyer Yayıncılık.

Baş, T., & Akturan, U. (2008). Nitel Araştırma Yöntemleri: NVivo İle Nitel Veri Analizi. Ankara: Seçkin Yayıncılık.

Başaran, İ. E. (1996). *Eğitim Yönetimi*. Yargıcı Matbaası.

Basilaia, G., & Kvavadze, D. (2020). Transition to online education in schools during a SARS-CoV-2 coronavirus (COVID-19) pandemic in Georgia. *Pedagogical Research*, *5*(4), 10.

Baştaş, M., & Altinay, Z. (2019, November 2). Employment for Disability: Human Resources Management in Higher Education for Quality. *International Journal of Disability Development and Education*, *66*(6), 610–615. Advance online publication. doi:10.1080/1034912X.2019.1643456

Bavelas, A. (1942). A method for investigating individual and group ideology. *Sociometry*, *5*(4), 371–377. doi:10.2307/2785286

Bayraktaroğlu, S. (2003). *İnsan Kaynakları Yönetimi*. Sakarya Kitabevi.

BBC. (2020). Coronavirus: Only Go to Your Job If You Cannot Work from Home—Hancock. In *Coronavirus Pandemic*. BBC. https://www.bbc.co.uk/news/uk-52022417

Beatty, K. (2003). *Teaching and researching computer assisted language learning*. Pearson Education Limited.

Becker, K., Kehoe, J., & Tennent, B. (2007). Impact of personalised learning styles on online delivery and assessment. *Campus-Wide Information Systems*, *24*(2), 105–119. doi:10.1108/10650740710742718

Beck, J., Rainoldi, M., & Egger, R. (2019). Virtual Reality in Tourism: A State of the Art Review. *Tourism Review*, *74*(3), 586–612. doi:10.1108/TR-03-2017-0049

Bek, H. (2006). *İnsan Kaynakları Yönetiminde Eğitim ve Geliştirme Etkinliği*. Sosyal Bilimler Enstitüsü Dergisi.

Benckendorff, P. J., Xiang, Z., & Sheldon, P. J. (2019). *Tourism Information Technology*. Cabi. doi:10.1079/9781786393432.0000

Bentley, M. L., Ebert, S. E., & Ebert, C. (2007). *Teaching constructivist science*. SAGE Publications.

Berry, T. (2008). Pre-test assessment. *American Journal of Business Education*, *1*(1), 19–22. doi:10.19030/ajbe.v1i1.4633

Beutel, T., Jonas, J. M., & Moeslein, K. M. (2017). Co-creation and User Involvement in a Living Lab.: an Evaluation of Applied Methods. In Proceedings der (Vol. 13, pp. 1453-1464). Academic Press.

Bhatti, T. M. (2013). Teaching reading through computer-assisted language learning. *TESL-EJ*, *17*(2), 1–11.

Bijeesh, N. A. (2017). *Advantages and disadvantages of distance learning*. Retrieved May 13, 2022, from http://www. indiaeducation.net/online-education/articles/advantages-and-disadvantages-of-distancelearning.html

Bilgin, L., Taşcı, D., & Kağnıcıoğlu, D. V. (2004). İnsan Kaynakları Yönetimi. Eskişehir: Açık Öğretim Fakültesi Yayınları.

Birhanu, M. (2015). Perception of students and instructors toward students with disabilities: Issues, challenges, and opportunities to implement inclusive education. *Research Journal of Educational Studies and Review, 1*, 30–56. doi:10.4236/oalib.1103174

Biscop, S. (2018). *European strategy in the 21st century: New future for old power*. Routledge.

Bistaman, I. N. M., Idrus, S. Z. S., & Abd Rashid, S. (2018). Augmented reality technology for primary school education in Perlis, Malaysia. *Journal of Physics: Conference Series*, *1019*(1), 012064. doi:10.1088/1742-6596/1019/1/012064

Bjorn, P. M., Esbensen, M., Jensen, E., & Matthiesen, S. (2014). Does distance still matter? Revisiting the CSCW fundamentals on distributed collaboration. *ACM Transactions on Computer-Human Interaction, 21*(5), 27. doi:10.1145/2670534

Blake, R. (2015). The messy task of evaluating proficiency in online language courses. *Modern Language Journal*, *99*(2), 408–412. doi:10.1111/modl.12234_5

Blasco. (2014). Making the tacit explicit: Rethinking culturally inclusive pedagogy in international student academic adaptation. *Pedagogy, Culture, 23*(1), 1–22.

Bond, M. (2020). Schools and emergency remote education during the COVID-19 pandemic: A living rapid systematic review. *Asian Journal of Distance Education, 15*(2), 191–247.

Bong, W. K., & Chen, W. (2021). Increasing faculty's competence in digital accessibility for inclusive education: A systematic literature review. *International Journal of Inclusive Education*. Advance online publication. doi:10.1080/13603116.2021.1937344

Bonk, C. J., & King, K. S. (2012). Searching for learner-centered, constructivist and sociocultural components of collaborative educational learning tools. In *Electronic collaborators* (pp. 61–86). Routledge. doi:10.4324/9780203053805-10

Bortnik, B., Stozhko, N., Pervukhina, I., Tchernysheva, A., & Belysheva, G. (2017). Effect of virtual analytical chemistry laboratory on enhancing student research skills and practices. *Research in Learning Technology*, *25*(0). Advance online publication. doi:10.25304/rlt.v25.1968

Borup, J., Graham, C. R., & Davies, R. S. (2013). The nature of adolescent learner interaction in a virtual high school setting. *Journal of Computer Assisted Learning*, *29*(2), 153–167. doi:10.1111/j.1365-2729.2012.00479.x

Brieger, E., Arghode, V., & McLean, G. (2020). Connecting theory and practice: Reviewing six learning theories to inform online instruction. *European Journal of Training and Development*, *27*(5), 1843–1860. doi:10.1108/EJTD-07-2019-0116

Brink, R., & Lautenbach, G. (2011). Electronic assessment in higher education. *Educational Studies, 37*(5), 503–512. doi:10.1080/03055698.2010.539733

Brinson, J. R. (2015). Learning outcome achievement in non-traditional (virtual and remote) versus traditional (hands-on) laboratories: A review of the empirical research. *Computers & Education, 87*, 218–237. doi:10.1016/j.compedu.2015.07.003

Brockett, R. G., & Hiemstra, R. (1991). *Self-direction in adult learning: Perspectives of theory, research and practice.* Routledge.

Bulut, Y., Duruel, M., Kara, M., & Bílbay, Ö. F. (2016). Yerel Yönetimlerde İnsan Kaynaklarının Etkin Yönetimi: Hatay'da Bir Uygulama. *Strategic Public Management Journal, 3*(3), 1–24. doi:10.25069pmj.290497

Burdea, G. C., & Coiffet, P. (2003). *Virtual reality technology.* Wiley & Sons. doi:10.1162/105474603322955950

Burston, J. (2013). Mobile-assisted language learning: A selected annotated bibliography of implementation studies 1994-2012. *Language Learning & Technology, 17*(3), 157–225.

Butler-Henderson, K., Crawford, J., Rudolph, J., Lalani, K., & Sabu, K. M. (2020). COVID-19 in higher education literature database (CHELD V1): An open access systematic literature review database with coding rules. *Journal of Applied Learning & Teaching, 3*(2), 1–6.

Cain, W., Bell, J., & Cheng, C. (2016). Implementing robotic telepresence in a synchronous hybrid course. In *Advanced Learning Technologies (ICALT). 2016 IEEE 16th International Conference on.* IEEE. 10.1109/ICALT.2016.79

Çakmak, F. (2022). Review of Mobile assisted language learning across educational contexts. *Language Learning & Technology, 26*(1), 1–4.

Çalık, C., & Şehitoğlu, E.T. (2006). Okul müdürlerinin insan kaynakları yönetimi işlevlerini yerine getirebilme yeterlikleri. *Millî Eğitim Üç Aylık Eğitim ve Sosyal Bilimler Dergisi*, 170.

Cameron, K. S., & Quinn, R. E. (1999). *Diagnosing and Changing Organizational Culture Based on the Competing Values Framework.* Addison-Wesley Publishing Company, Inc.

Can, H., Akgün, A., & Kavuncubaşı, Ş. (2001). Kamu ve Özel Kesimde İnsan Kaynakları Yönetimi. Ankara: Siyasal Kitapevi.

Candy, P.C. (1991). *Self-direction for life-long learning.* Jossey-Bass.

Candy, P. (1991). *Self-direction for lifelong learning.* Jossey-Bass.

Can, H. (2002). *Organizasyon ve Yönetim.* Siyasal Kitabevi.

Cao, W., Fang, Z., Hou, G., Han, M., Xu, X., Dong, J., & Zheng, J. (2020). The Psychological Impact of the COVID-19 Epidemic on College Students in China. *Psychiatry Research, 2020*(287), 112934. doi:10.1016/j.psychres.2020.112934 PMID:32229390

Carlon, S., Bennett-Woods, D., Berg, B., Claywell, L., LeDuc, K., & Marcisz, N. (2012). The community of inquiry instrument: Validation and results in online health care disciplines. *Computer Education*, *59*, 215–221.

Carolan, C., Davies, C. L., Crookes, P., McGhee, S., & Rox-Burgh, M. (2020). COVID 19: Disruptive impacts and transformative opportunities in undergraduate nurse education. *Nurse Education in Practice*, *46*, 215–223.

Carrier, M., & Pashler, H. (1992). The influence of retrieval on retention. *Memory & Cognition*, *20*(6), 633–642. doi:10.3758/BF03202713 PMID:1435266

Carroll, J. (2002). *A handbook for deterring plagiarism in higher education*. Oxford Centre for Staff and Learning Development.

Carroll, J., & Appleton, J. (2001). *Plagiarism: A good practice guide*. Oxford Brookes University Press.

Carrozzino, M., & Bergamasco, M. (2010). Beyond virtual museums: Experiencing immersive virtual reality in real museums. *Journal of Cultural Heritage*, *11*(4), 452–458. doi:10.1016/j.culher.2010.04.001

Çelik, S., & Aytin, K. (2014). Teachers' Views on Digital Educational Tools in English Language Learning: Benefits and Challenges in the Turkish Context. *Tesl-Ej*, *18*(2), n2.

Çelik, V. (2003). *Eğitimsel Liderlik*. Pegem A Yayınları.

Cengiz, E. (2010). Taşımalı İnsan Kaynakları Yönetiminde Öğretmenlerin Örgütlenme Hakkı (Yüksek Lisans Tezi). Beykent Üniversitesi, Sosyal Bilimleri Enstitüsü, İstanbul.

Cent, H. (2007). Özel Okullarda İnsan Kaynakları Yönetimi Uygulamalarının İncelenmesi (Yüksek Lisans Tezi). Yıldız Teknik Üniversitesi / Sosyal Bilimler Enstitüsü, İstanbul.

Chalmers, D. J. (2022). *Reality+: Virtual Worlds and the Problems of Philosophy*. W. W. Norton.

Chambers, E. A. (1992). Workload and the quality of student learning. *Studies in Higher Education*, *17*(2), 141–152. doi:10.1080/03075079212331382627

Chambers, E. A. (1994). Assessing learners' workload. In F. Lockwood (Ed.), *Materials production in open and distance learning*. Chapman.

Charitos, D., Lepouras, G., Vassilakis, C., Katifori, V., & Halatsi, L. (2000). An Approach to Designing and Implementing Virtual Museums. *Proceedings of the Seventh UK VR-SIG Conference*.

Chaturvedi, S., Rizvi, I. A., & Pasipanodya, E. T. (2019). How Can Leaders Make Their Followers to Commit to the Organization? the Importance of Influence Tactics. *Global Business Review*, *20*(6), 1462–1474.

Checa, D., & Bustillo, A. (2019). A review of immersive virtual reality serious games to enhance learning and training. *Multimedia Tools and Applications*, *79*(9-10), 5501–5527. doi:10.100711042-019-08348-9

Cheong, R. (1995). The virtual threat to travel and tourism. *Tourism Management, 16*(6), 417–422. doi:10.1016/0261-5177(95)00049-T

Chiarini, A. (2021). Industry 4.0 technologies in the manufacturing sector: Are we sure they are all relevant for environmental performance? *Business Strategy and the Environment, 30*(7), 3194–3207. doi:10.1002/bse.2797

Choy, J. L. F., & Choon, L. Q. (2016). Modelling relationships between students' academic achievement and community of inquiry in an online learning environment for a blended course. *Australasian Journal of Educational Technology, 32*, 106–124.

Chui, M., Manyika, J., & Miremadi, M. (2016, July). Where machines could replace humans and where they can't (yet): The technical potential for automation differs dramatically across sectors and activities. *McKinsey Quarterly.*

Chu, S. K. W., Reynolds, R. B., Tavares, N. J., Notari, M., & Lee, C. W. Y. (2017). *21st century skills development through inquiry-based learning: From theory to practice.* Springer. doi:10.1007/978-981-10-2481-8

Cigir, K. (2018). Creating a Living Lab. Model for Tourism and Hospitality Businesses to Stimulate CSR and Sustainability Innovations. *WIT Transactions on Ecology and the Environment, 217*, 569–583. doi:10.2495/SDP180491

Cignoni, P., & Scopigno, R. (2008). Sampled 3D models for CH applications: A viable and enabling new medium or just a technological exercise? *Journal on Computing and Cultural Heritage, 1*(1), 1–23. doi:10.1145/1367080.1367082

Cimnaghi, E., & Mussini, P. (2015). An application of tourism carrying capacity assessment at two Italian cultural heritage sites. *Journal of Heritage Tourism, 10*(3), 302–313. doi:10.1080/1743873X.2014.988158

Çınar, M., Doğan, D., & Tüzün, H. (2020). The effect of design tasks on the cognitive load level of instructional designers in 3D MUVEs. *International Journal of Technology and Design Education*, 1–18.

Clariana, R., & Wallace, P. (2002). Paper–based versus computer–based assessment: Key factors associated with the test mode effect. *British Journal of Educational Technology, 33*(5), 593–602.

Clevaland, J. N., Murphy, K. R., & Williams, R. E. (1989). Multiple Uses of Performance Appraisal: Prevelance and Correlates. *The Journal of Applied Psychology, 74*(1), 20. doi:10.1037/0021-9010.74.1.130

Cliburn, D. (n.d.). Incorporating Virtual Reality Concepts into the Introductory Computer Graphics Course. In *Proceedings of the SIGCSE.* ACM.

Code, J., Ralph, R., & Forde, K. (2020). Pandemic Designs for the Future: Perspectives of Technology Education Teachers during COVID-19. *Inf. Learn. Sci., 2020*(121), 419–431. doi:10.1108/ILS-04-2020-0112

Cogo, A. (2012). English as a lingua franca: Concepts, use and implications. *ELT Journal, 66*(1), 97–105. doi:10.1093/elt/ccr069

Collins, A., Azmat, F., & Rentschler, R. (2018). Bringing everyone on the same journey: Revisiting inclusion in higher education. *Studies in Higher Education, 44*, 1475–1487. doi:10.1080/03075079.2018.1450852

Comito, C., & Pizzuti, C. (2022). Artificial intelligence for forecasting and diagnosing COVID-19 pandemic: A focused review. *Artificial Intelligence in Medicine, 128*, 102286. doi:10.1016/j.artmed.2022.102286 PMID:35534142

Committee W.C.H. (2019). *Wuhan Municipal Health and Health Commission's briefing on the current pneumonia epidemic situation.* Author.

Constance, M. F. (1984). An Examination of Teachers Attitudes Toward Women in Education Administration (Yayımlanmamış Doktora Tezi). University of Massachusetts.

Cooper, A., & Reimann, R. (2003). *About-face 2.0: the essentials of interaction design.* Wiley Publishing, Inc.

Corbetta, P. (2003). *Social Research: Theory Methods and Techniques.* SAGE Publications Ltd. doi:10.4135/9781849209922

Costan, E., Gonzales, G., Gonzales, R., Enriquez, L., Costan, F., Suladay, D., Atibing, N. M., Aro, J. L., Evangelista, S. S., Maturan, F., Selerio, E. Jr, & Ocampo, L. (2021). Education 4.0 in developing economies: A systematic literature review of implementation barriers and future research agenda. *Sustainability, 13*(22), 12763. doi:10.3390u132212763

Cotton, D. R., Nash, T., & Kneale, P. (2017). Supporting the retention of non-traditional students in higher education using a resilience framework. *European Educational Research Journal, 16*(1), 62–79.

Creswell, J. W., & Poth, C. N. (2017). *Qualitative inquiry and research design: Choosing among five approaches.* Sage publications.

Crompton, H. (2013). A historical overview of mobile learning: toward learner-centered education. In Z. L. Berge & L. Y. Muilenburg (Eds.), *Handbook of Mobile Learning* (pp. 3–14). Routledge.

Cullwick, D. (1975). Positioning Demarketing Strategy: Marketers must integrate the changes in the business environment into effective new product, pricing, distribution, and promotion strategies. *Journal of Marketing, 39*(2), 51–57. doi:10.1177/002224297503900209

Dachapally, P. R. (2017). *Facial Emotion Detection Using Convolutional Neural Networks and Representational Autoencoder Units.* Academic Press.

Dağdeler, K. O., Konca, M. Y., & Demiröz, H. (2020). The effect of mobile-assisted language learning (MALL) on EFL learners' collocation learning. *Journal of Language and Linguistic Studies, 16*(1), 489–509. doi:10.17263/jlls.712891

Dampitakse, K., Kungvantip, V., Jermsittiparsert, K., & Chienwattanasook, K. (2021). The Impact of Economic Growth, Financial Development, Financial Performance and Capital Growth on the Adoption of Artificial Intelligence in the ASEAN Countries. *Journal of Management Information and Decision Sciences, 24*(4), 1–14.

Danışman, A. (2008). *Türkiye'de İnsan Kaynakları Yönetimi Uygulamaları.* Nobel Yayınevi.

Darmawati, D. (2018). Improving Speaking Skill Through Mobile-Assisted Language Learning (MALL). *Jurnal Teknologi Sistem Informasi dan Aplikasi, 1*(1), 24-30.

David, M., & Sutton, C.D. (2004) Social Research: the basics. London: Sage Publications.

De Leon, M. P., Hribernik, K. A., & Eriksson, M. (2008). The Living Labs Approach to a Virtual Lab. Environment. In *Encyclopedia of Networked and Virtual Organizations* (pp. 818–821). IGI Global. doi:10.4018/978-1-59904-885-7.ch108

Delen, D. (2011). Predicting Student Attrition with Data Mining Methods. *Journal of College Student Retention, 13*(1), 17–35. doi:10.2190/CS.13.1.b

Deniz, M., & Ünal, A. (2007). İnsan Kaynaklarının Bir Fonksiyonu Olarak Örgütsel Kariyer Yönetimi ve Bir Uygulama. *E-Journal of New World Sciences Academy.*

DePape, A., Barnes, M., & Petryschuk, J. (2019). Students' Experiences in Higher Education with Virtual and Augmented Reality: A Qualitative Systematic Review. *Innovative Practice in Higher Education, 3*(3), 22–57.

Dever, D. A., & Azevedo, R. (2019). Autonomy and types of informational text presentations in game-based learning environments. In S. Isotani, E. Millán, A. Ogan, P. Hastings, B. McLaren, & R. Luckin (Eds.), *AIED'19: Proceedings of the 20th International Conference on Artificial Intelligence in Education* (pp. 110-120). Springer.

Dewey, J. (1959). *My pedagogic creed. In Dewey on Education.* Teachers College, Columbia University.

Dhawan, S. (2020). *Online Learning: A Panacea in the Time of COVID-19 Crisis.* Academic Press.

Dhawan, S. (2020). Online Learning: A Panacea in the Time of COVID-19 Crisis. *Journal of Educational Technology Systems, 2020*(49), 5–22. doi:10.1177/0047239520934018

Dias, L., & Victor, A. (2017). Teaching and learning with mobile devices in the 21st century digital world: Benefits and challenges. *European Journal of Multidisciplinary Studies, 2*(5), 339–344. doi:10.26417/ejms.v5i1.p339-344

Dibbell, J. (1998). *My tiny life: Crime and passion in a virtual world. New York.* Holt.

Dimock, M. (2019). *Defining generations: Where millennials end and generation z begins.* Pew Research Centre. https://pewrsr.ch/2szqtJz

Din, R., Norman, H., Karim, A., Shah, P., Rahmat, F. R., & Kamarulzaman, F. (2012). Hybrid e-training assessment tool for higher education. *WSEAS Transactions on Advances in Engineering Education, 2*(9), 52-61. https://www.wseas.org/multimedia/journals/education/2012/55-353.pdf

Din, R., Nordin, M. S., Kassim, N. A., Ahmad, T. B. T., Jusoff, K., Johar, N. A., Zaman, M. F. K., Zakaria, M. S., Ahmad, M., Karim, A. A., & Mastor, K. A. (2010). Development and validation of meaningful hybrid e-training model for computer education. *International Journal of Computer Science and Information Technologies, 1*(3), 179–184. http://www.ijcsit.com/ijcsit-issue3.php

Din, R., Nordin, N., Jusoff, K., Nordin, M. S., Zakaria, M. S., Mastor, K. A., & Embi, M. A. (2011). Hybrid e-training measurement tool: Reliability and validity (2011). *Middle East Journal of Scientific Research, 7*(2), 184–188. http://www.idosi.org/mejsr/mejsr7(2)11/10.pdf

Disabled Students Sector Leadership Group (DSSLG). (2017). *Inclusive teaching and learning in higher education as a route to excellence.* London: Department for education. Available Online: https://www.gov.uk/government/uploads/system/uploads/attachment_data/file/58 7221/ Inclusive_Teaching_and_Learning_in_Higher_Education_as_a_route_to excellence.pdf

Doğan, E., Apaydın, Ç., & Önen, Ö. (2006). Eğitim hizmetlerinde toplam kalite yönetimi ve kalite politikası. *Mehmet Akif Ersoy Üniversitesi Eğitim Bilimleri Dergisi, 11*, 59–79.

Dong, C., Cao, S., & Li, H. (2020). Young children's online learning during COVID-19 pandemic: Chinese parents' beliefs and attitudes. *Children and Youth Services Review, 118*, 118. doi:10.1016/j.childyouth.2020.105440 PMID:32921857

Doucet, A., Netolicky, D., Timmers, K., Tuscano, F. J. (2020). *Thinking about pedagogy in an unfolding pandemic* (An Independent Report on Approaches to Distance Learning during COVID-19 School Closure). Work of Education International and UNESCO.

Doughty, C. (2015). Accountability of foreign language programs. *Modern Language Journal, 99*(2), 412–415. doi:10.1111/modl.12234_6

Dovigo, Dovigo, & Janssen. (2017). Special educational needs and inclusive practices. Sense Publishers.

Doyle, O. (2020). *COVID-19: Exacerbating educational inequalities?* Retrieved April 5, 2022, from http://publicpolicy.ie/ papers/covid-19-exacerbating-educational-inequalities/

Dudwick, N., Kuehnast, K., Jones, V., & Woolcock, M. (2006). *Analyzing social capital in context: A Guide to using qualitative methods and data. World Bank.* The International Bank for Reconstruction and Development/the World Bank.

Duimering, P. R., Ran, B., Derbentseva, N., & Poile, C. (2006). The effects of ambiguity on project task structure in new product development. *Knowledge and Process Management, 13*(4), 239–251. doi:10.1002/kpm.260

Dumford, A. D., & Miller, A. L. (2018). Online learning in higher education: Exploring advantages and disadvantages for engagement. *Journal of Computing in Higher Education, 30*(3), 452–465. doi:10.100712528-018-9179-z

Dutta, S., & Lanvin, B. (2020). *The Network Readiness Index 2020: Accelerating Digital Transformation in a post-COVID Global Economy*. Academic Press.

Dwivedi, A., Dwivedi, P., Bobek, S., & Sternad Zabukovšek, S. (2019). Factors affecting students' engagement with online content in blended learning. *Kybernetes*, *48*(7), 1500–1515. doi:10.1108/K-10-2018-0559

Dwivedi, Y., Hughes, L., Coombs, C., Constantiou, I., Duan, Y., & Edwards, J. (2020). Impact of COVID-19 pandemic on information management research and practice: Transforming education, work and life. *International Journal of Information Management*, 55.

EasyLMS. (2022). *Advantages and disadvantages of online assessments*. Retrieved from https://www.onlineassessmenttool.com/knowledge-center/online-assessment-center/advantages-and-disadvantages-of-online-assessments/item12518

Eleyyan, S. (2021). The future of education according to the fourth industrial revolution. *Journal of Educational Technology & Online Learning*, *4*(1), 23–30. https://dergipark.org.tr/jetol

Ellahi, R. M., Khan, M. U. A., & Shah, A. (2019). Redesigning curriculum in line with Industry 4.0. *Procedia Computer Science*, *151*, 699–708. doi:10.1016/j.procs.2019.04.093

Encarnacion, R. E., Galang, A. D., & Hallar, B. A. (2021). The impact and effectiveness of e-learning on teaching and learning. *International Journal of Computing Sciences Research*, *5*(1), 383–397. doi:10.25147/ijcsr.2017.001.1.47

Erdoğan, İ. (1991). *İşletmelerde Personel Seçimi ve Başarı Değerleme Teknikleri*. İ.Ü. İşletme Fakültesi Yayınları.

Erdoğan, İ. (2002). *Okul Yönetimi Öğretim Liderliği*. Sistem Yayıncılık.

Eren, E. (2001). *Örgütsel Davranış ve Yönetim Psikolojisi*. Beta Basım Yayım.

Erlam, G., Garrett, N., Gasteiger, N., Lau, K., Hoare, K., Agarwal, S., & Haxell, A. (2021). What really matters: Experiences of emergency remote teaching in university teaching and learning during the COVID-19 pandemic. *Frontiers in Education*, *6*, 639842. doi:10.3389/feduc.2021.639842

Ermi, L., & Mäyrä, F. (2005). Fundamental Components of the Gameplay Experience: Analysing Immersion. *Proceedings of the DiGRA Conference on Changing Views: Worlds in Play*.

Ertmer, P. A., & Newby, T. J. (2013). Behaviorism, cognitivism, constructivism: Comparing critical features from an instructional design perspective. *Performance Improvement Quarterly*, *26*(2), 43–71. doi:10.1002/piq.21143

Eysenck, M. W. (2004). *Psychology: An international perspective*. Taylor & Francis.

Farooq, L., Ali, A., Mahmood, S., Farzand, M., Masood, H., & Mujahid, S. (2019). Association between excessive use of mobile phone and insomnia among pakistani teenagers cross sectional study. *American International Journal of Multidisciplinary Scientific Research*, *5*(4), 10–15. doi:10.46281/aijmsr.v5i4.406

Feldhus, N., Ravichandran, A. M., & Möller, S. (2022). *Mediators: Conversational Agents Explaining NLP Model Behavior*. Academic Press.

Felix, U. (2005). E-learning pedagogy in the third millennium: The need for combining social and cognitive constructivist approaches. *ReCALL, 17*(1), 85–100. doi:10.1017/S0958344005000716

Fernandez, S. (2008). *Teaching and learning languages other than English (LOTE) in Victorian schools*. Office for Policy, Research and Innovation, Department of Education and Early Childhood *Development.*

Ferri, F., Grifoni, P., & Guzzo, T. (2020). Online learning and emergency remote teaching: Opportunities and challenges in emergency situations. *Societies (Basel, Switzerland), 10*(4), 86. doi:10.3390oc10040086

Filizöz, B. (2003). İnsan Kaynakları Yönetiminde Uluslar Arası Yaklaşım Gerekliliği. *Cumhuriyet Üniversitesi İktisadi ve İdari Bilimler Dergisi, 4*(1).

Fiore, A. (2017). *How can a theory guide or inform practice?* http://annemariefiore.com/connectivism/

Fithriani, R. (2021). The utilization of mobile-assisted gamification for vocabulary learning: Its efficacy and perceived benefits. *Computer Assisted Language Learning Electronic Journal (CALL-EJ), 22*(3), 146-163.

Flack, C. B., Walker, L., Bickerstaff, A., Earle, H., & Margetts, C. (2020). *Educator perspectives on the impact of COVID-19 on teaching and learning in Australia and New Zealand*. Retrieved April 4, 2022, from https://www.pivotpl.com/wpcontent/uploads/2020/04/Pivot_StateofEducation_2020_White-Paper-1.pdf

Florian, L., & Linklater, H. (2010). Preparing teachers for inclusive education: Using inclusive pedagogy to enhance teaching and learning for all. *Cambridge Journal of Education, 40*(4), 369–386.

Florian, L., & Spratt, J. (2013). Enacting inclusion: A framework for interrogating inclusive practice. *European Journal of Special Needs Education, 28*(2), 119–135. doi:10.1080/08856257.2013.778111

Flowerday, T., Schraw, G., & Stevens, J. (2004). The Role of Choice and Interest in Reader Engagement. *Journal of Experimental Education, 72*(2), 93–114. doi:10.3200/JEXE.72.2.93-114

Foot, K. A. (2001). Cultural-historical activity theory as practice theory: Illuminating the development of a conflict-monitoring network. *Communication Theory, 11*(1), 56–83. doi:10.1111/j.1468-2885.2001.tb00233.x

Foster, D., & Layman, H. (2013). *Online proctoring systems compared*. Retrieved from https://caveon.com/wp-content/uploads/2013/03/Online-Proctoring-Systems-Compared-Mar-13-2013.pdf

Francois, E. J. (2015). *Education and society: Building global education with a local perspective*. Palgrave Macmillan. doi:10.1057/9781137386779_1

Friesen, S. (2008). *Effective teaching practices – A framework*. Canadian Education Association.

Galkienė, A., & Monkevičienė, O. (2021). Preconditions of transforming the educational process by applying inclusive education strategies: Theoretical background. In *Improving Inclusive Education Through Universal Design for Learning* (Vol. 5, pp. 1–21). Springer.

García Botero, G., Nguyet Diep, A., García Botero, J., Zhu, C., & Questier, F. (2022). Acceptance and Use of Mobile-Assisted Language Learning by Higher Education Language Teachers. *Lenguaje*, *50*(1), 66–92. doi:10.25100/lenguaje.v50i1.11006

Garrison, D. R., & Anderson, T. (2003). E-learning in the 21st century: A framework for research and practice. Routledge.

Garrison, D. R., Anderson, T., & Archer, W. (2000). Critical inquiry in a text-based environment: Computer conferencing in higher education. *The Internet and Higher Education*, *2*(2-3), 87–105.

Garrison, D. R., Anderson, T., & Archer, W. (2001). Critical thinking, cognitive presence, and computer conferencing in distance education. *American Journal of Distance Education*, *15*(1), 7–23.

Garrison, D. R., Anderson, T., & Archer, W. (2004). Student Role Adjustment in Online Communities of Inquiry: Model And Instrument Validation. *Journal of Asynchronous Learning Networks*, *8*(2), 61–74.

Garrison, D. R., & Arbaugh, J. B. (2007). Researching the community of inquiry model: Review, issues, and future directions. *The Internet and Higher Education*, *10*, 157–172.

Garrison, D. R., & Archer, W. (2000). *A transactional perspective on teaching and learning: A framework for adult and higher education*. Pergamon.

Gee, J. P. (2003). *What video games have to teach us about learning and literacy*. Palgrave Macmillan.

Genç, Y., & Çat, G. (2013). Engellilerin İstihdamı ve Sosyal İçerme İlişkisi. *Akademik İncelemeler Dergisi*, *8*(1).

George, M. L. (2020). Effective Teaching and Examination Strategies for Undergraduate Learning during COVID-19 School Restrictions. *Journal of Educational Technology Systems*, *49*(1), 23–48.

Georgiev, T., Georgieva, E., & Smrikarov, A. (2004). *M-learning – a new stage of e-learning*. Paper presented at the International Conference on Computer Systems and Technologies – CompSysTech' 2004.

Georgiev, T., Georgieva, E., & Smrikarov, A. (2004). M-learning: a new stage of e-learning, *Proceedings of the International Conference on Computer Systems and Technologies (CompSysTech)*, *4*(28), 1–4.

Gerstein, J. (2014). Moving from Education 1.0 through education 2.0 towards education 3.0. In L. M. Blaschke, C. Kenyon, & S. Hase (Eds.), *Experiences in self-determined learning* (pp. 83–99). Create Space Independent Publishing Platform.

Gharehblagh, N. M., & Nasri, N. (2020). Developing EFL elementary learners' writing skills through mobile-assisted language learning (MALL). *Teaching English with Technology, 20*(1), 104–121.

Ghorbani, N., & Ebadi, S. (2020). Exploring learners' grammatical development in mobile assisted language learning. *Cogent Education, 7*(1), 1704599. doi:10.1080/2331186X.2019.1704599

Gibbs, G. (1995). *Assessing student-centred courses.* Oxford Centre for Staff Development, Oxford Brooks University.

Gigante, G., & Zago, A. (2022). *DARQ technologies in the financial sector: artificial intelligence applications in personalized banking.* Qualitative Research in Financial Markets. doi:10.1108/QRFM-02-2021-0025

Girija Shankar Behera. (2020, December 24). *Face Detection with Haar Cascade.* Towardsdatascience.

Gök, S. (2006). *21. Yüzyılda İnsan Kaynakları Yönetimi.* Beta Yayıncılık.

Gouedard, P., Pont, B., & Viennet, R. (2020). *Education responses to COVID-19: Implementing a way forward.* OECD Education Working Paper No. 224.

Govindarajan, V., & Srivastava, A. (2020). What the Shift to Virtual Learning Could Mean for the Future of Higher Education. *Harvard Business Review.*

Gray, K., & Ulbrich, F. (2017). Ambiguity acceptance and translation skills in the project management literature. *International Journal of Managing Projects in Business, 10*(2), 423–450. doi:10.1108/IJMPB-05-2016-0044

Grudin, J. (1993). Interface: An evolving concept. *Communications of the ACM, 36*(4), 110–119. doi:10.1145/255950.153585

Gudjonsdottir, H., & Óskarsdóttir, E. (2016). Inclusive education, pedagogy, and practice. Culturally responsive teaching practices. In S. Markic & S. Abels (Eds.), *Science Education Towards Inclusion* (pp. 7–22). Nova Science Publishers.

Gürüz, D., & Yaylacı, G. Ö. (2004). *İletişimci Gözüyle İnsan Kaynakları Yönetimi.* Kapital.

Guttentag, D. A. (2010). Virtual reality: Applications and implications for tourism. *Tourism Management, 31*(5), 637–651. doi:10.1016/j.tourman.2009.07.003

Häfner, P., Häfner, V., & Ovtcharova, J. (2013). Teaching methodology for virtual reality practical course in engineering education. *Procedia Computer Science, 25*, 251–260.

Hales, R., & Jennings, G. (2017). Transformation for sustainability: The role of complexity in tourism students' understanding of sustainable tourism. *Journal of Hospitality, Leisure, Sport and Tourism Education, 21*, 185–194. doi:10.1016/j.jhlste.2017.08.001

Halili, S. H., & Sulaiman, S. (2021). Students' perception to integrate education 4.0 in Science program. *Multidisciplinary Journal for Education, Social and Technological Sciences, 8*(1), 45–57. doi:10.4995/muse.2021.14768

Hanlon, B., & Larget, B. (2011). *Analysis of variance.* Department of Statistic, University of Wisconsin-Madison.

Hartshorn, K. J., & McMurry, B. L. (2020). The Effects of the COVID-19 pandemic on ESL learners and TESOL practitioners in the United States. *International Journal of TESOL Studies, 2*(2), 140–156.

Haseeb, M., Hussain, H., Slusarczyk, B., & Jermsittiparsert, K. (2019). Industry 4.0: A Solution towards Technology Challenges of Sustainable Business Performance. *Social Sciences, 8*(5), 184. doi:10.3390ocsci8050154

Haseeb, M., Sasmoko, Mihardjo, L. W. W., Gill, A. R., & Jermsittiparsert, K. (2019). Economic Impact of Artificial Intelligence: New Look for the Macroeconomic Assessment in Asia-Pacific Region. *International Journal of Computational Intelligence Systems, 12*(2), 1295. doi:10.2991/ijcis.d.191025.001

Hassan, W. U., Nawaz, M. T., Syed, T. H., Arfeen, M. I., Naseem, A., & Noor, S. (2015). Investigating students' behavioral intention towards adoption of mobile learning in higher education institutions of Pakistan. *University of Engineering and Technology Taxila Technical Journal, 20*(3), 34.

Hendrawan, M. R., & Bafadhal, A. S. (2022). Virtual Museum. In D. Buhalis (Ed.), *Encyclopedia of Tourism Management and Marketing*. Edward Elgar Publishing.

Heriyanto, Satori, D., Komariah, A., & Suryana, A. (2019). Character education in the era of industrial revolution 4.0 and its relevance to the high school learning transformation process. *Utopía y Praxis Latinoamericana, 24*(5), 327-339. https://www.redalyc.org/articulo.oa?id=27962050036

Herrington, J., Oliver, R., & Reeves, T. C. (2003). Patterns of engagement in authentic online learning environments. *Australasian Journal of Educational Technology, 19*(1). Advance online publication. doi:10.14742/ajet.1701

Higgins, S. (2014). Critical thinking for 21st-century education: A cyber-tooth curriculum? *Prospects, 44*(4), 559–574.

Hilliard, L. P., & Stewart, M. K. (2019). Time well spent: Creating a community of inquiry in blended first-year writing courses. *Internet Higher Education., 41*, 11–24.

Hodges, C., Moore, S., Lockee, B., Trust, T., & Bond, A. (2020). The difference between emergency remote teaching and online learning. *EDUCAUSE Review.*

Hoffman, J., & Leafstedt, J. (2014). Understanding the Use of Technology for Facilitating Inquiry-Based Learning. *Inquiry-based Learning for Faculty and Institutional Development: A Conceptual and Practical Resource for Educators* (*Innovations in Higher Education Teaching and Learning, 1*, 421-437. doi:10.1108/S2055-364120140000001021

Holla, S., & Katti, M. M. (2012). Android based mobile application development and its security. *International Journal of Computer Trends and Technology, 3*(3), 486–490.

Hricko, M., & Howell, S. L. (2006). *Online assessment and measurement.* IGI Global. doi:10.4018/978-1-59140-720-1

Huang, J., Shlobin, N. A., Lam, S. K., & DeCuypere, M. (2022). Artificial Intelligence Applications in Pediatric Brain Tumor Imaging: A Systematic Review. *World Neurosurgery, 157*, 99–105. doi:10.1016/j.wneu.2021.10.068 PMID:34648981

Huang, Y. C., Backman, S. J., Backman, K. F., & Moore, D. (2013). Exploring user acceptance of 3D virtual worlds in travel and tourism marketing. *Tourism Management, 36*, 490–501. doi:10.1016/j.tourman.2012.09.009

Huarcaya-Victoria, J. (2020). Mental health considerations about the COVID-19 pandemic. *Revista Peruana de Medicina Experimental y Salud Pública, 37*, 327–334.

Hughes, C. E., & Moshell, J. M. (1997). Shared Virtual Worlds for Education: The Explore Net Experiment. *Multimedia Systems, 5*(2), 145–154. doi:10.1007005300050050

Hu, W., Liu, G. P., & Zhou, H. (2012). Web-based 3-D control laboratory for remote real-time experimentation. *IEEE Transactions on Industrial Electronics, 60*(10), 4673–4682. doi:10.1109/TIE.2012.2208440

Hymes, D. H. (1972). On communicative competence. In J. B. Pride & J. Holmes (Eds.), *Sociolinguistics. Selected Readings*. Penguin.

İnce, M. (2000). Değişim Olgusu ve Örgütlerde İnsan Kaynakları Yönetiminin Değişen Fonksiyonları. *Selçuk Üniversitesi Sosyal Bilimler Dergisi, 11*, 319–340.

Inkpen, K., Booth, K., Klawe, M., & Upitis, R. (1995). Playing together beats playing apart, especially for girls. In J. Schnase, & E. Cunnius (Eds.), *Proceedings of CSCL 1995: The First International Conference on Computer Support for Collaborative Learning* (pp. 177– 181). Hillsdale, NJ: Erlbaum.

Intelitek. (2018). *The education 4.0 revolution: An analysis of industry 4.0 and its effect on education.* https://intelitek.com/2018/05/11/what-is-education-4-0/

IPAG Business School. (2021). *What is digital learning?* Retrieved from https://www.ipag.edu/en/blog/definition-digital-learning

Iriondo, R., & Shukla, P. (2022, May 6). *What is Machine Learning (ML)?* Towards AI. https://towardsai.net/p/machine-learning/what-is-machine-learning-ml-b58162f97ec7

Irshad, S., & Ghani, M. (2015). Benefits of CALL in ESL pedagogy in Pakistan: A case study. *ELF Annual Research Journal*, *17*, 1–22.

Islam, R., Islam, R., & Mazumder, T. (2010). Mobile application and its global impact. *IACSIT International Journal of Engineering and Technology*, *10*(6), 72–78.

Ismailov, M., & Chiu, T. (2022). Catering to Inclusion and diversity with universal design for learning in asynchronous online education: A self-determination theory perspective. *Frontiers in Psychology*, *13*, 819–884. doi:10.3389/fpsyg.2022.819884 PMID:35265016

Itow, R. C. (2020). Fostering Valuable Learning Experiences by Transforming Current Teaching Practices: Practical Pedagogical Approaches from Online Practitioners. *Inf. Learn. Sci.*, *2020*(121), 443–452. doi:10.1108/ILS-04-2020-0106

Izard, S. G., Juanes, M. J. A., & Palomera, P. R. (2017). Virtual Reality Educational Tool for Human Anatomy. *Journal of Medical Systems*, *41*(5), 76. doi:10.100710916-017-0723-6 PMID:28326490

Izci, D., & Ekinci, S. (2022). *A Novel Hybrid ASO-NM Algorithm and Its Application to Automobile Cruise Control System*. doi:10.1007/978-981-16-6332-1_29

Jachova, Z., Kovačević, J., & Hasanbegović, H. (2018). Individual education plan foundation of a quality inclusive education. *Journal Human Research in Rehabilitation*, *8*(2), 88–93. doi:10.21554/HRR.091811

Jackson, L. B., Ryndak, D. L., & Wehmeyer, M. L. (2008). The dynamic relationship between context, curriculum, and student learning: A case for inclusive education as a research-based practice. *Research and Practice for Persons with Severe Disabilities*, *34*(1), 175–195.

Jadoul, M. (2021). How industry 4.0 is transforming higher education. *Education Technology*. https://edtechnology.co.uk/comments/how-industry-4-0-transforming-higher-education/

Jahanzaib, R., & Zeeshan, M. (2017). University Teachers' and Students' Beliefs about Grammar Translation Method and Communicative Language Teaching in Quetta, Balochistan, Pakistan. *International Journal of English Linguistics*, *7*(2), 151. doi:10.5539/ijel.v7n2p151

Jayathirtha, G., Fields, D., Kafai, Y. B., & Chipps, J. (2020). Supporting Making Online: The Role of Artifact, Teacher, and Peer Interactions in Crafting Electronic Textiles. *Inf. Learn. Sci.*, *2020*(121), 381–390. doi:10.1108/ILS-04-2020-0111

Jensen, T. (2019). Higher Education in the Digital Era: The Current State of Transformation Around the World. International Association of Universities (IAU). *Journal of Educational Technology Systems*, *49*(1), 5–22.

Johnson, N., Seaman, J., & Veletsianos, G. (2021). Teaching during a pandemic: Spring transition, fall continuation, winter evaluation. *Bayview Analytics*. Retrieved May 17, 2022, from https://www.bayviewanalytics.com/reports/teaching-duringapandemic.pdf

Jones, A., & Issroff, K. (2007). Motivation and mobile devices: Exploring the role of appropriation and coping strategies. *Association for Learning Technology, 15*(3), 247–258. doi:10.3402/rlt.v15i3.10934

Joughin, G. (2009). Assessment, learning and judgement in higher education: a critical review. In G. Joughin (Ed.), *Assessment, learning and judgement in higher education* (pp. 13–27). Springer Netherlands. doi:10.1007/978-1-4020-8905-3_2

Jurāne-Brēmane, A. (2021). The digital transformation of assessment: Challenges and opportunities. *Human, Technologies and Quality of Education*, 352.

Justis, N., Litts, B.K., Reina, L., & Rhodes, S. (2020). Cultivating Staff Culture Online: How Edith Bowen Laboratory School Responded to COVID-19. *Inf. Learn. Sci. 2020.*

Kandroudi, M., & Bratitsis, T. (2012). Exploring the Educational Perspectives of XBOX Kinect Based Video Games. *Proc.ECGBL 2012*, 219-227.

Kao, F. C., Tung, Y. L., & Chang, W. Y. (2008). *183 The Design of 3D Virtual Collaborative Learning System with Circuit-Measuring Function*. Academic Press.

Kaplan, A. M., & Haenlein, M. (2016). Higher education and the digital revolution: About MOOCs, SPOCs, social media, and the Cookie Monster. *Business Horizons, 59*(4), 441–450. doi:10.1016/j.bushor.2016.03.008

Karaca, D. 2009. İlköğretim Okullarında Yöneticilerin İnsan Kaynakları Yönetimi İşlevlerini Yerine Getirebilme Yeterlikleri ile Öğretmenlerin Örgütsel Bağlılıkları Arasındaki İlişki (Yüksek Lisans Tezi). Akdeniz Üniversitesi/Sosyal Bilimler Enstitüsü, Antalya.

Karakose, T. (2021). The impact of the COVID-19 epidemic on higher education: Opportunities and implications for policy and practice. *Educational Process: International Journal, 10*(1), 7–12. doi:10.22521/edupij.2021.101.1

Karasar, N. (2008). Bilimsel araştırma yöntemi. Ankara: Nobel Yayın Dağıtım.

Karcıoğlu, H., & Öztürk, Ü. (2009). İşletmelerde Performans Değerleme İle İnsan Kaynakları Bilgi Sistemleri (İKBS) Arasındaki İlişkisi, İstanbul İlinde Bir Araştırma. *Atatürk Üniversitesi Sosyal Bilimler Enstitüsü Dergisi, 13*(1), 343–366.

Kardan, A. A., Sadeghi, H., Ghidary, S. S., & Sani, M. R. F. (2013). Prediction of student course selection in online higher education institutes using neural network. *Computer Education, 65*, 1–11.

Kardan, A. A., Sadeghi, H., Ghidary, S. S., & Sani, M. R. F. (2013). Prediction of student course selection in online higher education institutes using neural network. *Computers & Education, 65*, 1–11. doi:10.1016/j.compedu.2013.01.015

Kaya, E. N., & Taş, İ.E. (2015). Personel Yönetimi-İnsan Kaynakları Yönetimi Ayrımı. *KSÜ İİBF Dergisi, 5*(1). 21-28.

Kayıkçı, K. (2001). Yönetici yetiştirme sorunu. *Millî Eğitim Dergisi*, 150.

Kemps, S. (2020). *Report: Most important data on digital audience during coronavirus*. Growth Quarter – The Next Web. https://thenextweb.com/growth-quarters/2020/04/24/report-most-important-data-on-digital-audiences-during-coronavirus/

Kent, M. (2015). Disability and e-learning: Opportunities and barriers. *Disability Studies Quarterly*, *35*(1), 1–15. doi:10.18061/dsq.v35i1

Kerckhove, D. (1995). *The Skin of Culture: Investigating the new electronic reality*. Kogan Page.

Keskin, A., & Keskin, B. (2005). *Eğitimde toplam kalite- okul yönetiminin kalite arayışı*. Samsun: Deniz Kültür Yayınları.

Keskin, N. O., & Metcalf, D. (2011). The current perspectives, theories and practices of mobile learning. *Turkish Online Journal of Educational Technology-TOJET*, *10*(2), 202–208.

Kessler, A. Barnes, S. Rajagopal, K. Rankin, J. Pouchak, L. Silis, M. & Esser, W. (2020). Saving a Semester of Learning: MIT's Emergency Transition to Online Instruction. *Inf. Learn. Sci.*

Khan, M. Y., & Tufail, H. (2020). *An Investigation into the Effectiveness of MALL during COVID-19 at the Higher*. Academic Press.

Khan, I., Ahmad, A. R., Jabeur, N., & Mahdi, M. N. (2021). An AI approach to monitor student performance and devise preventive measures. *Smart Learning Environments*, *8*(1), 17. doi:10.118640561-021-00161-y

Kiakalayeh, M. (2022). 'Military Use of Artificial Intelligence under International Humanitarian Law: Insights from Canada'. World Academy of Science, Engineering and Technology, Open Science Index 184. *International Journal of Law and Political Sciences*, *16*(4), 213–217.

Kiel, E., Muckenthaler, M., & Weiß, S. (2020). Students with emotional and behavioral problems in inclusive classes: A critical incident analysis. *Journal of Emotional and Behavioral Disorders*, *29*(4), 213-225. doi:https://doi:29.10.1177/1063426620967286

Kiernan, J. E. (2020). Pedagogical commentary: Teaching through a pandemic. *Social Sciences & Humanities Open*, *2*(1), 1–5. doi:10.1016/j.ssaho.2020.100071

Kirkman, B. L., Rosen, B., Gibson, C. B., Tesluk, P. E., & McPherson, S. O. (2002). Five challenges to virtual team success: Lessons from Sabre, Inc. *The Academy of Management Perspectives*, *16*(3), 67–79. doi:10.5465/ame.2002.8540322

Kivirand, T., Leijen, Ä., Lepp, L., & Tammemäe, T. (2021). Designing and implementing an in-service training course for school teams on inclusive education: Reflections from participants. *Education Sciences*, *11*(4), 166. doi:10.3390/educsci11040166

Klang, N., Olsson, I., Wilder, J., Lindqvist, G., Fohlin, N., & Nilholm, C. (2020). A cooperative learning intervention to promote social inclusion in heterogeneous classrooms. *Frontiers in Psychology*, *11*, 586–489. doi:10.3389/fpsyg.2020.586489 PMID:33414744

Knapp, E. & Yu, D. (1999). Understanding organizational culture: how culture helps or hinders the flow of knowledge. *Knowledge Management Review*, 16-21.

Kraut, R. E., & Streeter, L. A. (1995). Coordination in Software Development. *Communications of the ACM, 38*(3), 69–81.

Krishnamurthy, S. (2020). The future of business education: A commentary in the shadow of the Covid-19 pandemic. *Journal of Business Research, 117*, 1–5.

Krishnamurthy, S. (2020). The Future of Business Education: A Commentary in the Shadow of the Covid-19 Pandemic. *Journal of Business Research, 2020*(117), 1–5.

Kroeze, J. H. (2012). Postmodernism, interpretivism and formal ontologies. In Research methodologies, innovations and philosophies in software systems engineering and information systems. Information Science Reference. doi:10.4018/978-1-4666-0179-6.ch003

Küçükkaya, G. (2006). İnsan Kaynakları Yönetiminde Personel Seçimi ve Bir Uygulama (Yüksek Lisans Tezi). Marmara Üniversitesi, Sosyal Bilimler Enstitüsü, İstanbul.

Kuensel. (2020). *First confirmed coronavirus case in Bhutan.* Kuensel. https:// kuenselonline.com/first-confirmed-coronavirus-case-in-bhutan

Kuimova, M., Burleigh, D., Uzunboylu, H., & Bazhenov, R. (2018). Positive effects of mobile learning on foreign language learning. *TEM Journal, 7*(4), 837-841.

Kuimova, M., Kiyanitsyna, A., & Truntyagin, A. (2016). E-learning as a means to improve the quality of higher education. *SHS Web of Conferences, 28,* 01129. 10.1051hsconf/20162801129

Kukulska-Hulme, A. (2009). Will mobile learning change language learning? *ReCALL, 21*(2), 157–165. doi:10.1017/S0958344009000202

Kukulska-Hulme, A. (2013). Mobile-assisted language learning. In C. Chapelle (Ed.), *The encyclopedia of applied linguistics*. Wiley.

Kukulska-Hulme, A., Arús-Hita, J., Hou, Z., & Aryadoust, V. (2021). García Laborda, J. (2021). Mobile, Open and Social Language Learning Designs and Architectures. *Journal of Universal Computer Science*, *27*(5), 413–424. doi:10.3897/jucs.68852

Kuş, E. (2009). Nicel-nitel araştırma teknikleri: Sosyal bilimlerde araştırma teknikleri nicel mi? Nitel mi? Ankara: Anı Yayıncılık.

Küsmen, B. (2010). Kurumsal İletişim Ve İnsan Kaynakları Yönetimi İlişkisi (Yüksek Lisans Tezi). Marmara Üniversitesi, Sosyal Bilimler Enstitüsü, İstanbul.

Kye, B., Han, N., Kim, E., Park, Y., & Jo, S. (2021). Educational Applications of Metaverse: Possibilities and Limitations. *Journal of Educational Evaluation for Health Professions*, *18*, 18. doi:10.3352/jeehp.2021.18.32 PMID:34897242

Laine, T. H., & Joy, M. (2009). Survey on Context-Aware Pervasive Learning Environments. *International Journal of Interactive Mobile Technology*, *3*(1), 70–76.

Lakhal, S., Mukamurera, J., Bédard, M. E., Heilporn, G., & Chauret, M. (2020). Features fostering academic and social integration in blended synchronous courses in graduateprograms. *International Journal of Educational Technology in Higher Education, 17*(1), 1–22. doi:10.118641239-020-0180-z

Lane, H. C., & D'Mello, S. K. (2019). Uses of physiological monitoring in intelligent learning environments: A review of research, evidence, and technologies. In T. Parsons, L. Lin, & D. Cockerham (Eds.), *Mind, brain and technology. Educational Communications and Technology: Issues and Innovations*. Springer.

Laouris, Y., & Eteokleous, N. (2005). *We need an educational relevant definition of mobile learning*. Academic Press.

Laouris, Y., & Laouri, R. (2006).Can Information and Mobile Technologies serve to close the gap and accelerate development? *Proceedings of MLearn 2006.*

Law, R., Buhalis, D., & Cobanoğlu, C. (2014). Progress on Information and Communication Technologies in Hospitality and Tourism. *International Journal of Contemporary Hospitality Management, 26*(5), 727–750. doi:10.1108/IJCHM-08-2013-0367

Lawrence, R., Fung Ching, L., & Haslinda, A. (2019). Strengths and weaknesses of education 4.0 in the higher education institution. *International Journal of Innovative Technology and Exploring Engineering (IJITEE), 9*(2S3), 511 – 519. doi:10.35940/ijitee.B1122.1292S319

Lawrie, G., Marquis, E., Fuller, E., Newman, T., Qui, M., Nomikoudis, M., Roelofs, F., & van Dam, L. (2017). Moving towards inclusive learning and teaching: A synthesis of recent literature. *Teaching & Learning Inquiry, 5*(1), 9–21. doi:10.20343/teachlearninqu.5.1.3

Lee, B. W., & Lee, J. H. (2022). *Auto-Select Reading Passages in English Assessment Tests?* Academic Press.

Lee, J., Kim, Y., Ahn, E., & Kim, G. J. (2012). Applying "out of the body" funneling and saltation to interaction with virtual and augmented objects. In *2012 IEEE VR Workshop on Perceptual Illusions in Virtual Environments* (pp. 7-9). IEEE. 10.1109/PIVE.2012.6229793

Legard, R., Keegan, J., & Ward, K. (2003). In-depth interviews. In Qualitative Research Practice (pp. 139-168). London: Sage.

Lei, X., Fathi, J., Noorbakhsh, S., & Rahimi, M. (2022). The Impact of Mobile-Assisted Language Learning on English as a Foreign Language Learners' Vocabulary Learning Attitudes and Self-Regulatory Capacity. *Frontiers in Psychology, 13*, 13. doi:10.3389/fpsyg.2022.872922 PMID:35800918

Leonard, D. C. (2002). *Learning theories, A-Z.* Greenwood Press.

Lichtblau, K., Stich, V., Bertenrath, R., Blum, R., Bleider, M., Millack, A., Schmitt, K., Schmitz, E., & Schröter, M. (2015). *Industrie 4.0 Readiness*. Impuls-Stiftung.

Lieberman, L. J., Ball, L., Beach, P., & Perreault, M. (2022). A Qualitative Inquiry of a Three-Month Virtual Practicum Program on Youth with Visual Impairments and Their Coaches. *International Journal of Environmental Research and Public Health*, *19*(2), 841. doi:10.3390/ijerph19020841 PMID:35055663

Li, F., Fan, S., & Wang, Y. (2022). Mobile-assisted language learning in Chinese higher education context: A systematic review from the perspective of the situated learning theory. *Education and Information Technologies*, *27*(7), 1–24. doi:10.100710639-022-11025-4

Liguori, E., & Winkler, C. (2020). *From offline to online: Challenges and opportunities for entrepreneurship education following the COVID-19 pandemic*. Sage.

Lin & Yuxin. (2022). *Rhetoric, Writing, and Anexact Architecture: The Experiment of Natural Language Processing (NLP) and Computer Vision (CV) in Architectural Design*. Academic Press.

Liou, S. (2008). An Analysis of the Concept of Organizational Commitment. *Nursing ForumNo.*, *43*(3), 116–125. doi:10.1111/j.1744-6198.2008.00103.x PMID:18715344

Lipka, O., Forkosh-Baruch, A., & Meer, Y. (2019). Academic support model for post-secondary school students with learning disabilities: Student and instructor perceptions. *International Journal of Inclusive Education*, *23*(2), 142–157.

Li, R. (2022). Effects of mobile-assisted language learning on EFL/ESL reading comprehension. *Journal of Educational Technology & Society*, *25*(3), 15–29.

Li, W., Liao, J., Li, Q., Baskota, M., Wang, X., Tang, Y., Zhou, Q., Wang, X., Luo, X., Ma, Y., Fukuoka, T., Ahn, H. S., Lee, M. S., Chen, Y., Luo, Z., & Liu, E. (2020). Public Health Education for Parents during the Outbreak of COVID-19: A Rapid Review. *Annals of Translational Medicine*, *2020*(8), 628. doi:10.21037/atm-20-3312 PMID:32566565

Lok Lee, Y., & Vitartas, P. (2001, November 15). *Teaching and learning in Asia.* Unpublished Seminar hosted by Teaching and Learning Centre, Southern Cross University.

Lomicka, L. L. (2020). Creating and sustaining virtual language communities. *Foreign Language Annals*, *53*(2), 306–313. doi:10.1111/flan.12456

Longhurst, G. J., Stone, D. M., Dulohery, K., Scully, D., Campbell, T., & Smith, C. F. (2020). Strength, Weakness, Opportunity, Threat (SWOT) Analysis of the Adaptations to Anatomical Education in the United Kingdom and Republic of Ireland in Response to the Covid-19 Pandemic. *Anatomical Sciences Education*, *2020*(13), 301–311. doi:10.1002/ase.1967 PMID:32306550

Lynch, K. (1981). *A Theory of Good City Form.* MIT Press.

Majanja, M. K. (2020). The Status of Electronic Teaching within South African LIS Education. *Library Management*, *2020*(41), 317–337. doi:10.1108/LM-05-2020-0084

Mäkiö, E., Azmat, F., Ahmad, B., Harrison, R., & Colombo, A. W. (2021). T-CHAT educational framework for teaching cyber-physical system engineering. *European Journal of Engineering Education.* Advance online publication. doi:10.1080/03043797.2021.2008879

Maloney, S., Hass, R., Keating, J. L., Molloy, E., Jolly, B., Sims, J., Morgan, P., & Haines, T. (2012). Breakeven, Cost Benefit, Cost Effectiveness, and Willingness to Pay for Web-Based Versus Face-to-Face Education Delivery for Health Professionals. *Journal of Medical Internet Research, 14*(2), 1–16.

Manimuthu, A., Venkatesh, V. G., Shi, Y., Sreedharan, V. R., & Koh, S. C. L. (2022). Design and development of automobile assembly model using federated artificial intelligence with smart contract. *International Journal of Production Research, 60*(1), 111–135. doi:10.1080/00207543.2021.1988750

Maqsood, L. (2015). *Use of mobile technology among rural women in Pakistan for agricultural extension information*. Michigan State University.

Marcon, T., & Gopal, A. (2005). *Uncertain knowledge, uncertain time*. ASAC.

Marinoni, G., Van't Land, H., & Jensen, T. (2020). *The Impact of Covid-19 on Higher Education Around the World.* IAU Global Survey Report.

Market Trends. (2021, May 27). *Use cases of AI in diverse sectors*. Analytics Insight.

Martinelli, A., Mina, A., & Moggi, M. (2020). The enabling technologies of industry 4.0: Examining the seeds of the fourth industrial revolution. *Industrial and Corporate Change*.

Martinez, J. (2020). Take this pandemic moment to improve education. *EduSource*. Retrieved May 17, 2022, from https://edsource.org/2020/take-this-pandemic-moment-to-improveeducation/633500

Mastelic, J., Sahakian, M., & Bonazzi, R. (2015). How to keep a living lab alive? *Info, 17*(4), 12–25. doi:10.1108/info-01-2015-0012

Mattew, Joro & Manasseh. (2015). The role of information and communication technology in Nigeria educational system. *International Journal of Research in Humanities and Social Studies, 2*(2), 64–68.

Maurin, E., & McNally, S. (2008). Vive la révolution! Long-term educational returns of 1968 to the angry students. *Journal of Labor Economics, 26*(1), 1–33.

McFarlane, A., Sparrowhawk, A., & Heald, Y. (2002) Report on the educational use of games: an exploration by TEEM of the contribution which games can make to the education process in Cambridge. *U.K. TEEM (Teachers Evaluating Educational Multimedia), 27.*

McFarlane, A., Sparrowhawk, A., & Heald, Y. (2002). *Report on the Educational Use of Games. TEEM*. Teachers Evaluating Educational Multimedia.

McLoughlin, C. (2001). Inclusivity and alignment: Principles of pedagogy, task, and assessment design for effective cross-cultural online learning. *Distance Education, 22*(1), 7–29. doi:10.1080/0158791010220102

McLoughlin, C., & Luca, J. (2000). Assessment methodologies in transition: Changing practices in Web-based learning. *ASET-HERDSA, 5*, 16–526.

Mcmahon, C.J., Heying, R., & Budts, W. (2022). Paediatric and adult congenital cardiology education and training in Europe. *Cardiol Young*, 1-18.

Meijer, C., Soriano, V., & Watkins, A. (2007). Inclusive education across Europe: Reflections upon 10 years of work from the European agency for development in special needs education. *Childhood Education, 83*(6), 361–365. doi:10.1080/00094056.2007.10522951

Mercin, L. (2005). İnsan Kaynakları Yönetimi'nin Eğitim Kurumları Açısından Gerekliliği ve Geliştirme Etkinliği. *Elektronik Sosyal Bilimler Dergisi, 4*(14), 128–144.

Meskhi, B., Ponomareva, S., & Ugnich, E. (2019). E-learning in higher inclusive education: Needs, opportunities, and limitations. *International Journal of Educational Management, 33*(3), 424–437. doi:10.1108/IJEM-09-2018-0282

Mhlanga, D. (2020). Industry 4.0: The challenges associated with the digital transformation of education in South Africa. In Ö. Aydin (Ed.), *The impacts of digital transformation* (pp. 13–26). Efeacademy.

Mhlanga, D., & Moloi, T. (2020b). COVID-19 and the digital transformation of education: What are we learning on 4IR in South Africa? *Education Sciences, 10*(7), 180. doi:10.3390/educsci10070180

Miles, M. B., & Huberman, A. M. (1994). Qualitative data analysis: An expanded sourcebook. Sage.

Miles, M. B., & Huberman, A. M. (1994). *Qualitative Data Analysis: An Expanded Sourcebook* (2nd ed.). Sage.

Miranda, J., Navarrete, C., Noguez, J., Molina-Espinosa, J., Ramirez-Montoya, M., Navarro-Tuch, S., Bustamante-Bello, M., Rosas-Fernandez, J., & Molina, A. (2021). The core components of education 4.0 in higher education: Three case studies in engineering education. *Computers & Electrical Engineering, 93*(107278), 107278. Advance online publication. doi:10.1016/j.compeleceng.2021.107278

Mircea, M., Stoica, M., & Ghilic-Micu, B. (2021). Investigating the impact of the internet of things in higher education environment. *IEEE Access: Practical Innovations, Open Solutions, 9*, 33396–33409. doi:10.1109/ACCESS.2021.3060964

Mishra, L., Gupta, T., & Shree, A. (2020). Online teaching-learning in higher education during lockdown period of COVID-19 pandemic. *International Journal of Educational Research Open*, 1–24, doi:10.1016/j.ijedro.2020.100012

Mishra, L., Gupta, T., & Shree, A. (2020). Online teaching-learning in higher education during lockdown period of COVID-19 pandemic. *International Journal of Educational Research, 1*, 12–34.

Mishra, P., & Koehler, M. (2009). Too cool for school? No way! Using the TPACK framework: You can have your hot tools and teach with them, too. *Learning and Leading with Technology, 36*(7), 14–18.

Mohanta, B., Nanda, P., & Patnaik, S. (2019). *Management of V.U.C.A. (volatility, uncertainty, complexity and ambiguity) using machine learning techniques in industry 4.0 paradigm. Studies in Big Data, 64*. doi:10.1007/978-3-030-25778-1_1

Mohite, M. (2020). Covid 19 and use of ICT in education. *Educational Resurgence Journal, 2*(4), 17–23.

Mohsen, M. A., & Mahdi, H. S. (2021). Partial versus full captioning mode to improve L2 vocabulary acquisition in a mobile-assisted language learning setting: Words pronunciation domain. *Journal of Computing in Higher Education, 33*(2), 524–543. doi:10.100712528-021-09276-0

Montacute, R. (2020). *Social mobility and COVID-19*. Retrieved May 17, 2022, from https://www.suttontrust.com/wpcontent/ uploads/2020/04/COVID-19-and-Social-Mobility-1.pdf

Moore, M. G. (1989). Three types of interaction. *American Journal of Distance Education, 3*(2), 1–6. doi:10.1080/08923648909526659

Moraes, E. B., Kipper, L. M., Hackenhaar Kellermann, A. C., Austria, L., Leivas, P., Moraes, J. A. R., & Witczak, M. (2022). Integration of industry 4.0 technologies with education 4.0: Advantages for improvements in learning. Interactive Technology and Smart Education. doi:10.1108/ITSE-11-2021-0201

Morgana, V., & Kukulska-Hulme, A. (Eds.). (2021). *Mobile assisted language learning across educational contexts*. Routledge. doi:10.4324/9781003087984

Morgan, C., & O'Reilly, M. (2005). Ten key qualities of assessment online. In *Online assessment and measurement: Foundations and challenges* (pp. 86–101). IGI Global. doi:10.4018/978-1-59140-720-1.ch004

Moriña, A. (2017). Inclusive education in higher education: Challenges and opportunities. *European Journal of Special Needs Education, 32*(1), 3–17. doi:10.1080/08856257.2016.1254964

Moser, K., Wei, T., & Brenner, D. (2021). Remote teaching during COVID-19: Impli-cations from a national survey of language educators. *System, 97*, 1–15. doi:10.1016/j.system.2020.102431

Mostakhdemin-Hosseini, A., & Najafabadi, N. (2006). *The Mobile Phone Constitutive Effect on Student Life in Finland*. IEEE-IMCL, Interactive Mobile.

Mukhopadhyay, M., Pal, S., Nayyar, A., Pramanik, P. K. D., Dasgupta, N., & Choudhury, P. (2020). Facial Emotion Detection to Assess Learner's State of Mind in an Online Learning System. *Proceedings of the 2020 5th International Conference on Intelligent Information Technology*, 107–115. 10.1145/3385209.3385231

Munar, A. M. (2010). Digital exhibitionism: The age of exposure. *Culture Unbound, 2*(3), 401–422. doi:10.3384/cu.2000.1525.10223401

Mvududu, N., & Burgess, J. T. (2012). Constructivism in practice: The case for English language learners. *International Journal of Education, 4*(4), 3. doi:10.5296/ije.v4i3.2223

Mystakidis, S. (2021). Deep meaningful learning. *Encyclopedia*, *1*(3), 988–997. doi:10.3390/encyclopedia1030075

Mystakidis, S., Berki, E., & Valtanen, J. P. (2021). Deep and meaningful e-learning with social virtual reality environments in higher education: A systematic literature review. *Applied Sciences (Basel, Switzerland)*, *11*(5), 2412. doi:10.3390/app11052412

Nagrale, P. (2013). *Advantages and disadvantages of distance education*. Retrieved May 17, 2022, from https://surejob.in/ advantages-anddisadvantages-of-distance-education.html

Neaga, I. (2019). Applying industry 4.0 and education 4.0 to engineering education. *Proceedings 2019 Canadian Engineering Education Association (CEEA-ACEG19) Conference*, 1-6. 10.24908/pceea.vi0.13859

Nesenbergs, K., Abolins, V., Ormanis, J., & Mednis, A. (2021). Use of Augmented and Virtual Reality in Remote Higher Education: A Systematic Umbrella Review. *Education in Science*, *11*(8), 1–12.

Neuhofer, B., Buhalis, D., & Ladkin, A. (2015). Smart Technologies for Personalized Experiences: A Case Study in the Hospitality Domain. *Electronic Markets*, *25*(3), 243–254. doi:10.100712525-015-0182-1

Newstead, S. E., & Dennis, I. (1994). The reliability of exam marking in psychology: Examiners examined. *The Psychologist*, 216–219.

Ng, H.-W., Nguyen, V. D., Vonikakis, V., & Winkler, S. (2015). Deep Learning for Emotion Recognition on Small Datasets using Transfer Learning. *Proceedings of the 2015 ACM on International Conference on Multimodal Interaction*, 443–449. 10.1145/2818346.2830593

Nigam, A., Pasricha, R., Singh, T., & Churi, P. (2021). A Systematic Review on AI-based Proctoring Systems: Past, Present and Future. *Education and Information Technologies*, *26*(5), 6421–6445. doi:10.100710639-021-10597-x PMID:34177348

Noe, A. R. (1999). İnsan Kaynaklarının Eğitim ve Gelişimi. İstanbul: Beta Yayıncılık.

Noh, S. C., & Abdul Karim, A. (2020). Design thinking mindset to enhance education 4.0 competitiveness in Malaysia. *International Journal of Evaluation and Research in Education*, *2*(2), 490–501. doi:10.11591/ijere.v10i2.20988

NortonLifeLock. (2020). *NortonLifeLock study: Majority of parents say their kids' screen time has skyrocketed during the COVID-19 pandemic*. NortonLifeLock. Retrieved May 17, 2022, from https://www.businesswire.com/news/home/20200831005132/en/

Nowacka, A., & Rzemieniak, M. (2022). The impact of the VUCA environment on the digital competences of managers in the Power Industry. *Energies*, *15*(1), 185. doi:10.3390/en15010185

NSW Government. (2021). *Approaches to assessment*. Retrieved from https://education.nsw.gov.au/teaching-and-learning/professional-learning/teacher-quality-and-accreditation/strong-start-great-teachers/refining-practice/aspects-of-assessment/approaches-to-assessment

Nyaupane, G. P., & Timothy, D. J. (2010). Heritage awareness and appreciation among community residents: Perspectives from Arizona, USA. *International Journal of Heritage Studies*, *16*(3), 225–239. doi:10.1080/13527251003620776

Oblinger, D. G. (2006). *Learning Spaces, Washington*. EDUCAUSE.

OECD. (2019). *OECD future of education and skills 2030*. OECD Publishing.

Ogunlade, O. O. (2014) Information and Communication Technology (ICT). In M. O. Yusuf & S. A. Onasanya (Eds.), Critical Issues in educational technology (pp. 98-104). Department of Education Technology, University of Ilorin.

Okongo, R. B., Ngao, G., Rop, N. K., & Wesonga, J. N. (2015). Effect of availability of teaching and learning resources on the implementation of inclusive education in pre-school centers in Nyamira North Sub-County, Nyamira County, Kenya. *Journal of Education and Practice*, *6*(35), 132–141. http://Hdl.Handle.Net/123456789/3198

Orhan, K. (2010). Amerika Birleşik Devletleri'nde ve Avrupa'da insan kaynakları yönetimi yaklaşımlarının bir karşılaştırılması: Avrupalı insan kaynakları yaklaşımı mümkün müdür? [A comparison of human resources management approches' in the United States and European Union: Is actually European approches of the human resources management possible?]. *Ege Academic Review*, *10*(1), 271–301.

Orr, D., Weller, M., & Farrow, R. (2018). *Models for Online, Open, Flexible and Technology Enhanced Higher Education Across the Globe: A Comparative Analysis*. International Council for Open and Distance Education.

Osuji, U. S. (2012). The use of e-assessments in the Nigerian higher education system. *Turkish Online Journal of Distance Education*, *13*(4), 140–152.

Outhwaite, L. (2020). *Inequalities in resources in the home learning environment (No. 2)*. Centre for Education Policy and Equalising Opportunities, UCL Institute of Education.

Ozan, O., Yamamoto, G. T., & Demiray, U. (2015). Mobile learning technologies and educational applications. *Mobile Learning Technologies and Educational Applications*, *9*(3-4), 97–109.

Özbayram, E. (2014). Türk Çalışma Hayatında Korumalı İşyerleri ve Engelli İstihdamı. Gazi Üniversitesi Sosyal Bilimler Enstitüsü Çalışma Ekonomisi Ve Endüstri İlişkileri Anabilim Dali Yüksek Lisans Tezi, Ankara, Özen, Şükrü (2002). Bağlam, Aktör, Söylem ve Kurumsal Değişim: Türkiye'de Toplam Kalite Yönetiminin Yayılım Süreci. *Yönetim Araştırmaları Dergisi*, *1/2*, 47–90.

Özdemir, E., & Akpınar A. T. (2002). Konaklama İşletmelerinde İnsan Kaynakları Yönetimi Çerçevesinde Alanya'daki Otel ve Tatil Köylerinde İnsan Kaynakları Profili. *Kocaeli Üniversitesi Sosyal Bilimler Enstitüsü Dergisi*, *2*(3), 85–105.

Özgen, H., Öztürk, A., & Yalçın, A. (Eds.). (2002). İnsan Kaynakları Yönetimi. Adana: Nobel Kitabevi.

Özmen, İ. (2003). Bilgi Sistemleri İş Stratejisi ve Ticari Avantaj Sağlamak İçin Kullanılması. *İstanbul Üniversitesi İşletme Fakültesi, İşletme İktisadı Enstitüsü Dergisi, 13*(45), 51.

Öztay, F. E. (2006). Eğitim Örgütlerinde İnsan Kaynakları Yönetimi İle Oluşturulmuş Kurum Kültürünün Öğretmen Motivasyonuna Etkisi (Yüksek Lisans Tezi). Yeditepe Üniversitesi/Sosyal Bilimler Enstitüsü, İstanbul.

Paccaud, A., Keller, R., Luder, R., Pastore, G., & Kunz, A. (2021). Satisfaction with the collaboration between families and schools - the parent's view. *Front. Educ.*, *6*, 86. doi:10.3389/feduc.2021.646878

Pal, K. (2019). Markov Decision Theory Based Crowdsourcing Software Process Model. In Crowdsourcing and Probabilistic Decision-Making in Software Engineering: Emerging Research and Opportunities. IGI Global.

Pal, K. (2020). Framework for Reusable Test Case Generation in Software Systems Testing. In Software Engineering for Agile Application Development. IGI Global.

Pal, K. (2022). Reflection on Teaching Practice for Agile Methodology Based Product Development Management. In Teaching Innovation in University Education: Case Studies and Main Practices. IGI Global.

Pal, K., & Karakostas, B. (2020). Software Testing Under Agile, Scrum, and DevOps. In Agile Scrum Implementation and Its Long-Term Impact on Organizations. IGI Publication.

Pal, K., & Williams, I. (2021). Software Development Knowledge Management System Using Web Portal. In Digital Technology Advancement in Knowledge Management. IGI Publication.

Panesar, K., Dodson, T., Lynch, J., Bryson-Cahn, C., Chew, L., & Dillon, J. (2020). Evolution of COVID-19 guidelines for University of Washington oral and maxillofacial surgery patient care. *Journal of Oral and Maxillofacial Surgery*, *78*(7), 1136–1146.

Papanicolau-Sengos, A., & Aldape, K. (2022). DNA Methylation Profiling: An Emerging Paradigm for Cancer Diagnosis. *Annual Review of Pathology: Mechanisms of Disease*, *17*(1), 295–321. doi:10.1146/annurev-pathol-042220-022304 PMID:34736341

Paris, T. N. S. T., Manap, N. A., Abas, H., & Ling, L. M. (2021). Mobile-Assisted Language Learning (MALL) in Language Learning. *Journal of ASIAN Behavioural Studies*, *6*(19), 61–73. doi:10.21834/jabs.v6i19.391

Park, M., & Jones, T. (2021). Going Virtual: The Impact of Covid-19 on Internships in Tourism, Events, and Hospitality Education. *Journal of Hospitality & Tourism Education*, *33*(3), 176–193. doi:10.1080/10963758.2021.1907198

Park, S. Y., Nam, M. W., & Cha, S. B. (2012). University students' behavioral intention to use mobile learning: Evaluating the technology acceptance model. *British Journal of Educational Technology*, *43*, 592–605.

Parsa, N., & Fatehi Rad, N. (2021). Impact of a Mobile-Assisted Language Learning (MALL) on EFL Learners' Grammar Achievement and Self-Efficacy. *International Journal of Language and Translation Research, 1*(4), 71–94.

Parsons, S., Beardon, L., Neale, H. R., Reynard, G., Eastgate, R., Wilson, J. R., Cobb, S. V., Benford, S. D., Mitchell, P., & Hopkins, E. (2000). Development of social skills amongst adults with Asperger's Syndrome using virtual environments: the 'AS Interactive' project. In *Proc. The 3rd International Conference on Disability, Virtual Reality and Associated Technologies, ICDVRAT 2000*, 163-170.

Parsons, C., & Castle, F. (1998). The cost of school exclusion in England. *International Journal of Inclusive Education, 2*(4), 277–294. doi:10.1080/1360311980020402

Patton, M. Q. (1987). *How to Use Qualitative Methods in Evaluation.* Sage Publications, Inc.

Paulsrud, D., & Nilholm, C. (2020). Teaching for inclusion: A review of research on the cooperation between regular teachers and special educators in the work with students in need of special support. *International Journal of Inclusive Education, 27*, 1–15. doi:10.1080/13603116.2020.1846799

Pechenkina, E., Laurence, D., Oates, G., Eldridge, D., & Hunter, D. (2017). Using a gamification mobile app to increase student engagement, retention and academic achievement. *International Journal of Educational Technology in Higher Education, 14*(13), 1–13.

Penfold, P. (2009). Learning through the world of second life—A hospitality and tourism experience. *Journal of Teaching in Travel & Tourism, 8*(2-3), 139–160. doi:10.1080/15313220802634224

Peng, S. (2019). A Study of the differences between EFL and ESL for English Classroom teaching in China. *IRA International Journal of Education and Multidisciplinary Studies, 15*(1), 32–35. doi:10.21013/jems.v15.n1.p4

Perez. (2018, August 30). *Recognizing human facial expressions with machine learning.* Thoughtworks.

Perry, K., Meissel, K., & Hill, M. F. (2022). Rebooting assessment. Exploring the challenges and benefits of shifting from pen-and-paper to computer in summative assessment. *Educational Research Review, 36*, 100451. doi:10.1016/j.edurev.2022.100451

Peterson, L., Scharber, C., Thuesen, A., & Baskin, K. (2020). A rapid response to COVID-19: One district's pivot from technology integration to distance learning. *Information and Learning Sciences, 121*(5/6), 461–469. doi:10.1108/ILS-04-2020-0131

Petretto, D. R., Carta, S. M., Cataudella, S., Masala, I., Mascia, M. L., Penna, M. P., Piras, P., Pistis, I., & Masala, C. (2021). The use of distance learning and e-learning in students with learning disabilities: A review on the effects and some hint of analysis on the use during covid-19 outbreak. Clinical practice and epidemiology in mental health. *Clinical Practice and Epidemiology in Mental Health, 17*, 92–102. doi:10.2174/1745017902117010092 PMID:34733348

Petrie, C. (2020). *Spotlight: Quality education for all during COVID-19 crisis* (hundred Research Report #01). United Nations. https://hundred.org/en/collections/qualityeducation-for-all-during-coronavirus

Pingping, G., Qiuyao, W., & Linyan, B. (2021). Enhancing Students' Mobile-Assisted Language Learning through Self-Assessment in a Chinese College EFL Context. *Journal of Education and e-Learning Research, 8*(2), 238-248.

Plöckinger, M., Aschauer, E., Hiebl, M. R. W., & Rohatschek, R. (2016). The Influence of Individual Executives on Corporate Financial Reporting: A Review and Outlook from the Perspective of Upper Echelons Theory. *Journal of Accounting Literature, 2016*(37), 55–75. doi:10.1016/j.acclit.2016.09.002

Pokhrel, S., & Chhetri, R. (2021). A Literature Review on Impact of COVID-19 Pandemic on Teaching and Learning. *Higher Education for the Future*, *8*(1), 133–141.

Ponomareva, S., & Ugnich, E. (2018). E-learning opportunities and limitations in inclusive higher education. In *SHS Web of Conferences* (Vol. 50, p. 01138). EDP Sciences. https://10.1051hsconf/20185001138

Popyk, A. (2020). The impact of distance learning on the social practices of schoolchildren during the COVID-19 pandemic: Reconstructing values of migrant children in Poland. *European Societies*, 1–15.

Poulova, P., Cerna, M., Hamtilova, J., Malý, F., Kozel, T., Kriz, P., & Ulrych, Z. (2020). Virtual hotel–gamification in the management of tourism education. In *International Conference on Remote Engineering and Virtual Instrumentation* (pp. 773-781). Springer.

Prathish, S., S., A. N., & Bijlani, K. (2016). An intelligent system for online exam monitoring. *2016 International Conference on Information Science (ICIS)*, 138–143. 10.1109/INFOSCI.2016.7845315

Pressman, R. S. (2000). *Software engineering: A Practitioner's Approach (European Adaption)* (5th ed.). McGraw-Hill International.

Prifti, L., Knigge, M., Kienegger, H., & Krcmar, H. (2017). A competency model for "industrie 4.0" Employees. In J. M. Leimeister & W. Brenner (Eds.), Proceedings der 13. Internationalen Tagung Wirtschaftsinformatik (WI 2017) (pp. 46–60). Academic Press.

Puangrimaggalatung, S. T. I. A., Yusriadi, Y., & Tahir, S. Z. B. (2022). MALL in Learning English through Social Networking Tools: Students' Perceptions on Instagram Feed-based Task and Peer Feedback. *Computer Assisted Language Learning*, *23*(2), 198–216.

Puebla, C., Fievet, T., Tsopanidi, M., & Clahsen, H. (2022). Mobile-assisted language learning in older adults: Chances and challenges. *ReCALL*, *34*(2), 169–184. doi:10.1017/S0958344021000276

Puebla, C., & Garcia, J. (2022). Advocating the inclusion of older adults in digital language learning technology and research: Some considerations. *Bilingualism: Language and Cognition*, *25*(3), 398–399. doi:10.1017/S1366728921000742

Puri, M., & Abraham, G. (Eds.). (2004). *Handbook of inclusive education for educators, administrators, and planners: Within walls, without boundaries*. Sage Publishing.

Putri, R., Purwanto, A., Pramono, R., Asbari, M., Wijayanti, L., & Hyun, C. (2020). Impact of the COVID19 pandemic on online home learning: An explorative study of primary schools in Indonesia. *International Journal of Advanced Science and Technology*, *29*(5), 4809–4818.

Quinn, C. (2000). *mLearning: mobile, wireless, in-your-pocket learning*. LineZine. www.linezine.com/2.1/features/cqmmwiyp.htm

Quinn, D., Shurville, S., McNamara, J., & Brown, C. (2009). Assessment of online discussion in work-integrated learning. *Campus-Wide Information Systems*, *26*(5), 413–423. doi:10.1108/10650740911004822

Quirke, M., McCarthy, P., Treanor, D., & McGuckin, C. (2019). Tomorrow's disability officer – a cornerstone on the universal design campus. *The Journal of Inclusive Practice in Further and Higher Education*, *11*(1), 29–42.

Raaper, R., & Brown, C. (2020). The Covid-19 Pandemic and the Dissolution of the University Campus: Implications for Student Support Practice. *Journal of Professional Capital and Community*, 2020.

Race, P., Brown, S., & Smith, B. (2005). *500 tips on assessment*. RoutledgeFalmer.

Raj, R. S. V., Narayanan, S. A., & Bijlani, K. (2015). Heuristic-Based Automatic Online Proctoring System. *2015 IEEE 15th International Conference on Advanced Learning Technologies*, 458–459. 10.1109/ICALT.2015.127

Rajasingham, L. (2011). *Will mobile learning bring a paradigm shift in higher education?* Education Research International.

Rajhans, V., Memon, U., Patil, V., & Goyal, A. (2020). Impact of COVID-19 on Academic Activities and Way Forward in Indian Optometry. *Journal of Optometry*, *2020*(13), 216–226. doi:10.1016/j.optom.2020.06.002 PMID:32703749

Ramberg, J., & Watkins, A. (2020). Exploring inclusive education across Europe: Some insights from the European agency statistics on inclusive education. In *FIRE, Forum for International Research in Education* (Vol. 6, pp. 85–101). Stockholm University. doi:10.32865/fire202061172

Ramsden, P. (1997). The context of learning in academic departments. In *The experience of learning* (2nd ed.). Scottish Academic Press.

Rap, S., Feldman-Maggor, Y., Aviran, E., Shvarts-Serebro, I., Easa, E., Yonai, E., Waldman, R., & Blonder, R. (2020). An applied research-based approach to support Chemistry teachers during the COVID-19 pandemic. *Journal of Chemical Education*, *97*(9), 3278–3284. doi:10.1021/acs.jchemed.0c00687 PMID:32952213

Rashid, S. (2018). *The effect of training in Mobile Assisted Language Learning on attitude, beliefs and practices of tertiary students in Pakistan*. Academic Press.

Raymond, N. A. (2009). İnsan Kaynaklarının Eğitimi Ve Geliştirilmesi. İstanbul: Beta Yayınları.

Reddy, M. S., Mahavidyalaya, P., & Hyderabad, K. (2016). Importance of English language in today's world. *International Journal of Academic Research*, *3*(4), 179–184.

Redinger, Cornia, & Tyler. (2020). Teaching during A Pandemic. *Journal of Graduate Medical Education, 12*(4), 403–405.

Regehr, C., & Goel, V. (2020). Managing COVID-19 in a Large Urban Research-Intensive University. *Journal of Loss and Trauma, 2020*(6-7), 1–17. doi:10.1080/15325024.2020.1771846

Renau-Renau, M. L. (2016). A review of the traditional and current language teaching methods. *International Journal of Innovation and Research in Educational Sciences*, *3*(2), 82–88.

Renninger, K. A., & Hidi, S. (2011). Revisiting the Conceptualization, Measurement, and Generation of Interest. *Educational Psychologist*, *46*(3), 168–184. doi:10.1080/00461520.2011.587723

Richards, J. C. (2008). *Communicative Language Teaching Today*. Paper Design Internationals.

Riehl, C. J. (2000). The principal's role in creating inclusive schools for diverse students: A review of normative, empirical, and critical literature on the practice of educational administration. *Review of Educational Research*, *70*(1), 55–81. doi:10.1177/0022057409189001-213

Rippe, Weisfeld-Spolter, & Yurova. (2021). Pandemic Pedagogy for the New Normal: Fostering Perceived Control During COVID-19. *Journal of Marketing Education*, *43*(2), 260–276.

RK. (2021). Real-time Attention Span Tracking in Online Education. Academic Press.

Robinson, N., Hardy, A., & Ertan, A. (2021). Estonia: A Curious and Cautious Approach to Artificial Intelligence and National Security. SSRN *Electronic Journal*. doi:10.2139/ssrn.4105328

Robinson, C. C., & Hullinger, H. (2008). New Benchmarks in Higher Education: Student Engagement in Online Learning. *Journal of Education for Business*, *84*(2), 101–109. doi:10.3200/JOEB.84.2.101-109

Rodrigues, A. R. D., Ferreira, F. A. F., Teixeira, F. J. C. S. N., & Zopounidis, C. (2022). Artificial intelligence, digital transformation and cybersecurity in the banking sector: A multi-stakeholder cognition-driven framework. *Research in International Business and Finance*, *60*, 101616. doi:10.1016/j.ribaf.2022.101616

Rodríguez-Hernández, C. F., Cascallar, E., & Kyndt, E. (2020). Socio-Economic Status and Academic Performance in Higher Education: A Systematic Review. *Educational Research Review*, *2020*(29), 100305. doi:10.1016/j.edurev.2019.100305

Rodriguez, N. (2016). Teaching virtual reality with affordable technologies. In *International Conference on Human-Computer Interaction* (pp. 89-97). Springer.

Rose, R., & Parsons, L. (1998). Supporting the subject coordinator through the process of curriculum monitoring in a special school. *Support for Learning*, *13*(1), 21–25. doi:10.1111/1467-9604.00050

Roussos, M., Johnson, A., Moher, T., Leigh, J., Vasilakis, C., & Barnes, C. (1999). Learning and building together in an immersive virtual world. *Presence (Cambridge, Mass.)*, *8*(3), 247–263. doi:10.1162/105474699566215

Roussou, M., Oliver, M., & Slater, M. (2006). The Virtual Playground: An educational virtual reality environment for evaluating interactivity and conceptual learning. *Virtual Reality (Waltham Cross)*, *10*(3-4), 227–240. doi:10.100710055-006-0035-5

Rowe, S. (2003). *A virtual classroom: What you CAN do to enrich the learning experience.* Paper presented at the NAWeb, New Brunswick, Canada.

Roy, D., Tripathy, S., Kar, S. K., Sharma, N., Verma, S. K., & Kaushal, V. (2020). Study of Knowledge, Attitude, Anxiety & Perceived Mental Healthcare Need in Indian Population during COVID-19 Pandemic. *Asian Journal of Psychiatry*, *2020*, 51. doi:10.1016/j.ajp.2020.102083 PMID:32283510

Rus, I., & Lindvall, M. (2002, June). Knowledge Management in Software Engineering. *IEEE Software*, *19*(3), 26–38. doi:10.1109/MS.2002.1003450

Russell, V. (2020). Language anxiety and the online learner. *Foreign Language Annals*, *53*(2), 338–352. doi:10.1111/flan.12461

Russell, V., & Murphy-Judy, K. (2020). *Teaching language online: A guide to designing, developing, and delivering online, blended, and flipped language courses.* Routledge. doi:10.4324/9780429426483

Sadullah, Ö. (2008). İnsan Kaynakları Yönetimine Giriş; İnsan Kaynakları Yönetiminin Tanımı, Önemi ve Çevresel Faktörler. In İnsan Kaynakları Yönetimi. İstanbul: Beta Basım Yayım.

Sae-Lim, P., & Jermsittiparsert, K. (2019). Is the Fourth Industrial Revolution a Panacea? Risks toward the Fourth Industrial Revolution: Evidence in the Thai Economy. *International Journal of Innovation. Creativity and Change*, *5*(2), 732–752.

Salih, A. H. (2019). Effects of mobile assisted language learning on developing listening skill to the department of English students in college of education for women at Al Iraqia University. *European Journal of Language and Literature, 5*(1), 31-38.

Salmi, J. (2018). *All around the world: Higher education equity policies across the globe*. The Lumina Foundation.

Salmi, J., & D'Addio, A. (2020). Policies for achieving inclusion in higher education. *Policy Reviews in Higher Education*, *5*(1), 47–72. doi:10.1080/23322969.2020.1835529

Salmon, G. (2019). May the fourth be with you: Creating education 4.0. *Journal of Learning for Development*, *6*(1), 95–115. doi:10.56059/jl4d.v6i2.352

Saran, M., Seferoglu, G., & Cagiltay, K. (2009). Mobile assisted language learning: English pronunciation at learners' fingertips. *Eurasian Journal of Educational Research*, *34*, 97–114.

Savolainen, H., Malinen, O.-P., & Schwab, S. (2020). Teachers' efficacy predicts teachers' attitudes towards inclusion - a longitudinal cross-lagged analysis. *International Journal of Inclusive Education*, *27*, 1–15. doi:10.1080/13603116.2020.1752826

Saylan, N. (2013). Özel İlköğretim Ve Ortaöğretim Okullarında İnsan Kaynakları Yönetimi İşlevlerinin Gerçekleşme Derecesi (Yüksek Lisans Tezi). Hacettepe Üniversitesi/Sosyal Bilimleri Enstitüsü, Ankara.

Schein, E. H. (1992). *Organizational Culture and Leadership* (2nd ed.). Jossey Bass.

Schleicher, A., & Reimers, F. (2020). Schooling Disrupted, Schooling Rethought: How the COVID-19 Pandemic is Changing Education. OECD.

Schultz, R. B., & DeMers, M. N. (2020). Transitioning from emergency remote learning to deep online learning experiences in Geography Education. *The Journal of Geography*, *119*(5), 142–146. doi:10.1080/00221341.2020.1813791

Schunk, D. H. (2012). *Learning theories an educational perspective*. Pearson.

Segond, F., Parmentier, T., Stock, R., Rosner, R., & Muela, M. U. (2005). Situational language training for hotel receptionists. In *Proceedings of the Second Workshop on Building Educational Applications Using NLP* (pp. 85-92). Academic Press.

Şen, M. (2018). Türkiye'de Engellilere Yönelik İstihdam Politikaları: Sorunlar ve Öneriler. *Sosyal Güvenlik Dergisi*, 129-152. . doi:10.32331/sgd.493016

Shahini, F. (2021). *Distance education: Challenges and opportunities in a post-pandemic world. Case of Kosovo* [Thesis]. Rochester Institute of Technology. https://scholarworks.rit.edu/theses

Sharan, Y. (2010). Cooperative learning for academic and social gains: Valued pedagogy, problematic practice. *European Journal of Education*, *45*, 300–313. doi:10.1111/j.1465-3435.2010.01430.x

Sharma, P., & Harkishan, M. (2022). Designing an intelligent tutoring system for computer programing in the Pacific. *Education and Information Technologies*, *27*(5), 6197–6209. Advance online publication. doi:10.100710639-021-10882-9 PMID:35002465

Sharma, U., Sokal, L., Wang, M., & Loreman, T. (2021). Measuring the use of inclusive practices among preservice educators: A multi-national study. *Teaching and Teacher Education*, *107*, 103506. doi:10.1016/j.tate.2021.103506

Sharples, M. (2000). The design of personal mobile technologies for lifelong learning. *Computer Education.*

Sharples, M., Taylor, J., & Vavoula, G. (2007). *A Theory of Learning for the Mobile Age. The Sage Handbook of E-learning Research*. Sage.

Shim, T. E., & Lee, S. Y. (2020). College students' experience of emergency remote teaching due to COVID-19. *Children and Youth Services Review, 119*, 1–7. doi:10.1016/j.childyouth.2020.105578 PMID:33071405

Sholihin, M., Sari, R. C., Yuniarti, N., & Ilyana, S. (2020). A new way of teaching business ethics: The evaluation of virtual reality-based learning media. *International Journal of Management Education, 18*(3), 100428. doi:10.1016/j.ijme.2020.100428

Shortt, M., Tilak, S., Kuznetcova, I., Martens, B., & Akinkuolie, B. (2021). Gamification in mobile-assisted language learning: A systematic review of Duolingo literature from public release of 2012 to early 2020. *Computer Assisted Language Learning*, 1–38. doi:10.1080/09588221.2021.1933540

Siemens, G. (2004). Connectivism: A learning theory for the digital age. *International Journal of Instructional Technology and Distance Learning, 2*. http://www.itdl.org/Journal/Jan_05/article01.htm

Siemens, G. (2012). *The future of higher education*. http://www.elearnspace.org/blog/2012/06/16/the-future-of-higher-education-and-other imponderables/

Singh, V., & Holt, L. (2013). Learning and best practices for learning in open-source software communities. *Computer Education, 63*, 98–108.

Sintema, E. J. (2020). Effect of COVID-19 on the performance of grade 12 students: Implications for STEM education. *Eurasia Journal of Mathematics, Science and Technology Education, 16*(7), 2–6.

Sjostrom, M., Lindholm, L., & Samuelsson, E. (2017). Mobile App for Treatment of Stress Urinary Incontinence: A Cost-Effectiveness Analysis. *Journal of Medical Internet Research, 19*(5), 1–12.

Skulmowski, A., & Rey, G. D. (2020). COVID-19 as an Accelerator for Digitalization at a German University: Establishing Hybrid Campuses in Times of Crisis. *Human Behavior and Emerging Technologies, 2020*(2), 212–216. doi:10.1002/hbe2.201 PMID:32838228

Slater, M., & Wilbur, S. (1997). A Framework for Immersive Virtual Environments (FIVE): Speculations on the Role of Presence in Virtual Environments. *Presence (Cambridge, Mass.), 6*(6), 603–616. doi:10.1162/pres.1997.6.6.603

Sommerville, I. (2001). *Software Engineering* (6th ed.). Addison-Wesley.

Sozudogru, O., Altinay, M., Dagli, G., Altinay, F., & Altinay, F. (2019). Examination of connectivist theory in English language learning: The role of online social networking tool. *The International Journal of Information and Learning Technology, 36*(4), 354–363. Advance online publication. doi:10.1108/IJILT-02-2019-0018

Sparrow, S. (n.d.). *Let's Talk About Adaptive Learning*. Smart Sparrow.

Squire, K. D. (2008). Video games and education: Designing learning systems for an interactive age. *Educational Technology, 48*(2), 17–26.

Srivani, V., Hariharasudan, A., Nawaz, N., & Ratajczak, S. (2022). Impact of education 4.0 among engineering students for learning English language. *PLoS One, 17*(2), e0261717. doi:10.1371/journal.pone.0261717 PMID:35108282

Ståhlbröst, A. (2008). *Forming future IT: the living lab way of user involvement* (Doctoral dissertation). Luleå tekniska universitet.

Stannard, R., & Basiel, A. (2013). A practice-based exploration of technology enhanced assessment for English language teaching. In G. Motteram (Ed.), *Innovations in Learning Technologies for English Language Teaching* (pp. 145–174). British Council.

Stansfield, S. (2005). An introductory VR course for undergraduates incorporating foundation, experience and capstone. In *Proceedings of the SIGCSE.* ACM. 10.1145/1047344.1047417

Stefani, L. (2009). Planning, Teaching and Learning: Curriculum design and development. In H. Fry, S. Ketteridge, & S. Marshall (Eds.), *A Handbook for teaching in learning in higher education: enhancing academic practices* (pp. 40–57). Routledge.

Stepaniuk, K., Bałakier, U., & Januszewska, A. (2014). Virtual tours in the opinion of the users of social networking sites in Poland and Belarus. *Ekonomia i Zarządzanie, 6*(1).

Stike, T. (2021, June 3). *What is Proctored Testing?* HonorLock. https://honorlock.com/blog/what-is-proctored-testing/

Stockwell, G. (2008). Investigating learner preparedness for and usage patterns of mobile learning. *ReCALL, 20*(3), 253–270. doi:10.1017/S0958344008000232

Stone, P., Brooks, R., Brynjolfsson, E., Calo, R., Etzioni, O., Hager, G., Hirschberg, J., Kalyanakrishnan, S., Kamar, E., Kraus, S., Leyton-Brown, K., Parkes, D., Press, W., Saxenian, A., Shah, J., Tambe, M., & Teller, A. (2016). *Artificial intelligence and life in 2030: One-hundred-year study on artificial intelligence. Report of the 2015-2016 Study Panel.* Stanford University. https://ai100.stanford.edu/2016-report

Strydom, H., Steyn, M. M., & Strydom, C. (2007). An adapted intervention research model: Suggestions for research and practice. *Social Work/Maatskaplike Werk, 43*(4).

Sturm, M., Kennel, T., McBride, R., & Kelly, M. (2009). The pedagogical implications of Web 2.0. In T. Michael (Ed.), *Handbook of research on web 2.0 and second language learning* (pp. 367–384). IGI Global. doi:10.4018/978-1-60566-190-2.ch020

Subedi, S., Nayaju, S., Subedi, S., Shah, S. K., & Shah, J. M. (2020). Impact of e-learning during COVID-19 pandemic among nurshing students and teachers of Nepal. *International Journal of Science and Healthcare Research, 5*(3), 9.

Sukiman, H. (2022). The pattern of hybrid learning to maintain learning effectiveness at the higher education level post-COVID-19 pandemic. *European Journal of Educational Research, 11*(1), 243–257. doi:10.12973/eu-jer.11.1.243

Suyaprom, S., & Manmee, T. (2018). Education Reform in Thailand 4.0: A True Story or a Soap Opera. *Asian Political Science Review*, *2*(2), 88–95.

Sveiby, K. E. (1997). *The New Organizational Wealth: Managing & Measuring Knowledge-Based Assets*. Berrett-Koehler Publishers, Inc.

Sweller, J. (2003). Evolution of human cognitive architecture. In B. Ross (Ed.), *The Psychology of learning and motivation*. Academic Press.

Syazali, M., Putra, F., Rinaldi, A., Utami, L., Umam, W. R., & Jermsittiparsert, K. (2019). Partial Correlation Analysis Using Multiple Linear Regression: Impact on Business Environment of Digital Marketing Interest in the Era of Industrial Revolution 4.0. *Management Science Letters*, *9*(11), 1875–1886. doi:10.5267/j.msl.2019.6.005

Talidong, K. J. B., & Toquero, C. M. D. (2020). Philippine Teachers' Practices to Deal with Anxiety amid COVID-19. *Journal of Loss and Trauma*, *2020*(6-7), 1–7. doi:10.1080/15325024.2020.1759225

Tanova, C., & Karadal, H. (2004). Kurumsal Strateji İle İnsan Kaynakları Politikaları Arasındaki İlişkinin Analizi. *Dokuz Eylül Üniversitesi İktisadi İdari Bilimler Fakültesi Dergisi*, *19*(2), 123–136.

Taymaz, H. (2009). *Okul Yönetimi*. Pegem A.

The World Bank. (2020). *The World Bank Report*. Retrieved May 17, 2022, from https://www.worldbank.org/en/topic/tertiaryeducation#1

Thomson, C., Brown, D., Jones, L., Walker, J., Moore, D. W., Anderson, A., Davies, T., Medcalf, J., Glynn, T. L., & Koegel, R. L. (2003). Resource teachers learning and behavior: Collaborative problem-solving to support inclusion. *Journal of Positive Behavior Interventions*, *5*(2), 101–111. doi:10.1177/10983007030050020501

Thornton, P., & Houser, C. (2005). Using mobile phones in English education in Japan. *Journal of Computer Assisted Learning*, *21*(3), 217–228. doi:10.1111/j.1365-2729.2005.00129.x

Timmis, S., Broadfoot, P., Sutherland, R., & Oldfield, A. (2016). Rethinking assessment in a digital age: Opportunities, challenges and risks. *British Educational Research Journal*, *42*(3), 454–476. doi:10.1002/berj.3215

Tonta, Y. (2008). Libraries and museums in the flat world: Are they becoming virtual destinations? *Library Collections, Acquisitions & Technical Services*, *32*(1), 1–9. doi:10.1080/14649055.2008.10766187

Topuz, A. C., Saka, E., Fatsa, Ö. F., & Kurşun, E. (2022). Emerging trends of online assessment systems in the emergency remote teaching period. *Smart Learning Environments*, *9*(1), 1–21. doi:10.118640561-022-00199-6

Tortop, N., Aykaç, B., Yayman, H., & Özer, M. A. (2013). İnsan Kaynakları Yönetimi. Ankara: Nobel Yayınları.

Tosun, Ü. (2002). *Onurlu disiplin*. Beyaz.

Treve, M. (2021). What COVID-19 has introduced into education: Challenges facing higher education institutions. *Higher Education Pedagogies*, *6*(1), 212–227. doi:10.1080/23752696.2021.1951616

Trinity College Dublin. (2022). *Advantages and disadvantages of online assessments*. Retrieved from https://www.tcd.ie/academicpractice/Gateway_to_Assessment/staff/digital_assessment_types

Trust, T., & Whalen, J. (2020). Should teachers be trained in Emergency Remote Teaching? Lessons learned from the COVID-19 pandemic. *Journal of Technology and Teacher Education*, *28*(2), 189–199.

Tryphon, A., & Vonèche, J. (1996). *Piaget-Vygotsky: The social genesis of thought*. Psychology Press.

Trzcioska-Król, M. (2020). Students with special educational needs in distance learning during the COVID-19 pandemic–parents' opinions. *Interdisciplinary Context of Special Pedagogy*, *29*(1), 173–191. doi:10.14746/ikps.2020.29.08

Türkel, A. (1984). *İşletme Yönetimi*. Okan Yayıncılık.

Türkmen, H. (2008). İlköğretim Okul Müdürlerinin Ġnsan Kaynaklarını Yönetme Yeterlilikleri (Yayımlanmamış Yüksek Lisans Tezi). Yeditepe Üniversitesi/Sosyal Bilimler Enstitüsü, İstanbul.

Tussyadiah, I. P., Wang, D., Jung, T. H., & Tom Dieck, M. C. (2018). Virtual reality, presence, and attitude change: Empirical evidence from tourism. *Tourism Management*, *66*, 140–154. doi:10.1016/j.tourman.2017.12.003

Tutar, H. (2003). *Örgütsel İletişim*. Seçkin Yayınları.

Uğur, A. (2008). *İnsan kaynakları yönetimi*. Sakarya: Sakarya Kitabevi.

Ülsever, C. (2005). *21. Yüzyılda İnsan Yönetimi*. Alfa.

Ünal, S. (2000). Okulda İnsan Kaynakları Yönetimi. *Milli Eğitim Dergisi*, 146.

United Nation. (2021). *Policy Brief: Education During Covid-19 and Beyond*. United Nation.

United Nations Industrial Development Organisation. (2016). Industry 4.0: Opportunities and challenges of the new industrial revolution for developing countries and economies in transition. UNIDO.

United Nations. (2020). Policy Brief: Education during COVID-19 and beyond. United Nations.

Unterhalter, E. (2019). The Many Meaning of Quality Education: Politics of Targets and Indicators in SDG4. *Global Policy*, *10*(1), 39–51.

Unterhalter, E., Longlands, H., & Vaughan, R. P. (2022). Article. *Journal of Human Development and Capabilities*, 1–30.

Veeckman, C., & Van Der Graaf, S. (2015). The City as Living Laboratory: Empowering Citizens with the Citadel Toolkit. *Technology Innovation Management Review*, *5*(3), 6–17. doi:10.22215/timreview/877

Veile, J., Kiel, D., Müller, J. M., & Voigt, K. (2018). How to implement Industry 4.0. An empirical analysis of lessons learned from best practices. *International Association for Management of Technology IAMOT 2018 Conference Proceedings*, 1-24.

Veitch, S., Strehlow, K., & Boyd, J. (2018). Supporting university students with socially challenging behaviours through professional development for teaching staff. *Journal of Academic Language and Learning*, *12*(1), 156–167.

Velinova-Sokolova, N. (2021). Higher education and COVID-19 in conditions of Education 4.0. *International Scientific Journal "Industry 4.0"*, *5*(4), 165-168.

Venkatesh, V., Morris, M. G., Davis, G. B., & Davis, F. D. (2003). User acceptance of information technology: Toward a unified view. *Management Information Systems Quarterly*, *27*, 425–478.

Verawardina, U., Asnur, L., Lubis, A. L., Hendriyani, Y., Ramadhani, D., Dewi, I. P., & Sriwahyuni, T. (2020). Reviewing online learning facing the Covid-19 outbreak. *Journal of Talent Development and Excellence*, *12*(3s), 385–392.

Viberg, O., Wasson, B., & Kukulska-Hulme, A. (2020). Mobile-assisted language learning through learning analytics for self-regulated learning (MALLAS): A conceptual framework. *Australasian Journal of Educational Technology*, *36*(6), 34–52. doi:10.14742/ajet.6494

Vlachopoulos, D. (2020). COVID-19: Threat or opportunity for online education? *Higher Learning Research Communications*, *10*(1), 16–19.

Vygotsky, L. (1962). *Thought and language*. The M.I.T Press. (Original work published 1934) doi:10.1037/11193-000

Vygotsky, L. S. (1978). *Mind in society*. Harvard University Press.

Walker, S. S., Ruggs, E. N., Morgan, W. B., & DeGrassi, S. W. (2019). Diverse perspectives on inclusion: Exploring the experiences of individuals in heterogeneous groups. *Equality, Diversity and Inclusion*, *38*(1), 2–19. doi:10.1108/EDI-11-2017-0250

Wall, J. E. (2000). *Technology-delivered assessment: Diamonds or rocks?* ERIC Clearinghouse on Counseling and Student Services.

Wang, C., Cheng, Z., Yue, X.-G., & McAleer, M. (2020). Risk management of COVID-19 by universities in China. *Journal of Risk and Financial Management*, *13*(2), 36. doi:10.3390/jrfm13020036

Wardak, M. (2020). *Mobile Assisted Language Learning (MALL): Teacher Uses of Smartphone Applications (Apps) to Support Undergraduate Students' English as a Foreign Language (EFL) Vocabulary Development*. Lancaster University.

Wästberg, S. B., Eriksson, T., Karlsson, G., Sunnerstam, M., Axelsson, M., & Billger, M. (2019). Design Considerations for Virtual Laboratories: A Comparative Study of Two Virtual Laboratories for Learning about Gas Solubility and Colour Appearance. *Education and Information Technologies, 24*(3), 2059–2080. doi:10.100710639-018-09857-0

Watermeyer, R., Crick, T., Knight, C., & Goodall, J. (2020). COVID-19 and Digital Disruption in UK Universities: Afflictions and Affordances of Emergency Online Migration. *Higher Education, 2020*(81), 623–641. PMID:32836334

Weiner, C. (2003). Key ingredients to online learning: Adolescent students study in cyberspace – The nature of the study. *International Journal on E-Learning, 2*(3), 44–50.

Weiser, M. (1991). The Computer for the 21 st Century. *Scientific American, 265*(3), 94–105. doi:10.1038cientificamerican0991-94 PMID:1675486

Westerlund, M., & Leminen, S. (2011). Managing the Challenges of Becoming an Open Innovation Company: Experiences from Living Labs. *Technology Innovation Management Review, 1*(1), 19–25. doi:10.22215/timreview/489

Whitton, N. & Moseley, A. (2012). *Using games to enhance learning and teaching: A beginner's guide.* London: Taylor and Francis.

Wong, H. W. L., Jhaveri, A. D., & Wong, L. T. (2015). *The dilemma of matching learning styles and teaching styles in English language classrooms. In English language education in a global world: Practices, issues and challenges.* Nova Science Publishers, Inc.

Wood, R., & Shirazi, S. (2020). A systematic review of audience response systems for teaching and learning in higher education: The student experience. *Computer Education.*

World Economic Forum. (2020). Schools of the future: Defining new models of education for the fourth industrial revolution. *Platform for Shaping the Future of the New Economy and Society.* https://www.weforum. org/platforms/shaping-the-future-of-the-new-economy-and-society

Wu, H. K., Lee, S. W. Y., Chang, H. Y., & Liang, J. C. (2013). Current status, opportunities and challenges of augmented reality in education. *Computer Education, 62*, 41–49.

Xiaolong, T., & Qian, K. (2022). Researching Into the Use of Real-Life Materials in Language Learning Apps: A Case Study of the HANZI App for Learning Chinese Characters. In Applying Mobile Technologies to Chinese Language Learning (pp. 91-122). IGI Global.

Xie, Y., Liu, Y., Zhang, F., & Zhou, P. (2022). Virtual Reality-Integrated Immersion-Based Teaching to English Language Learning Outcome. *Frontiers in Psychology, 12*, 767363. doi:10.3389/fpsyg.2021.767363 PMID:35211053

Xu, X., & Li, Y. (2018). Teaching method of tourism curriculum design based on practical teaching method. *Educational Sciences: Theory and Practice, 18*(6).

Yalçın, S. A. (2002). *Personel Yönetimi.* Beta Yayınları.

Yaman, E. (2007). Üniversitelerde Bir Eğitim Sorunu Olarak Öğretim Elemanının Maruz Kaldığı İnformal Cezalar (Doktora Tezi). T.C Marmara Üniversitesi Eğitim Bilimleri Enstitüsü, İstanbul.

Yaman, H. (2010). Türk öğrencilerinin yazma kaygısı: Ölçek geliştirme ve çeşitli değişkenler açısından yordama çalışması. *International Online Journal of Educational Sciences*, *2*(1), 267–289.

Yang, D., Alsadoon, A., Prasad, P. W. C., Singh, A. K., & Elchouemi, A. (2018). An Emotion Recognition Model Based on Facial Recognition in Virtual Learning Environment. *Procedia Computer Science*, *125*, 2–10. doi:10.1016/j.procs.2017.12.003

Yen, J.-C., Tsai, C.-H., & Wu, M. (2013). Augmented reality in the higher education: Students' science concept learning and academic achievement in astronomy. *Procedia: Social and Behavioral Sciences*, *103*, 165–173. doi:10.1016/j.sbspro.2013.10.322

Yen, T. T. F. (2020). The Performance of Online Teaching for Flipped Classroom Based on COVID-19 Aspect. *Asian J. Educ. Soc. Studies*, *2020*(8), 57–64. doi:10.9734/ajess/2020/v8i330229

Yıldırım, A., & Şimşek, H. (1999), Sosyal Bilimlerde Nitel Araştırma Yöntemleri. Ankara: Seçkin Yayıncılık.

Yıldırım, A., & Şimşek, H. (2008). Sosyal Bilimlerde Nitel Araştırma Yöntemleri. Ankara: Seçkin Yayıncılık.

Yıldırım, A., & Şimşek, H. (2011). Sosyal bilimlerde nitel araştırma yöntemleri. Ankara: Seçkin Yayıncılık.

Yıldırım, A., & Şimşek, H. (2011). Sosyal Bilimlerde Nitel Araştirma Yöntemleri. Seçkin Yayınevi.

Yıldırım, İ. (2001). *Öğretmen yetiştirme ve eğitimde kalite paneli*. MEB Öğretmen Yetiştirme ve Eğitimi Genel Müdürlüğü.

Yılmaz, G. (2006). Örgüt Kültürü ve İnsan Kaynakları Yönetimi (Yayınlanmamış Yüksek Lisans Tezi). Marmara Üniversitesi, İstanbul.

Yüceol, N. (2021). The steps to be taken in higher education for successful adaptation to industry 4.0. *Yükseköğretim Dergisi*, *11*(3), 563–577. doi:10.2399/yod.21.617715

Yüksel, Ö. (2000). *İnsan Kaynaklan Yönetimi*. Gazi Kitapevi.

Zaim, H. (2005). *Bilginin Artan önemi ve Bilgi Yönetimi*. İşaret.

Zainuddin, Z., Perera, C. J., Haruna, H., & Habiburrahim, H. (2020). Literacy in the New Norm: Stay-Home Game Plan for Parents. *Inf. Learn. Sci.*, *2020*(121), 645–653. doi:10.1108/ILS-04-2020-0069

Zakiah, W. G., Karsidi, R., & Yusuf, M. (2021). The implementation of inclusive educational policies in elementary school. *Jurnal Pendidikan dan Pengajaran*, *54*(1), doi:doi:130-140.10.23887/jpp.v54i1.32210

Zarzuela, M. M., Pernas, F. J. D., Calzón, S. M., Ortega, D. G., & Rodríguez, M. A. (2013). Educational tourism through a virtual reality platform. *Procedia Computer Science*, *25*, 382–388. doi:10.1016/j.procs.2013.11.047

Zhang, D., & Perez-Paredes, P. (2021). Chinese postgraduate EFL learners' self-directed use of mobile English learning resources. *Computer Assisted Language Learning*, *34*(8), 1128–1153. doi:10.1080/09588221.2019.1662455

Zhang, Y., & Lin, C. H. (2020). Student interaction and the role of the teacher in a state virtual high school: What predicts online learning satisfaction? *Technology, Pedagogy and Education*, *29*(1), 57–71. doi:10.1080/1475939X.2019.1694061

Zhao, F. (2003). Enhancing the quality of online higher education through measurement. *Quality Assurance in Education*, *11*(4), 214–221. doi:10.1108/09684880310501395

Zhou, J., Zuo, M., Yu, Y., & Chai, W. (2014). How fundamental and supplemental interactions affect users' knowledge sharing in virtual communities? A social cognitive perspective. *Internet Research*, *24*(5), 566–586. doi:10.1108/IntR-07-2013-0143

Zhou, L., Wu, S., Zhou, M., & Li, F. (2020). 'School's Out, But Class' On,' The Largest Online Education in the World Today: Taking China's Practical Exploration During The COVID-19 Epidemic Prevention and Control as an Example. *Best Evid. Chin. Edu.*, *2020*(4), 501–519. doi:10.15354/bece.20.ar023

Zhu, X., & Ramanan, D. (2012). Face detection, pose estimation, and landmark localization in the wild. *2012 IEEE Conference on Computer Vision and Pattern Recognition*, 2879–2886. 10.1109/CVPR.2012.6248014

Zimmerman, G. W., & Eber, D. E. (2001). When worlds collide!: an interdisciplinary course in virtual-reality art. In *Proceedings of SIGCSE*. ACM. 10.1145/364447.364545

Zimmerman, J. (2020). Coronavirus and the Great Online-Learning Experiment. *The Chronicle of Higher Education*, *6*(2), 122–138.

# About the Contributors

**Oytun Sözüdoğru** received his BA degree in English Language Teaching and MA degree in Educational Sciences at Eastern Mediterranean University. During his M.Ed studies, he also worked as a research assistant at the Department of Educational Sciences and English Language Teaching. After that he completed his PhD in Educational Administration, Supervision, Planning and Economics. Currently, he is currently working as a Professor in the Department of Educational Sciences. His research interests are English language teaching, curriculum design, multiple intelligence, materials development, educational technology, Web 2.0 tools, and e-learning.

**Bülent Akkaya** is Lecturer and Chair of the Department of Office Management & Secretary at Ahmetli VHS of the Manisa Celal Bayar University, Turkey. His research interests comprise networks and partnerships in diverse disciplines. He has been working on dynamic capabilities, agile leadership, industry 4.0 and 5.0 and quality of management in contemporary enterprises and higher education.

* * *

**Muhammad Mooneeb Ali** is a PhD in Applied Linguistics, he has authored 20 books on linguistics, literature, and general English. he has published more than 40 research publications. His areas of expertise are technology-based learning discourse analysis, and technology in education.

**Aniesa Samira Bafadhal** is a lecturer at the Department of Tourism at the Faculty of Administrative Science Brawijaya University, Indonesia. Since 2017 She serves as vice head of the Tourism Laboratory and is actively involved in the Tourism Research Center. Her research interests currently focus on a number of areas including virtual tourism, cultural heritage, visual culture, and tourism marketing.

**Oindrila Chakraborty** is currently working as the Assistant Professor at J.D.Birla Institute, affiliated to Jadavpur University. She has completed her PhD from University of Calcutta and secured her gold medal from Indian Institute of Social Welfare and Business Administration.

**Gokmen Dagli** is Dean of Faculty of Education, Vice Rector of University of Kyrenia.

**Nazan Dogruer** got her BA in English Language and Literature, (Hacettepe University, 1990); MA in English Language Teaching / Educational Studies (EMU, 2000); PhD in Educational Sciences (EMU, 2015). She holds RSA COTE, DOTE and CEELT II from Cambridge University.She has been an English instructor since 1992 and she has started teaching at Education Faculty since 2010. While working at Eastern Mediterranean University (EMU) she holds different extra responsibilities and currently she is the Assistant Director for Academic Affairs at Foreign Languages and English Preparatory School at EMU. Throughout her professional career she has attended many seminars, workshops, conferences, and educational training courses as an attendee or a presenter. She also has published book chapters and articles in the field of education.

**Halil Ercan** was born in 1988. He completed his primary education at Çatalköy Primary School, and his secondary and high school education at Girne Anafartalar High School. He completed his undergraduate education in the field of English Language Education at Near East University. Afterwards, he completed his military education and started his teaching career. During this period, he completed his master's degree in the Girne American University in the field of English Language Education by focusing on his studies in listening, applied linguistics, and pronunciation. In the same years, he completed the Cambridge University Local Examinations Association (UCLES) English Language Education one-year program with high success. Continuing his studies in the field, he presented his research studies as papers in many national and international conferences. He completed his doctoral education courses in the field of English Language Teaching at the Eastern Mediterranean University by focusing on phonetic studies. At the same time, he is the language and field editor of the Turkey-based journal in the field of Educational Sciences called Ilkogretim-online. He also works as a field and language editor for the Hiper Academy Punlishing. He worked as a library director at a private university in the TRNC for many years and contributed to many conferences in Turkey and abroad. He currently teaches linguistics, listening, speaking, effective writing, and pronunciation in educational science programs. His hobbies include organic beekeeping, organic farming, lavender cultivation, fishing, and archery. He is married and has two daughters.

**Ramadan Eyyam** got his BA in Linguistics, (Hacettepe University, 1989); MA in English Language Teaching / Educational Studies (EMU, 2000); PhD in Educational Sciences (EMU, 2014). He holds RSA COTE, DOTE and CEELT II from Cambridge University. He has been an English instructor since 1991 and he has started teaching at Education Faculty since 2010. While working at Eastern Mediterranean University (EMU)he holds different extra responsibilities and currently he is the Director of Foreign Languages and English Preparatory School at EMU. Throughout his professional career he has attended many seminars, workshops, conferences, and educational training courses as an attendee or a presenter. He also has published book chapters and articles in the field of education.

**Zehra Gazi** is teaching doctorate, graduate, and undergraduate degree courses in Ataturk Education Faculty at Near East University. Zehra Altınay is Vice Director of Institute of Educational Sciences. She is also board member of Distance Education Center. Further to this, Assoc. Prof. Dr. Zehra Altınay is the Director of Societal Research and Development Center. She is the section editor in education and science journal which is SSCI journal. Zehra Altınay has two national academic content books published by reputable publishing houses. Further to this, she has international academic content books. In addition, she has international book chapters published by reputable publishing house. Zehra Altınay has articles which were indexed at Social Sciences Index (SSCI), international book chapters and international articles that were indexed at the educational field indexes (British Education Index, ERIC, Science Direct, Scopus, etc.). She has national publications. There also are academic presentations and reports at international conferences. She worked as active researcher in research projects. She has editorial role in respected journals.

**Muhammad Rosyihan Hendrawan** is a lecturer at the Department of Library and Information Science at the Faculty of Administrative Science Brawijaya University, Indonesia. Currently, He serves as coordinator of information technology and communication infrastructure at the Faculty of Administrative Science Brawijaya University, Indonesia and is actively involved as a board in the Indonesian Library and Information Science Scholars Association. His research interests currently focus on a number of areas including information governance and digital humanities.

**Tanaya Krishna Jupalli** is pursuing a Bachelor of Technology in Computer Science with a specialization in Artificial Intelligence at VIT-AP University, Amaravati, India. He worked as a Research Assistant in the School of Computer Science Engineering (SCOPE) Research Department. He is well versed in the field of Artificial Intelligence, and has done various projects related to Machine Learning (ML) and Deep Learning. He has experience in Google Cloud and was a member of Google Developer Student Club (GDSC).

**Hameed Khan** received his B.E. degree from RGPV University Bhopal, in 2007 and M.Tech from RGPV Bhopal in 2012. Currently, he is pursuing PhD under the supervision of Dr Jitendra Singh Thakur Head department of CSE Jabalpur Engineering Collge Jabalpur, MP, India. His research area is Machine learning, Mobile Ad-hoc Networks.

**Hari Kishan Kondaveeti** is working as an Associate Professor in the School of Computer Science Engineering (SCOPE), acting as Deputy Director of Engineering Clinics, and acted as a Core Member of the Innovation and Incubation Center (IIC) at VIT-AP University, Amaravati, India. He is an IBM Certified Data Science Professional and NASSCOM Associate Analyst certified faculty and handling multiple Data Analytics courses. He worked as Research Associate in the Naval Science & Technological Laboratory, India. He is interested in teaching, scientific article writing, and developing IoT solutions. He has filed several patents and authored technical articles, conference papers, journals, and book chapters. He is acting as a reviewer in SCIE journals IEEE Sensors Journal, IET Image Processing, IET Electronics Letters, Frontiers of Computer Science, Journal of Super Computing and ESCI Journals International Journal of Information Technology Research (JITR), Journal of Information Retrieval Research (IJIRR) and served in the committees of several conferences such as ICCIDE-2021, ICECCME 2021, ISCDA-2020, ICCIDE-2020, RACSPA-2019, ICACCI-2017, ICCSA-2017, etc. Dr. Kishan attended, organized, and acted as a resource person in several FDPs, workshops, refresher courses, conferences, and technical talks in his domain and expertise. He received the Best Guru Male Award 2020 by GISR Foundation, Best Research with a patent award (2021), Beyond and Above Award (2019) by VIT-AP University, Amaravati, and Top 50 Tech-savvy Academicians in Higher Education Across India for the year 2019.

**Kamal Kushwaha** received PhD from RDVV University Jabalpur, in 2015. Currently, he is working as Head of Department in Department of Applied Physics, Govt. Engg. College, Jabalpur. Presently being in charge of the Nanoscience lab. Supervising various projects related to nanoscience, nanocomposites, nanofluids subjected to optical mechanical, and thermal applications. His expertise areas are material science, optoelectronic devices, analog & Digital communication, Artificial Intelligence, Machine Learning. He is a regular reviewer of various journals of international repute.

**Ipek Menevis** has been working at Eastern Mediterranean University (EMU) Foreign Languages and English Preparatory School (FLEPS) since 1999. She has contributed to various units in the school. She holds RSA CEELT II from Cambridge University. She completed her Master of Education degree in 2011. She was actively involved in many teams and committees within the institution and published book chapters and articles in the field of education. She is currently holding the position of Assistant Director for Student and Administrative Affairs at FLEPS. She is also doing her Ph.D. in the field of Psychological Counseling and Guidance.

**Kamalendu Pal** is with the Department of Computer Science, School of Science and Technology, City, University of London. Kamalendu received his BSc (Hons) degree in Physics from Calcutta University, India, Postgraduate Diploma in Computer Science from Pune, India, MSc degree in Software Systems Technology from the University of Sheffield, Postgraduate Diploma in Artificial Intelligence from Kingston University, MPhil degree in Computer Science from the University College London, and MBA degree from the University of Hull, United Kingdom. He has published over eighty international research articles (including book chapters) widely in the scientific community with research papers in the ACM SIGMIS Database, Expert Systems with Applications, Decision Support Systems, and conferences. His research interests include knowledge-based systems, decision support systems, teaching and learning practice gamification, blockchain technology, software engineering, service-oriented computing, sensor network simulation, and supply chain management. He is on the editorial board of an international computer science journal and is a member of the British Computer Society, the Institution of Engineering and Technology, and the IEEE Computer Society.

**Mulka Sai Tharun Reddy** is pursuing a Bachelor of Technology in Computer Science with a specialization in Networking and security at VIT-AP University, Amaravati, India. He worked as a Research Assistant in the School of Computer Science Engineering (SCOPE) Research Department. He is well versed in cybersecurity, has done various projects and built tools in that field. He has experience in Google Cloud and is part of the Google Developer Student Club (GDSC).

**Mutlu Soykurt** has been working in ELT since 1997. A naturally open person, she is passionate about learning what interests her students and how to help them through language. Her experience teaching people from a wide range of industries enables her to create a comfortable, accessible, and fun learning environment for her students, no matter whatever age they are and their focus may be. Parallel to teaching, she also continues to work on art and design projects. Her most recent initiative includes a book series that provides intimate life stories of people living in North Cyprus. She is an expert on creativity in foreign language teaching.

**Razge Sıla Zorba** was born in Famagusta in 1988. She completed her primary school, Gazi Primary School and Secondary School in Famagusta at the Turkish Maarif College. She graduated from Nicosia the Turkish Maarif College in 2005. She received her undergraduate degree in music from Anglia Ruskin University in Cambridge, England. Returning to Cyprus in 2008, she completed the Secondary Education Field Teaching Non-Thesis Master's Program at the Atatürk Teachers Academy until 2009. She also volunteered as a music teacher at special education schools in North Cyprus. In 2009, she was accepted to Anglia Ruskin University Music Therapy Master's education and won a European Union Scholarship. She graduated from this department in 2011 as a specialist music therapist. Returning to Cyprus in 2012, she established the Cyprus Music Therapy Center and started both music therapy and promotion of this profession. She gave music therapy seminars at various universities and brought music therapy together with university students. She worked as a volunteer music therapist with cancer patients at Umut Education and Culture House. She organized music therapy workshops by actively participating in bi-communal studies. She started to work as part-time in the Special Education Department of Cyprus International University in 2013. She started to work as a part-time lecturer at the Near East University Occupational Therapy and Audiology Departments in 2017. In these departments, Music Perception of the Hearing Impaired Lessons were given by her. After graduating from the Near East University Special Education Doctorate Program in 2020, she started to work as a full-time lecturer in the International Final University Special Education Teaching Program. She is still working as a special education teacher program manager at Final International University. She currently teaches Intellectual Disability and Autism Spectrum Disorder, Special Education, Learning Disability and Special Ability, Assessment in Special Education, Adaptation in Special Education, Supporting Language and Communication Skills in Special Education Institutions, Observation in Special Education Institutions, Literacy in Special Education, Reading Disability: Diagnosis and Intervention, Special Education Science and Social Studies Teaching, Teaching Social Adaptation Skills in Special Education, Play and Music in Special Education, School and Institution Experience in Special Education, Teaching Practice I, Teaching Practice II, Adolescence and Sex Education courses. She is interested in the fields of autism spectrum disorders, music therapy and special education and conducts her research in these fields.

# Index

## E



## F



## G



## H



## I



## L



## M

## N



## O



## P



## R



## S



## T



## V

CPSIA information can be obtained
at www.ICGtesting.com
Printed in the USA
LVHW060728100523
746513LV00005B/539